CW01430276

THE ANTI–CIVIL RIGHTS MOVEMENT

THE ANTI–CIVIL RIGHTS MOVEMENT

Affirmative Action as Wedge and Weapon

MIKE STEVE COLLINS

UNIVERSITY PRESS OF KANSAS

Published by the University Press of Kansas (Lawrence, Kansas 66045), which was organized by the Kansas Board of Regents and is operated and funded by Emporia State University, Fort Hays State University, Kansas State University, Pittsburg State University, the University of Kansas, and Wichita State University

Library of Congress Cataloging-in-Publication Data

Names: Collins, Mike Steve. (Writer on civil rights movement), author.
Title: The anti–civil rights movement : affirmative action as wedge and weapon / Mike Steve Collins.
Description: Lawrence : University Press of Kansas, 2024. | Includes bibliographical references and index.
Identifiers: LCCN 2023057852 (print) | LCCN 2023057853 (ebook)
ISBN 9780700637140 (cloth)
ISBN 9780700637133 (ebook)
Subjects: LCSH: Affirmative action programs—Law and legislation—United States—History. | Affirmative action programs in education—Law and legislation—United States—History. | African Americans—Civil rights—United States—History. | Asian Americans—Civil rights—United States—History. | Civil rights movements—United States—History. | Equality before the law—United States—History. | Political questions and judicial power—United States—History. | Marshall, Thurgood, 1908-1993. | Thomas, Clarence, 1948–
Classification: LCC KF4755.5 .C657 2024 (print) | LCC KF4755.5 (ebook) | DDC 342.7308/7—dc23/eng/20240326
LC record available at https://lccn.loc.gov/2023057852.
LC ebook record available at https://lccn.loc.gov/2023057853.

British Library Cataloguing-in-Publication Data is available.

Printed in the United States of America

10 9 8 7 6 5 4 3 2 1

The paper used in this publication is acid free and meets the minimum requirements of the American National Standard for Permanence of Paper for Printed Library Materials Z39.48-1992.

CONTENTS

ACKNOWLEDGMENTS

This book began in 2016 when James Marcus, then editor of *Harper's Magazine*, asked me to pitch some story ideas. He greenlit my proposal for an article on affirmative action and guided me through several drafts. By the time the article was published in 2017, I had started to think, with encouragement from Marcus, of expanding the essay into a book. My next stroke of luck came in 2019 when David Congdon, editor at the University Press of Kansas, took an interest in a book proposal I sent him. He then guided me through several versions of the manuscript and found anonymous readers who provided invaluable criticism and advice. To Marcus, Congdon, and the anonymous readers, I am eternally grateful.

Time is a critical factor when writing a long, complicated book, and a one-semester course release through an internal faculty fellowship from Texas A&M's Glasscock Center (though granted for another, shorter project) gave me a chance to do some indispensable moonlighting in affirmative action land.

As indispensable as time in completing a long project is the kindness of strangers, such as those who granted me interviews.

A final critical ingredient is encouragement, and there were always people out there, even if I did not contact them directly about this particular manuscript, who were rooting for me to live up to my potential and who, in the past, have written recommendation letters when I needed them most—people like Arnold Rampersad, Annie Dillard, Yusef Komunyakaa, Charles H. Rowell, and Catherine McCauliff.

I dedicate this book to my family, but I have to single out my late father, Raymond Collins, whose bookshelf was my second tutor (my great-grandmother Florence Kelly's Bible was my first), and my late mother, Beverly Collins. Their grace and enduring wit under extreme pressure during their last months were astounding, as were their courage, humor, kindness, and thirst for revelation in earlier years.

ABBREVIATIONS

AAMC	Association of American Medical Colleges
ACLU	American Civil Liberties Union
ACORN	Association of Community Organizations for Reform Now
ACRI	American Civil Rights Institute
ADL	Anti-Defamation League
AEI	American Enterprise Institute
AP	advanced placement
BAMN	Coalition to Defend Affirmative Action by Any Means Necessary
BLM	Black Lives Matter
CAA	Chinese for Affirmative Action
CADC	Chinese American Democratic Club
CEO	chief executive officer
CIA	Central Intelligence Agency
CIR	Center for Individual Rights
CNP	Council for National Policy
CORE	Congress of Racial Equality
CRT	critical race theory
DA	district attorney
DEI	diversity, equity, and inclusion
ECOA	Equal Credit Opportunity Act
EEOC	Equal Employment Opportunity Commission
ESL	English as a second language
FAIR	Fairness & Accuracy in Reporting

FAIR	Federation for American Immigration Reform
FCC	Federal Communications Commission
FEPC	Fair Employment Practice Committee
FOIA	Freedom of Information Act
GPA	grade point average
HEW	US Department of Health, Education, and Welfare
IEA	Institute for Educational Affairs
IRS	Internal Revenue Service
LCCR	Leadership Conference on Civil Rights (now Leadership Conference on Civil and Human Rights)
LSAT	Law School Admission Test
MCAT	Medical College Admission Test
MCRI	Michigan Civil Rights Initiative
MUD	municipal utility district
NAACP	National Association for the Advancement of Colored People
NAS	National Association of Scholars
NASA	National Aeronautics and Space Administration
NBER	National Bureau of Economic Research
NLCPI	National Legal Center for the Public Interest
NPR	National Public Radio
OCR	Office of Civil Rights
OFCCP	Office of Federal Contract Compliance Programs
PFR	Project on Fair Representation
PLF	Pacific Legal Foundation
POA	Police Officers Association (San Francisco)
ROTC	Reserve Officers' Training Corps
SFFA	Students for Fair Admissions
SFPD	San Francisco Police Department
SFUSD	San Francisco Unified School District
UC	University of California
UN	United Nations
UNC	University of North Carolina
UPI	United Press International
UT	University of Texas
VRA	Voting Rights Act
WEAL	Women's Equity Action League

INTRODUCTION: HUG-GATE AND OTHER HERMENEUTIC TRAPS

On a clear April 1990 afternoon in front of Harvard Law School's Bauhaus-style Harkness Commons building, Barack Obama, president of *Harvard Law Review* and future president of the United States, addressed about five hundred people gathered in front of Harkness or peering down from its second-floor windows. Perhaps to manage nerves, the lanky Obama—all but lost in a big blue shirt—thrust his right hand into his pants pocket before launching each perfectly calibrated thought about the man he was introducing: Professor Derrick Bell.

Obama drew titters from the crowd when he noted that Bell had not achieved his legendary status by the grace of "his good looks and easy charm, although he has both in ample measure." Nor had Bell done so because of his scholarship, which had "changed the standards of what legal writing is about." He had done so, Obama suggested, because of the tremendous ethical example he set.

The bespectacled fifty-nine-year-old Bell, wearing a gray suit over a blue shirt that nicely set off his dark brown skin, gave Obama a big hug that, years later, would become notorious. Pulling a page of notes from his jacket pocket, Bell mused that it "may be significant that the student stands here and delivers a mighty address without notes, while the teacher . . . "—here, the professor flashed his toothy grin, and the crowd laughed.

Getting down to business, Bell announced that he was taking an unpaid leave of absence from Harvard Law School to put an exclamation point on his demand that it give tenure to a woman of color. Though he could ill afford it financially (he omitted the fact that his wife was at home battling terminal cancer), Bell insisted on stepping into the breach. The leave was his way of paying forward the student activism that, he believed, had forced the university to make him the first Black pope of the law (as Harvard law professors have been called).[1] "I have not forgotten," he said,

> that my appointment represented the culmination of years of student struggle. I remember as well that for the first 150 years of its history, the faculty at Harvard Law, the oldest existing, most prestigious and in the view of many the best law school in the United States, was all white and all male. That is a horrible history not remediable by plaintive pleas of *mea culpa* combined with the token appointment of members of the victim class who are least likely to remind the school of its past racist hiring practices.[2]

Holding the law school's feet to the fire was central to Bell's approach as an activist scholar—so much so that eight years later he chastised Randall Kennedy, a younger colleague who had inherited a popular class created by Bell, for taking a less confrontational stance. Bell took special exception to a suggestion Kennedy made in his book *Race, Crime and the Law* that Blacks practice a politics of respectability to win white esteem. In a review, the exasperated Bell satirized Kennedy with the following quip: "We blacks have faults as well as rights. I concede the former and hope you will recognize the latter."[3] In other essays, Kennedy had taken the tough stance Bell preferred, and Bell advised him to "come home" and stop discussing African Americans' unequal treatment in the criminal justice system and elsewhere in tones of "sweet reason." Nevertheless, Bell conceded that if Kennedy could show that sweet reason "has brought about significant policy reform in the criminal justice system, perhaps we racial advocates should reconsider our practice of lambasting whites for the society's racism."[4]

Lambasting freely in 1990, Bell took his leave of absence and stayed away for two years. During that time, Harvard did not give tenure to a woman of color. Instead, it dismissed Bell for extending his leave too long. And there, but for the meteoric rise of Barack Obama and a small empire of right-wing lambasters eager to bring him down, the drama might have ended. But in 2012, the year after Bell died, Obama was running for reelection and the right-wing website Breitbart.com tried to blow up his campaign with the help of footage of Obama introducing and embracing Bell.[5]

Breitbart's gambit was not as far-fetched as it sounds. The website's founder, Andrew Breitbart, had wreaked more than his share of destruction with manufactured scandals. In 2010, for instance, he orchestrated the firing of an Obama administration official by deceptively editing some of her remarks. That same year, he bamboozled most of the American media and political class with a heavily fictionalized video that brought down a huge target—the Association of Community Organizations for Reform Now (ACORN), a national antipoverty and voter-registration organization for which Obama had briefly worked.[6]

Breitbart and his website suffered few consequences when this trickery was revealed. Instead, in 2011 they secured $10 million in funding from the reclusive tech billionaire Robert Mercer.[7] Breitbart collapsed and died of heart failure on a Los Angeles sidewalk before he could put the windfall to use, but those who worked for him pushed the Bell-Obama "bombshell" hug out into the media and made Bell such a villain that former GOP vice-presidential candidate Sarah Palin called him a "radical college *racist* professor," without fear of contradiction, on Fox's popular *Hannity* show.[8] Even the venerable, conservative Heritage Foundation got into the act, launching an investigation into whether Bell had ever visited the Obama White House.[9]

Of course, Obama was reelected anyway. But a seed had been planted, and a mighty tree sprang from it with the help of new Breitbart chief Steve Bannon. Bannon used Mercer's money to reach beyond Breitbart-world and build a political infrastructure (complete with cutting-edge and quasi-legal data analytics) that propelled Donald Trump into the White House, helped Trump move white grievances to the center of American politics, and, in the process, set the stage for a bigger and more insidious attack on critical race theory (CRT)—something vaguer and more easily demonized than the cherubic Bell with his high, earnest voice and thick-lensed eyeglasses.[10]

Having been fed a steady diet of alleged leftist malfeasance, Fox and its viewers, the Heritage Foundation, and the wider world of aggrieved Trump supporters were ready to burst a collective political blood vessel by the time a narrow-faced think tank intellectual named Christopher Rufo proclaimed, during an appearance on Fox's *Tucker Carlson Show*, that CRT had infiltrated government agencies and was threatening the republic. Rufo looked directly into the camera at one point and implored Trump—a regular Fox viewer—to issue an executive order banning CRT. The very next day, having contacted Rufo, the Trump administration began drafting Executive Order 13950: Combating Race and Sex Stereotyping.[11]

The irony is that CRT is hardly a race- and sex-stereotyping proposition. It strives to be the opposite. But following its arguments requires a greater appreciation for complexity than Rufo, Fox, and their audiences—ever eager for an outrage—allowed themselves. Cofounded by Derrick Bell and other legal scholars, CRT regularly pushes legal scholarship in the direction of autobiography, fiction, allegory, literary criticism, platonic dialogue, and, especially, hybrids of two or more genres.[12] But at its core, it is a relentlessly logical response to the civil rights movement's mysterious failure to win full equality for Blacks. In the words of a character Bell introduces in his 1987 classic *And We Are Not Saved*, "the once swiftly moving march toward racial equality through law reform has slowed to a walk, leaving millions of black Americans no better off than they were before the civil rights movement."[13]

It is hard to imagine that many Blacks would choose to time-travel back to the world before the civil rights movement (where, even at the height of legal reform in the mid-1960s, someone could reply to a query about equalizing employment opportunity by asserting that "he owned the so-and-so town, he owned all the so-and-so niggers, and he owned the so-and-so store where they traded with no credit").[14] Yet there is truth in the assertion by Bell's character. According to a 2017 National Bureau of Economic Research (NBER) working paper by William J. Collins and Marianne H. Wanamaker, the wage gap between Black and white men decreased between 1965 and 1975 but widened again after 1980, meaning that "the gains of the Civil Rights era have not translated into a sustained path toward economic equality."[15] In schools, segregation decreased between 1968 and the 1980s, but by 2018, 81 percent of Blacks attended mostly minority schools, with high rates of segregation associated with higher levels of poverty and less educational opportunity.[16]

About such phenomena, CRT asks why? Naturally, many of the answers CRT offers focus on race, just as an analysis of a drought would focus on water. Bell's version of CRT calls on whites to acknowledge the persistence of racial discrimination in everything from prison sentences to wages to infant mortality rates. But, in a move that the Rufos of the world refuse to acknowledge, Bell stressed that disadvantaged whites *as well as* disadvantaged minorities would benefit from a top-to-bottom reckoning with the way race structures opportunity in America. In his field-defining legal textbook *Race, Racism and American Law,* Bell laments that "the idea that racial remedies for blacks also help whites remains difficult to convey."[17]

It remains difficult to convey because of the enormous amount of disinformation generated by Rufo and other members of what I call the anti–civil rights movement. Their goal, in Rufo's words, is to have "the public read something crazy in the newspaper and immediately think 'critical race theory'"—or whatever organization or initiative Rufo and his peers are targeting for destruction on any given day. Rather than engaging with Bell's or other CRT theorists' texts, Rufo exulted in one tweet, "We have decodified the term [CRT] and will recodify it to annex the entire range of cultural constructions that are unpopular with Americans."[18]

Although Rufo focuses much more on the easy-to-mangle term "critical race theory" than on Bell himself, the late professor is still a useful foil for those eager to make another Harvard professor like Bell an impossibility. In a 2021 best seller, Mark Levin, a big-jawed, bald, pugnacious radio and television host and former Reagan administration lawyer, managed to both declare Bell unqualified for a position at Harvard—thus deploying an old anti–affirmative action and anti-Black trope—and call CRT a sort of "racist, anti-American" Bond villain ideology.[19] To complete this ideological hat trick, Levin twisted Bell's 1995 essay "Who's Afraid of Critical Race Theory" to make points Bell never conceived of.

Shielding his readers from knowledge as if from a dangerous virus, Levin is careful not to mention that Bell's essay was driven by dismay about the 1994 best-seller status of an 800-page, chart-packed, biceps-builder of a tome called *The Bell Curve*. The book's authors, Charles Murray and Richard J. Herrnstein, argue that because Blacks are usually intellectually inferior to whites, "aggressive affirmative action" is both unfair to whites and a waste of time.[20]

"Why," Bell asks in his essay, "did these two well-known men produce a book filled with rejected theories? Surely they must have known that the book would provide pseudoscientific support for racial hostilities that always worsen during times of economic stress and anxiety."[21] Ignoring this part of Bell's argument, Levin assures his readers that Bell-style CRT is a "Marxist-based ideology laced throughout with raw bigotry, antagonism and hate."[22] The impact of this sort of dishonesty has been and continues to be enormous, and it is the subject of this book.

The Trump executive order that Rufo demanded and got continues to influence American life, and it is very much a grape of the Rufo–Levin vineyard, albeit dressed up in legal language that dispenses with most of the hyperbole. Trump's order banned government agencies and government contractors from providing any diversity training "grounded in misrepresentations of our country's history," including the notion that the US government was built "by white men, for the benefit of white men." "Our Founding documents," the order intones, "rejected these racialized views of America."[23]

An instant classic of the anti–civil rights movement, this executive order co-opted the structure, the penalties, and some of the language of Lyndon Johnson's 1965 Executive Order 11246, a founding document of affirmative action. Trump's order also drew authority from the Civil Rights Act of 1964, the legislative root of contemporary affirmative action. Because it built on such landmark documents, there was much in Trump's executive order that no one could object to.[24] But it went far beyond its sources in banishing the historical reality that only white men of property could vote under the original Constitution and that enslaved Blacks were counted as three-fifths of a person to woo the South by boosting its population and therefore the number of representatives white southerners could elect.

Continuing on its merry way, the Trump executive order became a distillation of the work of Rufo, Levin, and many others in the anti–civil rights movement, which is an evolving coalition of aggrieved (and mostly white) citizens, activists, militias, theorists, politicians, and donors who have battled against Black and other minority civil rights since the era of Reconstruction.

The Trump order had immediate effects. The University of Iowa, "fearing a loss of federal research grants, paused programs across the university, including training for university employees on race or sex stereotyping and scapegoating."[25] (The order forbade any training indicating that "meritocracy or traits such as a hard work ethic are racist or sexist," though such training targets not the traits but the stereotype that Blacks and other minorities lack a proper Protestant work ethic and advance without true merit.) The Trump Department of Labor opened an investigation of the Microsoft Corporation because of its commitment to "double the number of Black employees in leadership posts by 2025."[26] The executive order helped change the national climate of opinion and prepare the ground for the Supreme Court to eviscerate affirmative action in higher education in June 2023. How did Rufo, Trump, Levin, and thousands like them gain such a stranglehold on American thought while using such transparently dishonest and even ridiculous methods? This book is my answer to that question. Although affirmative action was merely the bull's-eye and not the entire target of the anti–civil rights movement, this book keeps affirmative action at the center because the rest of the anti–civil rights agenda is inexplicable without it.

As is probably clear by now, my approach differs from that of most other writers on affirmative action. Randall Kennedy's eloquent *For Discrimination*, for instance, mentions *The Bell Curve* but does not discuss, as I will, the right-wing think tank infrastructure that helped make the Herrnstein–Murray monstrosity a best seller. Nor does it examine how anti–civil rights stalwarts like Levin co-opt the strategies of civil rights pioneers like Thurgood Marshall and turn them into zombies chewing away at the gray matter of civil rights thinking. Kennedy takes the traditional approach of tracing the contours of affirmative action along the Caucasian–African American racial continuum.

In contrast, this book strives for a more comprehensive evaluation of affirmative action, which directly benefits Asians and white women (and, on occasion, even white men) as well as the African Americans and Latinos who generally come to mind when the policy is discussed, whether by Kennedy, Bell, or Levin.[27]

This book differs, too, from Melvin I. Urofsky's comprehensive *The Affirmative Action Puzzle*, which discusses affirmative action for the disabled and for white women but does not discuss key anti–civil rights entities such as the National Association of Scholars, an obscure right-wing organization that helped end affirmative action in California and set the stage for its destruction in Michigan and, ultimately, at Harvard and the University of North Carolina (UNC).[28] Nor does Urofsky discuss the American Enterprise Institute, the home base of Edward Blum, who launched the legal missiles that struck Harvard and UNC.

One book that takes an approach closer to mine is 2021's *The Death of Affirmative Action? Racialized Framing and the Fight against Racial Preference in College Admissions*. The authors, J. Scott Carter and Cameron D. Lippard, analyze the habits of thought, or "frames," that are used and sometimes built by political leaders, advocacy groups, and media. In Shakespeare's *Othello*, for example, the silver-tongued Iago is passed over for promotion and exacts revenge by framing Othello's virtuous bride, Desdemona, as a "strumpet." Viewing his wife through this frame and seeing himself as a cuckold, the invincible general feels himself imploding under the "slow and moving finger" of scorn.[29] Iago, in short, places Desdemona in what Carter and Lippard call a "threat frame." The authors show that powerful defenders of the status quo—people like Rufo and Levin—can set the agenda for the nation by using their access to enormous political, social, and economic resources to impose threat frames on people's minds, just as Iago presses the false image of Desdemona on Othello's.[30]

Rufo, based at the influential Manhattan Institute, where Mercer's powerful daughter Rebekah is on the board of trustees, was able to take advantage of his appearance on the even more influential *Tucker Carlson Show* to demand an executive order that helped reset the national agenda on race relations, impacting everything from school board meetings and the fates of university presidents to gubernatorial races and briefs filed with the Supreme Court.[31]

The idea of "frames" is a powerful one, but this book views Rufo-style agenda setting more in terms of games than frames. Using a game heuristic is nothing new. Media accounts of affirmative action tend to frame it as a zero-sum game—that is, if Blacks win, whites must lose.[32] Rufo is playing a zero-sum game: if he wins, CRT (or whatever the target might be) must lose.

But the war in which Rufo's efforts are a front (in every sense of that word) is better described as a prisoner's dilemma—a game that models situations in which it seems logical to act in a way that makes everyone worse off. To see why, consider the Supreme Court case *DeFunis v. Odegaard* (1974), which exemplifies how affirmative action can become a wedge between erstwhile allies who, in true prisoner's dilemma fashion, get pushed into making decisions that put them in a worse-off position.

In briefs filed to influence the Supreme Court's decision in *DeFunis*, Jewish organizations were split, writes Ellen Messer-Davidow in her book *The Making of Reverse Discrimination: How* DeFunis *and* Bakke *Bleached Rasism from Equal Protection*. Some supported Marco DeFunis's claim that the affirmative action program at the University of Washington Law School discriminated against him, while others backed the law school.[33] This split reflected a fraying of the storied Black-Jewish alliance that had been so effective during the climax of the civil rights movement in the 1960s.[34] Some Jewish leaders declared that "a multiply victimized people who, after surviving virulent anti-Semitism to make good through talent and toil in America, were being revictimized by affirmative action quotas. . . . But African Americans also felt chronically victimized: after being enslaved, lynched, segregated, and pauperized, they were embittered to find their former Jewish allies opposing their efforts," writes Messer-Davidow, who, like me, is an English professor trained to look under the hood of arguments.[35] In this telling, both groups started to see former allies as adversaries and were tempted to abandon the fruits of future partnership. In game theory parlance, they were tempted to defect.

Among those who tried to keep the partnership intact was Jack

Greenberg, the idealistic, no-nonsense Jewish lawyer who led the NAACP Legal Defense Fund from 1961 to 1984.[36] Commenting on the *DeFunis* tensions in his autobiography, Greenberg argues that the small number of Blacks being admitted to top law schools had little impact on the prospects of Jewish applicants. But if Jews joined the vanguard of resistance to affirmative action, it could erode Black leaders' support for Israel. Concluding with a Derrick Bell–like point, Greenberg writes that whites "won't live in a decent society until Blacks do."[37]

If one accepts Greenberg's argument, affirmative action might have led to the ultimate payoff—a decent society. But in a world riddled with injustice, betting on the emergence of a decent society seems risky, while doubling down on whatever advantages one has in the unjust status quo may seem like a sure thing. The temptation to give up on the big payoff—to defect—can be overwhelming because small losses loom large, as Daniel Kahneman and Amos Tversky have shown.[38] Those supporting DeFunis saw deprivation looming large in the form of lost law school seats and a return to second-class citizenship. People like Greenberg, who subscribed to a school of Zionism he viewed as "a call for justice, equality and fairness for all people," saw a weaker Black-Jewish coalition, the loss of a cohort of Black lawyers, potential diminished support for Israel, and one less step toward a decent society.[39] The stark choices here resemble the choices of the aforementioned prisoner's dilemma. After all, unequal opportunity can seem like a burning building one has to escape, even if the rush for the door and the resulting mayhem make escape less likely.

THE PRISONER'S DILEMMA

Since playing the prisoner's dilemma in a building on fire is what social reform is all about, it makes sense to say a bit more about it here. It is usually illustrated by some version of the following story: Two partners in crime are apprehended and separated. Each is told that if he confesses, he will go free. But if he stays quiet and his partner confesses, he will get a brutal sentence. If both men stay silent, the police and the district attorney will be unable to prove either one guilty of the major crime they are suspected of committing, and both will get a slap on the wrist for some minor offense. If both confess, both will do hard time, but not the hardest. Game theorists conclude that, rather than risk the brutal sentence, it is rational for both men to confess and do some hard time, even though it would be better for both to keep their mouths shut, not "defect" from their alliance, and get a slap on the wrist.

Investigators in many fields have found that this type of dilemma is built into numerous human (and nonhuman) situations.[40] Back in 1974, social scientists Tom Burns and Walter Buckley modeled social domination with the help of the dilemma and found that "control agents"—people like Rufo, Breitbart, and especially Trump—are sometimes able to "structure relationships among the actors of a group so as to foster conflict of interest." History, they add, is full of "rulers exploiting racial, ethnic, or ideological cleavages so as to inhibit the organization of cooperation among subordinate groups"—groups such as Blacks and poor whites in the United States or Blacks and Jews in *DeFunis*.[41] Such control agents manipulate social rewards and punishments—called payoffs by game theorists—in such a way as to make conflict seem rational. Thus, they manufacture and benefit from prisoner's dilemmas.

The prisoner's dilemma is just one example of what I call a hermeneutic trap—a way of looking at a problem that makes the solution harder to reach or even to imagine.[42] Getting out of a trap like the prisoner's dilemma involves changing one's perspective not only from what is rational for an individual to what is rational for an alliance or a community but also from what makes sense in the short run to what makes sense in the long run (with Keynes's caveat that, in the long run, we are all dead). But of course, changes in perspective are always resisted to some extent.[43] There is always a Rufo around to caricature the arguments of a Bell. And in the long run, memories fade, are banished from school curricula, or are otherwise forced underground by, say, an executive order.

All this keeps inequality entrenched as both a social reality and a hermeneutic trap that makes a tycoon seem like a master of the universe and a homeless person seem like a walking affront who has brought disaster on himself.[44] Most of the possible solutions to inequality—redistributive taxes, aid to families with dependent children, housing for the poor in more affluent neighborhoods, affirmative action, and DEI education about systematic inequality itself—create prisoner's dilemmas that the Levins and Rufos of the world take advantage of.

These "conflict entrepreneurs" play the role of the police and the district attorney in the prisoner's dilemma as they pressure the "prisoners" to defect from the incipient society that redistributive taxes or affirmative action or new housing opportunities or knowledge of history might help bring about.[45] Of course, harmony entrepreneurs drive society in the other direction. This is why the foremost American battle is for the power to drive society in one direction or the other. This is why the thirst for agenda-setting power—which amounts to the ability to determine the future—may be the most intense thirst there is and why, from Bell's point of view, the greatest obstacle to equal opportunity for Blacks and other minorities is the "vested interest in superior status" among American elites (and aspiring elites).[46]

This is why prisoner's dilemma–style defection from interracial coalitions is not limited to the mainstream white community, as Bell often assumes. Such defection occurs among minority groups competing for the scarce resources of opportunity and power. Rufo, who has trouble keeping his id in check, crowed that, with his help, "the racial coalition is also breaking apart—Asian-Americans, in particular, are revolting against CRT."[47] The dart that brought down affirmative action in higher education in 2023 was tipped not with curare but with the inaccurate idea, crafted over decades, that affirmative action put people like Bell on perches they did not deserve and clouded the futures of model-minority Asian Americans.

THE INTEREST-CONVERGENCE DILEMMA

Whereas Bell writes of racism as a permanent feature of American society, this book focuses on the permanence of the prisoner's dilemma and other hermeneutic traps. In fact, one of Bell's most famous formulations—the interest-convergence dilemma—can be seen as a special case of the prisoner's dilemma.[48] "The interest of blacks in achieving racial equality," Bell theorizes, "will be accommodated only when it converges with the interests of whites; however, the fourteenth amendment, standing alone, will not authorize a judicial remedy providing effective racial equality for blacks where the remedy sought threatens the superior societal status of middle- or upper-class whites."[49]

Ironically, as Bell goes on to acknowledge, it is working-class whites who have been most susceptible to the anxiety caused by measures intended to boost the fortunes of minorities.[50] But the "police"—the conflict entrepreneurs—are in fact those who construct the prisoner's dilemma in which working-class whites are caught. A May 15, 2023, segment of *The Five*, a hit show on Fox News, provided a classic example of the workings of this sort of hermeneutic trap. Responding to a speech to Howard University graduates in which President Joe Biden called on the nation "to choose love over hate, unity over disunity," said that "racism has long torn us apart," and identified white supremacy as the main threat to the nation, the show's four überconservative panelists savaged the president. One argued that although white supremacists might commit mass murder a few times a year, the biggest threat to young Black men in the United States was other Black men with guns. It was regrettable, another opined, that Biden's words might rob innocent white children of any pride they had in themselves. When the token liberal on the show pushed back with some powerful points, one of the conservatives rhetorically obliterated everything she said and accused Biden of lying to Black people to keep them angry and tied to illusion.[51] For the show's conservative audience, Biden's plea to choose love over hate could be interpreted only as a call for racial hatred, child abuse, rage, and the brainwashing of Black people. For its core viewers, *The Five* had built an inescapable hermeneutic trap.[52]

To the extent they are conscious of this effect and not just working a room whose social rules were written before they were born, leaders of the anti–civil rights movement such as Rufo and the stars of *The Five* have taken, as their guiding philosophy, a sort of *interest-divergence* principle that works to preserve their and their allies' agenda-setting power. This may be why *The Five*'s panelists so energetically vivisected

Biden's speech: whatever anti–white supremacist agenda setting he might have had in mind at Howard was drowned in the spittle of conservative ire.

With the agenda-setting power of *The Five* in mind, we can reformulate Bell's principle from the point of view of the anti–civil rights movement as follows: the interests of Black Americans (and others) in achieving equal opportunity will be accommodated only when they converge with conservative elites' interest in maintaining agenda-setting power. To the extent that conservative elites' agenda-setting power is threatened by judicial and other remedies for inequality, those remedies will be buried at the bottom of hermeneutic traps.

Some of the cultural psychology behind *The Five* was described decades earlier in a book that probably influenced Bell and his interest-convergence principle (first laid out in his 1980 essay "*Brown* and the Interest-Convergence Dilemma"). That book, Gunnar Myrdal's massive 1944 study *An American Dilemma*, shaped American policymakers' thinking about race for decades and played a role in the Supreme Court's decision to rule school segregation unconstitutional.[53] Myrdal describes the paradoxical coexistence of white supremacy (and therefore interest divergence) and cherished ideals of liberty and equality:

> We shall find that even a poor and uneducated white person in some isolated and backward rural region of the Deep South, who is violently prejudiced against the Negro . . . has also a whole compartment in his valuation sphere housing the entire American Creed of liberty, equality, justice, and fair opportunity for everybody. . . . At the other end, there are few liberals, even in New England, who have not a well-furnished compartment of race prejudice, even if it is usually suppressed from conscious attention. Even the American Negroes share in this community of valuations.[54]

Anticipating the theory of cognitive dissonance, Myrdal adds, "Trying to defend their behaviors to others, and primarily to themselves, people will attempt to conceal the conflict between their different valuations of what is desirable and undesirable, right or wrong, by keeping away some valuations from awareness and by focusing attention on others, *people will twist and mutilate their beliefs of how social reality actually is.*"[55]

Recent American politics has been driven by the need for politicians, pundits, think tank intellectuals, and voters to twist reality in ways that trigger hermeneutic traps and the resulting bad, acrimonious decisions. Those caught in these traps slide down a chute of bad interpretations of national reality like ants sliding down funnels dug by insects called ant lions into the ant lions' jaws. These chutes of bad interpretations—these hermeneutic traps—deliver those caught in them into the jaws of a delusion or lead them to vote against their own interests.[56] Unfortunately for activists like Bell, life in a hermeneutic trap can feel very cozy and safe.

THE CONSPICUOUS CONSUMPTION OF WHITENESS

This is why, as Bell knew, changing the value of white status by diluting its hold on agenda-setting power can lead not only to the banning of parts of US racial history but also to bloodletting born of denial or ignorance of that history.[57] Tucker Carlson, who gave Rufo the launching pad for his CRT panic, also helped dig a hermeneutic trap so deep that a racist massacre may have grown out of it. That massacre happened in 2022 when an eighteen-year-old white man, motivated partly by fear of a conspiracy to replace white people (which Carlson regularly promoted on his show), killed ten people and wounded three in a Buffalo, New York, supermarket selected because many Black people shopped there.[58] Before the massacre, the gunman posted a long celebration of murder that, combined with scribblings on his weapons, invoked every anti–civil rights trope in the book, alongside racist ideas that would be disavowed by all but a tiny fringe of that movement.

Because they show what is ultimately at stake in this book's discussion of hermeneutic traps, and because they display some of what the real critical race theory aims to call out, it is worth examining some of the gunman's beliefs. Written on his assault rifle were taunts such as "buck status broken," which, according to the Anti-Defamation League (ADL), "is likely referring to 'buck breaking,' the use of brutal sexual violence by slave owners as punishment against enslaved Black men." Also written on the gun was "#BLM mogged"—"mogged" being internet slang for the assertion of dominance, in this case, over the Black Lives Matter movement. The ADL continues:

> Writing above the trigger of the AR-15 stock reads "James Watson," the name of the Nobel Prize–winning scientist who was stripped of his honorary titles in 2019 for linking race and IQ. . . . Writing on the stock of the assault rifle includes the phrase "here's your reparations!" This refers to the call for reparations for descendants of slaves in America and sometimes People of Color in general. . . . The bolt-action rifle includes similar references such as . . . "white lives matter" [an aggrieved reply to the Black Lives Matter movement, which is regularly demonized on Fox and among Republican politicians].[59]

Stripped of the virulent racism, many of the gunman's assertions can be found in anti–civil rights and anti–affirmative action rhetoric going back decades. *The Bell Curve*, for example, attempts to provide evidence for claims like Watson's. Affirmative action itself has been characterized as the replacement of deserving whites by undeserving Blacks.

The killer's assertions of dominance through violence and his celebration of the breaking of Black status are, of course, not part of the mainstream anti–civil rights movement. But a more sanitized, nonviolent version of the battle for agenda-setting dominance—which often makes violence unnecessary—is evident in Rufo's celebration of decodifying and recodifying CRT into something that would arouse instant outrage among "Americans"—a group that, in Rufo's imagination, does not include anyone who might take CRT seriously.

This book maintains a wall of separation between the gunman's views and those of the mainstream movement. But at the same time, my research shows that there are fewer degrees of separation between his opinions and those of the high-minded wing of the anti–civil rights movement than the high-minded would like to think. If a hermeneutic trap can deliver a person to the view that Derrick Bell is a "radical college *racist* professor," then, given a sufficient amount of disinformation, its bottom can fall out and deliver a person into a racist charnel house like the Buffalo gunman's mind.

Claiming to defend the truth, activists like Rufo clearly play fast and loose with racial distortions and have a good time doing it. But genuine defenders of the high Enlightenment quest to escape illusion—a quest at the core of America's founding documents that I endorse and that Bell's character Geneva Crenshaw pleads with the founders to protect by excluding slavery from the Constitution[60]—those defenders need to remember that the quest can be corrupted by payoffs paid in the coin of racial illusion.[61]

SCOPE OF THIS BOOK

Though the affirmative action debate is its bull's-eye, this book is also a guide to the personalities, funding, dilemmas, and traps that play a role in the contest between the civil rights and anti–civil rights movements. The sort of guide it is can be summarized by brief genealogies of two affirmative action–related cases: *Gratz v. Bollinger* (2003), which grew directly out of the money and maneuvering of major players in the anti–civil rights movement, and *Officers for Justice v. Civil Service Commission of the City and County of San Francisco* (1995), a long-running litigation that forced the San Francisco Police Department to hire more African Americans, Asian Americans, other minorities, and women of all races.

By "genealogy," I mean four things: (1) the series of court decisions that influence subsequent ones and become precedents; (2) the chain of outside influences, including financial support for lawsuits intended to alter government policy and briefs written by interested parties; (3) legislation passed in response to both civil rights and anti–civil rights campaigns; and (4) enforcement standards set by government agencies.

About legal precedents, current Supreme Court justice Amy Coney Barrett wrote in 2013, "Justices can more easily apply the Constitution's broad language because precedent offers them a framework for doing so."[62] When a precedent is judged to have been established in error, it can be overruled, as the Supreme Court's 1896 endorsement of segregation in *Plessy v. Ferguson* was overruled by *Brown v. Board of Education* in 1954. Part of the mission of the anti–civil rights movement is the overturning of key civil rights–related Supreme Court decisions.[63] As a result, the two movements and their precedents, legal and otherwise, are intertwined. Thus, although the *Gratz* genealogy in figure I.1 is an anti–civil rights genealogy, Thurgood Marshall, the legendary "Mr. Civil Rights," is central to it because his victory in *Brown* was the starting gun for the modern anti–civil rights movement.

Among those responding to that starting gun was *Richmond News Leader* editor James J. Kilpatrick. A firm believer in Black inferiority, Kilpatrick turned his newspaper's editorial page over to the legal theory that states could use their authority to block the mixing of Black and white schoolchildren. Though his message, along with the messages of powerful politicians such as Senator Strom Thurmond, was not equally successful everywhere, what mattered in the long run was that Kilpatrick, Thurmond, and others rode herd on the southern psyche at a time when some leaders in the region were looking for ways to live with *Brown*.[64] The result was that a number of state legislatures passed anti-*Brown* laws and funded segregation academics.

A key figure in the *Gratz* genealogy is Arizona senator and 1964 GOP presidential candidate Barry Goldwater. Goldwater added momentum to the anti–civil rights movement by claiming, in a book that became a "conservative bible," that the *Brown* decision violated the Constitution and should not be viewed as the law of the land, and he topped this by voting against the Civil Rights Act of 1964.[65] Goldwater's presidential campaign was the incubator for the political career of Ronald Reagan as well as the careers of a number of enormously influential political operatives who appear in the genealogy in figure I.1.

One such operative was Paul Weyrich, an organizational and strategic genius who was the intellectual father of the Heritage Foundation and a midwife of the Moral Majority—two organizations that energized the anti–civil rights movement. Through these and other institutions, Weyrich shaped the present as few others have, partly because he had a gift for picking partners such as the Reverend Jerry Falwell, the first leader of the Moral Majority. Falwell closed the loop between the original anti–civil rights movement sparked by the *Brown*

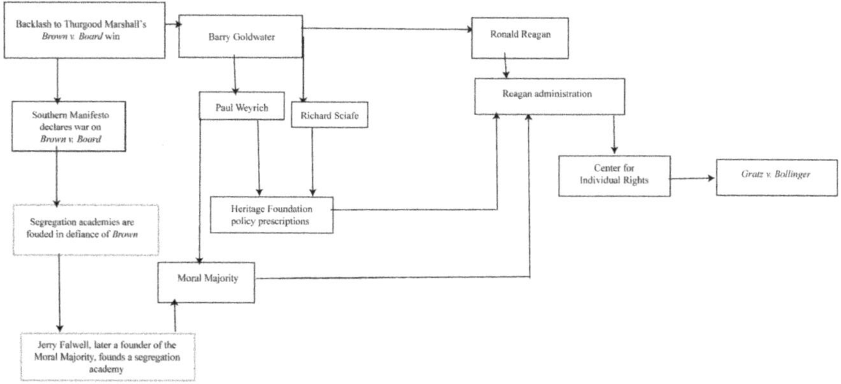

Figure I.1. Partial genealogy of *Gratz v. Bollinger*

The arrows in this genealogy connect a source of influence to the persons or entities influenced by that source. For example, Barry Goldwater got an electoral boost from the influential backlash against *Brown v. Board of Education*, and the Goldwater campaign was in turn a formative experience for donor Richard Scaife and political strategist Paul Weyrich, who helped found the Heritage Foundation and the Moral Majority. The latter helped Reagan win the presidency, and the former helped shape Reagan's policy agenda. Finally, Reagan administration alumni formed or litigated for the Center for Individual Rights, which brought major affirmative action cases, including *Gratz v. Bollinger*.

decision and the more mainstream movement whose face was Ronald Reagan.[66] Like Goldwater, Falwell condemned the *Brown* decision. He also condemned Martin Luther King Jr. and the 1964 Civil Rights Act and founded a "private school for white students."[67] But he lived to reverse his most extreme positions and remained a power broker for decades after helping Reagan win the presidency with Moral Majority votes. Reagan's presidency, in turn, created the climate of opinion and the legal approach from which *Gratz v. Bollinger* grew.

Figure I.1's brief genealogy is necessarily incomplete, as is this book's narrative of the road to *Gratz* and the key cases that followed it. Several volumes would be required to provide a complete account of the many larger-than-life characters, bank accounts, obsessions, and displays of genius that played a part in generating and winning cases like *Gratz*. In addition, this genealogy does not include a key illusion that tipped the anti–civil rights movement spear in the years after the *Gratz* case—the myth of Asian Americans as a "model minority" passed over in favor of lesser nonwhites by university admissions policies. The apotheosis of this use of the model minority, *Students for Fair Admissions v. Harvard* alleged that Asians with superior test scores and grade point averages (GPAs) were being admited to Harvard University at unjustly low rates because of their scores on a discriminatory "personal" rating. It thereby created the permission structure for a supermajority of six conservative Supreme Court justices to cut down all but a sliver of affirmative action on June 29, 2023. But an amicus curiae (friend of the court) brief written on behalf of 1,241 social scientists pushed back, arguing that the disproportionate number of high-scoring, high-GPA Asians applying to top US schools has more to do with immigration policy than anything else. For decades, the United States' selective immigration policy has favored people like educated Chinese and Indian immigrants—people who hold college and professional degrees at higher rates than the general populations in the United States or in India or China. But inevitably, in the hyperracialized US environment, this educational (and therefore income and opportunity) advantage is translated into the *racial* advantage of a model minority. Conservatives then use this advantage as evidence of the inadequacy or dysfunction of long-discriminated-against groups such as African Americans and Latinos.[68] This is not to say that Asians do not face real, ongoing discrimination and, in recent years, a spike in vicious assaults. But they are a diverse group that, as this book shows, does not fit the politically useful portrait the anti–civil rights movement paints.

The second genealogy (figure I.2) chronicles a confluence of civil rights triumphs that Thurgood Marshall played a major role in, whether as a lawyer and leader of the NAACP Legal Defense Fund or as a Supreme Court justice. Just as important to the second genealogy is A. Philip Randolph, a visionary with a voice so big it seemed to have its own echo. Randolph made his first indelible mark on America in 1925, when he organized the Brotherhood of Sleeping Car Porters. Eventually, its members became the highest-paid Black workers in the United States.[69] Convinced that "public opinion is the most powerful weapon in America," Randolph threatened to unleash it in 1941 with a March on Washington if President Franklin Roosevelt did not create a Fair Employment Practice Committee (FEPC) to fight "discrimination in employment related to the war effort."[70] Roosevelt formed the committee. Next, in 1950, Randolph cofounded a coalition of labor, civil rights, and religious organizations, the Leadership Conference on Civil Rights (LCCR), which lobbied President Harry Truman and his successors to make the FEPC permanent.[71]

As their movement built to a climax in the early 1960s, squabbling civil rights organizations settled on Randolph as a unifying figure and made him director of the 1963 March on Washington. That march, with Martin Luther King's "I Have a Dream" speech as the jewel in its crown, helped pressure Congress to pass the Civil Rights Act of 1964 (which occupies a central place in figure I.2). Titles VI and VII of the act paved the way for affirmative action as we know it, and each of them created its own drama.

Title VI was the brainchild of the hedonistic, movie-star-handsome, idol-smashing Black congressman Adam Clayton Powell (whose district was a result of a Randolph campaign to redistrict New York). It gave the federal government authority to refuse to "finance discrimination" by contractors and others receiving federal funds.[72] More than half a century later, Trump's executive order ironically drew some of its power from Powell's idea of withholding federal funds.

Title VII, whose basic language was drafted in a committee chaired by Powell, not only prohibited employment discrimination but also mandated the creation of the Equal Employment Opportunity Commission (EEOC), a successor to the FEPC with somewhat sharper teeth.[73] The combination of Title VII and EEOC regulations became the legal basis of a landmark win for affirmative action in *Griggs v. Duke Power Company* (1971). In turn, with *Griggs* as precedent, the integration of many construction sites, police departments, universities, and much else was accomplished.

Griggs is also partly a Thurgood Marshall story. Developed and argued before the Supreme Court by Jack Greenberg—Marshall's handpicked successor as head of the NAACP Legal Defense Fund—*Griggs* was a triumph that Marshall was on the court to vote for, and he lamented its "implicit" overruling by a later, more conservative court in a 1989 speech.[74] While *Griggs* retained its full power, however, it served as a precedent in a San Francisco case that helped open the door for minorities and women in the San Francisco Police Department. That case, the aforementioned *Officers for Justice v. Civil Service Commission of the City and County of San Francisco*, is a characteristic triumph of the civil rights movement and affirmative action in their heyday, and it is the culmination of the genealogy in figure I.2.

Meanwhile, the always lurking anti–civil rights movement is represented in the figure by Wickliff Draper, a textile heir whose fortune helped support the nastiest parts of that movement for decades. Aiming to strangle the Civil Rights Act of 1964 before it became law, Draper funded the Coordinating Committee for Fundamental American Freedoms—a lobbying outfit run by arch-segregationists who believed in Black inferiority. Although the committee folded after the civil rights bill passed, its members played important roles in promoting anti-*Brown* "segregation academies" (another project Draper helped fund).[75]

Also lurking in figure I.2 is Coordinating Committee alumnus James J. Kilpatrick, who exemplifies the strategy that has held the anti–civil rights movement together over the decades. After passage of the 1964 Civil Rights Act, Kilpatrick remade his public image and emerged as a nationally syndicated newspaper columnist and respected television personality. He helped blaze a trail followed by many other formerly open segregationists.[76] With his sins shrugged off by the newspapers across the nation that ran his column and by television's *60 Minutes*, where he was a regular, Kilpatrick set out to co-opt the rhetoric and the moral authority of the civil rights movement while keeping some of his old anti-Black attitudes at the ready, like palmed cards.

In one 1979 column he described Thurgood Marshall "rolling his eyes to heaven" as he wrote an opinion (something Kilpatrick could not have witnessed). With this offhand phrase, Kilpatrick summoned minstrel show caricatures of African Americans, which featured much eye rolling.[77] But then, lamenting an affirmative action case that upheld race-conscious assignments to a training program, Kilpatrick accused the Supreme Court of turning the clock back to 1896, when the "separate but equal" standard set by *Plessy v. Ferguson* (and overturned

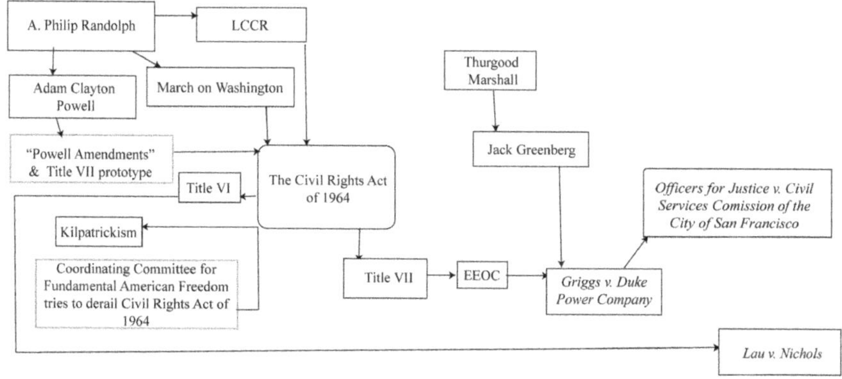

Figure I.2. Partial genealogy of *Officers for Justice v. San Francisco*

Central to this genealogy is the Civil Rights Act of 1964, elements of which African American heroes A. Philip Randolph and Adam Clayton Powell spent decades campaigning for. Opponents formed the Coordinating Committee for Fundamental Rights to try to derail the act. In defeat, some of them took refuge in "Kilpatrickism," a selective co-opting and zombification of civil rights movement ideals, rhetoric, and strategy. Out of the Civil Rights Act came major sources of affirmative action—Title VI, Title VII, and the EEOC. Other sources of affirmative action policy and practice included landmark cases such as *Griggs v. Duke Power Company*, a precedent cited in the *Officers for Justice* decision.

by *Brown*) was the law of the land.[78] Thus, Kilpatrick demeaned Marshall with a racist trope and then condemned racism a few lines later.

Riffing two years afterwards on an 1857 Supreme Court pronouncement that a Black person has no rights that a white person needs to respect, Kilpatrick asked whether, in "such areas as education, employment and voting rights, we approach the reverse of the proposition: Do whites have no rights that blacks are bound to respect?"[79] Endless repetition helped solidify Kilpatrick's anti–affirmative action position "into conventional wisdom," in the view of Ta-Nehisi Coates.[80]

But there was far more involved than mere repetition in the transformation of cries of Black inferiority into cries of reverse discrimination, and the parallel transformation of open expressions of contempt into the almost subliminal images of Marshall rolling his eyes toward heaven. "Kilpatrickism" epitomizes the journey into euphemism and the (sometimes) changed beliefs that have characterized the anti–civil rights movement since 1954. Its infiltration of the mainstream in the person of Kilpatrick (*60 Minutes* was the top TV show in the country during some of his years on the program) and many others no doubt added to the frustration evident in some of Marshall's Supreme Court dissents (more about this later). Although the Coordinating Committee for Fundamental American Freedom was soundly defeated by Marshall, Randolph, Powell, and other civil rights movement heroes, the forces behind it did not die; like Kilpatrick, they remade themselves.

Taken together, the two genealogies demonstrate my reasons for not discussing my core subject, affirmative action, in isolation but instead discussing it as a battlefield where the fighters and strategies are part of a larger war between the two movements. Indeed, the fact that Marshall appears in both genealogies tells us that the civil rights and anti–civil rights movements are engaged in a peculiar arms race, albeit one in which most of the intellectual weapons come from the civil rights side.

Because the anti–civil rights movement seeks to blur the lines between itself and its target, part of this book's mission is to distinguish between the original movement, led by people like Randolph, Powell, King, and Marshall, and the anti–civil rights movement, powered by activists such as Kilpatrick, Goldwater, Rufo, Weyrich, and Draper.[81] The willful blurring of the lines between the two movements often succeeds because the vocabulary of the civil rights movement has been captured by its opponent, zombified, and sent back to bite the original movement's heirs (including literal heirs such as Martin Luther King III).

That being said, it must be admitted that not all civil rights movement heirs see affirmative action as worth its unintended consequences. Derrick Bell saw it as a kind of bait and switch that lifts a few minorities up into the opportunity stratosphere at the cost of trapping the masses in a massive opportunity deprivation chamber.

Best-selling civil rights lawyer Michelle Alexander has questioned whether resources poured into defending affirmative action as a means of integrating elite schools might have been better used to combat mass incarceration. Affirmative action, Alexander adds, may even be counterproductive because high-visibility African American success stories "prove" that anyone can reach the top with enough hard work; therefore, those given draconian and often irrational prison sentences have only themselves to blame.[82] But, as the CRT panic and its successors show, anyone who accepts Rufo- or Levin-style "proof" would be susceptible to Rufo-like views, with or without affirmative action.

Still, civil rights energies are just as finite and in need of careful allocation and strategic deployment as Alexander thinks they are. Derrick Bell himself came to question the wisdom of his focus on desegregating schools when he was a young Justice Department and then NAACP lawyer.[83] "I too was insufficiently sensitive to how much would be lost when black schools were closed with most of the black teachers and principals dismissed," he writes in *Ethical Ambition*. "Worst of all, I knew that black children and their parents would have to seek the equal educational opportunity we lawyers promised them in often hostile and always alien schools."[84]

This admission is not, of course, a disavowal of integration as a means of democratizing access to opportunity and high status. Nor, as Bell's Harvard protest and his earlier resignation from the University of Oregon (when it refused to hire a top Asian candidate) show, is it a disavowal of turning affirmative action like a key in the door to agenda-setting power.[85] So, while the always questioning Bell wondered about making desegregation the holy grail, he clearly believed in integrating powerful institutions and in using affirmative action to do so.[86]

What he insisted on, then, was a cost-benefit analysis of integration, affirmative action, and other paths out of second-class citizenship. His interest-convergence test is a sort of generalization of the pragmatism that his mentor Thurgood Marshall admonished him to practice after Bell was arrested in 1961 for trying to use a telephone in a train station waiting room reserved for whites—with a white policeman glowering at him as he did so. "Damn, boy," Marshall later admonished him, "the black folks down South need good lawyering. They don't need dead heroes. They got plenty of them already. Understand? Do your protesting in the courtroom, not in the railroad station."[87]

Bell's disillusionment and self-questioning are due in part to the success of the anti–civil rights movement, which builds funhouse mirror after funhouse mirror to make interest convergence look like interest divergence. Even when affirmative action *did* crack open opportunity's gates, Bell found, the adjusted measures of merit that created the openings were used to renew old stigmas. Over time, the supposed magnanimity minorities were receiving morphed, in the minds of many whites (and some minorities), into a "badge of inferiority" that whites (and others) who were not accepted by their chosen colleges could place, like a discount sticker, on the academic records of Blacks but not, as Bell points out, on the records of legacy applicants and athletes who had been granted a nonacademic edge.[88]

By viewing the world with a practical eye, this book ends up seeing affirmative action—which even now is not quite dead—as a greater positive than Bell and Alexander do. After all, affirmative action helped place them, Barack Obama, and other movers and shakers in agenda-setting positions where they could call attention to and start to address the needs of the nonwhite underclass.

This book is therefore pro affirmative action, but not religiously so. After all, it is hard to be religious about an experiment, and affirmative action is nothing but a group of experiments in the creation of equal opportunity within the larger experiment of American democracy.[89] If there are better solutions to the prisoner's dilemma than the various race- and gender-conscious affirmative action experiments—including ads encouraging women and minorities to apply for positions, rewards for applicants who add to diversity, the use of federal dollars to pressure universities and companies, and the funding of minority-owned businesses—that is, if there are other plausible ways to make the path to agenda-setting power the same length for everyone, this book would embrace them. (Chapter 17, for instance, admiringly describes Texas's Top 10 Percent law as an ingenious stopgap workaround of an affirmative action ban, which it is. And the conclusion praises the University of California–Davis Medical School's use of a socioeconomic disadvantage score to build an exceptionally diverse class without directly considering race—with the caveat that such an approach may be unaffordable across California's, much less the nation's, educational system.)

But my main mission in these pages is to illuminate what affirmative action actually is by bulldozing the hermeneutical trap the anti–civil rights movement has placed it in. What I hope to encourage is a less ignorant, less bitter debate about affirmative action as it is—or, if the Supreme Court ends every form of it, which seems likely at the time of this writing, as it was. This clarification will matter even if all affirmative action is eliminated because the anti–civil rights movement's claims of antiwhite (or anti-Asian) discrimination are a transferable mythology, an intellectual virus that can infect CRT today and protests against racial violence tomorrow.[90]

One last bit of preliminary bulldozing is in order, and it concerns the reputations of Sandra Day O'Connor and anti–civil rights movement hero Antonin Scalia. O'Connor was elevated to the Supreme Court in large part because Ronald Reagan wanted to appoint a woman to that august body. O'Connor was therefore one of the most prominent beneficiaries of affirmative action in the twentieth century, even though she is never classified as such. Nor is Scalia, who was selected for the court in part because Reagan wanted to appoint an Italian. Indeed, Scalia railed so hard against affirmative action that O'Connor interrupted one of his rants by asking, "Nino, how do you think I got my job?"[91] But her remark was merely a quip, not a serious acknowledgment of having benefited from affirmative action. O'Connor, after all, was a rancher's daughter who resented the edge affirmative action gave Native Americans in their competition with ranchers over water rights.[92] As law professor Cheryl I. Harris argues, this sort of attitude grows out of a desire to hold on to the old advantages of being white, just as one holds on to property. Perhaps this explains why both Scalia and O'Connor felt free to judge affirmative action as if they were outside its sometimes charmed, sometimes cursed circle.[93] They thereby preserved their full quantum of agenda-setting power—their ability to "objectively" turn affirmative action toward the light of impartial judgment—and in Scalia's case, his full quantum of freedom to heap scorn on those who promoted the policy and pity on those who benefited from it. This was possible because of the persistence of race as a hermeneutic trap. Such traps endure because, as thinkers ranging from Nobel laureate Daniel Kahneman to philosopher Hans-Georg Gadamer have shown, humans are not omniscient and must rely on partially prefabricated understandings of the world—on prejudgments, as Gadamer calls them.[94] Such prejudgments can last for years or centuries because they seem to get agenda setters and aspiring agenda setters where they want to go.

But if something goes wrong with a prefabricated judgment about, for instance, race or merit or the US Constitution, the result might be a social upheaval that requires revising or perhaps discarding some prejudgments, even if they are enshrined in the Constitution or an established interpretation of it.[95] Under such circumstances, everyone is forced to practice some version of the philosophical art of hermeneutics, whose goal is to "distinguish the true [prejudgments], by which we *understand*, from the *false* ones," according to Gadamer.[96]

Unfortunately, in the political realm, bad prejudgments are reinforced by conflict entrepreneurs like Rufo, who make it more difficult to follow our better angels—our better judgments. Even without someone like Rufo around, it is "impossible to make ourselves aware of a [prejudgment] while it is constantly operating unnoticed," Gadamer writes.[97] As a result, even without a Rufo, we can end up falling into hermeneutic traps that keep us from rejecting bad judgements and cause us, like the conservatives on *The Five*, to see a call for love as a call for hatred or, as in the prisoner's dilemma, to feel compelled to betray a partner.

Because race as hermeneutic trap often operates unnoticed, affirmative action babies Scalia and O'Connor are usually treated as having landed on the Supreme Court entirely because of a transcendental merit untouched by prejudgment or history.

DESCRIPTION OF CHAPTERS

To fulfill its task of mapping the hermeneutic traps in which affirmative action and much else are caught, this book is divided into two parts. The first part focuses on the rise of affirmative action in the period before the Reagan administration, when the anti–civil rights movement was on its back foot. The second part covers the period during and after the Reagan administration, when the anti–civil rights movement not only put the civil rights movement on the defensive but also increasingly co-opted and zombified civil rights language and strategy.

Chapter 1 begins with Thurgood Marshall at the moment of his greatest triumph and proceeds to outline how this triumph inspired the fathers of the twentieth-century anti–civil rights movement to "run Thurgood ragged." Chapter 2 sketches some of the activists, lawyers, and officials who made memorable use of Title VI and changed American education with *Lau v. Nichols* (1974). Chapter 3 zeroes in on the work and impact of Ling-Chi Wang and Henry Der, a founder and an early leader, respectively, of the San Francisco civil rights organization Chinese for Affirmative Action. Chapter 4 explores how tensions in the prisoner's dilemma, massaged by well-funded conflict entrepreneurs, caused a split in the multiracial coalition of which Chinese for Affirmative Action was a part.

Chapter 5 is the first of a number of chapters that focus on the conflict entrepreneurs themselves. Chapters 6–9 explore the 1978 *Bakke* case, which both extended the life of affirmative action and locked it in a hermeneutic trap. Chapter 10 examines a post-*Bakke* incident at Cornell University and the still-resonating fury it inspired among conservatives.

Chapter 11 opens part II with a closer examination of the clashing conceptions of equality that fly like banners over most of the battles between the civil rights and anti–civil rights movements. Chapters 12 and 13 chronicle the Reagan administration's meteor-like impact on the intellectual foundations of the civil rights movement. Chapters 14 and 15 trace the rise of a key hermeneutic tool of the anti–civil rights movement—"originalism"—as the one true method of interpretation of the US Constitution.

Chapter 16 sketches the activities of Reagan administration alumnus Clint Bolick, a master zombifier of civil rights language. Chapter 17 describes the death of affirmative action in Texas and its sly resurrection at the hands of Latina Texas legislator Irma Rangel. Chapter 18 tells the story of one of the greatest triumphs of the anti–civil rights movement—Proposition 209, which ended affirmative action in California. Chapter 19 covers the philosophical metamorphosis and anti–civil rights movement initiation of Edward Blum, who superseded Bolick and everyone else as an anti–affirmative action warlord. Chapter 20 extends an analogy, introduced in chapter 19, between anti–affirmative action and anti–civil rights arguments and the three-card monte con game. The analogy shows how the lowest language of racial degradation is subliminally mixed into the high-minded rhetoric of equality and fairness used by Blum and other princes of the anti–civil rights movement.[98]

Chapters 21–23 chronicle landmark battles over affirmative action and the meaning of "merit" in Michigan. Chapter 24 tracks Blum as he bursts into the inner sanctum of the civil rights movement, delivering massive blows to voting rights and gathering himself to deliver the final blow to affirmative action with the equal protection clause of the Constitution and Title VI, which did so much to spread affirmative action across the United States in the first place. Finally, the conclusion considers options for equal opportunity that may be pursued with or without affirmative action.

PART I

THE LAST DAYS OF THE CIVIL RIGHTS ERA

On April 14, 1955, the last day of oral arguments in part 2 of *Brown v. Board of Education*, Thurgood Marshall rests his briefcase on a balustrade outside the northwest door of the Supreme Court and arranges his papers. (Photo by Bettmann; used by permission of Getty Images)

1

RUNNING THURGOOD RAGGED

After the Supreme Court handed him a victory with its Monday, May 17, 1954, decision in the *Brown v. Board of Education* school desegregation case, and after the court followed up with a 1955 ruling requiring the foot-dragging South to integrate classes "with all deliberate speed," Thurgood Marshall was feeling good.[1] On June 2, 1955, he phoned Carl Murphy, president of Baltimore's *Afro-American* newspaper, to crow a little. When Murphy suggested that segregationist resistance would collapse when the NAACP returned to southern courtrooms with the *Brown* decision and its 1955 affirmation in its pocket, Marshall agreed: "those white crackers are going to get tired of having Negro lawyers beating 'em every day in court."[2]

By then, Marshall loomed like a "bogey man" below the Mason–Dixon Line, according to journalist Harry Golden. At a meeting of city leaders in Charlotte, North Carolina, one lawyer worried out loud that if a certain problem were not solved, "we'll have Thurgood Marshall on our necks."[3] But Marshall later realized that while he was savoring victory and making some in the South tremble, others were taking steps to nullify everything he and the NAACP Legal Defense Fund had achieved.[4]

At the front of the pack of would-be nullifiers was Mississippi judge Tom P. Brady. In an October 28, 1954, speech in Sunflower County, Brady highlighted the claim of NAACP leader Walter White that the organization had been working toward *Brown* for fifty years. The white South had been outhustled and outfoxed, Brady lamented, and he issued a call to arms wrapped in history so delusional that it could have come out of an opium dream. The *Brown* decision was less a command to provide equal education than a command to practice miscegenation and destroy civilization, Brady said. The white men who had raised the pyramids in Egypt, written the Vedas in India, and established the Mayan and Incan empires in the Americas had dissolved themselves in the acid of race mixing, Brady warned.[5]

The miscegenation imperative of *Brown*, he explained, was the climax of a long journey into self-destruction that began when greedy New Englanders foisted a population of slaves on an innocent South. The final blow was the Fourteenth Amendment, the basis of *Brown* and other bad things, which had been adopted illegally and voted in not by true southerners but by "Scalawags . . . Carpetbaggers, the Northern troops, and the negroes."[6]

For Brady, a ray of light in all this darkness was *United States v. Cruikshank*, an 1875 case in which the Supreme Court limited the federal government's ability to enforce the Fourteenth Amendment and its progeny and undid congressional actions that, in Brady's mind, had humiliated his region: "It was rough," he sighed, "and the heel of the conqueror was placed on the neck of the vanquished."[7]

There is a grain of truth in Brady's lamentation. After the Civil War, legislators from the former Confederacy were barred from taking seats in Congress because the late Abraham Lincoln's Republican Party was trying to stop former rebels from gaining a majority in Congress and legislating a neo-Confederacy into existence. The South's power had been expanded by the Thirteenth Amendment's transformation of enslaved individuals from three-fifths to full personhood. This entitled the South to more seats in the House of Representatives, even though the freed people would not be allowed to vote for those representatives.[8] Put another way, the freed individuals had been relieved of bondage but not fully released from civil death—the condition of being shorn of civil rights.[9] Cementing this, President Andrew Johnson issued a Proclamation of Amnesty and Reconstruction in May 1865 that allowed ex-Confederates to return to power in the South and set up governments that locked Blacks in neo-slavery.[10] When Congress moved to remedy this civil death by passing civil rights bills, Johnson cried reverse discrimination—without, of course, using that twentieth-century term. For "the security of the colored race," Congress was forging "safeguards which go infinitely beyond any that the General Government have ever provided for the white race," Johnson claimed. "In fact, the distinction of race and color is by the bill made to operate in favor of the colored and against the white race."[11]

Congress decided to go around the president by changing the Constitution.[12] The drafting of the Fourteenth Amendment began in February 1866 and ended in June of that year. In between, a congressional election took place in which the amendment was, in effect, on the ballot, and the Republicans behind the bill won 143 of 192 seats. Nevertheless, the struggle to ratify the amendment stretched on for more than two years, in part because Johnson encouraged former slaveholders to defy congressional authority, removed those who sought to enforce that authority, and backed an alternative amendment that, in the name of federalism, would have allowed individual states to continue to deny Blacks their rights.[13]

Most important from Brady's point of view, Johnson and other Fourteenth Amendment opponents believed that because Congress passed the measure while barring the participation of representatives from former Confederate states, it lacked the legitimacy to alter the Constitution. Rubbing salt in the imagined wounds of ex-Confederates and their descendants for the next century, the amendment barred anyone who had "engaged in insurrection or rebellion against" the United States from serving in the House or Senate unless two-thirds of Congress voted to "remove such a disability." The amendment also declared that states' representation would not increase in proportion to their freed populations unless voting-age freed males were granted the franchise.

But Johnson, whose photographs show a face designed for sneering, continued to undermine every effort to grant civil life to former slaves. Shrugging off an impeachment effort that fell one vote short of removing him from office in 1868 (a presidential election year), he kept on handing out pardons to former Confederate officials like candy and earned praise from the anti-Black Democratic Party for keeping "negro supremacy" at bay.[14]

A parable-like moment in Johnson's resistance—a moment that

crystallizes the difference between civil life and civil death—came in a case brought by one of the men the president pardoned: Augustus Hill Garland. A narrow-eyed lawyer with a pillow-fluffy face who served in both the Confederate House and the Confederate Senate during the Civil War, Garland gleefully chronicled the restoration of his status in an autobiographical book: "after the row between the States had subsided, I called on President Johnson with much amiability, and requested pardon for my deeds of commission and omission, in that row. . . . I procured the pardon—it was large and capacious, and I hugged it closely and went off rejoicing, with exceeding great joy, as a *novus homo* would naturally do."[15] Aside from his reduction of the greatest bloodletting in American history to a "row," what is most striking about Garland's anecdote is his winking christening of himself as a *homo novus*—a new man, transmuted from outcast traitor to honorable citizen. The term *homo novus* has deep and, in a way, all-American significance. It is rooted in the words of Cicero, a persistent influence on American law, politics, and literature.[16] (A *homo novus* in Cicero's time was someone not born into the Roman nobility who nevertheless ascended into the aristocracy on the strength of his performance in public office.)[17]

Thus the pardoned Garland, washed clean of the walking corpsehood of civil death that was the fate of a traitor, reclaimed his position in the American equivalent of nobility: the society of white men with agenda-setting power.[18] A lawyer before the war, Garland applied for readmission to the Supreme Court bar, even though Congress had stripped ex-Confederate officials of the right to argue before the high court. Denied, Garland filed what turned out to be a landmark lawsuit alleging a violation of his rights. A six–three Supreme Court majority agreed that he had unconstitutionally been subjected to the elements of civil death that are part of a "bill of attainder"—literally, a bill that declares a person tainted.[19] But Justice Samuel Freeman Miller, a Lincoln appointee from Kentucky who had abandoned the practice of medicine for the law, dissented, arguing that the loyalty oath required of Garland and others was neither a bill of attainder nor the other iniquity claimed by Garland: an ex post facto law. Men like Garland, Miller asserted, were themselves sources of corruption who were rightly exiled from the bar, for weren't former rebels in the same class as lawyers disbarred for exhibiting moral turpitude?[20]

Ironically, despite his condemnation of "treasonable sentiments," Miller opposed the Fourteenth Amendment and led judicial efforts against it. In the process, he articulated views on which Brady later relied.[21] Miller even joined the majority opinion in Brady's cherished *United States v. Cruikshank*, which takes its name from the leader of a white mob that murdered more than two dozen Blacks taken prisoner during a battle the whites had started over an election in Grant Parish, Louisiana.[22]

Like a preacher recounting some miracle in the desert, Brady declared that *Cruikshank* "saved the South, and it saved the nation." But it was being menaced by *Brown* and related civil rights decisions and initiatives: "Anti–Poll Tax, Anti-Segregation, Anti-Lynching and the FEPC" stalked the land. With *Brown* coming down like a conqueror's heel, Brady summoned his audience to mortal—but legal and nonviolent—combat in defense of the southerner's right "to keep his blood white and pure," despite the Supreme Court's insistence that "you have got to sit a negro boy down by a white girl," in violation of "all the laws of eugenics and biology."[23]

That is what Thurgood Marshall was up against: a primordial thirst for superiority that was beyond the reach of reason and fact. And Brady was a great success. He gave speeches like the one in Sunflower County all across the United States. He developed those talks into a ninety-page manifesto that became both a bible and, through its sales, an endowment for a network of white Citizens Councils—a sort of Ku Klux Klan without the signature assassinations and cross burnings—which in turn became one of the sources of modern conservatism. Brady himself saw the Citizens Councils as the "nucleus for a conservative party in the United States," and he supported leaders of the anti–civil rights movement such as Alabama governor George Wallace and South Carolina senator Strom Thurmond. The latter set a still-standing record with a twenty-four-hour filibuster against a 1957 civil rights bill.[24]

The degrees of separation between those politicians and the contemporary Right are actually quite few. As conservative strategist Kevin P. Phillips has written, a massive race-driven realignment of US voting patterns arguably began in 1948, when, in response to the Democratic Party's endorsement of the desegregation of its national convention, southerners formed the States Rights Party and made Thurmond, then the governor of South Carolina, its presidential candidate. By 1972, Thurmond was a power in the Senate and his former aide, Harry Dent, was advising President Nixon on southern politics.[25] In the period between Thurmond's presidential run and the Nixon White House, Phillips writes, "the white South marched out of its historical alignment with the Democrats into a new alignment with the Republicans in presidential politics, and the race issue was probably the central reason."[26]

A turning point in this realignment came in 1956, when more than a hundred US senators and representatives signed the now-infamous Southern Manifesto (conceived by Thurmond), which demanded the nullification of *Brown.* The combination of Brady's Citizens Councils, the Southern Manifesto, and passage of legislation to fund white students' enrollment in segregated private schools helped preserve and defend a bifurcated and unequal educational system whose consequences continue to this day.[27]

As the NAACP and the Supreme Court fought to enforce *Brown,* Southern Manifesto supporters "shifted strategies" and crafted an argument that later became central to the affirmative action debate. They embraced a "neutered" version of *Brown,* insisting that *Brown,* "properly understood, actually mandated 'colorblind' policies" and "forbade districts from even voluntarily striving for meaningful integration if they considered the race of individual students in pursuing their goal," according to law professor Justin Driver.[28]

Strom Thurmond—womanizing, Miss South Carolina–marrying, exercise-obsessed, and destined to serve in the Senate until he was ninety-nine years old—was an early adopter of this and other key anti–civil rights movement strategies. Years before Brady lodged his complaints about the federal government's moves to end lynching, the poll tax, and employment discrimination, Thurmond temporarily broke with the Democratic Party to challenge Democratic president Harry Truman, whom A. Philip Randolph and others had pressured into integrating the armed forces and taking steps to combat hiring discrimination. Thurmond insisted that efforts like Truman's violated the federal system created by the Constitution. While accepting the presidential nomination of the aforementioned States Rights Party, Thurmond uncoiled a high tenor voice like a whip endowed with speech and attacked Truman's civil rights program as a step toward a police state.[29] Then, in 1964, Thurmond had a hand in founding the modern GOP when he permanently left the Democrats and declared himself a "Goldwater Republican." His support helped make Barry Goldwater the first of many Republican presidential candidates to carry the South.

Next, in 1967, from his perch as a senior member of the Senate Judiciary Committee, Thurmond staged a showdown with Thurgood Marshall during the latter's Supreme Court confirmation hearings. Trying to embarrass the man who had beaten the South, Thurmond fired a barrage of questions about the arcana of the Thirteenth and Fourteenth Amendments, which he characterized as Marshall's "area of expertise." "What committee," he asked at one point, "reported out the 14th amendment and who were its members?" Thurmond even tried to make Marshall admit that, in essence, outlawing segregation was contrary to the intent of the Fourteenth Amendment and its framers. Citing a statement made by the author of the amendment's equal protection clause that seemed to accept restrictions on voting and bans on school integration and miscegenation, Thurmond asked, "Do you find this remark relevant in interpreting the equal protection clause [of the Fourteenth Amendment] as it applies to the right to vote, enter desegregated schools, or engage in miscegenation?" Marshall played his ace: "All of this was litigated in the *Brown* case. Both sides, everybody, researched it. The Supreme Court found that there was nothing clearly derived from those debates."[30]

Thurmond turned to testing Marshall's commitment to what was later called an originalist interpretation of the Constitution: "Do you think that the Supreme Court must adhere to the original understanding of the Constitution as set forth by its framers, or may it ignore the intent of the framers and hold that a provision of the Constitution means whatever the Court chooses to have it mean at the moment?" Marshall's retort presaged a battle that would continue for decades: "You can't expect the Court to apply the Constitution to facts in 1967 that weren't in existence when the Constitution was drafted." After some back-and-forth, Marshall indicated that, in the rough-and-tumble of a history that had not stopped in 1787, faithfulness to the original intent of the Constitution was not incompatible with evolving interpretations of a document that was not a dead letter. After all, the justices would always be constrained in their interpretive innovations by their oath to defend the Constitution. "The question you propose," he told the unsatisfied Thurmond, "requires that Justices of the Supreme Court violate their oath, and that I can't suppose."[31]

In the end, all Thurmond could do was vote against the author of the South's "Black Monday." Marshall was confirmed by a vote of sixty-nine to eleven, with twenty senators not voting. Yet the Thurmond-influenced Republican Party and the anti–civil rights version of color blindness became, over time, an increasingly sharp thorn in Marshall's side. It helped teach Marshall, as he once ruefully admitted, that however much he crowed in the wake of the *Brown* victory, "You can't take a breather. If you do, that other guy will run you ragged."[32]

2

THE SEARCH FOR DEEP EQUALITY

In 1966 the California Supreme Court struck down Proposition 14, a wildly popular anti-integration ballot initiative that, like so much in the anti–civil rights movement, was the result of backlash—in this case, backlash against a 1963 ban on housing discrimination dubbed the Rumford Act after the African American state legislator, William Byron Rumford, who had pushed for its passage. Even after Proposition 14 was declared unconstitutional, the rage of the 4.5 million who had voted for it helped lift one of its best-known supporters, actor Ronald Reagan, into the California governor's mansion.[1]

A relative newcomer to electoral politics, Reagan helped himself during the gubernatorial campaign with masterful political footwork. At one point, he convinced an Associated Press reporter that he rejected both the Rumford Act *and* Proposition 14.[2] What he really stood for, he said, was the very "basis of our freedoms"—the "right to the ownership and control of our own property."[3] Balanced on that bedrock, Reagan felt free to tell one campaign audience that if "an individual wants to discriminate against Negroes or others in selling or renting his house, he has the right to do so."[4]

The whole dispute, and Reagan's chance to dance around it all the way to the pinnacle of California politics, began in 1963 when landlord Neil Reitman spoke on the phone with Dorothy Mulkey, a twenty-three-year-old navy veteran and apartment seeker. Reitman invited Mulkey and her husband, Lincoln, to view a brand-new apartment he was renting, but when the Mulkeys arrived and Reitman saw that they were Black, he claimed the apartment had already been rented.[5] Unbeknownst to Reitman, Dorothy and Lincoln were working with the NAACP, which, right behind the Mulkeys, sent a white couple to look at the apartment; Reitman immediately offered it to them.[6]

The Mulkeys sued the landlord, but because Proposition 14 was still in effect at the time, they lost in California Superior Court.[7] They won on appeal to the California Supreme Court, which ruled that Proposition 14 violated their Fourteenth Amendment right to equal protection under the law. Now it was Reitman's turn to appeal—to the US Supreme Court.[8]

In Washington, no less a personage than Thurgood Marshall appeared as a friend of the court to argue against Reitman. (President Lyndon Johnson had tapped Marshall to be solicitor general in 1965, in a sort of extended vetting for the Supreme Court.)[9] Marshall was in his prime, and his powerful baritone filled the courtroom as he seemed to engage in a kind of legal duet with Earl Warren, the former California governor who was now chief justice.[10] Making points that resonate strongly in the era of the Supreme Court's 2010 *Citizens United* decision, Marshall raised the specter of money as speech—as pure agenda-setting power that increases with the depth of the pockets from which it comes. Because Proposition 14 was now part of the California Constitution, it was no mere statute, Marshall argued. It could be removed only by a referendum voted on by the people of California. But, he said, "the people we are arguing about here are the underprivileged people in the State of California and I don't think anybody denied that you can't get [a] referendum by anyplace without hard earned cash and plenty of it." Marshall knew the campaign in favor of Proposition 14 had been funded by a California real estate industry that skillfully stoked white fear of neighborhood invasion by calling its organizing entity the Committee for Home Protection.[11]

In contrast, the arguments—rather than the cash—of minority groups had succeeded in pushing through both the Rumford Act and the related Unruh Act. But, as Marshall stressed, the victorious arguments had been buried under a mountain of opposition money.[12] The power of the US government had entered the courtroom with Marshall, however, and on May 29, 1967, the Supreme Court ruled the way Marshall wanted it to, voting five to four against Reitman.

But by then, the damage had been done. On his way to the governor's mansion, Reagan defended Proposition 14 supporters as honest folks living under the threat of being "accused of bigotry," and he helped extend the pro–Proposition 14 backlash by attacking University of California–Berkeley activists who were protesting on behalf of people like the Mulkeys, as well as against the Vietnam War and against a curriculum they saw as too Eurocentric. At tables in Sproul Plaza, the university's central gathering place, the activists established a nerve center for organizing and recruitment that the university administration, which was lobbied hard by the real estate industry, tried to shut down.[13] The students responded in 1964 with a full-blown free speech movement that by 1965 became a campus-wide "filthy speech" movement that deeply angered Reagan.[14]

"It began a year ago when the so-called 'free-speech advocates,' who in truth have no appreciation of freedom, were allowed to assault and humiliate an officer of the law," Reagan intoned in a career-defining speech at San Francisco's Cow Palace in 1966. (The 1964 protesters had surrounded the officer's car to stop him from arresting one of them. Then, one after another, they had climbed onto the car to make speeches.)[15] Their "ringleaders should have been taken by the scruff of the neck and thrown out of the university once and for all," Reagan said.[16]

When Berkeley's Black Student Union invited Stokely Carmichael, the activist firebrand who put the term "Black Power" on the map, to speak on campus on October 29, 1966, Reagan took full advantage: "We cannot have the university campus used as a base from which to foment riots," he warned in a press release, referencing the massive 1965 civil eruption in Watts, an African American neighborhood in Los Angeles.[17] Never mind that the explosion in Watts was due to long-standing frustration over police brutality as well as substandard housing, schools, and neighborhood resources. Reagan was watching polls that indicated white backlash was a power line for those who could plug it into their campaigns.[18] Not surprisingly, the Watts explosion ended up bolstering anti-Black stereotypes fed by that same power line and became evidence for a conclusion drawn by Proposition 14 supporters: "blacks 'haven't made themselves acceptable' for white neighborhoods."[19]

The enormous voltage in that power line illustrates not so much the "permanence of racism" (as Derrick Bells calls it) as the fact that race flows along lines of credit and discredit, organizing America's past and present by making all kinds of credit more accessible to white people, less accessible to most nonwhites, and especially difficult for Blacks to access. This business of pumping credit into white America and discredit into Black was most obvious under slavery, when stereotypes of Black moral and intellectual inferiority were planted deep in the national mind. Since slavery, it has been especially effective in walling large swaths of the Black community in discredit in the form of the systematic denial of bank loans, career advancement, and intergenerational wealth. Handing out credit and discredit, real estate organizations like those behind Proposition 14 shaped government policy far beyond California. Blessing and midwifing it all with disciminatory policies, federal regulators managed to regulate "every metropolitan area in the United States."[20]

This is why, despite court victories like *Brown* and the Mulkeys', schools became resegregated and minority neighborhoods continued to be poisoned by toxic waste, impoverished by punitive property taxation, and pierced by punitive (rather than protective) policing that cumulatively made poverty and dysfunction in the neighborhoods seem "natural," nobody's fault.[21]

LING-CHI WANG

Nevertheless, the civil rights movement was not without resources.[22] A little-noticed but important resource was L. Ling-Chi Wang, a young scholar of Semitic languages who arrived in San Francisco to meet his fiancée's parents in 1966 and was so shocked by the city's Chinatown that he helped found a new organization, Chinese for Affirmative Action, that soon made waves across the country. At the same time, Wang did academic work that helped alter the United States' understanding of its Asian American population.

History sometimes seems to ride like a moth on Wang's shoulder. He was born in Xiamen, China, on December 20, 1938. But in May 1949, after Mao's forces crossed the Yangtze River and took control of the city of Nanjing, the capital of Mao's opponents in the Chinese civil war, Wang's father decided to move his family to Hong Kong, where he was already in business. Wang finished secondary school there in 1958 and headed to the United States to complete his education. He earned an undergraduate degree at Princeton and entered the graduate program in Semitic languages and literature at the University of Chicago. He studied the Hebrew Bible in both Hebrew and Aramaic but took a special interest in Akkadian, the language of the Assyrian empire, Gilgamesh, and the Code of Hammurabi. He took a characteristic detour into Ugaritic, a Canaanite dialect, because all the Old Testament condemnations of the Canaanite fertility god Baal made him want "to know what the other side said," he told me in a 2021 interview.[23]

Even as he immersed himself in the ancient world, the upheavals raging around him were catching his attention. The University of Chicago adjoined an African American community notoriously walled in by housing discrimination and lacking in the very agenda-setting opportunities the university had been built to provide. The neighborhood had a relatively high crime rate, and when a number of students were robbed and assaulted, plans were made to move the institution to the suburbs. But a deal was struck: the university stayed, and the city of Chicago agreed to pursue urban renewal, which some activists of the era called "Negro removal."

All this gave Wang a crash course in American racial politics, poverty, crime, power, privilege, and bargaining. But his real education began in 1965, when he met Linda Ying, a graduate student at Chicago's School of Social Welfare, and she became his fiancée. In the summer of 1966 he made his fateful trip to San Francisco to meet her parents. The "experience of that summer, two and a half months in San Francisco, completely changed my outlook," Wang recalls. "You know the condition of Chinatown was actually worse than the Black ghettos. . . . And when Linda went back to Chicago to finish her degree, I stayed." Wang landed on his academic feet by gaining acceptance to the fortuitously located University of California–Berkeley program in Semitic studies.

But graduate school increasingly took a backseat to Chinatown, as Wang tried to fathom what had happened to the community there. The Chinese civilization, he told me—

> a great civilization—ended up being so discriminated against in America, and living in such horrible poverty conditions, and without any rights. And so, even before the summer was over, I started reading, looking for books in English and Chinese about the Chinese in the United States. And of course there was hardly anything at that time. And that's what [made me feel] a kind of moral imperative to do something about it.

In 1968 Berkeley granted Wang a fellowship that would have carried him through his Ph.D. and guaranteed two years of teaching afterward, but by 1970, he had dropped out of the doctoral program to plunge more deeply into efforts to improve conditions in Chinatown and to establish a new kind of American—the Asian American. He was among those who met in May 1968 in the Berkeley apartment of Japanese American Yuji Ichioka and Chinese American Emma Gee to discuss common issues facing Americans of Japanese, Korean, Chinese, and Filipino descent. The group settled on "Asian American" as an umbrella term for their identities and a sign of their "shared destiny."[24] They established a new organization, the Asian American Political Alliance, inspired by the very things that so alarmed Ronald Reagan. "Berkeley was in an uproar at that time, exploding every day," Wang recalls. "And in 1969, the students—Asian American students got together and decided they wanted to join African Americans and Latinos and Native Americans to form a coalition of minority students to ask for the founding of Ethnic Studies."[25] Wang ended up coteaching an experimental Asian American history course that was the seed of the Asian American Studies Department at Berkeley, which he eventually chaired.

As for Chinatown, Wang's efforts there are so severely underreported that it is worth quoting him at length about what he saw and what he did. "First of all," he recalled in 2021, "at that time San Francisco Chinatown was the densest populated area next only to Manhattan. And the housing was mostly built after the San Francisco earthquake. And they were all in terrible condition."

Going down the hallways, Wang saw "cubbyholes on each side. Mostly pensioners and retired people living by themselves. Because this is the remnants of the Chinese Exclusion immigration law. Because you know Chinese were not allowed to have families in the United States. So Chinatown was essentially a bachelor society—no family. Family was separated because of the Chinese Exclusion Law," first enacted in 1882. Under Lyndon Johnson, that law was replaced with one designed to foster family reunions and attract people with in-demand skills and education. Wang arrived in San Francisco the year after the new law took effect and found Chinatown "totally swamped with immigrants. People were living on top of each other . . . a whole family would be living in one room." Parents usually worked for low wages as waiters, waitresses, kitchen help, and cooks. Many got jobs in sweatshops as the garment industry mushroomed. But all this created a crisis for many children because, Wang recalls, often "both husband and wife worked both day and night, children were not supervised, and schools were not prepared to deal with non-English-speaking students." The result, he says, was "a lot of school dropouts. Which was unheard of, because the national news magazines, like *U.S. News and World Report* and *Newsweek* and *Time* had all been celebrating a successful model minority beginning. . . . Gang killings? And school dropouts? Delinquency? They were unheard of."

Responding to the "unheard of" that was in front of his eyes, Wang cofounded an organization: Chinese for Affirmative Action (CAA), which, at its 1970 inaugural news conference, vowed to press for the hiring of Chinese people in finance, insurance, journalism, civil service, and construction—industries that were largely closed to them at the time.[26]

Here, as everywhere, Wang did his research, scouting everything from a Hilton Hotel to restaurants on San Francisco's Fisherman's Wharf to department stores. Macy's department store, he discovered, would not hire Chinese retail clerks or cashiers "on the ground that they consider an Asian face a public relations risk." TV stations had similar views. But it was not long before CAA began to make a difference. In 1970,

Wang recalls, pressure by CAA led the local CBS affiliate to hire the first Asian American TV reporter in northern California—a Berkeley graduate named Christopher Chow who had completed an affirmative action summer program at Columbia University.

On Chow's first night, Wang remembers, media executives at CBS and around the Bay Area worried that audiences would switch channels at the sight of his face. When viewers kept watching, "the other stations started looking for Asian journalists," according to Wang. With the hiring of new journalists, coverage of Chinatown changed. Reporters had previously gone there mainly to cover sweatshop stories or gang violence. Now, journalists in San Francisco, with more knowledge about the neighborhood and more sympathy for it, expanded the spectrum of reporting.

Wang and CAA had advanced a key goal of any activist organization: resetting the media agenda and perhaps also the opportunity agenda. Agenda-setting theorists have long recognized that one of the most valuable commodities in any community is the attention of its members. Parts of Chinatown life that had once been invisible began to appear on TV.

LAU V. NICHOLS

Education (as the CRT panic of 2021–2022 showed) is a major agenda-setting arena. In their best-known effort, Wang and CAA helped set not only San Francisco's but also the nation's education agenda by teeing up a landmark Supreme Court case.

The spark for the case came when newly minted Stanford Law School graduate Edward Steinman arrived in Chinatown and set up shop in the local office of the Legal Services Program, a national organization launched by LBJ's Office of Economic Opportunity and endorsed by future Supreme Court justice Lewis Powell, then the American Bar Association president. Steinman was the recipient of a fellowship supporting efforts to solve problems caused by poverty. One day, in a historic bit of eavesdropping, he overheard Kam Wai Lau ask, through a translator, for help resolving a dispute with her landlord. When she mentioned that her son Kinmon was struggling to keep up in school because of his limited English, Steinman, who had been dreaming of finding a plaintiff for a language rights case, had a eureka moment.[27]

But, as a non-Chinese speaker, he knew he needed help. As luck would have it, Ling-Chi Wang was doing some work in the legal services office, and the two were soon working together to build a class-action lawsuit. Wang took Steinman to community meetings so the lawyer could soak up the realities faced by non-English-speaking students and their families. In the end, Steinman and Wang recruited a class of thirteen plaintiffs, including Kinmon Lau, to represent three thousand Chinese students in the school system whose language needs were not being met. The mischievous Steinman summed up the issue at a fortieth anniversary conference on the case: "Now Ling-Chi, you know you have been wrong for forty years," he told the bespectacled, hard-thinking Wang. "They *were* offering bilingual education. They defined bilingual as the teacher spoke English and the child spoke something else!"

Steinman filed suit in 1970, asking that the district court require San Francisco to hire teachers fluent in both English and Chinese. Some of Steinman's best ammunition was provided by the school district itself. It had conceded in 1969 that when students struggling with English were placed in grades that matched their age, "they are frustrated by their inability to understand the regular work." A Chinese student in secondary school was "almost doomed to be a dropout and another unemployable in the ghetto."[28]

Steinman, eager to make "constitutional history," went into district court with an argument bristling with references to violated amendments. The San Francisco Unified School District (SFUSD), he said, was not only violating the students' right to equal protection guaranteed by the Fourteenth Amendment but also falling foul of the Fifth Amendment's guarantee of due process and the Ninth Amendment's guarantee that the list of rights in the Constitution did not exhaust the protections people could claim. The school district, he concluded, was consigning these children to an educational twilight zone that separated them from political agency, good incomes, and proper self-respect.[29]

Still, Steinman "hedged his bets," according to Rachel Moran.[30] In addition to the constitutional amendments, he tied his case to one of the sources of affirmative action policy: Title VI of the Civil Rights Act of 1964, which forbade the use of race, color, or national origin to deny anyone equal participation in any program that received federal funding. Since the SFUSD relied on such financial assistance, Steinman said, it could not deny the benefits of a timely education to children who could not follow English-language lessons. He demanded "immediate affirmative action to guarantee them an education."[31]

Though well-hedged and brimming with confidence, Steinman had doubts about the Honorable Lloyd Burke, the judge assigned to the case. As a US attorney in the 1950s, Burke made a name for himself (and perhaps won his judgeship, according to Wang) in part by deporting Chinese immigrants and forcing a "substantial portion" of the Chinese families in San Francisco to prove they were American.[32] As Steinman expected, Burke ruled against him, despite the fact that, just before the case ended, the federal Office of Civil Rights (OCR)—and Richard Nixon's OCR at that—issued a memorandum that endorsed Steinman's conclusions.[33]

Steinman appealed, but the Ninth Circuit Court of Appeals also ruled against him. Writing for the majority of a three-judge panel, Judge Ozell Miller Trask argued that "the language deficiency suffered by appellants was not caused directly or indirectly by any State action. . . . [The school district's] responsibility to appellants under the Equal Protection Clause extends no further than to provide them with the same facilities, textbooks, teachers and curriculum as is provided to other children in the district."[34]

Steinman promptly appealed to the US Supreme Court, and when he rose before the justices in Washington, DC, on December 10, 1973, Steinman had a new advantage. In addition to the memorandum issued by Nixon's OCR, he had the author of that memorandum, former OCR head and now assistant attorney general J. Stanley Pottinger, on his side. Pottinger contributed a brief (coauthored by then–solicitor general Robert Bork, among others) and took part in the oral arguments as a friend of the court.

Asserting the power of the Department of Health, Education, and Welfare (HEW) to both interpret Title VI and enforce the interpretation,

Pottinger assured the justices that "San Francisco in this particular case has bound itself to compliance with Title VI and its regulations and all requirements of the Department of Health, Education and Welfare imposed pursuant to those regulations." At an opportune moment, Pottinger cited his own memo, telling the justices that HEW "has construed the meaning of Title VI in a national origin discrimination memorandum relevant to this case by stating that where inability to speak and understand the English language excludes national origin minority group children from effective participation in the educational program offered by the school district, the school must take affirmative steps to rectify the language deficiency." Going beyond the memo, Pottinger reminded the justices that some of their own decisions had acknowledged the need to defer to HEW's constructions of the Civil Rights Act.

The Supreme Court, which now included Thurgood Marshall, ruled unanimously in Lau's favor, and Justice William O. Douglass gave the Pottinger memo a certain pride of place in the opinion he wrote for the court. Just as the memo said, the SFUSD must rectify students' "linguistic deficiencies," he wrote.[35]

This opinion affirmed Steinman's contention, made back in October 1970 in his opening brief in the Ninth Circuit appeal, that the Chinese students were afforded only a "surface equality" consisting of identical facilities and instructors that nevertheless could not close the language gap.[36] Affirmative action was required to reach beneath the surface to shut off the source of the inequality.

The *Lau* ruling changed the nature of civil rights law by using Title VI to abolish surface equality as an acceptable policy and spotlighting the "disparate impact" that seemingly neutral policies can have in different communities.[37]

NIXON'S TWO MINDS

The *Lau* case, and Pottinger's role in it, opened a window into the Nixon administration's sometimes tortured political and philosophical thinking on race and into the bizarre symbiotic relationship that sometimes arises between the civil rights and anti–civil rights movements.

The Nixon administration was generally very supportive of affirmative action and bilingual education. Nixon believed that, in the wake of urban riots such as the one in Watts, affirmative action might be a way to buy social stability on the cheap by making the disenfranchised feel as if they had a stake in the US system.

Nixon allowed labor secretary George Shultz to try to unravel generations of racial segregation in the building trades unions by pressing those organizations—starting with the ones in Philadelphia—to voluntarily integrate the crews working under government-funded contracts.[38] According to Thomas J. Sugrue, Shultz's idea originated from below—from Philadelphia activists who had been demanding desegregation of the city's building trades for years. Sugrue argues that protests led by the NAACP, the Congress of Racial Equality (CORE), and others were a factor in John F. Kennedy's 1963 executive order on affirmative action and that the thinking behind the protests themselves could be traced all the way back to the 1930s and 1940s and to the strategies of leaders such as A. Philip Randolph and the hermeneutics of Myrdal's *An American Dilemma*.[39]

Believing that "blacks should benefit from $600 million in federal funds" earmarked for city projects, Shultz asked contractors to adopt the goal of raising their proportion of Black workers (in a 33 percent Black city) to 4 percent in 1970, 9 percent in 1971, 14 percent in 1972, and between 19 and 25 percent thereafter.[40] Nixon saw this as a golden opportunity to drive "a wedge through the Democratic coalition at its most vulnerable joint: between blacks and hard hats," and he endorsed this "Philadelphia Plan" as well as the 1970 extension of its provisions nationwide by his Department of Labor.[41] The strange combination of idealistic policy and Machiavellian calculation created a brief synthesis of the aims of the civil rights movement and those of one of its regular adversaries.

The reasons why the synthesis was brief were revealed in a 1986 joint interview with Pottinger and John Ehrlichman, who had been Nixon's domestic policy chief. Ehrlichman explained that Nixon was a virtuoso manipulator of the "passion issues"—abortion, race, and sometimes religion. According to Ehrlichman, these issues are "never solved, you never get equilibrium on them. It's up and down, up and down." And every "politician, I don't care which party, could be called Machiavellian because he copes with the passion issues at one time or another."[42]

The passion issues—those that slip the bonds of reason most easily—are so resistant to logical solutions that they keep American politics going in a perpetual circle of anxiety that perversely connects Nixon's Philadelphia Plan with Rufo's panic over critical race theory. Of course, the commitment to equal treatment that informs American ideals is also a long-term engine of this circle. In Nixon's case, concern for equality shaped by his Quaker upbringing was intertwined with racial contempt. Ehrlichman recalled that Nixon would sometimes philosophize in Quaker fashion and in the next breath "cuss somebody out and violate every Quaker precept known to the religion. He was described in his first year as zigzagging or tacking, and he's been described as . . . a closet liberal for the positions he's taken on civil rights and some other things. And all of that is true." Ultimately, facing a House and Senate controlled by Democrats, Nixon made the decision to tack against the political wind "to get something done rather than gridlock the government and sit down there behind a pile of sandbags and get nothing done," Ehrlichman said.[43]

With regard to the ultimate passion issue, race, Nixon's contradictions were at their ugliest. According to Ehrlichman, Nixon firmly believed in equality for all in the race for success, but he also "believed that blacks simply didn't have the genes to win the race. . . . I don't think he was a racist, but he had these kinds of paradoxical views that I think are shared by a multitude of people in our country." Pottinger immediately interrupted to say, "Not by me," and added, "If Nixon had those views, I would say that is pretty strong evidence of racism." In the gap between Nixon's racism and his desire to create a fair chance for everyone, and with the presence in his administration of both an Ehrlichman, who took racial bias for granted, and a Pottinger, who wanted to uproot bias, there was room for both the Philadelphia Plan and the *Lau* case.[44] There was also a gentlemen's agreement between Nixon and Strom Thurmond: in return for the senator's help in ensuring that Nixon carried the South in the 1968 election, Nixon would put the brakes on school desegregation.[45]

Pottinger said that, in an administration so at odds with itself, he expected to be fired on a daily basis for persisting in a "bizarre balancing act, trying to do liberal work in a conservative administration." But Pottinger was at his most powerful after Nixon made a strategic shift from his first-term push for affirmative action in employment (which failed to win him much love in a wary African American community) to a campaign season and second-term push for bilingual education to attract Latino votes, paired with a disavowal of quotas in hiring and an outright railing against integration via school busing—to the point of calling for a constitutional amendment against it.[46]

Pottinger's balancing act became possible in the first place because Nixon had fired his OCR predecessor for pushing busing too aggressively. The space this created in the OCR portfolio left Pottinger free to midwife bilingual education, to outline (with input from people like Wang) "*Lau* remedies" for schools challenged by significant numbers of students struggling with English, and to advance other sorts of affirmative action measures.[47]

In 1974 the dashing, divorced Pottinger began a nine-year relationship with feminist icon and affirmative action advocate Gloria Steinem. Carol Iannone of the anti–civil rights movement publication *Academic Questions* later groused (citing a miniseries that depicted their romance), that Steinem's nefarious influence was such that Pottinger tried "to increase his standing with her by becoming an affirmative action enforcer" in defiance of the Constitution and the Civil Rights Act of 1964, in Iannone's view.[48]

3

THE RISE OF CHINESE FOR AFFIRMATIVE ACTION

In the wake of *Lau*, Ling-Chi Wang found that the battle to create deep equality for Chinese students in particular, and for the Chinese community and other marginalized groups in general, was just beginning. On the one hand, the Supreme Court had remanded *Lau* to Judge Lloyd Burke's court to work out of the details. On the other hand, deciding what deep equality might be and how it might be achieved still needed to be negotiated among the school district, the court, and the bilingual education activists.

Wang recalls that when the *Lau* decision came down, "the communities with most to gain—the Chinese, Filipino, Japanese, Korean and Spanish-speaking communities—greeted the Supreme Court decision with jubilation and great expectation."[1] But then the Board of Education and its president Eugene Hopp, as well as superintendent of schools Steven P. Morena, pursued what Wang saw as the opposite of deep equality—a kind of hip, Bay Area version of the South's massive resistance to equality.

In February 1974 Hopp announced that the school district would consult with the community and develop a bilingual program that Judge Burke could approve. This was followed by months of near radio silence. Chinese for Affirmative Action led a group of community organizations demanding that the Board of Education appoint a Citizens Task Force on Bilingual Education to tackle the measures CAA and the others were proposing as ways to bring the San Franciso Unified School

District into compliance with the new *Lau* standard. The board was squandering a rare chance to take advantage of federal funds available for bilingual education, and worse, it was bringing the school system to the brink of losing "all its existing Federally funded programs due to non-compliance with Title VI of the Civil Rights Act of 1964 and the order of the U.S. Supreme Court," CAA alleged. There was no response until April 15, when forty-four citizens were summoned by Raymond Del Portillo, the city's director of bilingual education, to witness the unveiling of a secretly drafted fifty-three-page plan that offered no more than "maintenance and slight expansion of the *status quo*," according to Wang.[2]

Real movement began only after the Justice Department, at HEW's urging, filed a motion to enter the *Lau* case as a plaintiff, on the grounds that the case had national implications. Judge Burke scheduled a hearing for May 17, 1974, to consider the Justice Department's motion. On May 14 the Board of Education agreed to create the Citizens Task Force and to get technical assistance from the Center for Applied Linguistics in writing a bilingual education master plan. At the May 17 hearing, all was sweetness and light: the "previously warring factions" put on a display of amiability, according to journalists Dexter Waugh and Bruce Koon.[3]

But the harmony did not last. The superintendent continued to prefer fifty-minute-per-day English as a second language (ESL) classes for students not proficient in the language, while Wang and others believed that the true solution was the creation of a bilingual, bicultural program that sacrificed neither English-language acquisition nor students' proud rootedness in their own languages and cultures. Wang's suspicions about the ESL-only approach were confirmed when a San Francisco–area government watchdog proclaimed that "much of the trouble in our schools stems from a fundamental lack of understanding of our way of life," and therefore the solution to the bilingual issue was to bring non-English speakers "into the greatest harmony with our established ways."[4]

For Wang, this was an "inherently racist" guarantee that Asians and Mexicans would "lose on both sides. They cast away their culture and lose on that side, and then find they are not accepted in white society anyway." The Japanese Americans driven from their homes and placed in internment camps during World War II were a case in point: "These were people who thought they were patriotic Americans—and look what happened to them."[5]

The SFUSD was unable to grasp what was obvious to Wang and his allies, but not only because of chauvinism. The district was facing a flurry of resource-consuming lawsuits brought against it and its leaders at the beginning of the 1970s. For example, *Johnson v. SFUSD*, initiated in 1971, demanded that the district desegregate itself, while another 1971 case, *Larry P. v. Riles*, demanded that the use of IQ test results to place Black children in classes for the mentally challenged be discontinued because the test was culturally biased. Yet another lawsuit, brought in 1970, was dropped the same year after the district took steps to more adequately fund schools with a mostly Spanish-speaking student body.[6]

Even without the lawsuits, the school district would have had its hands full. Fifty-six of the district's schools had been declared out of compliance with earthquake safety codes. In addition, a bond issue designed to end a budget crisis proved insufficient to head off a hiring freeze just when Wang and others were demanding the addition of bilingual teachers and other staff.[7] On top of all this, Morena, who was battling the Board of Education for the authority he needed to do his job, suffered a heart attack in 1973. Eager to retire, he suggested a replacement, but it took two years for the board to officially name one.

Contrary to Wang, scholar Doris R. Fine argues that the school board went astray by "submitting to the pressures of various interest groups" and adding new programs while neglecting "routine building maintenance" and the preservation of "programs that lacked visible, political support." With all this juggling, balls were dropped. At one point, Morena "admitted that the administration could not even determine the exact number of certified staff on the payroll."[8]

When Morena could finally announce his departure in June 1975, he was eloquent in his understatement, saying that San Francisco "is a vibrant city, eager for change, yet impatient with many of the traditional avenues for effecting such change. The schools of the city reflect such forces, and I might add, so do the weekly Board of Education meetings.

. . . I have tried my hardest."[9] In the minefield Morena was stepping out of, momentum swung in Wang's direction for a time. With input from him, the Office of Civil Rights issued the aforementioned *Lau* remedies in 1975. In 1976 the state of California essentially adopted San Francisco's plan, passing the Bilingual Bicultural Education Act.[10]

One evening in the early 1980s, Wang consolidated his gains when he invited the superintendent over for dinner. Wang's wife was pregnant at the time, and during the meal Wang pointed to her belly and said, "That child is going to come out. I would like to see he or she get into an immersion program from kindergarten on." The superintendent responded, "Ling-Chi, you can have it, on two conditions. Number one, that you must find enough parents who are interested in such a program. If you do not have enough parents, you cannot have this. And then number two, the immersion program must reflect the racial composition of San Francisco [since the schools were under a court order to integrate]." The always resourceful Wang made sure both conditions were met, and bilingual education became a fact of life in San Francisco.[11]

By this time, the leader of Chinese for Affirmative Action was a Stockton-born Stanford graduate named Henry Der, a handsome man with big cheekbones and lively eyes. Like Wang, Der is a soft-spoken, deep-thinking man with a will that has no kryptonite.[12] Taking over as executive director of CAA in 1974, Der kept the organization busy campaigning for affirmative action well beyond the San Francisco school system.

In 1975, for example, Der and CAA went to court to demand enforcement of a newly enacted voting rights provision that ballots and other election materials be made available in languages other than English. Then, in one of their most impactful moves, Der and CAA filed a Title VI complaint against the San Francisco Police Department (SFPD) because of its lack of bilingual officers. The Law Enforcement Assistant Administration (a Justice Department unit created by the Nixon administration to fund crime-fighting efforts across the nation) sent an agent to San Francisco to investigate the charges, and CAA was vindicated. The investigator discovered that "no police officer assigned to Chinatown, or the Richmond district could communicate effectively with the non-English-speaking Chinese population," Der later told the Commission on Civil Rights. As a result, Chinese speakers often waited hours for police to respond when they needed help.[13] Under Justice Department pressure, the SFPD agreed to publish announcements in both English and Chinese and to beef up the Chinese-language skills of the five bilingual officers on the force.[14]

The emergency need for such measures became clear in 1977 at Chinatown's Golden Dragon restaurant. There, in an attempt to kill the leader of a rival gang, members of the Joe Boys opened fire with two shotguns, a submachine gun, and a .38 pistol. They killed five and wounded eleven—all of them innocent bystanders.[15]

It turned out that knowledge of Cantonese and a CAA campaign were critical to cracking the case. Five years earlier, CAA had assisted recent high school graduate Fred Lau, who was desperate to become a police officer but was a quarter inch below the minimum height requirement. "There was this big article on the front page of the *San Francisco Chronicle*," Wang recalls, "with a photograph of him hanging down from the ceiling upside down and lifting weights upside down in order to stretch that quarter inch."[16] CAA and the wider Chinatown community got behind Lau, making their wishes known by holding rallies at city hall and elsewhere. The SFPD allowed Lau to enter the police academy in 1971, opening the door to a small number of people who were under the minimum height.[17]

This paid off after the Golden Dragon massacre. Lau and a recent police academy graduate named Heather Fong were placed on the Golden Dragon task force, and their language skills and knowledge of Chinatown, where Lau grew up, proved invaluable.[18] A determined, shy woman, Fong shut herself up in a "tiny, gray windowless room at the Hall of Justice, transcribing hundreds of hours of audiotapes gained from wiretaps of the gang members. . . . Her evidence-gathering led to four convictions," according to Jim Herron Zamora and Cicero Estrella.[19]

Fong's hiring, unlike Lau's, had nothing to do with waiving the height requirement. It came about due to a long-running affirmative action lawsuit, *Officers for Justice v. Civil Service Commission of the*

City and County of San Francisco, filed by a classic civil rights coalition—CAA, National Organization for Women, League of United Latin American Citizens, and the primary plaintiff, Officers for Justice.[20] A mostly African American group founded in 1968, Officers for Justice, joined by its coplaintiffs, accused the SFPD in 1973 of hiring and promoting on the basis of a discriminatory exam and discriminatory physical tests. District court judge Robert Francis Peckham issued a preliminary injunction barring the use of the tests and requiring the development of a new exam. Peckham found that the hiring and promotion exams were fatally flawed because, according to the testimony of an expert in psychometrics, no matter how wide the gap between applicants on entry tests, all performed equally well on tests given after training at the police academy. Worse, the tests themselves were not consistent because results in the same areas were weighted differently from test to test. Peckham concluded that the hiring exam had little or no proven relationship to performance in policing, and the exam for promotion to sergeant had similar shortcomings. He also accepted evidence from Officers for Justice that, although the population of San Francisco was 14 percent Black, 15 percent Latino, and 14 percent Asian, the police department was only 4.41 percent Black, 4.05 percent Latino, and 0.88 percent Asian.[21] Until the new exam arrived, he required the department to hire three minority applicants for every two white applicants.

Next, in 1975, Peckham responded to a motion from Officers for Justice by ordering that the minimum height requirement be scrapped, citing the landmark *Griggs v. Duke Power Co.* case.[22] In addition, he required the department to hire women to meet a temporary quota and ordered changes in physical fitness tests that disadvantaged women.[23] This paved the way for the hiring of women like Heather Fong.

Although the Golden Dragon case proved the value of such affirmative action, there was significant pushback from the SFPD rank and file. Sergeant Jerry Crowley growled that Judge Peckham had forced a system of "special privilege and political patronage" and delivered "a slap in the face to policemen in San Francisco."[24] Needless to say, Officers for Justice disagreed. One member, Earl Sanders (who eventually became police chief), reports that only one man who was not Irish held a rank of captain or higher at the time Officers for Justice filed suit, which the group did only after previous attempts to call attention to the pattern of racial discrimination within the department had been ignored.[25]

An SFPD sergeant named Anthony J. Balzer made the case against affirmative action with real academic skill in a 1977 article in *Public Administration Review*. "The second group of 15 woman officers is just completing recruit training and 'hitting the streets' to patrol," he wrote. But the lawsuit that won those women their jobs had caught the SFPD with its "empirical pants down." He saluted the effort of the usually "divided and bickering" Police Officers Association (POA) to pull those pants up by closing ranks "to support at least some standards of merit in the screening of SFPD applications and promotions, even though the sought-after 'merit' and 'standards' would undoubtedly be tough to define." It is this acknowledgment of the difficulty of defining "merit" and "standards," as well as the difficulty of defining the nature of good policing, that makes Balzer's essay timely forty-five years after it was written.[26]

Yet, having acknowledged this much, Balzer goes on the attack, arguing that "minority group quotas" do little but stir resentment and "produce potentially inferior police services." Before the lawsuit, he explains, competition for SFPD jobs had inspired an increase in the cutoff score on the civil service exam, which led to the hiring and promotion of "an increasing number of college-educated middle-class candidates—a phenomenon encouraged and acclaimed by many as a step toward more professional police services."[27] Here, without quite realizing it, Balzer makes the argument that the tests were biased in favor of people from white and middle-class backgrounds, since that demographic was most likely to have the advantages of a college education and middle-class status.[28] He cites as his authority for the importance of advanced education for police officers the famed Katzenbach Commission report on crime in a free society. However, he compounds his error by ignoring the commission's emphasis on diversity.[29]

When he turns to the subject of racial categorization, Balzer suffers a full-on attack of disingenuousness. He stresses the difficulty of determining "who is a minority group member and who is not" and accuses the EEOC of producing "arbitrary" racial requirements, such as the one that states "policemen claiming American Indian ancestry" must demonstrate "at least ¼ Indian blood and adoption of an essentially 'American Indian lifestyle.'"[30] For purposes of his argument, Balzer leaves out the backstory, which Sanders and Cohen are only too happy to provide: "In the department's initial count of minorities, prior to the preliminary ruling, there were only three Native Americans on the force. As the appeals process began, that number somehow swelled to sixty-three."[31]

Officers for Justice's lead lawyer, Robert Gnaizda, responded in court by congratulating the SFPD for achieving "one of the greatest feats in the history of affirmative action" by raising the number of Native Americans on the force "by over two thousand percent in only a few months." When Judge Peckham asked for suggestions about how to evaluate the increase, Gnaizda said the sixty-three Native American officers should go down to the San Francisco office of the EEOC to affirm their new identities. The judge agreed. Only nine officers showed up at the EEOC, and when they were later asked to make their claims under oath, some demurred, and the number of Native Americans on the SFPD was once again down to three.[32]

Balzer nevertheless asks, "why should we restrict our definition of minority groups to include only those groups exhibiting certain racial, ethnic, and sex characteristics?"[33] Sanders's experience provides the answer, for he had the third highest score out of the eight hundred applicants of all colors who took the SFPD entry exam in 1964, but the doctor who performed his physical pronounced him "unfit" for unspecified reasons and commented that the SFPD already had enough of "your kind."[34] Sanders got around the doctor by threatening to sue, but he discovered that his brush with discrimination was far from unique because bias was written into both the rules and the cognitive structure of the SFPD. Recruits were trained to stop interracial pairs or groups, and when some white officers "talked about blacks in the third person, they still called them niggers without so much as a second thought."[35]

Not long after Peckham handed down his preliminary injunction, the SFPD's need for more Black recruits became painfully evident. One night in October 1973, a white couple strolling down a San Francisco street were forced into a van, brutally assaulted by several Black men, and then thrown onto the railroad tracks. The man, Richard Hague, survived, but the woman, Quita, died. This was the first in a series of killings and attempted killings of whites—most of them carried out with a .32 pistol—that did not stop until April 1974, when members of a depraved splinter group of the Nation of Islam who wanted to start a race war were captured—with the help of a twenty-eight-person detail of Black officers who kept the suspects under surveillance—and eventually convicted of the murders.[36]

In the months of mayhem, the city was in such a panic that the mayor ordered all Black men who resembled the composite sketch compiled from survivor accounts stopped and searched. Stumped day after day, week after week, the SFPD grew sufficiently desperate to give Sanders and his partner Rotea "Gil" Gilford prominent positions on a task force assembled to track down the killers. "Because of the Officers for Justice lawsuit, most of the brass hated our guts," Sanders asserts, but "now they needed us." Gilford and Sanders "had the connections and knew the area where killings were taking place better than anyone else on the force."[37] No doubt, that sort of knowledge was not being tested on SFPD examinations.

Unfortunately, their contacts knew little about who the killers might be, but Sanders and Gilford were now in a position to try to educate the department. As the killings dragged on for months, the mayor announced the stop-and-frisk campaign that gave the episode its name. Once a man had been questioned and cleared as a suspect, he was given a "Zebra card" (based on the Z, or Zebra, police radio band assigned to the case). If he was stopped again, the man could present the card as proof he was not a suspect. Sanders and Gilford tried in vain to explain what a bad, not to mention illegal, idea this was. "I mean, this was the United States of America, and they were telling us we're going to issue identification cards based on race," Sanders writes. "We both stood up and tried to say . . . that we'd alienate the very community we were trying to get information from."[38]

Six hundred Black men had been stopped and searched by the time a court issued a preliminary injunction to stop the searches, which violated the Fourth Amendment's prohibition of unreasonable searches and seizures as well as the Fourteenth Amendment's guarantee of due process and equal protection. The SFPD finally conceded that the effort was "a waste of time."[39] It was also an example of the discriminatory habits of thought and decision making—the opposite of affirmative action—that the Officers for Justice lawsuit aimed to end or at least hamper—the sort of thinking Balzer sometimes falls into in his essay.

One of the things Balzer does put his finger on is the difficulty of reconciling the two perspectives in the lawsuit. Both sides, he writes, "sincerely claim to champion the cause of equality. Their respective positions on this issue implicitly reflect a broader on-going struggle for dominance in all of our social institutions between two ostensibly conflicting models of 'equality': 'equality of opportunity' and 'equality of results.'"[40] In pointing out this distinction, Balzer makes a familiar anti–civil rights movement error, for even the court-orchestrated consent decree's hiring ratios could not create equality of results. Sanders eventually ascended to the position of police chief, yet he was still subjected to what, in retrospect, appears to be a trumped-up criminal conspiracy indictment—suggesting that even at the top, he did not achieve equality.[41]

In truth, there *are* two kinds of equality: surface equality and deep equality. The often unacknowledged gap between them is part of what makes it possible for antagonists on both sides of the civil rights debate to claim to be championing the same value. And part of what prevents people from acknowledging the gap is the struggle for dominance that Balzer refers to. In that struggle, the concept of equality becomes a weapon that is too valuable to be analyzed. Seeking dominance for the POA perspective while acknowledging (in a surface way) the justice of minority access to the police department, Balzer splits equality into "equality of opportunity" and "equality of results" without stopping to consider whether the equality of opportunity he refers to goes deeper than superficial police department application forms.

In the end, Balzer returns to his view that quotas disregard the realities of intellectual and physical differences. He concludes that the inequality of results is a valuable incentive to greater individual productivity and self-improvement and that quotas are "arbitrary, degrading, alienating, resented, and largely self-defeating."[42] Here again,

Balzer anticipates future debates in general and the characterization of quotas as evil in particular. But the question remains: were the quotas the judge imposed an effort to dislodge a *deep* inequality that was beyond the reach of Balzer-approved surface measures such as the intensive recruitment of minorities combined with a training program open to both minorities and whites?

Deep inequality can be defined as an inequality so tightly woven into the social fabric that it becomes invisible to many, even as it affects everyone. Exams that have no provable relationship to job performance and that test class and cultural status as much as anything else are an example of deep inequality in disguise. So are height requirements that have no clear relationship to the ability to perform a job.

The question of whether goals and quotas are the best tools to reach into the social depths and undo inequality remains unanswered.[43] But the aggressive recruitment and the open-to-all training program Balzer ends up endorsing are midrange measures at best if they do not consider the different obstacles people encounter on the way to the recruiting office—and, in Sanders's case, in the hiring and promotion process. (Sanders and Cohen dismiss the idea of a recruitment drive—which the SFPD announced—as a head feint.)[44] Unlike quotas, which are no doubt controversial, midrange measures have little chance of reaching into the depths of cultures like the old SFPD's. The Golden Dragon massacre and the Zebra killings exposed the social depths to which affirmative action had to go.

Temporal depth is also involved, as time is a component of inequality. For example, the time it took for police to respond to calls from Chinatown was an element of inequality there. So was the time it took to find a translator or to hire and train an officer who understood the language of a complainant. Similarly, the time required to identify, hire, and promote officers who could build a network of contacts in the African American community was a measure of the depth of inequality between that community and more advantaged ones—and a measure of the shallowness of the proposed remedies. Sensitive to all this, Judge Peckham demanded a reversal of "the history of discrimination caused by the use of examinations which have not been properly validated."[45]

Under the judge's watchful eye, and with the help of CAA's efforts to recruit community members to apply and prepare for the SFPD's entry-level test, a 1979 consent decree to which the POA reluctantly agreed was hammered out.[46] Testifying before the Commission on Civil Rights that year, Henry Der summed up what had been achieved after six years of litigation: "a 50 percent hiring goal of minorities at the entry level. A total of 29 Chinese bilingual police officers will be hired by 1984, in addition to those who are on the police force now."[47] As it turned out, not only Earl Sanders but also Heather Fong and Fred Lau eventually rose to the position of police chief.

Unfortunately, the Officers for Justice lawsuit (along with a similar case against the San Francisco Fire Department) was probably the high point of the convergence of interests and efforts across San Francisco's always evolving racial and ethnic spectrum. In the educational arena, things had already become very, very complicated, and the racial coalition had begun to split.

4

THE COALITION SPLITS

Complications started on July 9, 1971, when Judge Stanley Weigel handed down his ruling in *Johnson v. San Francisco Unified School District*, a case brought by the San Francisco NAACP in an effort to end de facto segregation in the city's classrooms. Taking his lead from the Supreme Court, Weigel agreed with the plaintiffs that drawing school district lines that enhanced students' racial isolation violated their constitutional rights.[1] In the tradition of *Brown*, Weigel insisted that desegregation would improve the education of all students and would promote social harmony because opposition to desegregation "fosters false concepts of racial superiority and of racial inferiority" and "works to prevent the kind of exchange in formative years which can best inoculate against racial hatred."[2]

Weigel approved the Horseshoe Plan, which divided the city into seven zones where the schools would be integrated with the help of busing, which, Weigel avowed, "students enjoy." Anticipating objections from some of the families represented in the *Lau* case, Weigel stressed that "bilingual classes are not proscribed. They may be provided in any manner which does not create, maintain or foster segregation." Nevertheless, the ruling enraged many in the white and Chinese communities, where anger had been at such a boil for two years that a police presence was required at school board meetings to maintain order. At the meeting where the board adopted the Horseshoe Plan, the audience demanded to know, "Is Judge Weigel God?" and broke into the chant, "We want Freedom too!"[3]

This seeming reference to the African American freedom movement, implying that African American liberty might come at the cost of freedom for others, is a trope that recurs throughout the history of desegregation and affirmative action. It captures a moment of prisoner's dilemma–style defection from the multiracial coalition that Judge Weigel saw himself strengthening.[4] To mix metaphors, it suggests that even education can be a psychological zero-sum game, despite being an everybody-wins, positive-sum game in theory, in rhetoric, and, if budgets allow, in reality.[5] Polls at the time suggested that an overwhelming majority of San Francisco residents was against busing to accomplish desegregation. One poll found that more than 50 percent of African Americans were against busing, but at the epicenter of antibusing sentiment was the Chinese American community, where disapproval reached 92 percent.[6]

Like most defections, this one has iceberg depths that are worth exploring. In what one participant called awakening a sleeping giant, antibusing sentiment had been whipped to a white heat in Chinatown. Dentist Zuretti Goosby, the harmony-seeking African American head of the school board, surmised that emotions in Chinatown were being stoked by people like Joseph L. Alioto, San Francisco's antibusing mayor. "Local politicians who hole up and hope that the desegregation order of Judge Stanley A. Weigel is going to be reversed help to keep the Chinatown area in turmoil," Goosby told United Press International.[7]

Irate Chinatown parents arranged for ambitious Harvard Law School alumnus Quentin Kopp (along with cocounsel Jack Chow) to intervene on their behalf in the *Johnson* case.[8] "We were treated shabbily by Judge Weigel in his imperiousness and he denied our application to intervene," Kopp later complained.[9] So he filed a motion in the Ninth Circuit Court of Appeals arguing that, although the state of California and the city of San Francisco had long discriminated against Chinese students by forcing them to attend segregated schools, these students now rejected a cure—"attending schools which are not predominantly Chinese"—that they believed was worse than the disease. Therefore, Kopp argued, Chinese schools should be exempt from the desegregation plan.[10] The parents cherished the fact that neighborhood schools were overwhelmingly Chinese—456 of 482 students in one school, 230 of 289 in another, and 1,074 of 1,111 in a third—because "important cultural values could not be passed on to future generations if the children were dispersed through the city."[11]

The appeals court granted a temporary stay of Judge Weigel's order, but the NAACP's lawyers moved for a reconsideration, and the court lifted its stay after only four days. Forced to return to Weigel's courtroom, the jowly, bespectacled, cleft-chinned Kopp argued in vain that integration "will do violence to the San Francisco Chinese community unmatched by any legislation or executive action in the history of the state."[12] Denied again, Kopp and Chow petitioned the Supreme Court in August 1971, using parent Guey Heung Lee and others to get them through the high court's doors in the case of *Guey Heung Lee v. Johnson.* The Supreme Court was not in session, so on August 13 Kopp mailed the appeal to Justice William O. Douglas, the circuit justice for the San Francisco area.[13] According to Kopp, Douglas "was hiking somewhere in the wilds of the state of Washington," but he interrupted his trek long enough to rule in Judge Weigel's favor.[14]

Contrary to the findings in *Brown v. Board of Education*, and contrary to the arguments Ed Steinman was making in the *Lau* case, Kopp and his clients claimed that the segregated Chinese "are not at all intimidated or have a feeling of suppression or inferiority by attendance at a school in their neighborhood."[15] Justice Douglas, however, kept the case firmly within the interpretive framework established by *Brown* and by later reinforcements of that case, such as *Swann v. Charlotte-Mecklenburg Board of Education*.[16] "Schools once segregated by state action," Douglas said, "must be desegregated by state action, at least until the force of the earlier segregation policy has been dissipated." He added, in one of the most famous lines of his opinion, that "*Brown v. Board of Education* was not written for blacks alone. It rests on the Equal Protection Clause of the Fourteenth Amendment, one of the first beneficiaries of which were the Chinese people of San Francisco [in *Yick Wo v. Hopkins*]."[17] Douglas even endorsed Weigel's findings that integration would not strip the children of their knowledge of Chinese culture and language, since bilingual classes "are not proscribed" and there is "no prohibition of courses teaching the cultural background and heritages of various racial and ethnic groups." Perhaps most tellingly,

Douglas endorsed a key pro-coalition conclusion reached by Weigel: "The Judgment and Decree now to be entered is of less consequence than the spirit of community response. In the end, that response may well be decisive in determining whether San Francisco is to be divided into hostile racial camps."[18] Kopp dismissed this as an "imperious" example of "exactly the kind of paternalistic thinking I expected."[19] Douglas had crafted "a dangerous order," Kopp warned.[20] The fight against busing had to and would go on.[21]

By this time, Kopp had already decided to run for office, taking advantage of the notoriety he had gained from representing the Chinese parents. Days after mailing the Supreme Court appeal, he announced his candidacy for San Francisco's Board of Supervisors at the Commodore Stockton School in Chinatown. He was elected with the help of heavy Chinese support.[22]

Meanwhile, perhaps taking a cue from Kopp's remark to a reporter that Douglas might have "invited" a boycott with his rejection of their appeal, Chinese parents organized to keep their children out of public school.[23] In Chinatown, "Freedom Schools" were created, built on the foundation provided by existing after-school programs focused on Chinese language and culture. Pharmacist Dennis Wong, one of the leaders of the boycott, said parents were prepared to continue their protest "for years, if necessary."[24] Wong insisted that those after-school language and culture classes would be lost and generational continuity would be broken if Chinese children were bused out of Chinatown.[25] Remarks by some of the Chinese parents, however, suggested that there was more to the story than Wong admitted. One young mother told UPI, "We Chinese usually do what the law says, but this time I will not obey. . . . With busing, we have heard of so much violence already. There's also been a lot of serious bus accidents."[26] School officials claimed there was no evidence of either violence or accidents. "To tell the truth," one bank official stated, "some of it is racial prejudice." Robert Strand of UPI reported on what remains, in 2023, an inescapable reality: Chinese supporters of the desegregation plan "blame the resistance on skillful exploitation of the issue by political conservatives."[27] In February 1972 San Francisco superintendent of schools Thomas A. Shaheen was shouted down and menaced with "waving fists and swinging picket signs" when he stood up to answer questions about busing at a meeting in Chinatown. Goosby blamed not only Mayor Alioto but also newly elected Board of Supervisors member Kopp. Kopp and the rest of the board heightened emotions (or perhaps rode and reinforced already high anxieties) by moving to amend the city charter to rein in Shaheen, as though, Goosby said derisively, "if we get rid of Shaheen the federal court order doesn't have to be obeyed."[28]

Finally, contrary to reports that Chinatown was unanimous in its opposition to busing, Ling-Chi Wang claimed that those who forced Shaheen to make a quick exit represented only a "small die-hard faction." That faction included representatives of traditional Chinatown power centers that Wang himself had battled when he helped establish CAA and other organizations. They were the tip of "a loosely organized coalition of the city's long-standing anti-busing groups and confused white and Chinese parents," according to education journalist Rob Moskowitz.[29] Wang himself, in his early thirties at the time but looking a decade younger, was accused by one Freedom School vice chairman of not being a parent, being "pro-Shaheen [and] pro-busing," and, with his "Affirmative Action group," generally doing more harm than good.[30]

At one school board meeting, Wang recalled in 2021:

> I thought I was going to be lynched by the Chinese parents. I mean, they were just shouting obscenities at me, yelling at me, and pointing fingers at me, and God—because I spoke out against boycotting. I said that these so-called Freedom Schools that the Chinatown establishment set up were nothing but glorified babysitting facilities. And they were really pissed off at me. But you know I worried that they were going to lose out—the students, if they got taken out of school.[31]

With the *Lau* case, Wang had hoped to build the best of both worlds—integrated public schools with strong bilingual and bicultural components.[32]

Those favoring the boycott had a more splintered vision and a narrower agenda. The first to push the idea of Freedom Schools were thirty or forty "generally American-born [Chinese] . . . from a professional or semi-professional background" who wanted to defend the private bilingual and bicultural programs in Chinatown, according to Philip A. Lum. The problem was that the people developing a curriculum for the Freedom Schools "struggled at the onset to create some identifiable core not provided by the public schools. . . . The classes used state textbooks, but sponsoring organizations fought over what to teach beyond the basics," Lum writes. This was partly because some of the subjects touched on the tricky geopolitics of the contest between the People's Republic of China and Taiwan. Tensions were so high that Wang was showered with cries of "Get out, communist" as he was forced from the headquarters of Chinatown's Six Companies in advance of a press conference called to lambaste Taiwan's replacement by the People's Republic of China in the UN—something Wang supported.[33] All this, combined with low pay, led to a huge turnover among teachers.[34]

Helping to light the fuse on this situation was Proposition 21, a statewide ballot measure that blatantly rejected the integration of Black students into formerly all-white or almost-all-white schools. It sailed to passage in 1972.[35] And although the leaders of the Freedom Schools strongly denied that they harbored similar sentiments and were reluctant to send their children to school with Black youngsters, Lum insists that "anti-Black sentiment . . . played a fundamental role in the maintenance of the Freedom Schools beyond the first year, when the Chinese Consolidated Benevolent Association, commonly known as the Six Companies, undertook their sponsorship. During this period, Chinatown newspapers such as the *Chinese Times* hinted [at] the adverse effects of busing Black children into Chinatown and busing Chinese children into Black neighborhoods."[36]

Wang sent his own children to both integrated schools and after-school classes in Chinatown. Looking back on these events in 2021, the eighty-three-year-old Wang, despite being one of the lions of the civil rights movement, said he feared going outdoors because of the increasingly frequent and brutal attacks on Asian people (including a disproportionate number of the elderly) by perpetrators who included African Americans. Commenting on the sometimes mutual hostility of groups that should be allies, he remarked that "the relationship between Chinese and Blacks . . . has a very, very long history in this country—the tension and the racial prejudice. Blacks have prejudice against Chinese, Chinese have prejudice against Blacks. And all because each group . . . emulates and reflects the wider society's attitude toward Blacks or toward Chinese."[37]

At one point, the Freedom Schools found themselves in a vicious hermeneutic trap when they accepted support from an organization called the Liberty Lobby. In return, the Liberty Lobby asked that the schools send two representatives to Washington to campaign against integration.[38] Little did the Freedom Schools know that the organization's founder was a tycoon of American racism, Willis Carto, who kept four busts of Adolf Hitler in his office. Carto's empire eventually included a publishing house, a magazine with 300,000 subscribers, broadcasts on 470 radio stations, a political party that became the home of former Klan potentate David Duke's 1988 presidential campaign, and an institute dedicated to promoting scholarship that denied the Holocaust.[39] The Chinatown parents broke with the Liberty Lobby when they discovered that its priorities included "restrictive immigration quotas and support of causes detrimental to the well-being of Asian Americans."[40] (Carto's attitudes were reflected in a "dire warning" published in one of his magazines in the 1960s that "a rapidly expanding Asian population . . . would eventually invade America." Therefore, new immigration restrictions were urgently needed.)[41]

The American mind-set epitomized by the Liberty Lobby turned up in San Francisco again in 1983, this time in direct alliance with Quentin Kopp (who, like the Chinese parents, probably had no idea who he was getting in bed with). The organization this time was U.S. English. It arrived in San Francisco bearing a gift, Proposition O, which aimed to undo one of CAA's triumphs: the printing of ballots and other election materials in Spanish and Chinese in addition to English.[42] If passed, it would require the San Francisco Board of Supervisors and the mayor to demand that the federal government eliminate the requirement for trilingual ballots.

Kopp had just lost a run for mayor of San Francisco, but he remained on the Board of Supervisors and lent his name and energy to the collection of the 14,440 signatures needed to put Proposition O on the ballot (though only 12,400 of them were found to be valid). Kopp then contributed to a voter information pamphlet that described bilingual ballots by a series of epithets that spelled out the word "RIDICULOUS," epithets including "racist"; "discriminatory" to Italians, Jews, Greeks, and others who might not be native speakers; and "impediments" to social integration. Chiming in on the jeremiad and repurposing the word "racist" was U.S. English's West Coast director Stanley Diamond, who wrote that "singling out people for special treatment based on skin color, surname or language group is inherently racist."[43] On the other side, Ling-Chi Wang and Henry Der endorsed a voter information pamphlet asserting that "voting is a fundamental, constitutional right, not to be left to popularity contests. Not even in the deep south have local officials thrown the voting rights of minorities to a plebiscite."[44] Der had previously helped oust San Francisco registrar of voters Thomas P. Kearney, who declared, "If they're going to vote, they should know English. . . . Goddamn Chinks."[45]

But U.S. English executive director Gerda Bikales told the *Washington Post* that multilingual ballots make voting "too easy": "We demand a little bit, at least the ability to function well enough in our language." Asked if the intention of the proposition was to suppress the votes of Asians and Latinos who helped liberals and liberal causes (such as bilingual education) succeed, Kopp said, "They'll continue to vote, but they'll vote in English." Proposition O passed with the support of 62 percent of San Francisco voters.[46]

Because it was only advisory, Proposition O changed nothing in the short term. But U.S. English took the victory in a diverse city like San Francisco as a good sign that its long-term goals of ending government funding for bilingual education and making English the official language of the United States were possible. Underneath it all was a molten lava of resentment exemplified by a question posed by Michigan ophthalmologist and U.S. English national chairman John Tanton: "Whites see their power and control over their lives declining, will they simply go quietly into the night? Or will there be an explosion?"[47]

Because Tanton, in classic anti–civil rights movement fashion, maintained a moderate façade, he was able to get Linda Chavez, a well-known mainstream Latina conservative, to sign on as director of U.S.

English. But Chavez resigned when Tanton's memo about a white explosion was leaked and it was revealed that his moderate organizational fig leaf, the Federation for American Immigration Reform (FAIR)—with newsman Walter Cronkite on its board and regular appearances on outlets such as CNN on its résumé—had pocketed about $1.2 million from the devoutly racist Pioneer Fund between 1985 and 1994.[48]

The Pioneer Fund, which would become one of the underground engines in the movement against affirmative action in higher education in the 1990s, was founded in 1937 by textile heir Wickliffe Draper, whose heart's desire was to preserve and cultivate the genetic stock of the nation's white founders. By the 1980s, the Pioneer Fund was supporting the work of researchers seeking to prove not only that Blacks were less intelligent than whites but also that desegregation was harmful to the intellectual development of white students.[49]

In the nasty little network that emerged out of or was energized by all this, Roger Pearson, a professional anti-Semite and racist, moved from Britain to the United States to work with Willis Carto in the 1960s. A veritable mendicant priest going from diocese to diocese in the far-flung ecclesiae of white supremacy, Pearson once wrote that it was better for a superior race to exterminate an inferior one than to mingle with it. He went on to teach at a scattering of universities, work for anti–civil rights movement senator Jesse Helms, and obtain $1.2 million from the Pioneer Fund between 1973 and 1999. He founded (with Draper's money) various organizations and publications, published articles defending racial prejudice as an aid to evolution, and, as editor of the Pioneer-linked *Mankind Quarterly*, disseminated works on the evils of integration.[50] Last but not least, Pearson collaborated with Carto's Liberty Lobby.[51] Thus, the Chinatown parents came closer than they knew to the heart of American racism—a heart made up of a weird mix of money and hate that pumped no small amount of blood through the veins of the anti–civil rights movement. (See figure 4.1.)

I trace these connections not just to show they exist but also as a reminder of the scope of the network of organizations, funded by exceedingly deep-pocketed people, that challenged the gains made by CAA and similar groups. The Ford Foundation contributed $3 million in start-up funds to Public Advocates (the firm that won the *Officers for*

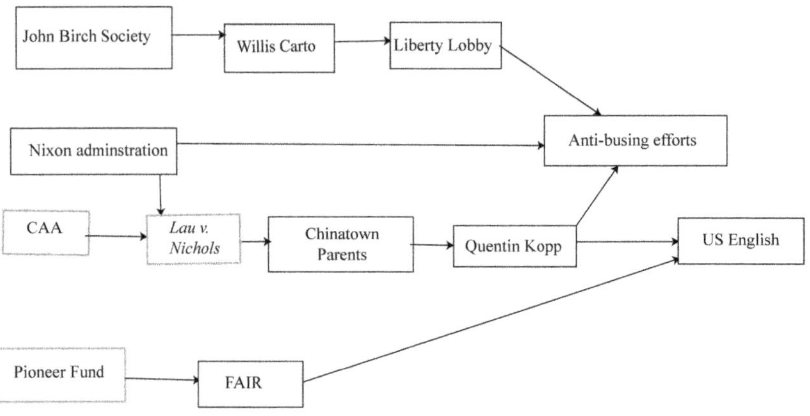

Figure 4.1. Genealogy of a hermeneutic trap.

This genealogy highlights how nefarious agendas can influence people while remaining out of sight (and out of mind). Thus, the Chinatown parents in the middle of the genealogy are unaware of their partners' connection to the Pioneer Fund or the antibusing ancestry of the John Birch Society. Hermeneutic traps work best when key parts of them are hidden.

Justice case), and the Carnegie Corporation funded the agenda-setting American Dilemma project, but over time, those determined to undo efforts to create deep equality in America marshaled a tsunami of funds and built an anti–civil rights network so big that some of its members and fellow travelers were, like the Chinese parents, unaware that a portion of their intellectual ammunition came from people like Pearson and that some of their efforts helped breathe life into his agenda.

The whole ecosystem was watered by a river of money turned to speech. Bank heiress Cordelia Scaife May and her Colcom Foundation, for instance, funneled tens of millions of dollars into eleven Tanton organizations—almost $57 million into FAIR alone by 2019 (another estimate puts the sum at $138 million).[52]

"For those on the far right, it's a waiting game," Angela Saini explains. "As long as they can survive and maintain their networks, it's only a matter of time before politics swings around and provides an entry point once more."[53] Of course, those on the left also bide their time, marshal resources, and watch history's every move. But since the founding of Chinese for Affirmative Action, the resources and passion have shifted to the anti–affirmative action and anti–civil rights side. In addition, the anti–affirmative action side has taken advantage of the peculiar legitimacy obtained by co-opting language and strategies from civil rights groups—whose own key strategists and wordsmiths the Pioneer Fund spent millions to prove inferior. This hidden history of co-option and contempt resides like a paradox wrapped inside a self-own inside the affirmative action debate.

It also helps explain why affirmative action in the popular imagination has little to do with the complexities of enforcing Titles VI and VII and related laws and executive orders. Instead, affirmative action has come to mean, almost exclusively, preferences granted to questionably qualified Black and sometimes Latino people. This focus tends to "white out" Asian and white female (and some white male) beneficiaries of affirmative action and, for reasons rooted in the activities of organizations like the Pioneer Fund, makes it easier to condemn affirmative action as reverse discrimination and as racism itself.

5

BACKLASH INC.

Reaching a peak of influence in the 1960s and 1970s, activists such as the young Ling-Chi Wang issued withering critiques of the American status structure and its infection with ideas like those emanating from the Pioneer Fund. In one undated essay from around 1968, Wang calls for a more militant Chinese American community in language reminiscent of one of his heroes, Malcolm X: Chinese people, he wrote, have long been stereotyped as "hard-working, inscrutable, patient, quiet, non-militant"—a stereotype that has been used by the Chinatown establishment, middle-class Chinese, and the white power structure to dismiss people like Wang who demanded change. But as long as "those who 'made it' maintain a hands-off 'Uncle Tom' attitude, the Chinese will continue to be exploited," he concluded.[1]

As we have seen, the stars aligned for Wang and his associates in the early 1970s: Wang testified before Congress and helped craft legislation. A legal aid office opened as part of Lyndon Johnson's War on Poverty lured Ed Steinman to Chinatown. Stanley Pottinger of the Nixon administration weighed in on Wang and Steinman's side of the bilingual education struggle. The Ford Foundation funded Public Advocates, the public-interest law firm that helped force the San Francisco Police Department to admit more minorities and women. The possibility of revising the whole status structure must have started to seem real to Wang, Steinman, Henry Der, and Earl Sanders.

It certainly seemed real to those perched at the top of the 1970s status hierarchy. Some of them felt the tremors coming up from below and decided they needed to counter the sudden power emanating from Chinatown, Black San Francisco, the chambers of the Supreme Court, and the executive branch of the national government. Massive resistance to *Brown* in particular and to desegregation in general erupted across the South, but it also emerged in the North and West in the form of campaigns like the one for Proposition 14 and backlash against efforts to desegregate San Francisco's schools.

Perhaps the most important element of this massive resistance emerged from the aftershocks of Barry Goldwater's 1964 presidential campaign and Ronald Reagan's transition from California chair of Goldwater's campaign to governor of California and future president. Goldwater's humiliating defeat by Lyndon Johnson in the 1964 election was a major birth pang of what later became known as the New Right and a major step toward Reagan's ascension as torchbearer of don't-tread-on-me conservatism.

William J. Baroody of the American Enterprise Institute (AEI) became a catalyst of the New Right's rise by scheming and maneuvering his way into authoring Goldwater's losing message in 1964. Although that message was buried under votes for Johnson in the short run, in the long run it helped mainstream the anti–civil rights vision. As scholar Jason Stahl explains, Baroody and his associates were behind a televised address on the "free society" that Goldwater delivered toward the end of the campaign. That speech not only condemned "racial quotas," busing, and government efforts to quash private-sector discrimination but also equated civil rights demonstrations with street crime. It claimed the government's job was to "restore proper respect for law and order in this land," not to "call men into the streets to solve their problems."[2]

Goldwater's loss reinforced Baroody's determination to institutionalize the ideas expressed during the campaign—and to counter the Brookings Institution, the font of many of Johnson's Great Society programs. Already president of AEI, Baroody sought to make it the counterweight to Brookings (and to the Ford Foundation, another of his adversaries). To make this happen, Baroody needed money, and he got it from hard-drinking Yale washout and multimillionaire Richard Mellon Scaife, who was just as alarmed by Goldwater's defeat and Lyndon Johnson's policies as Baroody was. Scaife had previously given AEI smaller amounts, but through the Scaife Family Charitable Trust he poured $4 million into the think tank between 1972 and 1975.[3]

As the *Washington Post* explains, the year of Goldwater's defeat was a "turning point" for Scaife, who had flown Goldwater out to California on a private plane on the eve of the 1964 Republican convention. Scaife was among the conservatives who

> concluded that they could only win an election in the future by matching the enemy's firepower. . . . "We saw what the Democrats were doing and decided to do the mirror image, but do it better," [a Scaife] associate said. "In those days . . . you had the American Civil Liberties Union, the government-supported legal corporations [legal aid operations like the one Steinman worked for], a strong Democratic Party with strong labor support, the Brookings Institution, the *New York Times* and *Washington Post* and all these other people on the left—and nobody on the right."[4]

Scaife did not limit himself to pumping money into AEI. In 1973 he sent funds to the Pacific Legal Foundation, a new, soon-to-be-consequential conservative public-interest law firm. In 1974, the year of the *Lau* decision, he gave his first big cash infusion to the year-old Heritage Foundation. By 1998, Scaife had injected $23 million into Heritage.[5]

The Heritage Foundation went on to eclipse AEI, not just because of its deep pockets but also because of the vision of Paul Weyrich, the blond, bespectacled political genius who dreamed it up.[6] Like Baroody, Weyrich was stunned by the power of the Democratic network that, in his view, had bound and gagged the real America. While working part time for Colorado senator Gordon Allot (a pro–civil rights lawmaker who, according to Weyrich, was fed up with civil rights leaders), Weyrich went in the senator's stead to a meeting of the Leadership Conference on Civil Rights—the organization cofounded by A. Philip Randolph—and had an experience akin to a Freudian primal scene when a child witnesses his parents having sex.[7] In this case, Weyrich witnessed his opponents organizing his and his compatriots' next defeat. "Before my eyes," he told CSPAN in a statement worth quoting at length, they rolled out a plan. . . . Nixon had just become president. And they had a defector [from Nixon's camp] who came . . . and he said, these are Nixon's plans with respect to housing. He wants to roll back the Civil Rights Bill on housing and make it possible for somebody who has, say, a 10-room house or apartment building to discriminate, if he wishes.

. . . . And every liberal group imaginable was there at that meeting. And I watched this interplay. I mean, first they got [Senator] Birch Bayh to cosponsor [legislation to counter Nixon, and] a brand-new Republican, Mac Mathias—he was a liberal Republican—to cosponsor it so it would be "bipartisan."

And then the ACLU said they would file a lawsuit not because of any aggrieved party, but in order to control the polemics of the issue. This was something I had never heard before. . . . Carl Rowan was there. He had just left the Johnson administration and was writing a column for the *Post*. . . . They had the Methodist Church there. . . .

There were black groups there. They wanted to have demonstrations. . . . And finally it was agreed that they should have demonstrations in Washington, but not in the rest of the country, because there might be backlash if they had them in the rest of the country, and so on.

. . . . The Brookings Institute guy was there, and he said, well, we've got a study coming up on housing. . . .

And I'm looking at this. And I said, that's how they do it. I mean, I had watched conservatives getting killed on the floor of the United States Senate. And I didn't know how it was done. . . . All of a sudden I was granted the opportunity to see the mechanics. . . . That was 1969. And from that day forward, I was insufferable. Wherever I went I said, "We've got to do something about this. We've got to have our own organizations."[8]

Weyrich took advantage of another bit of serendipity to make contact with beer magnate Joseph Coors, who provided the seed money for the Heritage Foundation, which Scaife later almost buried in dollars. In Congress, Weyrich brought Strom Thurmond and several other senators and House members together to strategize. A business plan for what became the Heritage Foundation had already been drawn up by a Weyrich associate in Thurmond's office, creating a wonkish fig leaf of high-minded abstractions to cover sentiments that were still bigoted.[9] Years earlier, Weyrich had dropped out of college to start a brief career in journalism, so he was probably familiar with the ways of mainstream communication, and this helped him and Heritage give Thurmond and others what is referred to in the movie *Casino* as a "morality carwash."[10] Thurmond went in tattooed with segregationist dogma and came out looking to some like one whose commitment to freedom and justice for all had simply been misunderstood.

After serving as its first president in 1977, Weyrich left the Heritage Foundation and continued to create new conservative organizations, as though the powerful, hydra-headed liberal coalition were breathing down his neck, about to devour all he had done.[11] A strict Catholic, he helped launch a movement that proved to be a powerful political and rhetorical counterweight to the religious elements within the Leadership Conference on Civil Rights and to influential political offspring of Martin Luther King, such as the Reverend Jesse Jackson and the Reverend Andrew Young. King had been able to deploy the language and the highest values of Christianity in a way that changed the American political landscape. So Weyrich partnered with data and direct-mail maven Richard Viguerie (another refugee of the Goldwater campaign) and the Reverend Jerry Falwell, a Protestant evangelical, to form the Moral Majority (whose name Weyrich coined). In turn, the Moral Majority played a critical role in Reagan's transformation from governor to president.[12] By 1980, Anne Nelson writes, "Weyrich's complex machine was under construction, with the Heritage Foundation to program policy, the Republican Study Committee [cofounded by Weyrich] to wrangle congressional votes, the American Legislative Exchange Council (ALEC) [also cofounded by Weyrich] to draft state-level legislation, and the Moral Majority to mobilize the masses."[13]

A final piece of the puzzle was put in place in 1981, when Weyrich became a charter member of the Council for National Policy (CNP), a Viguerie start-up. At the launch event, Reagan's director of the Office of Management and Budget was given the "Thomas Jefferson Award" to honor his efforts to "de-fund . . . the Left." But the CNP's broader purpose was to leverage the efforts of master strategists like Weyrich and deep-pocketed donors like Coors to shift the national agenda by changing the media landscape, guiding gerrymandering, and impacting decisions in statehouses.[14] As if to avoid giving away secrets like the ones Weyrich had discovered at the Leadership Conference on Civil Rights, the CNP adopted a commandment: the "media should not know when or where we meet or who takes part in our programs, before or after a meeting."[15]

In short, even as the CAA triumphed in *Lau* and other cases, bilingual education spread across the country, the SFPD and many other entities became racially integrated and more gender inclusive through affirmative action, and the Leadership Conference on Civil Rights worked to keep presidents' eyes on the prize of deep equality for all, a massive agenda-capturing counteroffensive steered by brilliant and determined operatives was taking shape.

In the affirmative action arena, one of the first public indications of this counteroffensive was a relatively obscure amicus brief submitted by the Pacific Legal Foundation in the landmark case of *Regents of the University of California v. Bakke*, the subject of the next chapter.

6

BAKKE: THE MAKING OF A DAGGER

On July 23, 2002, Dr. Patrick Chavis bought an ice cream cone at a Foster's Freeze restaurant in Hawthorne, California, and headed across the parking lot toward his Mercedes-Benz. Before he could get into the vehicle, he was accosted by three would-be carjackers with whom he exchanged words before being fatally shot. The trio fled without taking the car. It was probably a case of "the wrong guy with the wrong kind of car in the wrong place," detective Donna Cheek concluded.[1] This sort of amateur-hour evil rarely makes the national news. But Chavis's death stirred up a feeding frenzy of stories and op-eds in everything from the *Washington Post* and the *Los Angeles Times* to a neo-Nazi website. A *Wall Street Journal* op-ed summed up the reasons why: Chavis's story, which was once touted as a triumph of affirmative action, was now "more likely to be cited as a cautionary tale about the dangers of preferential treatment."[2] Conservative Valkyrie Michelle Malkin was less restrained: "Dr. Patrick Chavis is dead," she announced in her own op-ed. "Will the liberal politicians and gullible media who made him a poster boy for government-imposed affirmative action shed a single tear, or will they continue to ignore what a shameful tragedy his life became?"[3] Malkin took the full plunge into schadenfreude when she turned to her real target—a 1995 *New York Times Magazine* article that compared Chavis favorably with his fellow University of California–Davis alumnus Allan Bakke. Bakke achieved legal immortality when he sued the university for violating his constitutional rights after it rejected him in 1974 (for the second time) while admitting minorities he deemed less qualified than he was. Chavis had entered UC–Davis in 1973, one of five Black students (along with Chicano and Asian students) admitted under an affirmative action program designed to draw up to 16 percent of each incoming class from the ranks of the disadvantaged.[4] The *New York Times Magazine* article Malkin targeted was not the pure hagiography of Chavis she suggested, but its author, Nicholas Lemann, *did* compare Bakke's career unfavorably with Chavis's. After making the wildly inaccurate claim that Chavis "took Allan Bakke's place at U.C. Davis med school," Lemann justified the alleged usurpation by arguing that Bakke "does not seem to have set the world on fire as a doctor," as he had established no private practice in the Minnesota town where he lived and had landed no full-time staff position at a hospital. Chavis, in contrast, had made the most of his medical degree in the same community where he had grown up, "the eldest of five children of a welfare mother." Chavis had established a thriving obstetric and gynecological practice in a poor Black neighborhood that otherwise would have had no ob-gyn of any color. Here, Malkin has a point, for in his eagerness to do some pro–affirmative action agenda setting, Lemann did not dig deeply enough into Chavis's psyche.[5]

A few years after Lemann interviewed him, Chavis destroyed his own career and became exhibit A in the case against affirmative action. He took a four-day crash course in cosmetic surgery (a popular and profitable venture for many doctors at the time) and opened a clinic where he performed cosmetic procedures in exchange for cash from low-income patients.[6] In relatively short order the Medical Board of California suspended Chavis's license, pronouncing him unable to "perform some of the most basic duties required of a physician."[7] Administrative court judge Samuel Reyes affirmed this conclusion, ruling that Chavis would be a threat to public health, safety, and welfare if he were allowed to continue practicing.

No one, except for Chavis himself, could have disagreed with the ruling. He had caused the death of one woman and badly injured two others during botched and bloody "tumescent liposuction" procedures. Malkin could not have dreamed of a more perfect dagger to plunge into the heart of affirmative action and its champions. Ward Connerly, the African American who became the face of the anti–affirmative action movement in the 1990s and early 2000s, could not resist waving the flag of Chavis's downfall in the 2007 edition of his autobiography. Recalling that a "self-confident black man" named Cornelius Hopper had lectured him about the benefits of educating minority doctors who could then serve in minority communities, Connerly all but chortled in print: "I remembered Hopper's comments a couple of years later when the case of Patrick Chavis burst into the news. . . . I felt like calling Hopper to ask him what he thought the moral of the story was."[8]

And yet, as the go-to anecdote first for supporters of affirmative action and then for opponents, Chavis's story revealed more about those who used his rise and fall to bolster their own worldviews than it did about affirmative action itself. Chavis's malpractice could certainly serve as an example of incompetence, negligence, and lack of empathy. (On one occasion, he chastised a woman who was screaming in pain for talking "to the doctor while he is working." On another occasion, he left a woman bleeding in his office while he ran to check on another badly injured patient he had hidden away in his home.) But Chavis's actions testify more to a downward personal spiral than to the merits of any university or government policy. A psychiatrist who examined him for the California Medical Board found that Chavis "would lock himself in a closet for hours and then emerge in an angry mood because no one had bothered to check on him, and . . . he would leave the house to sleep outside in nearby fields." By then, Chavis had been divorced twice, been sued for child support, survived twenty-one malpractice suits, declared bankruptcy, and accused medical board investigators of conspiring against him with the Catholic Church. One of his ex-wives warned that if his license were taken away he would kill himself, "but only after he killed someone else."[9]

In light of all this, the *Wall Street Journal*'s conclusion—that Chavis's metamorphosis into a political symbol exemplified the effects of devaluing "merit in the name of 'diversity'"—could be reached only after some truly heroic avoidance of the obvious. This avoidance becomes clear when one considers that Chavis's first wife, Toni Johnson-Chavis, had been admitted to UC–Davis under the same affirmative action program, and to this day, she is a thriving pediatrician in the Compton neighborhood of Los Angeles where she grew up. To the extent that her ex-husband's story is a cautionary tale, it cautions against using any one successful (or failed) career to assess the value of affirmative action.

Nevertheless, Toni Johnson-Chavis's story *is* one of affirmative action working as intended. She grew up in Compton and attended a high school staffed by dedicated teachers who had so little in the way of resources that "simple things such as using slide rules [were not] taught." She earned straight A's in high school, but when she was admitted to Stanford she felt "really ill-prepared as compared to the other students even though I had fairly high SAT scores," she told interviewers for the documentary *Eyes on the Prize*.[10] Still, she graduated from Stanford in three years with a 3.2 GPA, while weathering racist hostility that included swastikas painted on her dormitory door and a cross set aflame outside her residence. In the end, she told *Eyes on the Prize*, she and two other African American women were moved, for their own safety, into a trailer usually reserved for upperclassmen. But Johnson-Chavis never missed an academic beat. Admitted to UC–Davis Medical School, she was at first unaware that she was a beneficiary of affirmative action, chosen by the relatively new Task Force on Medical Education for Underprivileged Citizens. She recalls white students who had been admitted with GPAs and MCAT scores much lower than hers. She adds:

> They certainly hadn't finished a curriculum in three years. . . . So, I took [being admitted under affirmative action] as an affront. That I, in some way, was given a spot . . . that I should not have had, that in some way I was not prepared, or that someone did me a favor. . . . How was somebody with a GPA above 3.0 who finished in three years at Stanford and who had contributed as much [in extracurricular community service] as I had, how is that affirmative action?[11]

Here, Johnson-Chavis is clearly using the definition of "affirmative action" created by the anti–civil rights movement.

In the *Bakke* turmoil, that meaning was very much in the headlines. Angry at news stories that described her and others admitted through the medical school's affirmative action program as obviously less qualified than Bakke, Johnson-Chavis asked rhetorically about Orel Knight, a Black classmate who won the award "given by the graduating class to the student who has demonstrated in his clinical work the qualities most likely to produce an outstanding physician."[12] Knight has since made headlines mainly as an obstetrician who handles difficult pregnancies and who performed the first successful in vitro fertilization in Sacramento, where he practices.[13] If "supporters of Bakke had had their say," Johnson-Chavis told *Eyes on the Prize*, "Dr. Knight would not have been [admitted to Davis]."[14]

On the whole, although some of the affirmative action students struggled, it "appears they either caught up rapidly or that they were more competent than the admissions scores showed," according to one faculty member.[15] Knight drew the obvious conclusion: "If admissions were based only on G.P.A. . . . med schools could turn out very intelligent medical computers. But they wouldn't be doctors."[16]

For Malkin and the rest, the stories of Johnson-Chavis and Knight and the overall success of the other task force admittees are not just passed over in silence. Their stories are treated as unworthy of recognition and perhaps even counterproductive, since they contradict the story line of Black incompetence and affirmative action's threat to public safety. Equally unworthy in the opinion of anti–affirmative action warriors are notable 1990s malpractice cases against whites and the fact that cosmetic surgery in that decade was like the Wild West. The quickest scalpel made the most money because "hundreds of thousands of baby boomers [wanted] face lifts, breasts implants, liposuction and other procedures," even though "a growing number of patients suffer disappointment, disfigurement and even death from what are billed as simple, low-risk procedures."[17]

When Chavis died, those who rushed to write about him asked no questions about how nonminority cosmetic surgeons who botched operations had managed to get into medical school. The *Journal of Blacks in Higher Education* ascribes the see-no-evil attitude toward whites and the seek-out-evil attitude toward Blacks to the tendency to dismiss whatever challenges one's preconceptions, a phenomenon known as confirmation bias.[18] As social psychologist Jonathan Haidt explains, "Each individual reasoner is really good at one thing: finding evidence to support the position he or she already holds. . . . We should not expect individuals to produce good, open-minded, truth-seeking reasoning, particularly when self-interest or reputational concerns are in play."[19] In the United States, of course, race is in some ways the ultimate reputational concern.

The volume of opinion devoted to the Chavis story eclipsed another important bit of data: a study that found no difference "in completion of residency training or evaluation of performance" between affirmative action beneficiaries and nonbeneficiaries who graduated from Chavis's and Bakke's alma mater between 1968 and 1987. Affirmative action "shows no evidence of diluting the quality of the graduates," the authors concluded.[20] Although this was only one study and not the last word on the subject, this article in a major medical journal was rendered invisible by the confirmation bias of affirmative action opponents. The complexities of why this was, and the effort to unlock hermeneutic traps (of which confirmation bias can be a key component) that is part of this book's mission, require a closer look at Bakke himself.

WHO WAS ALLAN BAKKE?

Tall, blue-eyed, and balding, Minnesota-born Allan Bakke was a Vietnam veteran who was working as a NASA engineer in the early 1970s when he applied to the University of California–Davis Medical School. He had higher test scores than most of those admitted to Davis, whether Black or white. But it is irrational to conclude that someone like Johnson-Chavis, who went from an underresourced Compton high school to Stanford to UC–Davis Medical School, "took" a seat that had "Bakke" written on it.[21]

There is no doubt that Bakke benefited from what has been called "white affirmative action," despite his humble beginnings as the child of a mailman and a high school teacher.[22] After his family moved to Florida, he graduated from segregated Coral Gables High School in 1958.[23] Even in 1965, by which time the high school had been integrated and a Black football star was playing quarterback on the team, some white parents withdrew their children from the school, and white players initially refused to block for their Black teammate. Decades later, the football player regretfully recalled how his academic performance suffered after a guidance counselor discouraged him from pursuing his dream of being a chemist because he had taken too few math classes at the segregated Black school he had attended previously.[24] The education Bakke got at Coral Gables clearly came gift-wrapped in a freedom to choose dreams without fear or favor that was not available to Black students until much later. And although Coral Gables was not Compton, Johnson-Chavis's time at Stanford suggests that her experience was closer to the football player's than to Bakke's.

For college, Bakke went back north to the University of Minnesota and defrayed costs by joining the ROTC, which paid his tuition and expenses in exchange for a four-year commitment to serve in the military after graduation. Earning a mechanical engineering degree with a 3.51 GPA in 1962, Bakke fulfilled part of his military commitment with a seven-month tour in Vietnam, where he commanded an antiaircraft missile unit, rose to the rank of captain, and took an interest in how medics treated the wounded.[25]

Back home, he spent a year in graduate school before taking a job at a NASA research center in Palo Alto, California. Working alongside physicians studying such subjects as the effects of space missions on the body, Bakke was mesmerized. He decided to become a doctor and enrolled in premed classes at San Jose State University and Stanford. He also volunteered in the emergency room of a nearby hospital, where he asked to be assigned to car wreck survivors and other difficult cases, all while holding down his job with NASA.[26]

In 1972, ten years after graduating from college, Bakke earned top scores on the MCAT and applied to eleven medical schools. He was interviewed at Stanford, the University of Minnesota, the Mayo Clinic, and the University of California–Davis, but none of those schools accepted him. Most of the rejection letters noted that intense competition created by a sharp rise in applicants forced them to reject some impressive candidates. Davis went so far as to say that the "number of applicants for each available position in each of our classes for the past several years has continued to increase in almost geometric proportions." The University of Minnesota observed that it favored in-state residents, and the Mayo Clinic confided that the applicants it admitted had better qualifications.[27]

At Davis, the least prestigious of the schools that interviewed Bakke, he had come close to acceptance, impressing his interviewer and earning 468 out of a possible 500 points in the rating system used by the admissions committee. That was only two points away from the 470 score that usually secured automatic admission, but because he was caring for his mother-in-law, who had lung cancer, Bakke had submitted his application late in the admissions cycle, when most seats had already been offered to others.[28]

After reading his rejection letter, Bakke wrote to Dr. George Lowrey, the square-jawed UC–Davis chairman of admissions, pleading for reconsideration. When no answer came, Bakke wrote again, making what are now classic anti–affirmative action arguments:

> Applicants chosen to be our doctors should be those presenting the best qualifications, both academic and personal. Most are selected according to this standard, but I am convinced that a significant fraction is judged by a separate criteria. I am referring to quotas, open or covert, for racial minorities. I realize that the rationale for these quotas is that they attempt to atone for past racial discrimination; but insisting on a new racial bias in favor of minorities is not a just situation. . . . [This is] reverse discrimination.[29]

Bakke also advised Lowrey that he was reviewing his legal options and consulting with people he knew in the federal and state governments. Lowrey passed the letter on to assistant dean Peter C. Storandt, who had come to work at Davis in 1972 and was charged with massaging the feelings of rejected applicants.[30]

Storandt quickly fell under Bakke's spell. During an exchange of letters in which Bakke announced his desire to challenge "the concept of racial quotas," Storandt did not question Bakke's characterization of the Davis admissions policy, which was based only on a goal, not a strict quota. Storandt even suggested that the University of California might be engaging in subterfuge in its efforts to enroll minorities: "I don't know whether you would consider our procedure to have the overtones of quota or not, certainly its design has been to avoid any such designation, but the fact remains that most applicants to such a program are members of ethnic minority groups."[31] The extraordinary leap of logic required to transform the race and ethnicity of a group of applicants into evidence of a covert quota is a marvel of confirmation bias and a sign that Bakke had found a friend.

THE CASE AGAINST THE UNIVERSITY

The climate of opinion that contributed to both Storandt's and Bakke's logic was shaped by intellectuals such as Paul Seabury, a professor at the University of California–Berkeley who took to the pages of *Commentary* in 1972 to attack Order 4 of the Nixon Labor Department, which expanded the Philadelphia Plan and has been called the "women's employment Magna Carta."[32] Seabury wrote that since 1967 (the year Lyndon Johnson's Executive Order 11375 added gender discrimination to the practices government contractors could not indulge in), "single-minded pursuers of an ideal of equality [have begun to] overrun and trample the ideal itself, while injuring innocent bystanders as well." The University of California, he lamented, was currently receiving $72 million in federal contract funds, but there were strings attached in the form of race and gender hiring goals.[33]

Seabury and, more surprisingly, Storandt seemed oblivious to the fact that, prior to the Civil Rights Act of 1964, the typical Black community was a "medical wasteland, bereft of medical services."[34] Across the nation, Black doctors—those most likely to establish practices in the medical wasteland—accounted for only 2.5 percent of physicians at a time when Blacks made up 11 percent of the population.[35]

The 1968 Kerner Commission report—widely covered by the media and very influential—suggested that one cure for the frustrations and humiliations that led to urban explosions like the one in Watts might be a "major upgrading in the employment status of Negro men" that would remedy their concentration at "the lowest end of the occupational scale." Those men needed access to well-paying, high-status work, which would require steep skills upgrades, equal access to higher education, and a "drastic reduction of discriminatory hiring and promotion."[36] Davis's decision to launch an affirmative action program, therefore, was not just a response to the nearly all-white composition of its first two medical school classes or to the specter of losing millions in federal funds. It was a response to a nationally sounded alarm.[37]

Though surely aware of at least some of this, Storandt was somehow able to dismiss it from his mind and make himself Bakke's Sherpa in the Minnesotan's quest to either win admission or bring the medical school to its knees. Bakke had such confidence in Storandt's support that he pumped him for nonpublic information about minority students in an April 7, 1973, letter:

1. Do they require special tutoring?
2. Do they take longer to complete medical school and therefore use more resources?
3. Do they perform adequately on national evaluation examinations?[38]

Among other things, Bakke's questions demonstrate why he might not have been the best choice to treat a community of diverse patients. His presumption of minority incompetence, slowness, and unreliability demonstrates bias, which, in a clinical setting, can lead to misdiagnoses and inadequate care for people suffering from serious conditions such as cancer or thrombosis.[39]

Nevertheless, Storandt went the extra mile (or two or three) for Bakke, and it eventually got him fired. He gave Bakke inside information about the academic performance of minority students at Davis and about their success rates in passing the national boards the first time around, which was almost certainly unavailable to other applicants. And given that Davis's affirmative action task force had been operating for just three years, this must have been a small and unscientific sample on which to base such large conclusions.[40] Storandt even advised Bakke to go to court if he were rejected again and told him about Marco DeFunis, a law school applicant whose challenge to affirmative action was on the fast track to the Supreme Court. Bakke began to correspond with DeFunis, who joined the circle of Bakke advisers.[41]

Bakke reapplied to Davis in 1974, and although the number of applicants had increased from 2,500 to 3,737, he again made it to the interview stage—this time under a revised admissions system whereby finalists were interviewed twice, once by a medical student and once by a faculty member. Another change was that those applying as "disadvantaged" were asked whether they were Black, Chicano, Asian, American Indian, or white/Caucasian.[42] The student who interviewed Bakke was quite impressed and awarded him 94 out of 100 points. But the faculty member—Dr. Lowrey himself—found Bakke wanting. Subtly using Bakke as an example of the need for doctors who understood minority perspectives, Lowrey concluded that Bakke's moral imagination was not powerful enough to escape his overachiever's high self-regard:

> He was very unsympathetic to the concept of recruiting minority students so that they hopefully would go back to practice in presently neglected areas of the country: one of his reasons for being against such programs was that they decrease his own chances. . . . My own impression of Mr. Bakke is that he is a rather rigidly oriented young man who has a tendency to arrive at conclusions based more upon his personal impressions than upon thoughtful processes using available sources of information.[43]

Despite Bakke's MCAT scores in the 97th percentile on scientific knowledge, 94th percentile on quantitative analysis, and 96th percentile on verbal ability, Lowrey was implying that Bakke's ability to tackle an unprecedented problem—how to reverse centuries of discrimination and ramp up the number of minority doctors to meet the enormous unmet demand for health care in minority communities—was more in line with his 72nd percentile score on the general information portion of the MCAT.

Lowrey's evaluation proved decisive, and Bakke was rejected for a second time. As planned, he sued, having already retained Reynold H. Colvin, who had gone to court in 1972 and blocked a San Francisco Unified School District plan to exempt minority administrators from layoffs in order to preserve diversity.[44] Colvin filed Bakke's suit in California Superior Court on June 20, 1973, and sixty-seven-year-old judge

Leslie Manker was brought out of retirement to preside over the case at the Yolo County courthouse. Manker ruled that the university had violated Bakke's rights under both the Fourteenth Amendment's equal protection clause and Title VII of the Civil Rights Act of 1964 because it had fixed the number of seats he could compete for based solely on race. But Manker refused to order Davis to admit Bakke because, as the university's lawyer argued, he might not have been accepted even if there were no affirmative action program.[45]

Manker disregarded some important issues. He failed to consider that, when Bakke applied to Davis, applicant age was an important factor in admissions decisions. Indeed, Bakke's age (thirty-three years) was the deciding factor for the ten other medical schools that rejected him.[46] The judge also lacked some crucial information that would have forced him to rethink his wildly inaccurate finding that the set-asides diminished Bakke's chances of admission by 16 percent. The judge stumbled into a hermeneutic trap that scholar Goodwin Liu, now a judge himself, calls the "causation fallacy"—the "mistaken notion that when white applicants like Allan Bakke fail to gain admission ahead of minority applicants with equal or lesser qualifications, the likely cause is affirmative action." Although "the sixteen-seat set-aside lowered Bakke's chances of admission," Liu explains, it lowered those chances by only half a percent, since scrapping the task force program and allowing everyone to compete for one hundred seats instead of eighty-four would lower the likelihood of rejection only from 97.3 percent to 96.8 percent.[47]

The judge was pushed deeper into the trap by other missing information. For example, the people who were most insulated from the competition for admission to UC–Davis were white. The dean of the medical school had the power to unilaterally grant admission to five applicants, most of whom were children of the well connected and the well-off. One white woman was reportedly accepted by the dean even after the admissions committee concluded that she was "emotionally unqualified to be a physician." A *Washington Post* article goes so far as to suggest that the University of California's general counsel, Donald L. Reidhaar, changed his courtroom strategy to shield the dean's activities. If this was indeed the case, it was not the last of the advantages the university gave to Bakke and the canny Colvin, who won again in California Supreme Court on September 16, 1976. Two weeks later, Reidhaar added to Colvin's victory by stipulating that the medical school "cannot meet the burden of proving that the special admission program did not result in Mr. Bakke's failure to be admitted."[48] The next step was for the university to decide whether to accept defeat or appeal to the Supreme Court of the United States.

The Bakke Case and Education

WHAT WERE THE CONCRETE CIRCUMSTANCES OF ALLAN BAKKE'S REJECTION BY MEDICAL SCHOOLS?

ARE SPECIAL ADMISSIONS PROGRAMS FOR MINORITY STUDENTS JUSTIFIABLE?

WAS BAKKE MORE QUALIFIED THAN THE SPECIAL ADMISSIONS STUDENTS?

DOES TESTING PROVIDE EQUAL OPPORTUNITY?

by the National Committee to Overturn the Bakke Decision

Cover of a pamphlet published in advance of the Supreme Court's *Bakke* ruling by the National Committee to Overturn the Bakke Decision, which was organized in Berkeley, California, in 1977. The pamphlet offered a point-by-point challenge to Bakke's arguments and warned that if the Supreme Court did not reject Bakke's lawsuit, "there will be a monumental backlash against this country's minorities and women." (Courtesy of Smithsonian National Museum of African American History and Culture)

7
THE STIPULATION

The university's defeat in the California Supreme Court led to withering criticism of Donald Reidhaar. A 1976 friend-of-the-court brief from the NAACP accused the university, and therefore Reidhaar, of launching a paper airplane of a case with nothing to keep it aloft, not even oral testimony from the obvious witnesses—aspiring doctors or members of minority communities—he should have approached if he hoped to win.[1]

The question of what to do next was left to William Coblentz, a member of the University of California's Board of Regents and a power broke in the Bay Area. A joyous, teetotaling man whose huge grins had carved deep creases in his cheeks, Coblentz knew that even minority students who were sure the court's ruling was wrong did not want the case appealed.[2] They understood that a US Supreme Court decision would apply to the whole country, not just to one state. But Coblentz decided to appeal anyway:

> I thought we should try to resolve the issues, that we had a good case. . . . The question is, who should handle the case? I had great respect for Don, but in the eyes of perhaps the public at large he wasn't the distinguished constitutional lawyer who should carry the burden. So I took it upon myself, the chairman of the board, to [find a replacement, and Reidhaar] was very gracious and agreed that he would drop out if we got the appropriate person.[3]

Reidhaar, with his winning smile, may have been gracious, but losing the biggest case of his life and then being dismissed from the appeal due to public outcry apparently sent him into a downward spiral. According to Coblentz, some connect the fallout from *Bakke* to Reidhaar's fatal leap from San Francisco's Golden Gate Bridge nine years later. Still serving as the university's general counsel at the time, Reidhaar wrote a suicide note to his wife stating, "My mind refuses to think clearly, and I am unable to cope. I wish with all my heart and soul there was some other way out of this terrible torment."[4]

In the end, Coblentz tapped Archibald Cox to take over as lead counsel on the *Bakke* case.[5] A lanky, six-foot-tall, bow tie–wearing descendant of a signer of the Declaration of Independence, Cox had been a boy wonder Harvard law professor, US solicitor general (until Nixon fired him for defying orders to call off the Watergate investigation), and Watergate special prosecutor. At the time of the *Bakke* case, he was said to be "more at home in the Supreme Court than any of the justices."[6]

One of Reidhaar's last acts on the case was to seek and win a thirty-day stay of the California Supreme Court's order to admit Bakke to Davis Medical School. He (and three coauthors) also petitioned the US Supreme Court to issue a writ of certiorari ordering that the *Bakke* case be brought before it. Here, Reidhaar and his team were acting more as corporate lawyers than as engineers of educational opportunity. As education expert Anthony P. Carnevale likes to stress, universities are businesses, and they are willing to waive requirements for a wealthy Jared Kushner without compunction but are probably less excited about admitting applicants from poor minority backgrounds.[7] The business side of the University of California was very much in evidence in Reidhaar's decision to stipulate that the Task Force on Medical Education for Underprivileged Citizens excluded whites—a stipulation that contradicted accounts of task force members.[8] Most tellingly, Reidhaar and his coauthors did not so much craft a relentless defense of the task force program as argue that the lower court's fallacious and fanciful insistence that the racial integration of educational opportunity be achieved without considering race, combined with contradictory legal standards established by decisions in *DeFunis*, *Bakke*, and a third case, was a kind of matador's swirling cape that drew the university and the entire legacy of *Brown* toward disaster in the form of "continual litigative testing of, and judicial intervention in, the administrative policies and practices of state graduate and professional schools." In short, Reidhaar and his coauthors pleaded with the high court to help the university manage risk by correcting "the mischief of the approach taken below and to give the issue the kind of treatment that, on a matter of such fundamental importance, the country so vitally needs and deserves."[9]

The Supreme Court took the case.

8

CERTIORARI

At the October 12, 1977, oral arguments for *Bakke*, Jimmy Stewart–soundalike Cox easily outclassed Colvin, a mere "trial lawyer from San Francisco, clearly unfamiliar with the Supreme Court," according to the *Washington Post*.[1] It is true that the justices sometimes switched to tutor mode with Colvin, but he managed to land some real blows against Cox. This is because he had a real strategy: he aimed to keep the justices focused on the details of Bakke's case as he, Colvin, framed them and avoid social and constitutional issues as much as possible. "I know, and we all know," he said, "that there are cases that are deemed to be [about] societal discrimination [affecting] millions and tens of millions of people. . . . *That is not this case!*"[2]

Cox, who was accustomed to dazzling the justices, attempted to do so by summoning the largest constitutional issues. Challenged by Justice Lewis Powell to state whether Davis's 16 percent minority goal was a quota, Cox made a philosophical argument, noting that the sixteen-seat goal "doesn't point the finger at any group. It doesn't say to any group you are inferior. It doesn't promise taking people regardless of their qualifications." The sixteen seats should be viewed not as a quota but as a measure of the urgency of including disadvantaged minorities in professional schools, he said. Such inclusion would make the professions aware of the existence of qualified minorities and would thereby help deprive race of "its present unfortunate significance."

Cox's problem was that he was trying to build a philosophical palace on the shakiest of foundations. He was attempting to work his magic on the same underdeveloped record the NAACP had complained about—"a trial record not of his own making" whose deficiencies "he could not correct," according to Dreyfuss and Lawrence. Key realities, such as the fact that the sixteen-seat "quota" had not always been filled, were not part of the record and therefore unavailable to Cox.[3] Also missing was the fact that the dean of the medical school had admitted white students with far lower grades than Bakke's and, in at least one instance, grades lower than the average GPA of task force admittees.[4]

Colvin, by contrast, had helped shape the record and knew exactly which parts he wanted to emphasize. Without going so far as to call himself a simple country lawyer, Colvin stressed that his was a simple narrative, "not an exercise in a law review article or a bar examination question." Instead, he said, "this is a question of getting Mr. Bakke into the medical school! And that's the name of the game and we have to do that." Colvin barely missed a beat when Justice Thurgood Marshall pressed him on whether some of his arguments were based on hearsay (and therefore inadmissible in court). He just kept pointing to the knots into which the university had tied itself. For example, he noted that the university had denied "that they had a racial quota. I think that's disappeared from the case. Secondly, they denied that Mr. Bakke would have been admitted even had there been no racial quota and as I will indicate at some length I hope later on, that's disappeared from the case." Weaving through questions from the justices, Colvin took care to twist the knife Reidhaar had handed him: "The ultimate fact in this case no matter how you turn it is that Mr. Bakke was deprived of an opportunity to attend the school by reason of his race. This is not a matter of conjecture. This is a stipulation by the Regents of the University of California."

Colvin even stood his ground when Marshall forced him to consider rights other than Bakke's by engaging him in a Socratic exchange. "You're arguing about keeping somebody out," Marshall began, "and the other side is arguing about getting somebody in?" When Colvin said that was true, Marshall responded, "So it depends on which way you look at it, doesn't it?" When Colvin conceded this point, Marshall focused on what the emphasis on Bakke was concealing: "You're talking about your client's rights. Don't these underprivileged people have some rights?" Colvin balked, insisting that the underprivileged "have the right to compete, they have the right to equal competition. . . . They have the right to compete not only upon the basis of grades, they have the right to compete on the basis of disadvantage."

Through it all, Colvin put on a display of lung strength, speaking in a voice that rarely dipped below the decibel level of a shout. He roared right through an acid comment Marshall injected after the first "they have the right to. . . . " "To eat cake," Marshall said in a quiet voice that nonetheless cut through Colvin's verbiage. Marshall thereby brought into court the legend of Marie Antionette saying of the masses of people begging for bread on the eve of the French Revolution, "Let them eat cake." The reference implied that Colvin was being equally cruel by saying that those who had spent their lives paying the stereotype tax—the costly presumption that they are unworthy—should eat equality.

Bulldozing along, Colvin refused to grant any primacy to rights other than Bakke's. Under questioning from Powell, he hedged a little, saying that his argument was based "not upon the ground that Mr. Bakke is attempting to tell the school what the qualifications are nor upon the ground that we as his counsel can somehow set up a rule which will tell us who is qualified to go to medical school." All he meant to prove, he concluded, was that the school had violated its own criteria by being high on quotas and blind to individual privileges and immunities. Here, Colvin danced around age, geography, and other typical elements of admissions decisions. "There are all kinds of other factors of economic and educational diversity," he stipulated. "We have no problem with that. The problem . . . is that we look at the Fourteenth Amendment and as we look at 2000(d),[5] the fact of the matter is that it is race itself, it is the discrimination on the ground of race itself . . . which is forbidden."

9

THE CONTEST INSIDE THE COURT

Two days after oral arguments, the nine justices—Thurgood Marshall, Lewis Powell, Potter Stewart, William Rehnquist, William Brennan, John Paul Stevens, Harry Blackmun, Byron White, and Chief Justice Warren Burger—held their first conference on the *Bakke* case. Justice White drove the agenda. He had circulated a memo the day before asking whether their decision should or could be guided by Title VI of the Civil Rights Act of 1964, which states: "no person in the United States shall, on the ground of race, color, or national origin, be excluded from participation in, be denied the benefits of, or be subjected to discrimination under any program or activity receiving Federal financial assistance."

White's problem was that neither Cox nor Colvin had relied on Title VI. Therefore, he suggested, "we should call for further briefs on the Title VI issue."[1] Over the objections of Marshall, Brennan, Stewart, and Powell, the court did just that on October 17, 1977. Cox, Colvin, and US solicitor general Wade H. McCree (who had joined oral arguments on the side of the University of California) immediately got to work writing briefs on whether Title VI applied to the *Bakke* case. Predictably, Colvin and coauthor Robert Links argued in their brief that Title VI gave the Supreme Court another way to find in Bakke's favor. The justices, they wrote, should ignore HEW interpretations that made affirmative action programs consistent with Title VI.[2]

Cox (joined by Donald Reidhaar, Paul J. Mishkin, and Jack B. Owens) took the opposite tack, arguing that the case should be decided entirely on the basis of the Fourteenth Amendment and that Title VI should not be a factor in the justices' decision, since even Bakke's legal team had not invoked it. However, if the justices did decide to bring Title VI into the case, Cox and his coauthors stated, using it to close the doors opened by affirmative action would "stand the Civil Rights Act of 1964 on its head."[3] McCree, joined by his boss, Attorney General Griffin Bell, and seven others, bolstered Cox by stressing that HEW interpretations of Title VI "are entitled to the greatest respect."[4]

After receiving the briefs in November 1977, the justices wrestled with *Bakke* for another seven months. In the streets, efforts to sway them had ramped up in October: three thousand demonstrators demanded that the Davis plan be upheld, and American Nazi Party members countered with chants of "White Power Now!"[5]

Inside the court, legal philosophizing sometimes mixed with sniping as Marshall tried to cobble together a majority. At one point late in the process, Powell's clerk Bob Comfort dismissed a Marshall draft opinion with a handwritten comment: "I cannot envision a need to respond to this very personal statement." Comfort was reacting to a particularly sharp passage in which Marshall attacked "Mr. Justice Powell's view that 'it is far too late to argue that the guarantee of equal protection to all persons permits the recognition of special wards'" entitled to extra protection. Powell's words, Marshall continued, "bear a discomforting relationship to those of the Court in the [nineteenth-century] Civil Rights Cases [where] the Court . . . wrote that the Negro emerging from slavery must cease 'to be the special favorite of the laws.'"[6]

"This is a not-so-subtle suggestion that you are a racist," Comfort advised Powell, "but I'm not sure we should dignify it by replying."[7] Comfort was not entirely wrong about Marshall's implication, but he ignored Marshall's substance and undermined Mr. Civil Rights' authority as the prime mover of *Brown* by suggesting that Marshall was guided not by reason but by emotions that had gotten the better of him. Comfort's dismissal is consistent with *Bakke*-era Washinton, DC, gossip about Marshall's work ethic and intellect. According to Juan Williams, the ailing Marshall was subject to ridicule by "white lawyers in top firms and law schools [who] had never been convinced that [Marshall had] a strong legal mind, and their snide private digs at him began getting into the public debate."[8] Even Cox joined in the fun, observing at one point that "Marshall may not be very bright or hard-working but he deserves credit for picking the best law clerks in town."[9]

Despite this derision, Marshall came close to engineering a majority that would uphold the university's affirmative action program early in the deliberations. At one point, Marshall needed just one more vote to consolidate a five–four majority, but, cleverly cajoled by Chief Justice Burger, Powell defected from Marshall's coalition.[10] Although there is no proof, it is hard to dismiss the idea that gossip about Marshall's supposed intellectual shortcomings—including the suggestion that his thinking was driven by emotion rather than reason—lowered Marshall's status and played a role in his failure to sway enough colleagues in an area of the law where he was the court's leading authority.[11]

None of this is meant to suggest that Marshall's arguments in the *Bakke* case were without flaw. His closest friend on the court, Justice Brennan, confided to a clerk that Marshall's draft opinion might have done more harm than good because Marshall argued that if an 1896 court had affirmed color blindness, "we would not be faced with this dilemma in 1978." This boiled down to, "'Goddammit, you owe us,'" Brennan concluded.[12]

Marshall's real point, of course, was that color blindness was being selectively invoked—as if the combination of hydrogen and oxygen were selectively invoked as *the* distinguishing feature of water, and assertions that a drink of hydrogen peroxide (H_2O_2) is not the same as a drink of water (H_2O) were "very personal" statements. Marshall was insisting that invoking color blindness after a hundred years of systematic racial discrimination and exclusion is not the same as invoking color blindness in the absence of such history. He was saying not "you owe us" but "you're still asking us to drink hydrogen peroxide." For Marshall, a prerequisite of true color blindness would be the removal of lingering elements of Black civil death, just as converting hydrogen peroxide to water requires the removal of an atom of oxygen. The problem, then, was not a contradiction in Marshall's argument but a willful shallowness in the thinking of those who scoffed at it or, in Brennan's case, the failure to see that extra atom of oxygen.

At the time, Justice Stevens averred in an opinion joined by Burger, Rehnquist, and Stewart that Title VI invalidated the Davis Medical School's affirmative action program.[13] But years later he not only came around to Marshall's point of view but became convinced that the final version of Marshall's opinion was a classic of American jurisprudence that "should be required reading for every high school in the country, for it tells a story that should be, but regrettably is not familiar to many Americans." It summarized "the impact of the Constitution as originally enacted on black Americans as well as the Supreme Court's role in reducing the force of the three amendments [Thirteenth, Fourteenth, and Fifteenth] adopted after the Civil War."[14]

In 1978, though, Powell carried the day by penning what became the plurality opinion after he defected from Marshall. Close to being Marshall's opposite, Powell was a tall, gaunt southerner who grew up steeped in the myth of the Lost Cause. Before Richard Nixon elevated him to the Supreme Court alongside Marshall, Powell served as chairman of the Richmond School Board in the wake of Marshall's 1954 victory in *Brown*. In 1959, with an eye on the many communities that had closed public schools rather than integrate them, Powell suggested delaying integration in the public schools that remained open.[15] As a result, "only 2 of 23,000 black children in Richmond [were] attending school with whites" when Powell left his post in 1960, according to Andres Walker.[16]

If Powell stopped short of advocating open defiance of *Brown*, it was for the same reason that he attacked Martin Luther King's use of nonviolent civil disobedience to defy unjust laws based on segregation: a rigid belief in obeying at least the letter of the laws on the books.[17] Though "the Negro has had, until recent years, little reason to respect the law" because the law was used against him, Powell believed that King's defiance of unjust laws in favor of God's moral law put him in the same boat as ardent segregationists who believed they were defending the law of nature.[18]

The logic Powell followed in condemning King shaped his controlling opinion in the *Bakke* case. With four justices to the right of him and Marshall and three others to the left, Powell found not a middle ground but an end run around the whole logic of the civil rights movement. Although Marshall disagreed with King's tactics and, more generally, was not pleased that his position as Mr. Civil Rights had been usurped by King, the jurist shared the civil rights leader's conception of injustice and recognized that the synergy between his own lawyering and King's protests advanced African Americans in the direction of equal rights.[19]

Unconcerned with that synergy, Powell used his *Bakke* opinion to invalidate Marshall's (and King's) vision of affirmative action as a corrective for past and present discrimination. He substituted an affirmative action built on the concept of diversity. For him, compensation for the past was a nonstarter because social inequality was "a fact of life and a possible source of creative ferment," according to Walker.[20]

Indeed, Powell insisted that if anyone had been burdened by disadvantage, it was Bakke. Yet the justice also believed that people like Bakke could benefit from the intellectual ferment at a school with a diverse student body—albeit a student body that exhibited "genuine diversity" rather than just "ethnic diversity." The quantum of difference an applicant could add to that fermentation was a plus in the same way that the ability to add long columns of figures in one's head or to execute a perfect corner kick in soccer was a plus. But this plus was a kind of Platonic entity, independent of the past. In a footnote addressing a competing opinion signed by Marshall, Brennan, White, and Blackmun, Powell scoffed at their use of stigma as the "crucial element in analyzing racial classifications." The Fourteenth Amendment's equal protection clause "is not framed in terms of 'stigma,'" he wrote. "Certainly the word has no clearly defined constitutional meaning. It reflects subjective judgment that is standardless."[21]

Yet in the same footnote, in a contradiction of Whitmanesque proportions, Powell invoked something utterly subjective and without constitutional meaning: the "deep resentment" felt by those on the losing end of affirmative action. Perhaps because of his experience managing a segregated school system, Powell was more sympathetic to the psychology of resentment than to the sting of stigma. Picking and choosing his history very carefully to whiten the meaning of stigma, Powell wrote that "the white 'majority' itself is composed of various minority groups, most of which can lay claim to a history of prior discrimination." Powell glossed over, or did not consider, the fact that white ethnics, after facing initial discrimination, could enter the "melting pot" and "become" white, while Blacks (except in borderline cases) and other longtime outsiders could not.[22]

In the passage Marshall took exception to, Powell wrote that the "clock of our liberties . . . cannot be turned back to 1868"—the year of the Fourteenth Amendment's ratification.[23] No turning back of the clock was needed, replied Brennan, Marshall, White, and Blackmun in an opinion penned mostly by Brennan.[24] Racial inequalities persisted in K–12 schools in California, the homeland of the *Bakke* case, and "many minority group members living in California were born and reared [like Bakke] in school districts in Southern States segregated by law."[25]

Powell swatted all this aside in favor of diversity as a sort of transcendental credit line cut off from history and accumulated disadvantage—a credit line that could pay for a new, narrow form of affirmative action. He made the Stevens group happy by striking down the existing task force program and ordering Bakke admitted. And yet, he saved affirmative action when he might have destroyed it. Added to the stronger endorsement of the policy signed by Brennan, Marshall, White, and Blackmun, his opinion reversed the California Supreme Court's prohibition of race-conscious admissions decisions.[26]

Unhappy with this half loaf, Marshall's final opinion focused on the grim results of the Supreme Court's chipping away at the Thirteenth, Fourteenth, and Fifteenth Amendments in many of its decisions:

> A Negro child today has a life expectancy which is shorter by more than five years than that of a white child. The Negro child's mother is over three times more likely to die of complications in childbirth, and the infant mortality rate for Negroes is nearly twice that for whites. The median income of the Negro family is only 60% that of the median of a white family. . . . For Negro adults, the unemployment rate is twice that of whites. . . . Although Negroes represent 11.5% of the population, they are only 1.2% of the lawyers

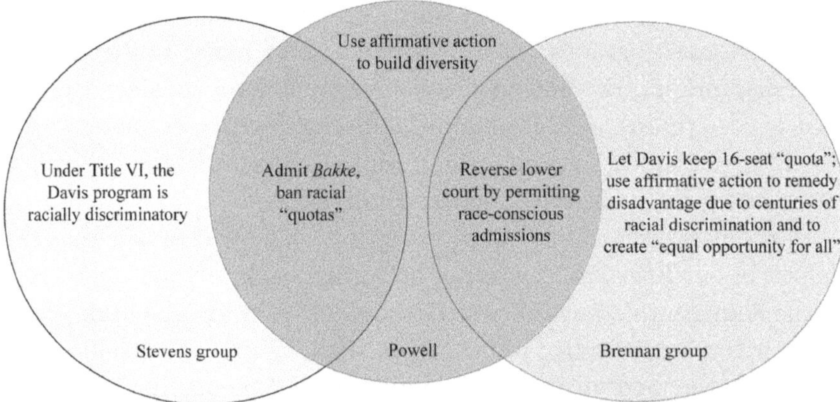

Figure 9.2. The *Bakke* decision established diversity as the basis of affirmative action in higher education from 1978 until the 2023 Supreme Court decisions in *SFFA v. Harvard* and *SFFA v. UNC* (discussed in chapter 24).

> and judges, 2% of the physicians, 2.3% of the dentists, 1.1% of the engineers and 2.6% of the college and university professors.
>
> The relationship between these figures and the history of unequal treatment afforded to the Negro cannot be denied. At every point from birth to death the impact of the past is reflected in the still disfavored position of the Negro. . . . I do not believe that the Fourteenth Amendment requires us to accept this fate. Neither its history nor our past cases lend any support to the conclusion that a university may not remedy the cumulative effects of society's discrimination by giving consideration to race.[27]

Powell was nevertheless the court's king for a day when the *Bakke* decision was announced to an eager public.[28] Having struck down Davis's affirmative action program, as the Stevens group desired, and having threaded affirmative action through the equal protection provisions of the Constitution, as the Brennan group insisted (see figure 9.1), Powell read from his controlling decision, beginning with a preamble that marveled at the interest in the case, albeit in a voice that was, as *Time* magazine observed, an "emotionless monotone."[29]

As for the tight-lipped Bakke, he waited thirty-seven years before suddenly joining Twitter to relive his application, rejection, lawsuit, and victory in a series of emotional 2015 posts that climaxed with: "I WON! #yes #happy #makingadifference #finally equal."[30]

10

THE AMERICAN MIND AFTER *BAKKE*

Maybe Allan Bakke and everybody won, as the *Washington Post* announced, but Thurgood Marshall viewed Lewis Powell's triumph as "tragic" for Black Americans, and he was not alone.[1] Civil rights legend Julian Bond said the court's message was: "We gave these people enough. They can sit in the front of the bus, they can sit downstairs in the movie theater, they can register to vote. Why aren't they happy with that?"[2] African American law professor Ralph Smith wrote that the decision "signaled the acceleration of a malignant retreat from the concessions extracted at such great cost in the 1960s."[3]

Others got to work stamping a favorable meaning on the decision. Eleanor Holmes Norton, head of the EEOC, which was handling eighty thousand job discrimination complaints each year, insisted that there was "nothing in today's decision that would keep the courts from ordering quotas" in hiring programs.[4] But in July 1978, when a Senate subcommittee decided that the *Bakke* decision made even the "presumption" of Black and Hispanic disadvantage unconstitutional and deleted an amendment to the Small Business Act of 1958 based on that presumption, she insisted that the subcommittee was mistaken.[5] Griffin Bell, the attorney general when *Bakke* was decided, backed Norton's position but said, "The court could have been a lot more forceful and made the whole thing more clear." Jack Greenberg, the NAACP Legal Defense Fund chief who expanded the scope of affirmative action by winning *Griggs* in 1971, resigned himself to the reality that the "matter will be subjected to continued litigation."[6]

With that litigious future hanging over everyone's head, some UC–Davis alumni tried to champion affirmative action as they had known it. James Mendez, a Chicano admitted to Davis Medical School under the affirmative action program, was working at a Fresno, California, hospital where more than one-third of the patients were Spanish speaking. He told CBS News that if the task force had not existed, "I wouldn't have applied, and it's that simple. Because prior to [the] affirmative action program, there were virtually no Chicanos in medical school." There was a level of empathy between him and Latino patients, he said, that he did not observe between Latino patients and white doctors.[7]

What the nation wanted to focus on, however, was not Mendez and his patients but Bakke's victory. *Time* magazine highlighted the case with a double headline on its cover: "Quotas: No [illustrated by a photograph of a smiling Bakke]—Race: Yes [illustrated by a photograph of a pensive African American man]." With stories like Mendez's eclipsed by such coverage, it is not surprising that a 1977 Gallup survey found that 81 percent of the public opposed any "preferential treatment" (a loaded term that provoked a more negative response than "affirmative action"), even if it was meant to compensate for past discrimination.[8]

In 1976 presidential candidate Ronald Reagan, once again both riding and shaping public opinion, appeared in an infomercial that heralded the full-blown modern anti–civil rights movement he would usher in four years later: "If you happen to belong to an ethnic group not recognized by the federal government as entitled to special treatment, you are a victim of reverse discrimination," Reagan said. "I'd like an opportunity to put an end to this federal distortion of the principle of equal rights."[9] Perhaps Reagan and his advisers were aware that the ambient white animus went well beyond resentment of preferential treatment. At the time of the *Bakke* decision, almost 60 percent of whites opposed laws that would stop them from practicing racial discrimination when selling their homes, and well over 30 percent believed they had the right to live in segregated neighborhoods.[10] Whites also showed significant resistance to sending their children to schools with large numbers of Black students.

This was part of the "haven't we given them enough" school of thought, or what sociologist Lawrence D. Bobo calls the "ideology of bounded racial change"—the boundary being the point at which "the existing distribution of power, wealth and status" starts to erode.[11] As Derrick Bell's convergence principle predicts, this means that even whites who endorse the ideal of racial equality resist concrete efforts to bring it about. As Bobo observes, "Whites, on average, have a real stake in maintaining race relations as they are and no benefits to gain by implementing equal opportunity policies. . . . A belief system that tends to espouse only constrained or 'bounded' racial change has resulted." Affirmative action and other efforts to lift the status of Blacks and others can cause whites to feel "status threat"—fear of lost position, esteem, and power—Bobo argues. Thus, northern whites who might have cheered the *Brown* decision and subsequent efforts to desegregate southern schools were not so happy when desegregation spread into their own towns and neighborhoods in the form of affirmative action in general and "forced busing" to integrate schools in particular.[12]

It is one thing for the Joneses if everyone tries to keep up with them; it is quite another thing for the Joneses if the rules are changed to make their enviable position easier for others to reach. Under these circumstances, defection from solidarity with the Black freedom struggle seems like the righteous option. In 1970s Boston, for instance, busing provoked a burst of "white flight" to what the *New York Times* described as "private antidesegregation academies" like those in the South. Parents of 17,760 white students pulled their children out of public schools within eighteen months of court-ordered integration by busing.[13]

To avoid cognitive dissonance, many whites (probably including those white parents in Boston) assert that whatever traces of racism remain in America have nothing to do with them. Asked to respond to the multiple-choice proposition that, on average, "blacks have worse jobs, income and housing than white people" because of (a) discrimination, (b) less inborn ability, (c) less educational opportunity, or (d) "lack of *motivation* or will power to pull themselves out of poverty," 66.2 percent of non-Hispanic whites chose "lack of *motivation* or will power" in 1977, the year before the *Bakke* decision and a year marked by the antibusing protests in Boston. The unambiguously racist "less inborn ability" was chosen by 26.2 percent.[14] Not surprisingly, that same year, Gallup found that just 9 percent of whites believed that "women and members of minority groups should be given preferential treatment [again, that loaded phrase] in getting jobs and places in college."[15]

Ironically, only fourteen years earlier, almost half of whites were inclined to say that the Black community's difficulties were due to discrimination, and almost half believed that a Black person had less chance of landing a job for which he or she was qualified than a white person did. But by 1978, 82 percent of whites believed a qualified Black person had just as good a chance of landing a job as a qualified white person. Backlash against ideological and rhetorical shifts in the civil rights movement contributed to the change. Howard Schuman and Maria Krysan argue that the contrast between the murders and lesser brutalities visited on civil rights activists, on the one hand, and King's emphasis on nonviolent protest, on the other, had won the sympathy and admiration of many whites during the years leading up to the Voting Rights Act of 1965. But the fiery rhetoric and raised-fist symbolism of the Black Power movement, combined with the outbursts of rage, window smashing, and greater or lesser degrees of looting in the wake of events like King's assassination, frightened and angered many whites.[16]

King's dramatizations of injustice were masterworks in "the use of media to explain a cause to the general public of a nation," said Birmingham, Alabama, attorney David Vann.[17] There were no two ways of interpreting the police assaults on schoolchildren that occurred during King's campaign to end segregation in Birmingham in 1960. But riots have no spokespeople and no clear message. They are subject to interpretation by people who are unsympathetic to and uncomprehending of the rioters' grievances. There are always some unjustifiable—even reprehensible—actions by those who take to the streets. And there are always skilled politicians like Reagan and Nixon who rally whites by promising to smother the chaos.[18] For many whites, the fact that the post-King social explosions were sparked by the literal gunning down of the voice of nonviolence was lost in a flood of scary TV images that cemented the presumption noted by Julian Bond—that white society had already paid its debt.[19] Lost in the condemnations of chaos and the promises to restore "law and order" was an old back-of-the-envelope equation that A. Philip Randolph concocted in the 1940s—unemployment plus hunger minus hope equals riots—an equation that still captured the conditions in some of the communities that exploded. Indeed, similar equations inspired affirmative action. But Reagan-style words about both riots and affirmative action helped keep all of that out of sight and out of mind for many people.[20]

In short, whether intentionally or not, Justice Powell was channeling mainstream America when he wrote that Blacks faced no extraordinary discrimination. The offense his law clerk took on his behalf at the suggestion that Powell might have racist attitudes—the sort of offense politicians like Reagan encouraged people to take—jibes with the attitudes of that era's Gallup-polled whites.[21] Thus, as Charlotte Steeh and Maria Krysan observe, except for "a short time in the 1960s, affirmative action policy has been portrayed in political discourse, in the media, and in polls primarily as preference or reverse discrimination or quotas."[22] It is no wonder that, in the heat of the *Bakke* debate, civil rights leader Jesse Jackson accused the media of hermeneutic malpractice that stacked "the deck against understanding."[23]

Some of the key elements of institutionalized hermeneutic malpractice as it has come down to us—in phenomena such as the panic over critical race theory—were a response to an eruption that occurred on April 19, 1969, during Parents' Weekend at the idyllic, gorge-dotted Cornell University campus in Ithaca, New York. A group of Black students, some brandishing rifles, took over the university's Willard Straight Hall. The bare fact of the takeover is just about the only thing those who have written about the event agree on.

The students who took over the hall saw the occupation as the best way to underscore their unmet demands that Cornell stop investing in South Africa, where apartheid was the law of the land. One faction of students was also pressing for the creation of a Black studies program. Others were demanding the firing of a visiting economics professor who had made remarks in class that some deemed racist. The Willard Straight Hall takeover was the culmination of a series of protests that included disrupting a basketball game, carrying toy guns into an administration building, knocking books off library shelves, and even grabbing the university president by the collar and dragging him away from the podium during an event about divesting from South Africa.

Thomas W. Jones, a leader of Cornell's Afro-American Society, disapproved of some of the more extreme actions, such as the assault on the president, and he initially voted against the idea of occupying Willard Straight Hall because by then, the university had agreed to create a Black studies program. But he changed his mind out of a desire to express solidarity with the protest movement and out of concern that the university was dragging its feet on launching the new program. On April 20, rifle in hand, he ended up being the last one to exit the building, which for him symbolized the heart of white power.[24]

For a number of influential conservatives, the seizure of Willard Straight Hall was the last straw. Almost two decades later, Allan Bloom, a philosophy professor at Cornell at the time of the takeover, was still fuming in the pages of his surprise 1987 best seller *The Closing of the American Mind* (which one reviewer advised government officials to read). Bloom condemned not only the takeover but also the idea of Black studies, assuring his readers that the African Americans recruited by Cornell were not only "unqualified and unprepared" but also humiliated and angered by their inability to keep up. Black studies was little more than a face-saving way out of the resulting academic catastrophe and a "license for a new segregationism," Bloom concluded.[25] A student like Thomas W. Jones—who graduated from Cornell, earned an MBA, became an enormously successful investment banker, and eventually landed a seat on Cornell's Board of Trustees—was inconceivable in Bloom's philosophy.

Impacting history and not just the best-seller list was the fury of wealthy Cornell alumnus John M. Olin, a chemist with deep-set eyes that could both twinkle and intimidate. Olin took a family fortune built on arms manufacturing (an area in which he held several patents) and expanded his company until it dealt in everything from pharmaceuticals to paper bags. Olin also hunted, sent boxes of salmon he caught to Richard Nixon, bred a Kentucky Derby–winning horse, and won prizes for dog breeding. "Show me a good loser and I'll show you a loser" was his motto, and he was convinced that Cornell had allowed itself to be defeated by a ragtag group of radicals who had unwisely been admitted to the university due to lowered standards.[26] His response, even at the age of eighty-one, was to pump enormous sums into the Olin Foundation, an outwardly traditional outfit that donated to organizations such as the Episcopal Church and Cornell (which opened the John M. Olin Library in 1961) but also helped disguise a CIA campaign to fund anti-communist efforts in the United States, Africa, and beyond through what the *New York Times* called a "worldwide propaganda network."[27] So in 1973, when Olin gave his foundation a new task—to use "strategic philanthropy" to create a "counterintelligentsia" that could break "the creeping stranglehold that socialism has gained here since World War II"—he could likely leverage expertise in shaping scholarship and public opinion that he gained from his association with the CIA.[28] Bloom became part of Olin's plans when he agreed to head a pilot foundation designed to "connect policymakers with political theory." The pilot project grew into the new John M. Olin Center for the Inquiry into the Theory and Practice of Democracy, which Bloom codirected even as funds from the center's $1.1 million three-year budget supported his writing of *The Closing of the American Mind*.[29]

The Olin strategy for a counterintelligentsia converged with that of another person upset by the Willard Straight takeover and other campus showdowns: Lewis Powell. Before his elevation to the Supreme Court, Powell addressed a now-famous 1971 memo on the "Attack on the American Free Enterprise System" to the Chamber of Commerce. Without using the words "foundation" or "think tank," Powell called on the chamber to enlist a contingent of scholars and speakers to push back against leftist academics who had captured higher education and were churning out anti–free enterprise students. Two years later, Olin's foundation began altering America's mind and politics by supporting people like Bloom and helping to launch major conservative think tanks and public-interest law firms that were everything Powell could have dreamed of.

PART II

TRIUMPH OF THE ANTI–CIVIL RIGHTS MOVEMENT

Celebrating her warp-speed confirmation to the Supreme Court after President Donald Trump nominated her to fill the seat of Ruth Bader Ginsburg (who died September 18, 2020, a little more than five weeks before), Amy Coney Barrett leads Trump and Supreme Court Associate Justice Clarence Thomas to the White House South Lawn, where Thomas will swear Barrett in using the constitutional oath. The current 6–3 conservative Supreme Court supermajority was officially created the next day, when, in a more traditional ceremony, Barrett was sworn in with the judicial oath by Chief Justice John Roberts. Barrett's confirmation path is discussed in the conclusion of this book. (Photo used by permission of Alamy.)

11
THE EQUALITY MATRIX

While John Olin and others like him were growing their counterintelligentsia, affirmative action law remained in the muddle noted by both Griffin Bell and Jack Greenberg. In an eloquent 1981 essay, Vanderbilt Law School professor Robert Belton mapped that muddle, explaining that the problem with affirmative action decisions was their struggle to reconcile two largely contradictory conceptions of equality: the equality of opportunity for groups, and the equal treatment of persons.[1]

Congress, the EEOC, the Office of Federal Contract Compliance, and the Supreme Court (in *Griggs* and other decisions) found that equality of opportunity can be estimated using statistics about a company's percentage of minority employees and the percentage of potential minority workers in the community where the company is located. In some decisions, the Supreme Court emphasized equality of opportunity for groups; in others, it emphasized an individual's right to equal treatment. For Thurgood Marshall, there was no contradiction. He always had his eye on deep equality, where equal treatment and equality of opportunity would rhyme, and he crafted decisions like a kind of prosody to get competing perspectives to interlace. But in 1979, when Marshall and three other justices signed on to William Brennan's opinion in *United Steelworkers v. Weber*, William Rehnquist tried to use Marshall's own words in an earlier case against him.

In *Weber*, Brennan found that a training program for Blacks (who had long been barred from skilled work at a Louisiana aluminum plant) did not violate the Title VII rights of Brian Weber, a white laboratory technician who had sued over his exclusion from the program. Rehnquist not only dissented but also cited the Marshall-penned majority opinion in *McDonald v. Santa Fe Trail Transportation Company*. In that case, the court ruled in favor of two white workers who had been fired for misconduct while a Black worker who participated in the misconduct kept his job. "Title VII prohibits racial discrimination against the white petitioners in this case upon the same standards as would be applicable were they Negroes and Jackson [the retained Black worker] white," Marshall wrote for a unanimous court.[2] Pointedly quoting Marshall's words in his *Weber* dissent, Rehnquist accused the majority of an "Orwellian" misreading of Title VII.[3] Rehnquist breathed so much fire that he burned to ashes (in his own mind, at least) a crucial footnote in Marshall's opinion. That footnote sought to head off the type of attack mounted by Rehnquist by stressing that since the firing of the white workers was not a result of any affirmative action program, *McDonald v. Santa Fe Trail* had nothing to do with affirmative action.[4] Here, Marshall was drawing a distinction between the deep historical inequality addressed by affirmative action and a surface inequality in the disparate punishment of workers for identical recent deeds. But the distinction was an exceedingly delicate one that some feared would leave "the lingering vestiges of centuries of discrimination to be resolved on a case-by-case basis."[5] This may be why, after the *Bakke* case, the Supreme Court sometimes split the difference between equality of opportunity and equal treatment by substituting "diversity" (defined as beneficial for everyone) for race. In 1990's *Metro Broadcasting Inc. v. Federal Communications Commission*, for instance, the court upheld an FCC ruling that gave an edge in the competition for a broadcast licenses to minority-owned companies. Brennan invoked *Bakke* in his majority opinion, writing that just "as a 'diverse student body' contributing to a 'robust exchange of ideas' is a 'constitutionally permissible goal' [as established by *Bakke*]," so "diversity of views and information on the airways serves important First Amendment values. . . . The benefits of such diversity are not limited to members of minority groups who gain access to the broadcasting industry . . . [but pertain to] all members of the listening and viewing audience."[6]

There remained, however, no general formula for resolving affirmative action disputes. This was true because parties to a dispute, seeking different outcomes, almost always made their arguments under the banner of either equality of opportunity or equal treatment. The intractability of this clash is illustrated by the matrix in figure 11.1. The matrix consists of choices available to two parties to a lawsuit—party A and party B. Each party has a choice: try to expand equality of opportunity or try to enforce strictly equal treatment, regardless of its effect on opportunity or its dissonance with history. In the matrix, I refer to a Rehnquist-like enforcement of equal treatment as "emphasizing surface equality." If both parties always choose to emphasize surface equality, they both accept something close to the status quo, do not support affirmative action except in individual cases of clear discrimination, and therefore do not become parties (or partisans) in a lawsuit. If both emphasize equal opportunity, they both support affirmative action that favors members of groups with less access to agenda-setting opportunities and, as a result, have a greater likelihood of bringing diversity to institutions full of individuals from more privileged groups. Because they agree, they do not take each other to court.[7] However, if one wants to cultivate a deep equality of opportunity and the other wants to cultivate surface equality, one of them files a lawsuit, perhaps against the other. Bakke, emphasizing surface equality, filed suit against Davis Medical School. Toni Johnson-Chavis, who filed no lawsuit, stresses the need for the deep equality pursued by the Davis task force: "Ten years after *Bakke*," she told one interviewer, "there are only two black pediatricians existing in Compton, California. . . . One guy who came out of the inner city, Indianapolis, Indiana, and myself, who came from Compton. . . . If the two of us had not been trained in that era and were not here, who would fill the void now?"[8] Thus, Johnson-Chavis endorses the policy Bakke sought to destroy. In this way, the two doctors are perfect embodiments of the choices depicted in the matrix.

Of course, sometimes surface equality is enough (as Marshall acknowledged). It is enough when deep equality already exists and, as on a team, it is just a matter of providing everyone with the same uniforms. But affirmative action arose because deep inequality (like that between medical care in Compton and medical care in wealthy

	Emphasize equal opportunity	Emphasize surface equality
Emphasize equal opportunity	affirmative action	lawsuit
Emphasize surface equality	lawsuit	no affirmative action

Figure 11.1. Equality matrix.

As of 2023, the Supreme Court has largely shifted the future of American higher education into the lower right-hand cell of this matrix, making it easier for devotees of surface equality to win lawsuits. These developments are discussed in chapter 24.

suburbs) has been the rule rather than the exception throughout much of US history. The country has practiced what political scientist Ira Katznelson calls "white affirmative action" in housing, education, credit, and agenda-setting power.[9] The result has been a never-ending inequality pandemic prolonged by interest-divergence entrepreneurs like Christopher Rufo.

12

SEA CHANGE

The counterintelligentsia began to take charge of the Supreme Court in 1981, when Ronald Reagan swept into the White House and appointed former Goldwater stalwart Sandra Day O'Connor to the court. In 1986 Reagan elevated the even more conservative William Rehnquist to the position of chief justice.[1] That same year, in an unacknowledged affirmative action posting that echoed O'Connor's, Reagan appointed the acerbic, überconservative Antonin Scalia partly because he wanted to be "the first president to nominate an Italian American to the Supreme Court."[2]

Just as important as these conservative judicial appointments was the fact that Reagan kept anti–civil rights movement innovators like Edwin Meese III and William French Smith close to him. Both men had been with Reagan since his gubernatorial days, and in 1973 they were among the founders of the Pacific Legal Foundation (PLF), a sort of pearl grown out of a combination of Lewis Powell's 1971 memo to the Chamber of Commerce (see chapter 10), strategic investments by the chamber and the Olin and Scaife Foundations, and, above all, the sheer aggravation of Meese and others in Reagan's gubernatorial orbit over lawsuits that blocked their efforts to achieve "total welfare reform" and loosen California's environmental regulations.[3] Smith served as attorney general during Reagan's first term and Meese during his second. But it was Meese who hit the Thurgood Marshall wing of the civil rights movement like a meteor, maneuvering to elevate O'Connor and Rehnquist and a host of conservative judges in the lower courts and leading an intellectual movement aiming to show that, in effect, surface equality is the only equality.

Increasingly, Meese and organizations like the PLF delivered combination blows to the civil rights movement. Early on, the PLF established itself in legal battles against environmentalists' efforts to protect air quality, the California coastline, and fragile species. The environmentalists, Reagan charged in a 1977 opinion piece, threatened to "unwind the U.S. economy—or stop it altogether."[4]

Robert Gnaizda, the witty, mustachioed lawyer who represented the Officers for Justice, battled the PLF in a case in which he argued that California's school financing arrangement hurt the poor. He later accused the PLF of being "a wolf in sheep's clothing" because the "true public interest firms represent the unrepresented—the views of minorities, the poor and others which otherwise would not be represented. The corporate view is already being well-expressed by big, well-financed corporations."[5] Indeed, Ronald A. Zumbrum, the PLF's dimple-cheeked executive director, argued that "many public interests" and environmental ones should not eclipse business ones. But the PLF became a deeper thorn in the civil rights movement's side when it filed an amicus brief and contributed in other ways to a major defeat for Marshall in the 1989 case *City of Richmond v. J. A. Croson Company.* Joining the brief writing was a network of similar organizations: the Mountain States Legal Foundation, the Southeastern Legal Foundation, and the Washington Legal Foundation.[6] Except for the PLF, which was the prototype, all these outfits had been spun off by the National Legal Center for the Public Interest (NLCPI), a sort of legal mothership created with funds from Richard Mellon Scaife; J. Simon Flour, an engineering and construction tycoon; and, to a lesser extent, John Olin. By the time liberals, accustomed to victory in the courts and the culture, were rudely awakened by the "debacle" of Reagan's election, they were all but surrounded. A 1981 *Washington Post* article noted that the "conventional wisdom about many issues appears to be changing. . . . And there is no doubt that the conservative network now provides the intellectual underpinning for these shifts."[7] Inside the Supreme Court, Marshall felt increasingly surrounded and isolated as the new conservatives on the court fed intellectually on the amicus briefs submitted by conservative legal networks and foundations. This was clear in the interplay of what became the O'Connor plurality opinion and the Marshall dissent in *Richmond v. Croson*.[8]

The case grew out of a challenge to the 1983 adoption by the City Council of Richmond, Virginia, of a Minority Business Utilization Plan that, between 1983 and 1988, aimed to set aside 30 percent of the city's construction business for companies with at least 51 percent minority ownership. The 30 percent target was inspired by a study showing that although Richmond was 50 percent African American, just 0.67 percent of its prime construction contracts went to minority-owned companies between 1978 and 1983. The city believed it was on solid legal footing because, in 1980's *Fullilove v. Klutznick*, the Supreme Court ruled that 10 percent of federal funds for local projects could be set aside for minority-owned companies (as mandated by the Public Works Employment Act of 1977).[9]

The first test of the Minority Business Utilization Plan came in September 1983, when the city requested bids for a job to install water closets and stainless-steel urinals in the Richmond jail. The nonminority-owned J. A. Croson Company put in a bid but had difficulty finding the required minority subcontractor.[10] Croson had been in talks with minority-owned Continental Metal Hose, but the deal went off the rails when Melvin Brown, who ran Continental, tried to obtain the $80,000 in specialty fixtures needed for the job and the manufacturer refused to grant him credit for such a large purchase. When Brown finally struck a deal for the parts and submitted a bid, it was more than $6,000 higher than one from a nonminority subcontractor. Furthermore, the manufacturer refused to certify Continental Metal Hose as a supplier, so Croson threw up its hands and asked Richmond to waive the minority subcontractor requirement. The city refused this request, and it also refused to let Croson raise its bid to cover the extra $6,000. Instead, the city announced that it would seek new bids. A month later, the manufacturer agreed to approve Continental as a distributor if it got the subcontract. But Croson filed a lawsuit anyway, claiming the city had violated its equal protection rights, unjustly disadvantaging it despite the fact that it bore "no responsibility for whatever harm the minorities included in the coverage of the City's ordinance are thought to have suffered," Croson's lawyer, Walter H. Ryland, argued in his Supreme Court brief.[11]

When oral arguments were heard on October 5, 1988, the city's lead lawyer, John A. Payton, argued that Richmond had "a closed business system"—an old-boy network of nonminority contractors and subcontractors who dealt opportunities to one another like cards. Antidiscrimination laws had thus far failed to breach that circle of favors.[12] In short, the Croson side insisted that the court focus on surface equality and ignore whatever discrimination minority businesses had suffered, and the Richmond side asked the court to focus on the twisted roots of the city's business practices.

As the oral arguments continued, Justice Scalia tossed Ryland a softball, asking whether those who had imposed the 30 percent set-aside were representing not the *minority* of the Richmond population but the majority, which by definition already possessed the agenda-setting power that affirmative action is supposed to make possible. Ryland took a good swing:

> Yes, one of the amicus briefs filed some Census data which showed that the actual minority percentage in Richmond was more than 50 percent. It was known that a majority of the people on the City Council were black.
>
> . . . . [But] it seemed to us that the tendency to adopt an ordinance for the wrong reason would be there any time you were dealing with a significant political interest group, without regard to whether it was the majority or not.[13]

Justice John Paul Stevens interrupted to say that the transcript of the crucial hearing before the City Council showed that the city was split down the middle, 50 percent Black and 50 percent white. But Scalia had made his point and likely that of the Reagan administration. It is not clear which brief Ryland was referring to, but a likely candidate was the one coauthored by Reagan's solicitor general Charles Fried, along with Roger Clegg, William Bradford Reynolds, and other surface equality devotees. On the first page of that document, Fried and the others asserted that "the City of Richmond, Virginia, has a population that is over 50% minority, of which blacks are by far the largest group."[14] The PLF attacked from another direction, writing that "absent a clear showing of racial discrimination, a governmentally imposed racial preference is an arbitrary and capricious act and itself constitutes invidious discrimination."[15]

Meanwhile, the Mountain States Legal Foundation, a PLF sibling, reminded the court that in the 1986 case of *Wygant v. Jackson Board of Education* (a Marshall loss discussed in chapter 13), the majority asserted not only that "societal discrimination alone is insufficient to justify a racial classification" but also that any affirmative action must be shown by "strict scrutiny" to be "narrowly tailored" to a problem the government had a "compelling" interest in solving.[16] In Richmond's set-aside, the Mountain States Legal Foundation insisted, there was no discernible governmental interest.

The Southeastern Legal Foundation offered the Court the weapon of *Associated General Contractors of California, Inc. v. City and County of San Francisco*, a 1987 case engineered and steered to victory by the PLF.[17] In her majority opinion in *Croson*, Justice O'Connor likely pleased the entire conservative network and those who bankrolled it when she invoked *Associated General Contractors* as she questioned Richmond's very right to put the Fourteenth Amendment to work to protect minorities:

> That Congress may identify and redress the effects of society-wide discrimination does not mean that, *a fortiori*, the States and their political subdivisions are free to decide that such remedies are appropriate. . . . To hold otherwise would be to cede control of the content of the Equal Protection Clause to the 50 state legislatures and their myriad political subdivisions. The mere recitation of a benign or compensatory purpose for the use of racial classification would essentially entitle the states to exercise the full power of Congress. . . . We believe that such a result would be contrary to the intentions of the Framers of the Fourteenth Amendment, who desired to place clear limits on the States' use of race as a criterion for legislative ac-

> tion, and to have federal courts enforce those limitations. See *Associated General Contractors of Cal. v. City and Cty. of San Francisco.*[18]

Marshall took on O'Connor's argument in a lengthy dissent joined by Justices William Brennan and Harry Blackmun. There was plenty of evidence supporting the city's position, including "pervasive discrimination in the Nation's tight-knit construction industry," Marshall insisted. Furthermore, the Richmond City Council had heard testimony "from city officials as to the exclusionary history of the local construction industry," and it had factored into its planning the results of congressional studies that documented a nationwide pattern of "racially exclusionary practices in the business world."[19]

Marshall was careful to quote a statement also quoted by O'Connor, but with the opposite interpretation. That statement, made by City Council member and former Richmond mayor Henry Marsh, stressed "that the general conduct of the construction industry in this area, and the State and around the nation, is one in which race discrimination and exclusion on the basis of race is widespread." O'Connor countered Marsh by noting that "some of the representatives of the local contractors' organizations indicated that they did not discriminate on the basis of race," adding that it was "sheer speculation how many minority firms there would be in Richmond absent past societal discrimination, just as it was sheer speculation how many minority medical students would have been admitted to the medical school at Davis absent past discrimination in educational opportunities."[20] Marshall went at this reasoning with hammer and tongs: "I find deep irony," he began,

> in second-guessing Richmond's judgment on this point. As much as any municipality in the United States, Richmond knows what racial discrimination is; a century of decisions by this and other federal courts has richly documented the city's disgraceful history of public and private racial discrimination. In any event, the Richmond City Council has supported its determination that minorities have been wrongly excluded from local construction contracting

> . . . [with] precisely the types of statistical and testimonial evidence which, until today, this Court had credited in cases approving race-conscious measures designed to remedy past discrimination.[21]

As for O'Conner's dismissal of the testimony of people like the former mayor, that was "armchair cynicism."[22]

But in this and other cases, there was no armchair cynicism like that of Justice Scalia—even though, where Marshall and his legendary pre–Supreme Court career were concerned, Scalia was a little intimidated. "He was always in the conference a visible representation of a past we wanted to get away from," Scalia told Juan Williams. "And you knew that as a private lawyer he had done so much to undo racism or at least its manifestation in and through government. Anyone who spoke in conference on one of these race issues had to be looking at Thurgood when you're speaking. You know you're talking in the presence of someone who devoted his life to that matter. Therefore, you'd better be doggone sure about it."[23]

Of course, it is no fun being intimidated, and one can detect a bit of kill-the-father Oedipal animus in Scalia's concurring opinion in *Croson*. To move Marshall's weighty presence aside, Scalia invoked James Madison, in particular Madison's pronouncement that, in small societies, majorities more easily carry out a "plan of oppression." This was what happened in Richmond, Scalia averred, because the set-aside was "clearly and directly beneficial to the dominant political group, which happens also to be the dominant racial group."[24] Hitting back, Marshall wrote, "Justice Scalia's artful distinction allows him to avoid having to repudiate 'our school desegregation cases' . . . but, like the arbitrary limitation on race-conscious relief adopted by the majority, his approach 'would freeze the status quo that is the very target' of the remedial actions of states and localities."[25]

Scalia, however, had an ambush to spring. After allowing that "actual victims of discrimination" could be compensated, he asserted that, for this very reason, racial classifications of such victims amounted to locking them up in a hermeneutic trap from which there is no escape because "overcoming the effects of past discrimination is as nothing compared with the difficulty of eradicating from our society the source of those effects, which is the tendency—fatal to a Nation such as ours—to classify and judge men and women on the basis of their country of origin or the color of their skin."[26]

It is hard to deny that racial terms—saturated as they are with myths, insults, and presumptions of superiority—can cage the mind and drive thoughts and deeds in disastrous directions, wiping neighborhoods, even whole peoples, clean of credit.[27] For Marshall, though, it made no sense to treat the traps in which millions remained caught as if a Scalia syllogism could open them all.

For Marshall, even "strict scrutiny"—the hermeneutic technique the majority settled on as a way out of the traps set by race—had no business being used in the Richmond case despite the fact that Marshall himself had helped tease out the meaning of the concept, which can be traced back to at least 1944. The concept as we know it began to emerge during World War II when, in a fit of racist paranoia, the US government ordered Japanese Americans to abandon their homes and report to internment camps. To avoid internment, a welder named Fred Korematsu had plastic surgery on his eyelids and hid out in Oakland, California, but was eventually caught. The ACLU stepped in to represent him, and at the end of the resulting legal action, Justice Hugo Black, writing for the majority in *Korematsu v. United States*, stressed that "restrictions which curtail the civil rights of a single ethnic racial group are immediately suspect" and must be subjected "to the most rigid scrutiny."[28] Rigid scrutiny in this case failed to find the obvious—a racist policy—and upheld the internment of Japanese Americans as a wartime necessity.

"Modern strict scrutiny" emerged in cases such as *Oregon v. Mitchell*, which asked whether provisions of the 1970 Voting Rights Act amendments usurped powers properly reserved to the states. Here, Justices Marshall, Brennan, and White asserted that "governmental action may withstand constitutional scrutiny only upon a clear showing that the burden imposed is necessary to protect a compelling and substantial governmental interest."[29]

In a 1972 case involving out-of-wedlock children who wished to claim their father's death benefits, Justice Powell wrote for the court in support of the children, reasoning that, "when state statutory classifications approach sensitive and fundamental personal rights, this Court exercises a stricter scrutiny. . . . The essential inquiry . . . is, however, inevitably a dual one: What legitimate state interest does the classification [of children as illegitimate] promote? What fundamental personal rights might the classification endanger?"[30]

Powell put this dual formulation to use six years later in *Bakke*. There, he conceded that strict scrutiny is an "inexact term" but suggested that there is little alternative where race is concerned because courts are not equipped to decide which groups suffer more prejudice than others and which groups should therefore "be entitled to preferential classifications" that are "free from exacting judicial scrutiny."[31]

Powell took another stab at strict scrutiny in the aforementioned 1980 case initiated by H. Earl Fullilove and other nonminority contractors to challenge a congressional set-aside for minorities (defined as "Negroes, Spanish-speaking, Orientals, Indians, Eskimos, and Aleuts").[32] In *Fullilove v. Klutznick*, Powell wrote that although "racial classifications require strict judicial scrutiny," the congressional set-aside passed muster because it "serves the compelling interest in eradicating the continuing effects of past discrimination identified by Congress."[33] Thus Powell, like Marshall, joined the six–three majority (led by Chief Justice Warren Burger) that handed a loss not only to H. Earl Fullilove but also to the PLF, which had filed an amicus brief stating, in anticipation of arguments that would eventually seize center stage in the court, that strict scrutiny would render the set-aside unconstitutional. In another glimpse of things to come, the PLF cited not only *Bakke* but also a 1972 majority opinion by Marshall that mandated precise tailoring of judgments affecting constitutional rights.[34]

Marshall, needless to say, did not agree. Instead, in a concurring opinion in *Fullilove*, he picked up where he had left off in *Bakke* to draw what he believed were the proper boundaries of strict scrutiny:

> My resolution of the constitutional issue in this case is governed by the separate opinion I coauthored in *University of California Regents v. Bakke*. . . . [W]e firmly adhered to "the cardinal principle that racial classifications that stigmatize—because they are drawn

> on the presumption that one race is inferior to another or because they put the weight of government behind racial hatred and separatism—are invalid". . . . We recognized, however, that these principles outlawing the irrelevant or pernicious use of race were inappropriate to racial classifications that provide benefits to minorities for the purpose of remedying the present effects of past discrimination. Such classifications may disadvantage some whites, but whites as a class lack the "traditional indicia of suspectness: the class is not saddled with such disabilities, or subjected to such a history of purposeful unequal treatment, or relegated to such a position of political powerlessness as to command extraordinary protection from the majoritarian political process." . . . Because the consideration of race is relevant to remedying the continuing effects of past racial discrimination, and because governmental programs employing racial classifications for remedial purposes can be crafted to avoid stigmatization, we concluded that such programs should not be subjected to conventional "strict scrutiny"—scrutiny that is strict in theory, but fatal [to programs like the set-aside] in fact.[35]

Ending his *Fullilove* concurrence on a satisfied note, Marshall praised his colleagues for seeing beyond what I have been calling surface equality by allowing Congress to move "our society toward a state of meaningful equality of opportunity, not an abstract version of equality in which the effects of past discrimination would be forever frozen into our social fabric."[36]

13
REAGAN JUSTICE

For Thurgood Marshall, *Croson* was an unwelcome return to the surface eight years after the deep dive of *Fullilove*. Indeed, by 1986, the chill Marshall feared when he wrote about discrimination frozen into the social fabric—leaving disadvantaged people trapped below the surface of agenda-setting power like those frozen in the miles-deep ice Dante walks on in the last canto of the *Inferno*—was finally arriving. Earl Warren, under whose leadership the Supreme Court had started to formulate a strict scrutiny doctrine Marshall could live with and who had done much to anger the anti–civil rights movement into organizational and intellectual overdrive, had retired in 1969 and been replaced as chief justice by Nixon appointee Warren Burger.[1] But Marshall had his victories on the Burger court, with *Fullilove*, penned by Burger himself, prominent among them.

The Supreme Court's center of gravity did not truly shift to the right until the arrival of Sandra Day O'Connor and, later, Antonin Scalia and the promotion of William Rehnquist. Orchestrating it all was a Reagan Justice Department determined to remedy what it saw as the excesses of the Warren court. Rehnquist's comfort level rose as Marshall's declined: "I came to the court sensing . . . that there were some excesses in terms of constitutional adjudication during the era of the so-called Warren Court," Rehnquist told the *New York Times* in 1985. "So I felt that at the time I came on the Court [in 1972], the boat was kind of heeling over in one direction. Interpreting the oath as I saw it, I felt that my job was, where those sorts of situations arose, to kind of lean the other way." By the time of the *New York Times* profile, Rehnquist was "finding himself far more frequently in the majority."[2]

Key to this sea change was the Reagan Justice Department's conviction that "the law—whether statutory (Title VII) or constitutional (the Fourteenth Amendment's Equal Protection Clause)—is color-blind," in the words of Justice Department spokesperson Terry Eastland.[3] To enforce color blindness, the Justice Department participated as a plaintiff in some Title VII cases and as a friend of the court in others. Justice Scalia obliged in *Croson* by dismissing color sightedness as a vengeful effort to "even the score" that could only lead to injustice.[4]

WYGANT

Marshall, meanwhile, had formulated a flexible, sliding scale of scrutiny that could be adjusted to fit the details of a particular case. Now he found himself not only pushing back against Scalia-style absolute color blindness but also arguing in key cases for a less rigid application of strict scrutiny. A telling loss for Marshall and a win for the Justice Department and Scalia came in the case of *Wygant v. Jackson Board of Education.*

The seed of the case was planted in 1972, when the Board of Education in Jackson, Michigan, stipulated in a collective bargaining agreement that "at no time will there be a greater percentage of minority personnel laid off than the current percentage of minority personnel employed at the time of the layoff."[5] This meant that some minority teachers would retain their jobs even if they had less seniority than some white teachers who were laid off. In 1981 Wendy Wygant, who had been laid off seven times since 1978 and thus felt the full weight of the quest for deep equality, went to court along with seven other white teachers to claim that their Fourteenth Amendment rights had been violated.

The Reagan Justice Department filed a friend-of-the-court brief supporting Wygant, citing both *Fullilove* and *Bakke* to bolster its argument that although "neither case produced a majority opinion, a plurality of the Court appears to have concluded that state action granting preferences to minorities must satisfy strict scrutiny. . . . We fully endorse this conclusion because we see no valid justification for more lenient judicial scrutiny of laws that discriminated in favor of some minorities and against a residual category of 'whites.'"[6]

Justice Lewis Powell came down on Wygant's side in yet another plurality opinion—this one joined by Rehnquist, O'Connor, and Chief Justice Burger—with Justice Byron White contributing the deciding vote and a concurring opinion. The "level of scrutiny does not change merely because the challenged classification operates against a group that historically has not been subjected to governmental discrimination," Powell wrote.[7]

In his exasperated dissent, Marshall conceded, "I, too, believe the layoffs are unfair. But unfairness ought not be confused with constitutional injury." Marshall noted that, in accordance with the convention that left the finding and verifying of facts to the trial courts, the plurality had based its decision on the admittedly incomplete and inadequate record compiled in the district court and the court of appeals. But since then, he added, both parties to the suit had added "voluminous" submissions, ranging from typescripts to statistical charts, that ought to be considered.[8] In a lengthy footnote, Powell took Marshall to task for doing just that. Marshall admitted, "We should not acquiesce in the parties' attempt to try their case before this Court. Yet it would be just as serious a mistake simply to ignore altogether, as the plurality has done, the compelling factual setting in which this case evidently has arisen."[9]

That factual setting included baked-in inequalities that began to change only after an order by the Michigan Civil Rights Commission increased minority representation from 3.9 percent to 8.8 percent of the faculty in Jackson schools between 1969 and 1971. However, layoffs in 1971 under a last-hired, first-fired scheme wiped out the increase, and in response to this situation and to spiking racial tensions in the schools, a deal to protect minority teachers from massive layoffs had been struck and ratified by a majority of the teachers employed at the time. Furthermore, "each of the six times that the contract has been renegotiated," Marshall wrote, the layoff deal was renewed.[10]

Marshall reached back to his joint opinion with Brennan, White, and

Blackmun in the *Bakke* case to back up his claim that Wygant's constitutional rights had not been violated since both Blacks and whites had been laid off, teachers as a body had repeatedly ratified the agreement, and whites were not a stigmatized class. As for Powell's rebuke, "I am at a loss," Marshall wrote, "as to why Justice Powell so glibly rejects the obvious solution of remanding for the factfinding he appears to recognize is necessary."[11]

LOCAL 28 SHEET METAL WORKERS

Two months later, in July 1986, Marshall's vision got something of a reprieve in *Local 28 Sheet Metal Workers v. EEOC*. The case was the culmination of a long-term judicial effort to compel a segregated union to admit minorities. In a textbook demonstration of why the federal government dreamed up affirmative action to knock down barriers to equal opportunity in the first place, the union had used subterfuge and outright defiance to resist court orders and shrug off fines. The case began in 1964 but shifted into high gear in 1971 when the Justice Department (soon replaced by the EEOC) sued Local 28 for violating Title VII and Lyndon Johnson's Executive Order 11246, which will be discussed in more detail in chapter 14.

As Justice Brennan explained in his sixty-page plurality opinion, Local 28 had a stranglehold on job opportunities in the sheet metal business in New York City, and it did everything it could to keep African Americans and Latinos out of its ranks. It provided "cram courses" for its entrance examination to friends and relatives but not to nonwhites. It allowed only whites to transfer into its ranks from sister organizations and refused "to administer journeyman examinations out of fear that minority candidates might do well."[12]

In 1975 a district court imposed a 29 percent minority hiring target on Local 28, but the union worked hard not to comply. It was found in contempt in 1982 and 1983, and the district court imposed a new 29.23 percent nonwhite membership goal to be met by 1987. No doubt hearing the anti–affirmative action noises coming from the Reagan administration, Local 28 appealed to the Supreme Court in

1985, claiming that its due process and equal protection rights had been violated.

Brennan decided otherwise. He cited *Wygant, Fullilove, Bakke,* and *Swann v. Charlotte-Mecklenburg* to show that the court had a record of allowing the use of racial classifications to remedy past discrimination. However, he conceded that the justices had not agreed on the "proper test"—strict scrutiny or something else—to use in judging such cases. "We need not resolve this dispute here," he added, "since we conclude that the relief ordered in the case passes even the most rigorous test—it is narrowly tailored to further the Government's compelling interest in remedying past discrimination."[13]

Not for the last time, Brennan stuck a bee in conservative bonnets by affirming that those receiving relief need not have suffered discrimination directly.[14] Stung, Rehnquist fired off a dissent based on the objections he raised in another case he lost the same day—*International Association of Firefighters v. City of Cleveland.* He accused his colleagues in the plurality of reading almost "out of existence" a key provision of Title VII that protected "innocent nonminority employees from the evil of court-sanctioned racial quotas."[15]

WHEN WINNING IS NOT ENOUGH

The irony of Rehnquist's vehemence is the extent to which his side was winning in the larger universe of American law. The scope of that victory can be measured by considering how much the Justice Department, the EEOC, and the Supreme Court had changed since 1972, when Rehnquist was appointed to the court. That year, the EEOC's budget was expanded to $29.5 million, up from the $13.2 million it received in 1968.[16] Under Reagan, the EEOC budget was cut.[17]

Policy shifts between Rehnquist's appointment as associate justice and his 1986 elevation to chief justice are clear if one recalls a 1973 EEOC victory over AT&T. At the time, only 2.7 percent of the company's 410,000 female employees held high-skilled jobs. William H. Brown III, the EEOC's wily African American chairman, compelled AT&T to sign a consent agreement that became an affirmative action model for other firms.[18] Private industry got the message, and "terms such as 'goals' and 'timetables' . . . entered the corporate lexicon," according to Dean J. Kotlowski.[19]

Admittedly, even in 1985, the civil rights edifice was such that when William Bradford Reynolds, the assistant attorney general for civil rights, was nominated to become associate attorney general, his appointment was torpedoed by charges such as those made by Senator Edward M. Kennedy, who said Reynolds had seized every opportunity

> to roll back the past 3 decades of progress on civil rights. The administration prides itself on cutting spending yet it has proposed the most unconscionable Federal subsidy of all—tax credits for segregated schools. And by all accounts, Mr. Reynolds was deeply involved in the administration's strategy to use the Bob Jones University case [involving tax-exempt status for a university that forbade interracial dating] to reverse the longstanding policy of the Internal Revenue Service against subsidizing racial discrimination.[20]

Reynolds, missing the forest for the trees, defended himself by saying the administration had been trying to rein in the IRS, which had not been granted the authority to deny tax-exempt status to a school.[21]

But Reynolds was able to look back on it all with satisfaction in a 1989 *Vanderbilt Law Review* article in which he presented the Reagan administration not as destroyers but as *rescuers* of a civil rights movement drowning in its own racial obsessions. When Reagan entered office in 1981, he explained,

> many forces within the civil rights movement had abandoned their moral dedication to equality for all and instead had embraced the concept of so-called "benign" discrimination. . . . Their chosen method was no longer an appeal to the conscience of all Americans, but rather a call to guilt for some, a promise of preference for others, and a reliance on the raw power of the three institutions that are least responsive to democratic forces—academia, the media, and especially the courts—to herd along a confused and reluctant population.[22]

This now familiar evil trinity for conservatives—academia, media, and "activist" courts—was the prime motivator for an ever-expanding conservative counterwave of think tanks, legal foundations, lawsuits, amicus briefs, media outfits, and court appointments. Reynolds even anticipated the "don't guilt us" cries of the anti-CRT movement.

He painted the 1970s as a sort of expulsion from the Eden of race blindness. "Forced busing" and attendant ills "drove white families to seek education for their children outside the very public-school systems whose integration the Nation sought. For many Americans civil rights [became] not a dream at all, but a shelter for the basest forms of group resentment and dictatorial power. It was left to the Reagan Justice Department," Reynolds added, to convince "the judiciary, and at least a few in academia and the media, that racial preferences are inherently discriminatory and cannot be countenanced under law except in the most extraordinary circumstances."[23]

Despite *Local 28 Sheet Metal Workers* and other bumps in the road, Reynolds was confident that the reversal of the 1970s remained on track: "The Department [of Justice] did not win every case or every policy argument, but it did not have to do so," he wrote. "The Department moved opinion in the cases and policy arguments it won and influenced the reasoning of members of the Supreme Court in the cases it lost."[24] That Reynolds-style reasoning (evident not only in *Croson* but also in an amicus brief coauthored by Reynolds, future Supreme Court justice Samuel Alito, and others who supported Local 28's view that the 29 percent hiring goal was improper and that a required fund to train minorities violated Title VII) may indeed have changed things is evidenced by the fact that the *Local 28* case dragged on for more than four decades, entering the headlines again in 2015 when the union was forced to establish a $12.7 million back-pay fund for nonwhites it had discriminated against.[25] For Reynolds, a climactic turning point was *Croson* (which may have also been a loophole for the continuation of practices like Local 28's).

"After a determined eight-year effort by the Reagan Justice Department to persuade the Supreme Court," Reynolds exulted,

> a comfortable majority of the Court in *City of Richmond v. J. A. Croson Co.* held, in clear and unequivocal terms, that all forms of

official preferences for members of any racial group, both those that suffered historically from discrimination and those that did not, are presumptively unconstitutional. . . . Fully embracing the main points of the *amicus curiae* brief filed by the Civil Rights Division and the Solicitor General, the Court held that racial preferences can overcome the presumption of constitutionality only when they survive . . . strict scrutiny.[26]

14

ORIGINALISM FROM STROM THURMOND TO EDWIN MEESE

Strict scrutiny was not the Reaganauts' only weapon. The need to forge new ones was clear to them by August 1985, when word leaked that they were planning to gut one of the foundations of post-1960s equal opportunity: Lyndon Johnson's Executive Order 11246, which required federal contractors of a certain size to use affirmative action to ensure equal job opportunity regardless of race or (after a supplemental executive order) gender. By mid-September, a classic showdown between the civil rights and anti–civil rights movements had erupted as 125 House and Senate members banded together to demand that the executive order be left alone.[1] William Bradford Reynolds and his boss Edwin Meese, the longtime Reagan aide installed as attorney general in February 1985, had had their eyes on 11246 since Reagan's first term.

As early as the transition period between the Carter and Reagan administrations, Meese had created a team that included future Supreme Court justice Clarence Thomas and tasked its members with evaluating the EEOC's antidiscrimination lawsuits under Title VII and suggesting what should be done with the agency. The team concluded that Executive Order 11246, enforced by the Department of Labor in coordination with the EEOC, had been "changed into a weapon to, in effect, endorse discriminatory hiring."[2] Nevertheless, the thirty-two-year-old Thomas's mind was not entirely made up at that point. He even pressured Texas to beef up affirmative action at its universities (by setting goals and timetables for the admission of minority graduate students) after he was confirmed in the summer of 1981 as assistant secretary of education in the Office of Civil Rights.[3] Tapped to chair the EEOC in 1982, Thomas called for an affirmative action plan for the New Orleans Police Department. This got him summoned to the White House, where Reynolds read him the riot act.[4]

Thereafter, through two terms as EEOC chairman, Thomas had little trouble pleasing his bosses, and the NAACP eventually called (unsuccessfully) for his resignation.[5] In 1985 Thomas ended his previous support for goals and timetables in EEOC lawsuits and settlements with employers.[6] He argued in 1986 that goals and timetables could backfire and leave people who were "actually discriminated against" out in the cold, without all the benefits they deserved and could obtain with proof of direct discrimination. Thomas scoffed at the business organizations "falling over each other to applaud the Court's approval of affirmative action" in *Johnson v. Santa Clara Transportation Agency*, where a statistical imbalance was used to show that women did not have the same opportunities as men.[7] Thomas's moves were very much in line with the defanging of Executive Order 11246 and other sources of affirmative action that Meese and Reynolds had partly achieved by the time of *Croson*.

Although Meese and Reynolds had mostly held back during Reagan's first term, with the president's landslide reelection in 1984 and no next election to worry about, they felt free to rewrite the executive order to prohibit what they believed were perversions of it by enforcers in the Department of Labor's Office of Federal Contract Compliance Programs (OFCCP).[8] Meese, Reynolds, and their peers believed the OFCCP was putting contractors in a straitjacket of "rigid quotas" that they managed to wriggle out of by hiring Blacks and then letting them go the minute it was convenient.[9]

At the EEOC, Thomas continued to roll back the use of the statistical tools that had lit up patterns of job discrimination like luminol and thereby triggered affirmative action by revealing places where minority workers were not being hired in proportion to their availability.[10] In doing so, he inverted the conception of affirmative action worked out in *Griggs* and, before *Griggs*, in the mind of Edward C. Sylvester Jr., the OFCCP's first director.[11] A tall World War II veteran who was part of the first wave of African Americans lifted into government by the civil rights tide, Sylvester was praised for using firmness, tact, and creativity to wrangle companies into diversifying. He explained the affirmative action ABCs to Congress in 1965, providing a brief history lesson in the process.[12]

According to Sylvester, the need for affirmative action with teeth grew out of the fact that an executive order issued by John F. Kennedy requesting voluntary compliance with equal employment opportunity goals had generated "no meaningful change" in minority hiring between 1961 and 1965.[13] So Sylvester and his team shifted from requesting more minority recruitment to enforcing it with the threat of the loss of federal contracts. He stressed to Congress that discrimination was a "structural thing" and not merely an individual misfortune. With seventy-five thousand contractors to be incentivized, Sylvester moved "to insure that contracts were dealt with on a mass and collective basis rather than on an ad hoc and individual" one, since the individual approach would have taken forever to make a mark on entrenched hiring patterns.[14]

Sylvester's conception of discrimination—which was extended as the Nixon administration strengthened the EEOC and the OFCCP and as the NAACP's Jack Greenberg made his winning arguments in *Griggs*—was exactly what Meese, Reynolds, Thomas, and the rest of the Reagan wing of the anti–civil rights movement wanted to declare unconstitutional. For Reynolds and Meese especially, "discrimination as a structural thing" was not tailored narrowly enough to avoid negative consequences for white workers and organizations that had not themselves discriminated. But, as Meese and those around him preferred not to acknowledge, the OFCCP had inherited a job market built on the back of racial and gender discrimination, and Sylvester had responded to that.[15] After Reynolds explained his opposition in a speech to the National Association of Manufacturers in 1985, its members pushed back, telling Reynolds that they feared a flood of *Bakke*-like reverse discrimination suits if the government washed its hands of affirmative action and made them solely responsible for diversifying their workforces.[16]

Ultimately, Sylvester's vision survived the 1980s largely because of the Leadership Conference on Civil Rights, led in the Reagan era on a $200,000 annual budget by a curly-haired white Catholic named Ralph G. Neas. Neas had once seriously considered becoming a priest, and he viewed political life as a secular ministry. After a bout of Guillain-Barré syndrome left him temporarily paralyzed, he gained extra motivation to make affirmative action and other rights for the disabled, minorities, and women a part of his ministry.[17] With tireless lobbying, networking, and cajoling, he managed to convince a little army of moderate and liberal members of Congress to join the civil rights movement in opposing Meese's and Reynolds's efforts. Also working in Neas's favor was a corporate America that had adapted to affirmative action and started to institutionalize it, albeit very imperfectly, in the form of equal opportunity departments, dedicated recruitment and training programs, sensitivity training (which has come under heavy attack since the CRT panic of the 2020s), and related innovations that at least scratched the surface of inequality.[18]

Reagan's own secretary of labor commissioned a study, published as *Workforce 2000*, that predicted a steep increase in the diversity of the American labor force. The study gave a shot in the arm to the idea that businesses should should prepare for and pursue the sort of diversity that, in the 2020s, Christopher Rufo and others have identified as the latest in an endless series of mortal threats to the true America.[19] In the pre-Rufo Reagan era, however, most of the cabinet "joined the civil rights community and its allies in Congress in opposing any reforms in affirmative action," and "Reagan quietly dropped his plans to change the program," according to scholar Nicholas Laham.[20]

This defeat did nothing to slow ongoing under-the-radar efforts to roll back affirmative action. Thomas did not reverse his EEOC policy shifts, the Justice Department penned anti–affirmative action amicus briefs like the one Reynolds celebrated, the solicitor general went to court to argue against the policy, and Reagan Supreme Court appointees crafted dissenting arguments that eventually took center stage in majority opinions of the Rehnquist court. Affirmative action was not taken out and shot, but Reagan officials and appointees weakened it with a thousand cuts and reconceptualizations.

Indeed, Reynolds and Meese, together with Meese's deputy Mark Levin and Thomas's aide Clint Bolick, set out to change the entire equal opportunity–centric network of interpretations in which the EEOC's and OFCCP's past practices, and the vocabulary of skilled political players like Neas, existed.[21] Levin and Bolick made their deepest marks after leaving the Reagan administration or after the administration itself ended. But Reynolds, like Thomas, wrote law review articles while still in office. Meese, however, was the one with the whip hand. As attorney general, he launched a powerful new legal weapon that he unveiled in headline-making speeches attacking the hermeneutic methods of the Supreme Court's increasingly embattled liberal brain trust—Thurgood Marshall and William Brennan.

Thus, in 1985, addressing and nurturing the three-year-old Federalist Society, Meese laid out a theory of interpreting the Constitution that was not entirely novel. But because he had the bully pulpit of attorney general, he helped transform the theory from an oddity into a shaper of American life. He argued that originalism—or, in his phrase, "a jurisprudence of original intention"—could rein in a Supreme Court that had become a kind of nine-headed warlock conjuring new rights out of thin air. In some cases, the justices of the Supreme Court had abandoned the Constitution entirely, Meese told the Federalist Society, and instead they "grounded their rulings in appeals to social theories, to moral philosophy or personal notions of human dignity, or to 'penumbras,' somehow emanating ghostlike from various provisions—identified and not identified—in the Bill of Rights." To counter this sort of heresy, Meese proposed a jurisprudence rooted in a Constitution whose meaning "can be known." Sketching his hermeneutic formula, he said:

> Where the language of the Constitution is specific, it must be obeyed. Where there is a demonstrable consensus among the Framers and ratifiers as to the principle stated or implied by the Constitution, it should be followed. Where there is ambiguity as to the precise meaning or reach of a constitutional provision, it should be interpreted and applied in a manner so as to at least not contradict the text of the Constitution itself.[22]

Meese's mention of "personal notions of human dignity" was a reference to a critique of Meese-style hermeneutics made a month earlier in a speech at Georgetown University by Justice Brennan. "It is arrogant," Brennan had said, "to pretend that from our vantage point we can gauge accurately the intent of the Framers on application of principle to specific, contemporary questions. . . . Typically, all that can be gleaned is that the Framers themselves did not agree about the application or meaning of particular constitutional provisions, and hid their differences in cloaks of generality." The task of changing those generalities into decisions, Brennan argued, left room for "a debate about how to read the text, about constraints on what is legitimate interpretation."[23]

Where the heavy-faced Meese emphasized fidelity to the meaning of the text of the Constitution and the intentions informing that text, the owlish Brennan stressed fidelity to the meaning of what the Constitution was built to protect: human dignity epitomized, Brennan believed, by the prohibition of cruel and unusual punishment, the writ of habeas corpus, the prohibition of the establishment of a state religion, and, "since the Civil War, the banishment of slavery and official race discrimination." By enshrining all these things, the Constitution, as "augmented by the Bill of Rights and the Civil War Amendments [Thirteenth, Fourteenth, and Fifteenth] . . . is a sparkling vision of the supremacy of the human dignity of every individual."[24]

Meese took aim not only at Brennan but also at the Supreme Court's agenda-setting power as a whole in a speech at Tulane University. Singling out *Cooper v. Aaron* (1958), Meese said it threatened the rule of law itself. The fact that *Cooper v. Aaron* was the court's exasperated effort to stop a wave of southern laws passed to nullify its *Brown* decision meant nothing to Meese. He raged against the court's declaration in *Cooper v. Aaron* that, since the Constitution is the supreme law of the land and since "the federal judiciary is supreme in the exposition of the law," the "interpretation of the Fourteenth Amendment enunciated by the Court in the *Brown* case is the supreme law of the land." Even as he condemned this as an enormous usurpation of power, the canny Meese took care to inoculate himself against charges of racial insensitivity by lambasting the Supreme Court's two worst race-related decisions: *Plessy v. Ferguson*, which green-lit racial segregation, and

Dred Scott v. Sandford, where Chief Justice Roger Taney wrote that Black people have no rights that whites must respect. Going for the checkmate, Meese called *Cooper v. Aaron* as bad as *Plessy* and *Dred Scott*. Thus immunized, Meese said *Cooper v. Aaron* was "at war with the Constitution, at war with the basic principles of democratic government, and at war with the very meaning of the rule of law."[25]

Since the Supreme Court's intention in *Cooper v. Aaron* had been to stop the nullification of "rights created and protected by the Federal Constitution," Meese could not have done more to corroborate Derrick Bell's view that Black gains become disposable when they inconvenience whites. Nevertheless, inoculated and boosted as he was, Meese felt free to assure his Tulane University audience that the Supreme Court needed to be kept in line by officials like himself who relied on the idea that "constitutional interpretation is not the business of the Court only, but also the business of all branches of government."[26]

Affirmation of the framers' original intention, which was the basis of Meese's diatribe, is the affirmation of an illusion, in the view of some scholars.[27] Raymond T. Diamond noted in 1989 that "reconciling differences in the framers' views, or deciding who deserves the title 'framer,' or how the words they set down were understood by themselves and their contemporaries may be an impossible task."[28] C. M. A. McCauliff points out that even the meaning of an all-American word like "equality" is hard to pin down, since when Thomas Jefferson wrote "equal" in the Declaration of Independence, the American slave market was thriving.[29]

Meese's originalism is a form of denial of this founding indeterminacy. Worse, Harry V. Jaffa shows in a 1987 essay (in which he hammers both Meese and Brennan) that Meese's reasoning leads not away from Taney and toward the true Constitution but back to the logic of Taney's denial of dignity and rights to Blacks: "no one, on or off the Court, has ever expounded on the theory of original intent with greater eloquence and conviction than Chief Justice Taney in the case of *Dred Scott*," Jaffa asserts.[30] Indeed, Taney plunges his sense of fidelity like a meat hook into the intentions of the framers and finds in their Constitution an obligation to affirm the rights of slave owners. "Barring amendment of the Constitution," Taney insisted, "it must be construed now as it was understood at the time of its adoption." Taney concluded that the 1787 Constitution commits the nation to protecting the right to own people "in all future times."[31] This is original intent with a vengeance, Jaffa writes.[32]

A more fainthearted originalist than Taney, Meese fatally wounds his own argument by insisting on an essential color blindness in the Constitution of 1787. Lawyering his way around the fact that a condition of the formation of the union was the capture of fugitive slaves—a condition backed by the full faith and credit of the framers—Meese insists that the framers were forced by "political realities" to "tolerate" slavery but made no "fundamental concessions to slavery at the level of principle." As proof, he cites the framers' refusal to include the words "slave" and "slavery" in the 1787 document. Thoroughly tangled up in Taneyism, Meese makes an off-balance leap from the conclusion that the Thirteenth, Fourteenth, and Fifteenth Amendments made the Constitution "officially 'color-blind'" to the conclusion that affirmative action amounts to racism in its elevation of "a perverted notion of equality and denies the original understanding that is our birthright."[33]

Without fully acknowledging or perhaps even knowing it, Meese was carrying forward a twentieth-century line of constitutional thought already present in the 1956 anti–*Brown v. Board of Education* "Declaration of Constitutional Principles," better known as the Southern Manifesto, spearheaded by Senator Strom Thurmond.[34]

Another senator, former North Carolina Supreme Court justice Sam Ervin, was reportedly the brains behind key passages of the manifesto, but the Harvard-educated Ervin liked to remind people—in a deep voice with a twang worthy of a single-coil bridge pickup on a Fender Stratocaster—that he was just a "country lawyer." Ervin developed legal arguments about the threat the Civil Rights Act of 1964 posed to individual liberties that eventually found a home in Meese's head.[35] Already in 1956, Ervin had "embraced a theory of constitutional originalism that foreshadowed the approach to today's conservative movement," according to Logan E. Sawyer III. In the following decades, Ervin used that theory

> to explain to both outsiders and southerners themselves how their shifting views of state authority were not self-serving responses to

> federal civil rights laws. . . . By easing the shift to new, individual rights–based conservatism, Ervin's constitutional arguments helped conservative Southern Democrats find common ground with anti–New Deal Republicans outside the South, some of whom were exploring similar constitutional arguments, and the vast majority of whom were happy to find new allies in their efforts to turn the GOP into a political vehicle for the conservative movement.[36]

Whether intentionally or not, Meese was picking up where Ervin and Thurmond (who, as chairman of the Senate Judiciary Committee, presided over the confirmation hearings of Scalia and Rehnquist), left off. As the next chapter shows, Meese was not alone in extending this peculiar legacy, not least because of his extraordinary success in creating intellectual progeny from the Federalist Society to the current Supreme Court supermajority.

15

WORLD MAKING, ORIGINALIST STYLE

The end of the Reagan administration did nothing to slow the originalists' quest to recast the world in their image of the Constitution. Even though Edward Sylvester had testified that a mere declaration of equal opportunity cannot undo centuries-old patterns of discrimination, in 1989, William Bradford Reynolds felt confident that "the obvious and not-so-obvious barriers that once marked blacks as inferior and second-class citizens largely have been eliminated."[1]

Seven years after Reynolds wrote this, unmistakable evidence of the persistence of racism made the headlines in the form of the $115 million in damages paid by oil and gas giant Texaco to compensate fourteen hundred Black employees who had been unjustly denied promotions, paid unequally for equal work, and, in some cases, subjected to racial slurs.[2] Thirty-three years later, Blacks were massacred in a supermarket in Buffalo, New York (see the introduction). In between, there have been countless episodes that underscore the large element of fantasy in the Reynolds-Meese view of the world.

Rendered invisible by this fantasy were the key lessons Texaco CEO Peter I. Bijur learned in the aftermath of the settlement: "We are a microcosm of society," he said. "We are 30,000 people, and these people have attitudes. And sometimes those attitudes, which they develop throughout their lives, are brought into the workplace."[3] Bijur decided to attack the problem at a systemic level. Though admittedly under court supervision, he set quantitative hiring and promotion goals and decided to track Texaco's progress in reaching them right alongside the company's achievement of profit and productivity targets. Although Bijur's efforts were spurred by a concrete finding of a pattern of discrimination rather than the detection of a pattern by statistics, the solution he settled on echoes Sylvester's conception of affirmative action as a rooting out of something bigger than individuals, and it directly contradicts the focus on particular people favored by Edwin Meese and Clarence Thomas and the rest of the Reagan brain trust. The key lesson here is that a system-level approach makes business sense. Sylvester said as much in his 1969 Senate testimony, stressing that goal setting

> is consistent with the way companies and employers and industry operates in almost any other activity that is of importance to them. . . . And my experience is very clear that in those areas and with those companies that did in fact set out objectives for themselves, the change was marked and visible. And in those areas where there was no objective, then the changes have been nominal if at all.[4]

Texaco's adoption of goal setting was viewed by many as concrete evidence of the continuing need for affirmative action.

But from the perspective of the Reagan brain trust, the story of Allan Bakke continued to matter much more than that of Bari-Ellen Roberts, the lead plaintiff in the Texaco case, who, admittedly, was part of a settlement at the district court level and therefore never came under the national klieg lights associated with a Supreme Court case about race.

TAKING IT TO THE MASSES

It was no surprise when Mark Levin, Meese's former chief of staff and the future best-selling author of *American Marxism* (discussed in the introduction), mixed the language of his radio talk-show host persona with the hard-charging originalist rhetoric of a Meese acolyte in his 2005 best seller *Men in Black*: "There's nothing in the Fourteenth Amendment about . . . diversity, and all the other judicial creations designed to get around the clear prohibition against racial discrimination," Levin declares, his authority enhanced by his position as president of a PLF cousin, the Landmark Legal Foundation. Picking up where Reynolds and Meese left off, but discarding all pretense of intellectual rigor, Levin mocks Thurgood Marshall's understanding of the Constitution as outlined in a speech Marshall gave on the bicentennial of that document. The Constitution, Marshall said,

> was defective from the start, requiring several amendments, a civil war and momentous social transformation to attain the system of constitutional government, and its respect for individual freedoms and human rights, we hold as fundamental today. . . . "We the people" no longer enslave, but the credit does not belong to the framers. It belongs to those who refused to acquiesce in outdated notions of "liberty," "justice" and "equality," and who strive to better them.[5]

Brushing such substance aside, Levin primes his audience to view Marshall as ridiculous by claiming that the justice sometimes spent more time in his Supreme Court chambers watching soap operas than reading briefs. Worse, Marshall disparaged the Constitution's framers, individuals Levin portrays as almost above criticism.[6]

At the climax of his bill of indictment, Levin proclaims that Marshall "couldn't have had a weaker grasp of the Constitution," since "discrimination, injustice, and inhumanity are not products of the Constitution" but are the results of "man's imperfection." This, of course, would have been news to those sold as slaves or captured and returned to their masters between the adoption of the Constitution and the ratification of the Thirteenth Amendment. But Levin's purpose in *Men in Black* is not to educate but to inoculate his readers against challenges to the system of thought in which he encloses them. This is why he sees no need to comment on Marshall's remarks about the Civil War, about Article I, section 9 (which declares that the international slave trade will not be interfered with until 1808), or about the fact that the 1787 framers' conception of liberty was defective.[7] Levin does not acknowledge at all the hole in originalism that Marshall highlights when he stresses that, since the framers made no provision for the end of slavery, it was a grave error to make "a blind pilgrimage to the shrine of the original document now stored in the vault in the National Archives. If we seek, instead, a sensitive understanding of the Constitution's inherent defects, and its promising evolution through 200 years of history, the celebration of the 'Miracle at Philadelphia' will, in my view, be a far more meaningful and humbling experience."[8] But Levin and other originalists brook no such humbling and are scandalized by the *e*-word ("evolution") and the *l*-word ("living") in connection with the Constitution.

Indeed, by popularizing originalism, running a conservative public-interest law firm, hosting a radio talk show, and publishing a book propelled to best-seller status with the help of an introduction by Rush Limbaugh, the god of right-wing talk radio, Levin was a kind of one-man answer to Reynolds's call for a conservative counter to "the raw power of the three institutions that are least responsive to democratic forces—academia, the media, and especially the courts."

The story of the post-Reagan era is the story of the rise of Levin-like figures across the media and legal landscapes and, to a lesser extent, the academic landscape—although the eclipsing of academic authority is part of the mission of the anti–civil rights movement.[9] Meese was at the center of much of this, nurturing not only Levin's career but also the extremely consequential careers of the founders of the Federalist Society.[10]

RISE OF THE FEDERALISTS

Like much of the anti–civil rights movement, the Federalist Society grew out of feelings of alienation—in this case, the alienation experienced by two law students at Yale and another at the University of Chicago who had all been undergraduates at Yale together. Trying to wrest the law from the forces Meese and Reynolds had railed against, these three organized conservative student groups on their campuses and networked with like-minded students at other top universities. They cast envious eyes at a major organization—the National Lawyers Guild—which they resented for being too liberal but hoped to re-create in conservative form.[11]

Their big-bang moment came in 1982, when the John M. Olin Foundation (which also funded Levin's Landmark Legal Foundation) and the Olin-supported Institute for Educational Affairs (IEA) funded the first Federalist Society conference. Neoconservative lion Irving Kristol later called the $15,000 contributed by IEA "the best money we ever spent."[12] Addressing the conference were Antonin Scalia and Ted Olson, then serving in the Reagan Justice Department but soon to play a key role in the campaign to destroy affirmative action. The Federalist Society collected $5.5 million from the Olin Foundation alone during the next twenty years, and others such as the Sarah Scaife and Bradley Foundations chipped in until annual donations reached $2.6 million by 1998.[13] Meese, true to his movement-builder instincts, "arranged for [the Federalist Society] founders to either get jobs in the [Reagan] White House or the [Department of Justice] after graduation from law school."[14]

With the young Federalists on board, the Justice Department became "a giant think tank where these passionate young conservative legal activists developed new legal theories to advance the Reagan agenda," according to Charles Savage.[15] It helped that the creed of the Federalists was originalism. Some of them viewed the Constitution as miraculous, a sort of virgin birth, and viewed originalism as the light by which to illuminate "timeless constitutional commands."[16]

A lightning strike moment came when this originalist sect closed ranks around its John the Baptist—Robert Bork, a sixty-year-old square-bearded Yale law professor with an intense green-eyed gaze. His critique of the bill that became the Civil Rights Act of 1964 had been cited approvingly by Sam Ervin in his own 1963 article accusing the act of being unconstitutional.[17]

But in a move that put a permanent bee in the Federalists' bonnet, the Democrats denied Bork a Supreme Court seat largely because of writings that suggested he would vote to overturn *Roe v. Wade*, the 1973 ruling that made abortion legal nationwide (until a Federalist-crafted supermajority struck *Roe* down in 2022). Despite assurances that his published opinions would not short-circuit his impartiality as a judge, Bork was subjected to an ideological immolation so intense that it created a verb—"borked." This borking became something the anti–civil rights movement "promised never to forget, never to forgive," according to Michael Avery.[18]

One of those who never forgot was Clint Bolick. His career trajectory is a case study in the cross-fertilization of the right-wing public-interest law network and the Reagan administration's policymaking apparatus. Bolick had litigated anti–affirmative action cases at the Mountain States Legal Foundation before going to work for Clarence Thomas at the EEOC. Thomas became a father figure who sharpened Bolick's sense that affirmative action and similar policies were patronizing and counterproductive.[19] Bolick had felt this way since attending the University of California–Davis Law School in the wake of *Bakke*. An indifferent law student, he honed his polemical skills by plunging into rancorous debates over race and educational standards at Davis—debates triggered by the high percentage of Black students among those dismissed from the school for poor grades.[20] In that era of delicate experiments in the creation of equal opportunity, Davis had clearly made some errors in the intense competition with other schools for talented Black and other minority students. But Black students claimed the expelled had been judged by unenlightened standards tainted by racism.

Bolick's response was to condemn the whole concept of affirmative action as racist and to argue (in a response to another student's opinion piece in the law school's newspaper) that his own "severe economic difficulties" (due to the sudden death of his father and his mother's struggle to support the family first as a cashier and then as an office worker) were on a par with the struggles of that other student—Duane E. Bennett. Bennett, an African American from an impoverished background, was the first Black person to graduate at the top of his class at the University of California–Santa Barbara. Although he struggled in law school, he traced Black students' difficulties to the law school's expectation that everyone view the law from a "white middle class perspective."[21]

Bennett (who went on to have a distinguished law career, despite needing three tries to pass the bar exam) overstated his case by describing the LSAT as a deliberately used "Nigger Weeder." But after law school he had an experience that put paid to the notion that Bolick's economic struggles placed them at comparable levels of disadvantage.

While working as a prosecutor in the mid-1980s, Bennett was pulled over by six police officers, handcuffed, and thrown to the ground while one officer held a gun to the back of his head. His crime, he concluded, was "driving while Black."[22] Meanwhile, Bolick was on the path that took him from the Mountain States Legal Foundation to Thomas's EEOC to Meese's Justice Department. After his harrowing experience with the police, Bennett worked within the system, serving as a city attorney, consulting with police departments around California, and writing a primer on illegal arrests and the illegal use of force.[23] Bolick, having worked at the top of the system, decided to remake it in such a way that it would be hard to distinguish between the private tragedy of his father's death and Bennett's encounter with agents of the state.

In the last full year of the Reagan administration, Bolick became the founding director of the Landmark Center for Civil Rights, a spinoff of the Landmark Legal Foundation, and he set out to apply a key lesson he had learned at Thomas's EEOC: the importance of controlling language.[24] Guided by Thomas's second in command, Ricky Silberman, Bolick learned to raise hackles and resentment by using the words "racial preferences" instead of "affirmative action" and "quotas" instead of "goals."[25] In his 1988 book *Changing Course*, Bolick announced that a "viable, forward-looking civil rights strategy . . . must begin by redefining the terms of the debate."[26]

16

CLINT BOLICK GOES TO WAR

Clint Bolick is a round-faced man with a cherubic smile, but long after his days in the Reagan administration, he added a bit of an edge to his appearance. He got a tattoo of a scorpion on his right index finger (the one he uses to type books, essays, and court filings) because the tiny predator, drawn with an outsized stinger, symbolizes his view of himself as a giant killer.[1] The tattoo can be traced to Bolick's passion for defending entrepreneurs and others against government regulations. After reading about a tattoo artist who had been blocked from opening a new parlor, Bolick got the block reversed and celebrated by getting his scorpion. But for Bolick, the policy that really deserved to be stung was affirmative action.

He administered that sting—in the form of an amicus brief—in *Board of Education of Oklahoma City Public Schools, Independent School District No. 89, Oklahoma County, Oklahoma v. Dowell.* Still based at the time at the Landmark Legal Foundation's Center for Civil Rights, which he founded in 1988, Bolick coauthored a brief supporting the dissolution of a school busing plan originally put in place to reduce wear and tear on Black students, even though the dissolution would steeply increase segregation. Rehnquist wrote a five–three majority opinion allowing the district court to end the injunction if, upon reexamining the case, it still believed the desegregation plan had achieved its purpose and the school board was "unlikely to return to its former [segregating] ways."[2] This majority opinion, according to Gary Orfield and Chungmei Lee, was a turning point in American education that resonated beyond Oklahoma City, clearing the way for a rolling wave of resegregation elsewhere.[3]

Foreseeing this very consequence, Thurgood Marshal offered a means of measuring the need for busing and other desegregation efforts in his *Oklahoma v. Dowell* dissent. "The concept of stigma," he wrote, "also gives us guidance as to what conditions must be eliminated before a [desegregation] decree can be deemed to have served its purpose." Therefore, in "assessing whether the task is complete, the dispositive question is whether vestiges capable of inflicting stigmatic harm exist in the system and whether all that can practicably be done to eliminate those vestiges has been done."[4]

This is the sort of nuanced rights argument Bolick set out to destroy in his 1988 book *Changing Course.* Whereas the architect of *Brown* continued to see Blacks as exiles within a school system that, by segregating them, treated them as fit only for their own company, Bolick believed that busing and other efforts to manufacture diverse student bodies turned *Brown* on its head.[5] Bolick held Marshall up as a symbol of the corruption of the civil rights establishment and offered as proof a quip, often cited in conservative circles, that William O. Douglas attributed to Marshall. "You guys have been practicing discrimination for years. Now it's our turn," Marshall allegedly said when Douglas implored him to help establish a color-blind standard in affirmative action.[6] With Mr. Civil Rights thus exposed as a mere score settler, it was up to Bolick and his fellow conservatives to raise the civil rights banner out of the muck.

Bolick took direct aim at the separate Brennan–Marshall–Blackmun–White opinion in the *Bakke* case and hammered away at Marshall's *Bakke* dissent because it distinguished between "abstract equality" and "genuine equality" (what I have been calling surface equality and deep equality). Bolick was even more incensed by the six–three majority (including O'Connor) in *Johnson v. Transportation Agency, Santa Clara County, California.* In this case, the majority upheld an affirmative action plan that allowed the Transportation Agency to fill a dispatcher's position with a white woman, Diane Joyce, instead of a white man, Paul Johnson. Johnson scored 75 on the test for the position and Joyce scored 73, but she had worked four years on a road crew, a prerequisite for the dispatcher's job, while Johnson had only a year and a half of road crew experience. After both candidates were interviewed, Johnson was recommended for the promotion. Joyce, whose personal motto was "the sin is not to try," went to the county affirmative action office to plead her case. She got the job.[7]

Now it was Johnson's turn to visit the affirmative action office. But right away he felt like he was in hostile territory. "The affirmative action man walks in," he later recalled, "and he's this big black guy. He can't tell me anything. He brings in this minority who can barely speak English. . . . I told them, 'You haven't heard the last of me.'"[8] Johnson retained a lawyer, who claimed that his client's Title VII rights had been violated. Johnson won in district court but lost in the Ninth Circuit Court of Appeals. Out of money and out of emotional gas, he was ready to drop the case, but his hopes were revived when he was made the judge of a "beauty contest" between the Pacific Legal Foundation and the Mountain States Legal Foundation, both eager to represent him. Mountain States won and brought Johnson's case before the US Supreme Court.[9]

The majority ruled against Johnson on the grounds that the Transportation Agency's affirmative action plan appropriately addressed "a conspicuous imbalance in job categories traditionally segregated by sex," and the affirmative action office's "moderate, flexible, case-by-case" approach was "effecting a gradual improvement in the representation of minorities and women in the Agency's work force."[10]

For some of the men employed by the Santa Clara Transportation Agency, this created an intolerable threat to their status. Joyce "thinks she is high class now that she's got her face on TV. Like we are dirt or something," one man told journalist Susan Faludi. Johnson himself (after retiring from the agency) sent newspapers an "Open Letter to the White Males of America." Sounding like someone from the 2020s, he wrote, "Fellow men, I believe it is time for us to object to our suppression."[11]

Though not going that far, Bolick saw the *Johnson* result as pure injustice, allowing "blacks and women who meet minimal qualifications to pass over more qualified applicants." In a telling slip, on the same page Bolick drops the reference to gender and declares *Johnson* "a major setback in the quest to eradicate consideration of race in American society. It squarely endorses coerced equality of result over equal opportunity, and group rights over individual liberty, inflicting painful divisions in a society badly in need of healing." While he mentions gender again on the next page, his focus shifts inexorably back to his true concern when he lists "the many human victims of the new racism" and mentions Wendy Wygant, who suddenly belongs to a class that contains no one who benefits from affirmative action.[12]

Bolick's slip highlights one of the recurring features of the affirmative action debate: the omission of white women beneficiaries and sometimes all non-Black minority beneficiaries from the discussion. This occurs in part because affirmative action grew out of the Black freedom struggle, but it is more a function of the American racial paradigm that defines civil death, the ultimate deviation from whiteness, first and foremost as Black.[13] This does not mean that women and other groups are not disadvantaged and susceptible to civil death. But the American racial paradigm is an addictive heuristic device that always leads back to Black and allows those who benefit from laws, policies, and constitutional amendments crafted with Blacks in mind to reap the benefits without necessarily being "charged" the price in resentment of them. Non-Blackness in this sense can be a get-out-of-jail-free card.[14] It is often (but not always) associated with a quantum of extra status that allows less restricted social mobility.

This is nowhere truer than in the case of white women, whose relative privilege can be measured by the ratio of benefits received from affirmative action to backlash related to those benefits.[15] There *has* been backlash for white women, as Joyce discovered, but the backlash-to-benefit ratio is much bigger for African Americans. In an essay aptly titled "Framing Affirmative Action"—both as an argument is framed and as an innocent person is framed—Kimberlé W. Crenshaw, one of the founders of critical race theory, explains that the vast majority of affirmative action news stories evaluated over a six-month period by FAIR (Fairness & Accuracy in Reporting) "failed to mention either white women or other people of color as beneficiaries of affirmative action. Most of the very few that did mention white women or other racial groups soon abandoned even this momentary recognition to focus exclusively on African Americans as the focus of the controversy."[16]

Of course, Clint Bolick seems to be sincere in his beliefs. He has ardently represented African American entrepreneurs stymied by government regulation, and in *Changing Course* he clearly calls for an end to the war on drugs because it disproportionately damages and hollows out minority communities.[17] His arguments lack the bad faith and bottomless malice of some of those put forward by Mark Levin or Chris Rufo. So it is hard to tell how conscious or unconscious his through-the-looking-glass framing of affirmative action is. About the inaccuracy of his framing, however, there can be no question.

The most striking element of this inaccuracy comes when Bolick argues that affirmative action and other parts of Lyndon Johnson's War on Poverty not only failed to meet their objectives but also wounded African Americans and the nation, producing a "new racism" whose victims are people like Wendy Wygant. Worse, it has produced a "new slavery" for African Americans. Eighty percent of the progress made between 1940 and 1980 took place "before 1965—before racial preferences, before massive busing, before skyrocketing welfare spending," Bolick writes, citing a Rand Corporation study. As Bolick tells it, everything after 1964 (including, apparently, the 1965 Voting Rights Act, full enforcement of the 1964 Civil Rights Act, and much else) had a net negative effect on the fortunes of the African American community.[18]

Here, Bolick not only ignores recessions, outsourcing, and other relevant contributors to post-1965 economic hardships but also leans heavily on the dubious scholarship of social scientist Charles Murray, telling his readers that "Murray traces the present predicament to the fundamental policy shift during the early 1960s from an emphasis on opportunity to a quick-fix effort to artificially produce equality of result. The trade-off . . . required abandoning 'those methods which have historically proven successful—self-reliance, work skills, education, business experience,' in favor of 'methods that are more immediate—job quotas, charity, subsidies, preferential treatment.'"[19]

As scholars such as Michael K. Brown have shown, this sort of argument is a rehash of blame-the-victim messages that have existed throughout the history of the welfare state, which has always lavished more benefits on whites but blamed Blacks for their dependence on—or, in Bolick's terminology, enslavement to—those benefits.[20] Indeed,

Brown demonstrates that the very struggles Bolick claims were created by the welfare state actually resulted from policies implemented during Bolick's beloved Reagan era—and elements of the Jekyll-and-Hyde Nixon era that preceded it—when "public investment in jobs, education, and neighborhoods was diminished at the same time that corporate disinvestment sucked jobs out of ghetto communities."[21]

Glossing over all this allows people like Murray to deploy the stigmatization of Blacks—a core element of American whiteness—as needed. Bolick is never whiter than when he uses the Black dependency argument to proclaim that civil rights leaders "have relinquished their claim to moral leadership."[22] Even Bolick's outbursts of genuine sympathy and his good ideas are poisoned by an impulse to stigmatize that is blind to arguments like Brown's and to the Reagan administration's own research on that sine qua non of Bolick's "new racism": affirmative action. A pair of studies ordered in 1981 by Reagan's OFCCP director Ellen Shong Bergman found that affirmative action was having a positive effect on the employment prospects of African Americans, white women, and Latinos. This was not good news for the anti–civil rights movement, and the Reagan administration refused to release the studies. Someone—apparently future Trump attorney general William Barr (who worked as deputy assistant director for legal policy in the Reagan White House in 1982–83)—suggested that the study was an "inside job" perpetrated by the OFCCP and that "impartial and competent social scientists" should reanalyze the studies' data and research methodology.[23]

Nevertheless, the author of one of the studies, Jonathan S. Leonard, published several essays in peer-reviewed journals based on the unreleased, three hundred-plus-page document. He reported that affirmative action had increased demand for Black males in high-skilled jobs and had helped Latino, Asian, and Native American males land white-collar jobs. But, in a finding that Bolick might have put to rhetorical use, Leonard also reported a "mixed and often negative impact on white females" when comparing their gains with those of white males.[24] Perhaps Bolick did not take this up because Leonard wrote in another essay that white women *did* experience gains in companies that, as federal government contractors, were required to have affirmative action plans. This suggested to Leonard that "affirmative action has actually been successful in promoting the employment of minorities and females, though less so in the case of white females. In the contractor sector, affirmative action has increased the demand relative to white males for black males by 6.5%, for nonblack minority males by 11.9%, and for white females by 3.5%."[25]

THE BIRTH OF TITLE IX

Of course, white women did not just passively allow themselves to be included in affirmative action programs; they demanded to be let in. A leader in this regard was Bernice Sandler. After completing her doctorate in education at the University of Maryland, Brooklyn-born Sandler started eyeing the seven jobs open in her department. When she was passed over, she asked a male professor why, and he told her, "You come on too strong for a woman." She had no language to express her devastation until her husband suggested that she had been subjected to sex discrimination. Sandler began reading discrimination law and eventually came across Lyndon Johnson's Executive Order 11246 and its 1967 follow-up, Executive Order 11375, which forbade recipients of federal contracts to practice gender discrimination. "I actually shrieked" while reading the order, she later recalled, "for I immediately realized that many universities and colleges had federal contracts [and] were therefore subject to the sex discrimination provisions of the Executive Order."[26]

Not entirely believing her own eyes, Sandler called the Labor Department and got on the line with OFCCP director Vincent Macaluso, who became a crucial ally. Sandler herself was soon the one-woman Federal Contract Compliance Committee for an organization called the Women's Equity Action League (WEAL). With Executive Order 11246 as her battering ram and Macaluso as her secret strategist, she set out to break up the old boys' network that controlled jobs in higher education. She initiated a class-action suit targeting 250 universities and colleges that benefited from federal funds. To do so, she used the very reading of Executive Order 11246 that Bolick, Meese, and the civil rights specialists in the Reagan administration tried to abolish. Specifically, she used the disparate impact option that had grown out of *Griggs*: to file suit, "you did not need to name a specific person who had been harmed by discrimination; you did not need to be part of the group that experienced discrimination; and you could file on the basis of statistical disparities." Sandler's filings drew the attention of women around the country. They helped her gather data on malfeasance at their own colleges, and the leaders of other women's groups joined her efforts. Advised by Macaluso to have those women write letters to their US representatives and senators, Sandler went to work: "We generated so much Congressional mail that the Department of Labor, and Health, Education and Welfare had to assign several full-time personnel to handle the letters." Investigations into sex discrimination at Harvard and the University of Michigan were begun. "Pandora's Box had finally been opened," Sandler crowed in 2007.[27]

The box was opened wider when members of Congress joined WEAL. One of them, Edith Green, had been looking for the data and the constituency she needed to justify proposing legislation against sex discrimination. Sandler's campaign provided both. Among the results were the Education Amendments of 1972, which brought academic institutions into the fold of federal contractors that had to obey the requirements of Title VII, Executive Order 11246, and a new addition to federal law: Title IX.

The crafting of Title IX was a kind of underground operation carried out in Congresswoman Green's office. It relied on likely opponents' ignorance of the title's implications. Green and WEAL adapted the wording of Title VI to cover gender discrimination in education. Together, these and a few other innovations created gender as a legal entity and an object of knowledge, according to Sandler.[28]

As he did so often in those years, Stanley Pottinger played a role. In October 1972 he was still the director of the Office of Civil Rights in the Nixon Department of Health, Education, and Welfare, and he sent a thick packet of information to college and university presidents explaining their new obligations, including the elimination of hiring and promotion criteria that were unrelated to job performance and tended to exclude women and minorities, plus the provision of child care as part of their affirmative action programs.[29]

Within sixteen years, a task force sponsored by the left-leaning Russell Sage Foundation affirmed the success of Sandler's and her associates' efforts, concluding that affirmative action "has been a premier force in theory and practice for women in higher education in their efforts to secure fair and equal treatment and to awaken community thought to the inequities inherent in long-accepted practices."[30] Looking back on it all in 2000, Kul B. Rai and John W. Critzer concluded that "white females were the greatest beneficiaries of faculty employment changes that, to a considerable extent, were a result of the implementation of affirmative action."[31] That was not all.

Analyzing data from 100,000 large private-sector firms for the period between 1973 and 2003, economist Fidan Ana Kurtulus concluded that affirmative action contributed to a 7.3 percent increase in white women working in "higher-paying skilled occupations," a 3.9 percent increase in Black women working in these areas, and 7.7 and 4.2 percent increases in Hispanic women's and Black men's employment in such occupations, respectively. Unfortunately, the advancement of minorities and white women "into the top echelons of firm structures subsided during the Reagan years," according to Kortulus.[32]

For Bolick, this subsidence, as affirmative action and other initiatives associated with the "frenzied expansion of the welfare state from the mid-1960s on" were reined in, represented justice. He therefore demanded a mea culpa from the civil rights establishment for its failure to admit that "government is not a solution but a cause of the [new] slavery."[33]

17

THE 10 PERCENT SOLUTION

Clint Bolick's and Mark Levin's books will not go down as classics in the same category as *The Federalist Papers* or *The Prince,* but they do not have to. They were part of a vast messaging and legal effort that, backed by well over $1 billion by the year 2000, reset the American agenda and changed the vocabulary used in discussions of affirmative action and related social policies. "When it comes to 'winning' political battles, ultimate success results less from who's doing the right thing, and more from whose view of reality dominates the battlefield. It does not take a rocket scientist to figure out that the millions spent by conservative think tanks have enabled them to virtually dictate the issues and terms of national debates," said Robert Bothwell, president of the Rockefeller Foundation–funded National Committee for Responsive Philanthropy in the 1990s.[1]

Those millions of dollars had an effect because, like people, societies—particularly democracies, which live on information (and sicken and die by misinformation)—have limited attention spans and many demands on their time. Borrowing a term from Nobel laureate Herbert Simon, Frank R. Baumgartner and Bryan D. Jones write that societies have *bounded rationality.* Lacking omniscience, they cannot gather and process all the information they need to make perfect decisions. "Instead, their decision-making procedures are incomplete and driven by severe limits on their attention spans. [They] can focus intensely only on a limited number of public policies."[2]

One result of this bounded social rationality is that it turns politics into a war to dominate the public's attention. The presidency's built-in advantages in this war allowed the Reagan administration to achieve some notable successes that did not always require it to "attack specific programs, as had the Nixonians," according to Baumgartner and Jones. Instead, the Reaganauts "attacked the entire philosophy of the positive state." Success came partly because Reagan's determination to "cut spending" on everything from affirmative action to food stamps to Medicare forced the Democrats "to defend only the programs generating the broadest popular appeal, and that was primarily Social Security [which, of course, benefits everyone, including white Republicans]."[3] The Democrats were put on the defensive so decisively not only because of master strategists like Meese inside the government and conservative foundations, think tanks, and public-interest law firms outside the government but also because of the ease with which centuries of stereotypes allowed debates about civil rights policies like affirmative action to be turned into hermeneutic traps.[4]

The notoriously Machiavellian, blues guitar–playing Reagan aide and campaign strategist Lee Atwater made no bones about using "the race thing" to woo white Democrats who resented some of the societal transformations wrought by the civil rights movement. "You start out—now, ya'all won't quote me now, on this?—you start out in 1954, by saying 'nigger, nigger, nigger,'" the thirty-year-old Atwater told an interviewer in 1981. "By 1968," he continued,

> you can't say "nigger"—that hurts you. Backfires. So you say stuff like forced busing, states' rights, and all that stuff. You're getting so abstract now [that] you're talking about cutting taxes, and all these things you're talking about are totally economic things and a byproduct of them is [that] blacks get hurt worse than whites. And subconsciously maybe that's part of it. I'm not saying that. But I'm saying that if it is getting that abstract, and that coded, that we are doing away with the racial problem one way or the other. You follow me—because obviously sitting around saying, "we want to cut this," is much more abstract than even the busing thing, and a hell of a lot more abstract than "nigger, nigger."[5]

In short, if Atwater is right, high-minded GOP attacks on "big government" and "tax-and-spend" Democrats have a genealogy that includes the racist backlash against *Brown* and the recoding of that backlash by people like Sam Ervin and Strom Thurmond. (Atwater worked for Thurmond early in his career, and the senator helped him get his job in the Reagan administration.)[6]

After all, government got big in a way that Reagan and other stalwarts of the anti–civil rights movement took exception to, largely as part of the effort to respond to the 1950s through 1970s civil rights movement as it gave rise to organizations ranging from Chinese for Affirmative Action to WEAL.[7] But if Atwater dispensed with ideological niceties in his unbuttoned and, he hoped, off-the-record comments (they were attached to his name only after his death), men like Meese and Bolick claimed to have a magic carpet that lifted them so high above race that they could clearly see how a small color-blind government would lift all boats, while policies like affirmative action would sink them. With people like the energetic Atwater doing the dirty work, philosopher kings like Meese and Bolick were free to pursue their goal of "redefining the terms" of the civil rights debate.[8] As Desmond S. King and Rogers M. Smith argue, race, race relations, and racial interests are ideas that can bind or shatter coalitions, depending on how those ideas, as well as race blindness, are defined.[9] In this context, the power to redefine is power itself.

Two consequential tools of redefinition were funded by the Olin Foundation. The first, the National Association of Scholars, was launched in 1987 with the aim of countering the university liberals that Lewis Powell and others identified as dangerous. In addition to Olin, the Smith Richardson Foundation helped the association spread from its home base in New York to California, where it unleashed a series of events that destroyed affirmative action in that state.[10] The second organization, the Center for Individual Rights, brought the curtain down on affirmative action in Texas and, eventually, Michigan, came within a whisker of ending affirmative action (at least in education) nationwide, and primed the pump for the case that finally unraveled much of the policy.

Like so much in the anti–civil rights movement, these two organizations were born of envy and frustration. The Center for Individual Rights (CIR) resulted from the interactions of Cornell University Department of Government professor Jeremy Rabkin, his graduate student Michael Greve, and the burgeoning post-Reagan conservative network. Rabkin dreamed and schemed to counter liberal public-interest law firms with firms whose litigation would work "to restrain the government instead of expand it."[11] Years later, in 1989, Greve and Michael McDonald, a lawyer groomed in two conservative public-interest law firms, decided to launch what became the CIR, and Rabkin agreed to join the board of directors. Like Rabkin, Greve and McDonald wanted to create the kryptonite for poweful liberal nonprofits such as the Sierra Club and the American Civil Liberties Union (where Ruth Bader Ginsburg was changing the face of American law for women). In their opinion, existing conservative firms such as the Washington Legal Foundation, where McDonald had worked as a lawyer and Greve as a fund-raiser, lacked the focus and strategic acumen needed to land the devastating body blows against liberal orthodoxy they wished to deliver, so they circulated a proposal for a leaner and meaner firm, and the Smith Richardson Foundation, the Olin Foundation, and the Bradley Foundation gave them a combined $250,000.[12] The CIR opened its doors in 1989. By 1997, it had an annual budget of $1.3 million and was in the middle of a case that earned national headlines.[13]

The case grew out of the rage of several white applicants rejected by the University of Texas Law School, which considered minority applicants under an elaborate affirmative action plan reminiscent of the effort at UC–Davis. Recruited by ambitious Austin lawyer Stephen Wayne Smith, the applicants—David Rogers, Kenneth Elliott, Douglas Carvell, and Cheryl Hopwood—sued the law school for rejecting them in 1992 in favor of, they claimed, less-qualified minorities. Hopwood, the lead plaintiff, was an accountant and the mother of a handicapped child, and she had worked twenty to thirty hours a week while putting herself through college. "Affirmative action should be used to help disadvantaged people of whatever background," Hopwood said in an interview. "You can find injustice anywhere. The fact that I have one severely handicapped child and another one died is an injustice. But nobody's helping me."[14] "African Americans," she argued in another interview, "are given full scholarships. I wasn't helped at all. . . . They didn't look at anything but race. And that's not fair."[15]

The four lost in district court, but CIR brought in former Reagan administration assistant attorney general Ted Olson to help with briefs and oral arguments for the appeal. The plaintiffs triumphed in New Orleans before a three-judge panel of the Fifth Circuit Court of Appeals.[16] Writing for the majority, Judge Jerry E. Smith relied on Justice Scalia's biting concurrence in *Richmond v. Croson*:

> Racial preferences appear to "even the score" . . . only if one embraces the proposition that our society is appropriately viewed as divided into races, making it right that an injustice rendered in the past to a black man should be compensated for by discriminating against . . . a white. *City of Richmond v. J. A. Croson Co., 488 U.S. 469 . . . (Scalia, J., concurring in the judgment).*[17]

Smith brushed aside the precedent the lower court relied on: Justice Powell's identification of diversity as an educational benefit in *Bakke*. Powell's view was not a precedent, Smith asserted, but an example of one hand clapping, since no other justice had signed on to the relevant portion of Powell's opinion.

In short, contrary to the finding of district court judge Sam Sparks, the law school's affirmative action program was unconstitutional, Smith concluded. Sparks had found the law school's admissions process fatally flawed (because in 1992 it placed nonminority and minority applicants in separate pools) but nevertheless constitutional along the lines established by Powell. The constitutional rights of the plaintiffs, who might not have been admitted even if there were no affirmative action, were intact, Sparks determined. Smith struck down Sparks's decision but did not order the four applicants admitted. Instead, he advised them to reapply, ordered the law school to rid its admissions process of its "constitutional infirmities," and ordered Sparks to reconsider the case in light of his and the rest of the majority's ruling.[18]

Sparks held a new trial but arrived at a bittersweet result for Hopwood and the others. The law school, he decided, "has proved by a preponderance of the evidence that none of the plaintiffs would have been admitted to the law school under a constitutional admissions system." As required, he forbade the University of Texas Law School to weigh race. He also granted the plaintiffs $703,992.29 plus interest in attorneys' fees. But he awarded only $1 each to Hopwood and the others, who had requested substantial damages for lost income and mental anguish.

The wavy-haired Hopwood was not only disappointed in the outcome but also hurt by the portion of Sparks's ruling that questioned whether anyone, male or female, would be able to get through law school while devoting enormous amounts of time to caring for a disabled daughter and commuting 150 miles to classes. "I'm not saying law school is a piece of cake," Hopwood responded. "But do not tell me that it would have been harder than anything I've had to face."[19]

CIR and attorney Smith went away happy, as they had achieved their main objective: ending affirmative action at the University of Texas Law School and beyond. An unexpected and controversial bonus came when Texas attorney general Dan Morales decided that the *Hopwood* ruling meant that affirmative action had to end at all Texas universities and that scholarships and other benefits earmarked for minorities had to cease.

Michael Greve took a victory lap in a *Pace Law Review* article. He mocked those hoping to find a way around the *Hopwood* ruling by quoting the tagline—"keep hope alive"—associated with the presidential campaign of civil rights icon Jesse Jackson. According to Greve, the racial diversity goals Powell permitted amounted to little more than a bait-and-switch operation that put race center stage and kept other forms of diversity, such as religious conservatism, out of sight and out of admissions officers' minds.[20]

Greve then turned to the meat of his argument: the law school's "Texas Index," built by combining LSAT scores and GPAs. The resulting numbers had been separated into three piles: "presumptive admit," "presumptive decline," and "discretionary zone." But, Greve declared, sounding like a prosecutor introducing the smoking gun into evidence, "the presumptive admit score for the preferred minorities (189) was lower than the presumptive deny score for the 'Others' (192)." Race, then, "was not a Powell-type 'plus-factor' or 'tie-breaker' in close cases;

it made all the difference in case after case." This put paid to "glib assurances" that nonminorities with lower scores than Hopwood and the other plaintiffs had been admitted. Only one conclusion could be drawn: "Cheryl Hopwood [who had the highest score among the four] and her fellow plaintiffs would have been admitted, had they been black." Crafting a conclusion that would make Atwater proud, Greve dismisses any diversity benefit minorities might bring because nonminorities "are unlikely to accept minority students as equals."[21]

Greve's argument is at its weakest when he dismisses the fact that whites with scores below 189 were admitted, that two of the whites admitted had scores lower than those of Blacks who were rejected, and that dozens of Mexican Americans who were rejected had higher scores than a number of whites who were admitted.[22] Lani Guinier (whose nomination to become Bill Clinton's attorney general was torpedoed by a Bolick op-ed that christened her and a Latina nominee "quota queens") reports that in 1992, when Hopwood and the others were rejected, "130 white students were admitted who had lower test scores and grade-point averages than she did." She concludes that "'merit' really reflects an overemphasis on quantitative measures," driven more by colleges' desire to do well in *U.S. News & World Report* education rankings (where small differences in admittees' test scores can change the rankings) than their desire to identify the most promising students.[23]

Even Greve takes out his rhetorical skinning knife for the schools competing in the *U.S. News & World Report* sweepstakes. The real issue, he writes, is that the University of Texas wanted to pack in high-scoring, high-GPA students—for Greve, the best students—because the law school wanted to improve its top-twenty ranking to a top-ten ranking. But "this ambition requires enrolling the very best students. Since few of these are members of the preferred minorities, UT turned to double standards."[24]

But in Texas, people like those Greve mocked were coming to quite different conclusions. Judge Sparks, for instance, had already identified some of the reasons why the records of Hopwood and the other plaintiffs were not necessarily the sort the law school was looking for. In his 1994 ruling, Sparks, who is famed for delivering "bench slaps" to lawyers who he decides are not up to their jobs, noted that Hopwood's application did not go much beyond her LSAT scores and GPA. She submitted no recommendation letters and no personal statement. In addition, her responses to questions on the application did not elaborate on her background and skills. Finally, after high school, Hopwood had been accepted to Princeton, but due to financial hardship, she went first to a community college and then to the University of Sacramento, which admissions officers viewed as a less rigorous and lower-status school than those attended by many of her fellow applicants. Last but not least, when she was offered a place on Texas's wait list, she declined because she feared it might be impossible to find child care if she were admitted.

One of the other plaintiffs, Kenneth Elliott, was placed on a waiting list and might have been admitted (the record is confusing and unclear), but communication between Elliott and the university broke down. Douglas Carvell ranked 98th in a class of 247 at a small and not especially prestigious college. David Rogers actually attended the University of Texas as an undergraduate but was dismissed because of poor academic performance. Although he received degrees in writing from the University of Houston and the University of Southern California, he was rejected outright.

Sparks concluded in 1994 and confirmed in 1998 that he saw "no disparities in the applications of admitted minorities when compared to those of the plaintiffs 'so apparent as virtually to jump off the page and slap [the court] in the face.'" After all, people like Greve did not consider how minorities might have answered the questions on the application, what they might have written in personal essays, how rigorous and prestigious their undergraduate institutions might have been, or what their recommendation letters might have said.

The fallout from Sparks's final word on the case in 1998 and from Morales's decision to apply the ruling across Texas led to developments that still reverberate. One source of these reverberations was a Texas state representative named Irma Rangel. Her father toiled as a migrant worker in cotton fields as a boy and did not attend school, and her mother did not study past the fifth grade, but they nevertheless founded several successful small businesses. Rangel grew up in Kingsville, in

South Texas, and spoke no English before starting elementary school, where she thrived, perhaps because of her awareness of the alternatives. Rangel's father put her and her two sisters to work in a cotton field for a week and then asked whether they wanted to continue or attend school. All three said, "School please."[25]

After graduating from Texas A&M–Kingsville in 1952 with both a degree in business administration and a teaching certificate, Rangel taught in Texas, Venezuela, and California.[26] Along the way, she wrote a guidebook on teaching Spanish to elementary students. Then she gave in to a secret ambition and earned a law degree in 1971. After working for a few years as an interpreter and law clerk for Judge Adrian Speers, she accepted an offer to become an assistant district attorney in Corpus Christi. Her status as a woman in the DA's office was so unusual that the *Corpus Christi Caller-Times* ran a story about it. Her biggest challenge, she told reporter Shelby Hodge, would be "to get jurors to accept a woman lawyer in the courtroom." Hodge took note of her relaxed, "rather jovial" demeanor and contrasted it with the stereotype of the stern prosecutor. Adjusting her image like a tightrope walker adjusting her posture, Rangel assured Hodge, "I'm much more firm in the courtroom."[27]

Rangel divided her time between the DA's office and the Corpus Christi Wife and Child Division, which she had discovered while clerking and translating for Judge Speers. In the DA's office, "I would get all the incest and rape cases," she later recalled. "They would come to me because I was the only woman there. The girls who were raped would get pregnant and cry and ask me what they were going to do. I couldn't tell them to get an abortion. Back then you could get two to 10 years in prison for getting an abortion."[28] As a politician, Rangel supported abortion rights despite her devout Catholicism. Her work in the Wife and Child Division familiarized her with the struggles of families on welfare, the problem of juvenile delinquency, the abortion issue (once again illegal in Texas as of 2022), and the suicide rate among women. All this may have factored into her decision to move from the prosecutorial side to the advocacy side of the law and hang up her own shingle, becoming the first Latina to practice in Kleberg County.[29]

Rangel turned to politics in 1976 and ran for state representative.

On the campaign trail, she used everything she had learned, flashing a guileless smile and stressing her experience as former chair of the Kleberg County Democratic Party and as the protector of consumers, working people, the aged, the needy, and the poor. Not least, she advertised her ability to "communicate with all of her potential constituents"—whether they spoke English or Spanish.[30] She won and became the first Latina to serve in the Texas House of Representatives. Entering a man's world once again, she built herself a shield as a founding member of the Texas Association of Elected Women, whose mission was to convince more women to enter politics. At a 1980 gathering of the group she shared her keys to success as a female politician: "maintain a sense of humor, avoid making the male mistake of acting pompous and arrogant, work together and [do] not be afraid to be women. . . . But one thing you'll find is that men are weak," yet they "will do their darndest to make you feel inferior and try to counsel you on tough decisions for their benefit."[31] Rangel regularly managed to turn the tables on men, who found themselves being, in quick succession, charmed (sometimes with a peck on the cheek), brushed back by her big brassy voice, and generally, as her colleagues termed it, "Irma-tized."[32] Among her accomplishments was securing $345 million to build universities in Texas border communities.

By the time the *Hopwood* decision came down and Morales had advanced his interpretation of it, Rangel was chair of the Higher Education Committee and perfectly positioned to push back against those who had guided *Hopwood* through the courts. Confronting attorney Stephen Wayne Smith at a hearing, she forced him to answer a key question that Michael Greve had ducked: "why is it that in your lawsuit you did not include Anglo students, only minority students: because it was very clear that Anglo students who had lesser results [than Hopwood's] had been accepted" (130 whites with weaker academic records than Hopwood's were admitted).[33] Smith's answer was a masterpiece of doublespeak:

> If you have a pool of Anglos that were admitted in 1992 with lower Texas indices than the Plaintiffs . . . then they fall into two catego-

> ries—one where the undergraduate institution and major was much better than the Plaintiffs'. Say the Plaintiffs went to an average college and somebody went to Yale, and I mean the GPA is going to be understated versus one from an average institution. So, it's not surprising that there would be Anglos admitted, with lower test scores based on other factors.[34]

As already noted, minorities who supposedly displaced Hopwood and the others were given no such benefit of the doubt. They were presumed to be inferior and unqualified. Smith went on to mention "a second group of Anglos" with lower Texas indices who were admitted based on their connections. This was not grounds for a lawsuit because the history of constitutional interpretation provides no basis, whereas prohibiting race discrimination "is essential to the Constitutional jurisprudence, so that's what we attacked."[35]

Here, the doublespeak, or perhaps the double blindness, has to do with the fact that admissions opportunities based on who one knows exist primarily in the Anglo population. Over time, this greater opportunity has led to the accumulation of more wealth, more positions of power, and, therefore, more access to those with the ability to wave in a well-connected student. This relative monopoly on access is itself an indication of continuing discrimination against minorities. Thus, the fact that the Constitution, as interpreted by CIR, by Smith, and by the whole conservative movement, does not recognize this ongoing discrimination keeps, in good working order, the hermeneutic traps that make such discrimination seem natural.

To get out of the trap in which *Hopwood* put their constituents, Rangel and her colleagues drafted a flurry of bills, most of which did not gain traction. But Rangel—who referred to her fellow legislators as "darling" or "sweetie" and sought support from colleagues by saying, "I have this sweet, wonderful bill that you are all going to love so much"—never gave up.[36] In the end, she coauthored State Bill 588, which mandated that any student who graduated in the top 10 percent of a Texas high school class be automatically admitted to a state college or university. If there were insufficient spots to accommodate all who qualified, the overflow qualifiers would be selected by lottery. For students not in the top 10 percent, the bill set forth eleven criteria for university admissions committees to consider, including the applicant's family income, whether the applicant spoke more than one language, and how well the applicant did on standardized tests.[37] "I got that bill passed by seven votes," Rangel recalled in 1998:

> I mean, this is really a race-neutral bill completely, and it passed by seven votes. I went to a Democratic friend of mine, and I said, "You find it very difficult to vote for the student's bill." And he said, "Well, now, Irma, if I had voted for your bill, you know I wouldn't be here, because I'd be beaten." And I said, "What the hell do we need you for anyway?" . . . So when we, as elected officials, stop thinking primarily about getting re-elected instead of doing the right thing . . . then the benefit not only is [to] our district but also the State of Texas.[38]

What became known as the top 10 percent law was signed by Governor George W. Bush and quickly became part of the fabric of Texas education.

For economist Anthony Carnevale, director of Georgetown University's Center for Education and the Workforce, Rangel's law was a stroke of genius because it took advantage of the lingering effects of discrimination that the Fifth Circuit, Stephen Wayne Smith, and even the Supreme Court refused to acknowledge: Texas schools had enough de facto segregation to guarantee that taking the top 10 percent of each school's graduates would automatically produce some degree of student diversity. "What is interesting to me," Carnevale said in 2017, "is that the politicians figured this out before the economists and the lawyers." They figured out that "the public is much more sympathetic to class than race" because race is so fraught it "is a secret we keep from ourselves."[39] It is true that some diversity was lost at the University of Texas and other prestigious Texas campuses after *Hopwood*, but Rangel's bill stopped the bleeding. What is more, the idea of automatically admitting top students was picked up in places like Florida, where Governor Jeb Bush ended affirmative action by executive order and then signed a top 20 percent bill into law.[40]

It is a testament to the growing nationwide power of the anti–civil rights movement that Jeb Bush made his move under pressure from the movement's new pope. To see the pope in action, we have to return to California.

18

PROPOSITION 209

The unlikely tip of the anti–civil rights movement spear in California was the National Association of Scholars (NAS). Horrified at the thought of a "radical generation of scholars [tightening] its grip on the academy every time an old professor retired from the faculty," the Olin and Smith Richardson Foundations gave modest grants to the NAS when it was still an academic start-up created by Professor Stephen Balch of John Jay College.[1] But with steadily increasing support from the foundations, the NAS evolved into a band of Ph.D.-wielding counterrevolutionaries who established franchises in many states in the name of restoring "intellectual substance, intellectual merit, and academic freedom in the university."[2] In California, the NAS became the point of contact between two frustrated and angry white scholars named Glynn Custred and Thomas Wood.

Custred, a professor of anthropology at California State University in Hayward, was alarmed by early efforts to diversify reading lists with writers such as Toni Morrison and by early efforts to diversify the Hayward faculty itself.[3] Like Christopher Rufo decades later, Custred and other NAS members saw such developments as an existential threat—nothing less than the 1960s riots being conducted by other means inside classrooms, as Custred and two coauthors argue in their 1999 book *The Ups and Downs of Affirmative Action Preferences*. In fact, the "New Left–black militant coalition has come a long way in capturing the university" with "a loose confederation of ideas known variously as the 'cultural left,' 'multiculturalism,' and advocates of 'diversity,'" they write.

In mortal danger from diversity was nothing less than what Ernest Gellner called "a common 'conceptual currency' . . . a shared language on which the consensus for public policy can be reached and maintained."[4]

Because it did not occur to Custred and the others that a common conceptual currency can be enriched by the expansion of its vocabulary and by the cultural blends created by diversity (one need only consider the roots of the personal computer business in 1960s youth culture to see why[5]), they dismissed multiculturalism and the rest as acids eating away at "the liberal vision that has long defined so successfully the American nation." Against this apocalyptic cloud, the NAS (with Custred taking the lead in California) was doing nothing less than riding to America's rescue and targeting the most corrosive force of all: affirmative action.[6]

Thomas Wood, the Robin to Custred's Batman, earned a Ph.D. in philosophy at the University of California at Berkeley but, despite years of effort, was unable to land a secure teaching job. He blamed that failure on affirmative action, claiming that a professor at one school told him he would have been a shoo-in there if his gender were different. When asked for confirmation, the professor in question said he did not recall the conversation. The head of the Philosophy Department at the time of Wood's job search told journalist Lydia Chávez that Wood had not even been a finalist.[7]

Nevertheless, the embittered Wood dreamed of eradicating affirmative action, and his eyes lit up when he saw a 1990 *Newsweek* story about a Wisconsin chapter of the National Association of Scholars that was about to officially condemn "minority hiring quotas being imposed" at a university there.[8] After Wood and Custred met at an NAS conference, they teamed up to draft an anti–affirmative action ballot initiative for California.[9]

Accustomed to the Lilliputian politics of academia, Custred had little idea how to bridge the gap between the issues he and Wood labored over and the mega-politics of a state as big as California. So Custred reached out to Stanley Diamond. In 1986, Diamond's determined campaign against bilingualism had resulted in a ballot initiative to undo much of the work of Ling-Chi Wang, Henry Der, and others by requiring the government to issue ballots only in English and to conduct all official business in English. "Our American heritage is now threatened by language conflicts and ethnic separatism. . . . This amendment establishes a broad principle: English is the official language of California. . . . No other language can have a similar status," Diamond, former senator S. I. Hayakawa, and businessman J. William Orozco wrote in a statement explaining the proposition.[10]

Diamand became the first in a series of political tutors for Wood and Custred as they wrote draft after draft. Along the way, they reached a conceptual fork in the road when they came under the tutelage of Lino Graglia, a UT–Austin law professor and member of NAS and the Federalist Society who, in the wake of the *Hopwood* decision, created a firestorm by declaring that Black and Latino students were culturally unequipped to compete academically with whites. Graglia advised Wood and Custred to avoid any mention of sex-based affirmative action in their proposition because "when you include sex, you run into a lot of problems that you don't run into with race."[11]

Graglia was right. As scholar Katharine T. Bartlett shows, stereotypes linked to race and gender are "numerous," but

> beliefs about race are more negative, and more significant in people's attitudes toward race-conscious affirmative action, than beliefs about sex are to people's attitudes about affirmative action for women. To start with, stereotypes about Blacks are virtually all negative. These negative stereotypes—that they are lazy and irresponsible—tend to support the same narrative as [the one claiming that] it is the fault of Blacks themselves that they lag behind whites [and are] "responsible for several major threats to the social order."[12]

Graglia, in short, was counseling them to maximize their initiative's chance of passing by riding the anti-Black and antiminority stereotypes that had trampled so many minorities' life chances into the dust.

Taking a stand that combined principle, strategy, and (on Wood's part) personal animus, Graglia's political pupils refused his advice. Custred explained that dropping

> gender from the initiative, when for the last thirty years it has been intimately linked with race and ethnicity, would suggest hypocrisy and a lack of principle. . . . There is a feeling in the black community that the greatest beneficiaries of affirmative action have been affluent white women at the expense of blacks. . . . To exclude gender preferences from the initiative would only reenforce this conviction, creating the belief that the initiative is in fact a racist measure.[13]

Here principle triumphed.

But Wood's grievance was clear in a memo he wrote: "White males need protection against discrimination on the basis of their sex even more than they need protection on the basis of their race. . . . Omitting gender from the initiative . . . would play right into the hands of the gender feminists and the radical feminists."[14]

In October 1993 Custred and Wood filed what they called the California Civil Rights Initiative. It quickly became apparent that Graglia need not have worried. Despite the inclusion of gender, the public debate focused on the racial portion of affirmative action. In February 1994, for example, once and future presidential candidate Pat Buchanan declared that Custred and Wood's initiative could help the GOP wrest the national agenda back from President Bill Clinton. "Politically, the initiative's appeal is obvious," Buchanan wrote. "Republicans in the 22 other states with ballot initiatives ought to be looking to put racial quotas to a popular vote; and the national GOP should write a version of the initiative into the 1996 party platform."[15]

Despite this endorsement and despite the fact that Larry Arnn, the well-connected cofounder and head of the Claremont Institute, signed on as chair in December 1994, the California Civil Rights Initiative was dead in the political water because its backers lacked the financial and political muscle to get it on the ballot.[16] This was not for lack of trying to create synergy with the rest of the right wing. In 1995, for instance, Arnn convened a three-day Claremont Institute symposium attended by seventeen power brokers—Edwin Meese, Ralph Reed of the Christian Coalition, Linda Chávez (former chair of U.S. English), and Pat Buchanan's sister Bay, among others. The product of the symposium was a manifesto calling for defense of "the moral and natural law" from the cultural forces smothering them.[17] Unfortunately, Arnn was not a good fund-raiser, and the initiative could not afford to hire the small army needed to collect the 693,000 signatures required to put it on the state ballot.[18]

The initiative took off only after Custred, Wood, and Arnn convinced businessman and University of California regent Ward Connerly to join them.[19] A round-faced fireplug of a man with a well-manicured mustache, Connerly had benefited heavily from affirmative action but made a political name for himself by campaigning to end it in California's university system. Among his many other qualities, Connerly possessed what columnist Carl Rowan called a "powerful black face." "For people who want to believe that there is something illegal or immoral about outreach programs to achieve fairness and diversity in education, employment and other areas of American life," Rowan wrote, "Connerly's face lends to them the false aura of gospel. If a black man says affirmative action hurts Caucasians and is morally wrong, then it surely has to be wrong."[20]

Connerly had come to Wood and Custred's attention when California governor Pete Wilson appointed him to the University of California Board of Regents to quell criticism that Wilson had appointed no nonwhites. Convinced that his business success and status as a longtime confidant of the governor canceled out the fact that his appointment was a classic example of affirmative action, Connerly began a dogged campaign against the policy.[21]

Civil rights leader Jesse Jackson flew in to oppose Connerly's efforts and brought the national spotlight with him. Because Wilson was nursing presidential ambitions at the time and saw his path leading straight through the underworld of white anxiety, he considered Jackson's arrival a gift. An African American would-be successor to Martin Luther King, Jackson constantly challenged the racial status quo but also made significant missteps during his own presidential campaign that in some ways set the stage for Barack Obama's triumphant run in 2008.[22] Lee Atwater had used Jackson to depress the poll numbers of the Democratic nominee during the 1988 presidential cycle. So the air was electric at what should have been another boring Board of Regents meeting in July 1995, where both Wilson and Jackson spoke, and Jackson insisted on leading the room in prayer. In the end, affirmative action in the university system was voted down.[23]

For a while, Wilson's political prospects rose like a kite in the wind. Connerly emerged as the voice of the anti–affirmative action movement. Wood and Custred courted Connerly assiduously because he had the governor's ear and the media spotlight. But "the fact that he was black was very important. It's like using affirmative action to defeat affirmative action. It's slightly unprincipled, but the fact was he brought some positive things like the full weight of the governor's office," according to Joe Gelman, who was part of the California Civil Rights Initiative for a time.[24]

The more circumspect Custred stressed that the aim of the initiative was to "reassert in clear terms the color-blind principles of Title VI of the 1964 Civil Rights Act." He emphasized Connerly's dedication to those principles as well as his business and political connections. But even Custred and his coauthors admitted that Connerly's "arguments carried more weight because [he] was black."[25] Connerly himself told the *New York Times* that his race "grants many whites a kind of absolution, allowing them to protest affirmative action 'without having to feel like they appear racist.'" But for Connerly, that was not what really mattered. Changing America into a postracial nation was paramount: "You can't unring the bell of slavery," he told the *Times*. "All you can do is make sure the next person who walks through the door, white or black, receives equal treatment." Of course, the basis of affirmative action as it was developed in the EEOC and OFCCP was that the bell of slavery continued to reverberate and shift opportunities away from certain groups and toward others. But for Connerly, affirmative action, "like an overused antibiotic, had become counterproductive" by the 1980s.[26]

Referencing the theory of "stereotype vulnerability," he told the *Times*, "Black kids don't go into an athletic competition thinking they're going to lose. They save those feelings of inferiority for the classroom. And do you know what reinforces the idea that they're inferior? Being told they need a preference to succeed." From Connerly's perspective, then, dismantling affirmative action meant not only putting a stop to "reverse discrimination" but also freeing young Blacks from self-doubt in a society that was well on its way to becoming postracial.[27] For him, the largest remnant of deep inequality seemed to be affirmative action itself.

Exhibiting all the discomfort of a man kidnapped and stuffed head-first into an artificial skin, Connerly explained to the *Times* that he is 25 percent Black, 37.5 percent Irish, 25 percent French, and 12.5 percent Choctaw. But in the United States, "one drop does it," so that made him Black. "I suppose I could claim to be Irish," he said, "but who wants to stand there and argue the point every time. So I'm black."[28] While the Irish, as Noel Ignatiev has argued, could become white, Connerly could not become Irish. But of course, his efforts to end affirmative action were a way of escaping from race by other means.

Taking over leadership of the initiative in November 1995, Connerly took care to keep the media engaged, to connect with the national Republican Party (1996 was a presidential election year), and to beat the bushes for donations. With Clint Bolick, Linda Chávez, and Pete Wilson in his ear, Bob Dole, the leading contender for the Republican nomination, was persuaded to drop his long-standing support for affirmative action and endorse the initiative in November 1995.[29]

Money began flooding into the California Republican Party, which put its weight behind the initiative. And even though Dole and the rest of the Republican establishment were clearly uncomfortable with their endorsement of the proposition, the amount of money they could bring in was mesmerizing.[30] Connerly, meanwhile, "spent all of December raising money," he reports in his autobiography. "By the end of the month I had $500,000 and Pete [Wilson] had raised another $100,000. Of this amount, much went to erase past debts the Wood and Custred operation had acquired, and the rest just barely got a signature-gathering firm back in the field."[31]

By February 21, 1996, the campaign had gathered more than a million signatures, far exceeding the 693,000 required. Connerly, Governor Wilson, and Quentin Kopp (who had tried unsuccessfully to pass legislation putting the initiative on the ballot) triumphantly turned the bundled forms over to the California secretary of state. The initiative was officially added to the 1996 ballot as Proposition 209. Meanwhile, as Dole was in the process of "betting the campaign" on winning California, his pro–affirmative action running mate, Jack Kemp, came out in favor of Proposition 209 in August 1996.[32]

Turning his attention to getting the proposition passed, Connerly redoubled his fund-raising and his efforts to corral the agenda-setting power of the news media. A high point came when he was granted an audience with the Australia-born media baron and political kingmaker on three continents, Rupert Murdoch. After their first meeting, Murdoch said he would back Connerly if he decided to run for office. At their second meeting, at the Republican National Convention in San Diego, Murdoch decided to donate $1 million to the California Republican Party, knowing that some of those dollars would go to the Proposition 209 campaign.

That same year, Murdoch made a move that strengthened the entire anti–civil rights movement. He summoned a media genius and master of the dark political arts named Roger Ailes and asked what it would take to create a cable news network that was "more patriotic and socially conservative" than outlets like CNN. Ailes said, "Nine hundred million to a billion. And you could lose it all." Murdoch said, "Go ahead and do it."[33]

So Ailes launched Fox News. A hemophiliac who drew a hard shell of fearlessness over his condition, Ailes allegedly had "two settings: attack and destroy." He molded Fox into a network that gradually became the mouthpiece and then the brain of the Republican Party.[34] Fox was determined to sweep away much of Lyndon Johnson's social safety net and all its philosophical underpinnings.[35] More than that, Fox became an unparallelled hermeneutic trap that captured the largest viewership in cable news, making it difficult for its audience to accept realities the network did not endorse, leaving its viewers less knowledgeable about current events than those who consumed no news at all, and priming them to participate in panics like the one surrounding CRT.[36]

Connerly seemed oblivious to all this in his autobiography, first published in 2000 but updated in 2007, when Fox's political clout was palpable. During the Proposition 209 campaign, Murdoch's million was just one victory in a heady mix of triumphs. Raising a total of $5,239,287, mostly from donors who gave more than $10,000, the

"Yes on Proposition 209" campaign was able to maintain a media blitz that overwhelmed the forces that, years late to the battle, scrambled to counter Connerly, Wood, and Custred.[37] But, contrary to Connerly's professed utopian desires (though perhaps not Murdoch's), the Proposition 209 campaign helped spread the message of white victimization and justified grievance (regularly paired with references to Black criminality and parasitism) that would become one of Fox's greatest products in the years between 1996 and the presidency of Donald Trump.[38]

One pro-209 radio ad featured a white woman who claimed to have suffered reverse discrimination because she was not allowed to take a vocational training class designed for Black students. Although the university she attended reported that she had neither preregistered nor taken the prerequisite for the class, the voice-over declared, "These programs are based not on merit, or even on need, but on race. . . . Janice Camarena Ingraham [the excluded student] now is one of many women *and* men leading the campaign for Proposition 209."[39] For Connerly, she was the campaign's symbol of "the injustice of preferences."[40]

Not content with the story of Ingraham's exclusion, the ad picked at the scab of white grievance by highlighting her tale of being laughed out of the classroom by the Black students when she was asked to leave. As Chávez points out, Ingraham "does not claim racial superiority but moral superiority."[41] And since the civil rights movement led by Martin Luther King rested on a claim of moral superiority to "vicious racists," the advertisement, like the entire Proposition 209 campaign, took an axe to the moral roots of affirmative action.[42]

In addition, the advertisement effectively undermined a key message of the campaign against Proposition 209: the idea that white women beneficiaries of affirmative action would be harmed if the proposition passed. Ingraham's powerful white face said otherwise, and she became the star of both TV and radio spots. Arnn's Claremont Institute added to the message by releasing a study featuring alleged victims of reverse discrimination, and Assemblyman Bernie Richter (who tried unsuccessfully to push through a legislative version of the initiative) announced that he would be holding hearings on antiwhite discrimination.[43]

Ironically, one of the few missteps in the 209 campaign arose from conservatives' ritual invocation of Martin Luther King as an inoculation against accusations of racial insensitivity. The national Republican Party ran a pro–Proposition 209 ad that featured a clip from King's "I Have a Dream" speech, and Connerly claimed to be appalled. "It was a naked act of opportunism in which the sinking Dole campaign tried desperately to hoist itself up onto the deck of 209 [by] . . . cynically summoning up the ghost of Martin Luther King," he writes in his autobiography.[44] But Connerly is protesting a bit too much here. It is true that when King's widow and son issued a statement condemning the misuse of his words and image, Connerly publicly disavowed the spot and said the person responsible for the ad had been fired. But the very next year he responded to criticism by Martin Luther King III with a letter that claimed, "Dr. King is not just your father." He added, "I truly hope that you do not blur the legacy of your father by becoming the spokesman for the 'preference cartel,' to such an extent that Americans begin to think of Dr. King as a proponent of color-conscious policies instead of remembering him as a champion of a color-blind society."[45]

For Connerly, as for all the ritual invokers of King, the reverend's actual words and thinking are unimportant in comparison to King the rhetorical device. When King's actual words began to unravel that rhetorical device, Connerly worked to knit it back together again. "I wrestled almost from the beginning of the campaign with the question of Martin Luther King," he writes:

> His 1963 speech was a great moment in our history because it summoned America in majestic terms to live up to one of its founding principles—that is, to strive for fairness, equity and colorblindness, and by doing this to create equal. . . . I knew too that at the end of his life King had been moving toward what would become affirmative action . . . and if he had lived he might well have wilted under the pressure from the preference cartel . . . I would still have revered [him] for the moral vision he had articulated in the past, but opposed him for how he had compromised that vision in the present.[46]

If Connerly knew King's life and thought as well as he suggests here, he had to realize that what he wrote was not true. By 1964 King was not only calling for what amounts to affirmative action but also answering the Ward Connerlys of that year: "It is impossible to create a formula for the future which does not take into account that our society has been doing something special against the Negro for hundreds of years," King writes in his classic book *Why We Can't Wait*:

> Whenever this issue of compensatory or preferential treatment for the Negro is raised, some of our friends recoil in horror. The Negro should be granted equality, they agree; but he should ask for nothing more. On the surface, this appears reasonable, but it is not realistic. For it is obvious that if a man is entered at the starting line of a race three hundred years after another man, the first would have to perform some impossible feat in order to catch up with his fellow runner.[47]

A year later, in a speech at Howard University that is generally recognized as outlining the rationale for affirmative action under Executive Order 11246, Lyndon Johnson paraphrased this same passage, including the metaphor of the runners starting a race centuries apart. Since none of this history advanced the arguments Connerly wished to make, it was treated as if it did not exist.

In short, Connerly's sharp response to the advertisement appears to be a reaction to a strategic error rather than an actual philosophical disagreement. Getting into a fight with the King family, Connerly saw, was not going to help the Proposition 209 campaign. Furthermore, the Dole campaign and the Republican National Committee swooping in with their $2 million ad buy threatened to involve the 209 effort in the complex calculations of a presidential campaign rather than the zero-sum choice that Connerly, Wood, Custred, and their supporters had worked so hard to trap Californians in.[48]

It was essential to the campaign that the deep equality King envisioned be flattened into the language of Proposition 209, which was so careful to avoid complexity that it did not even include the term "affirmative action." Having labored for years over every syllable, Custred and Wood were well aware that voters disliked "preferences" but favored "affirmative action." So when Wood and Custred first submitted the initiative to the California attorney general's office in 1993, they were irate when the attorney general issued a summary stating that the initiative would eliminate affirmative action. When the Connerly-championed version of the proposition finally appeared on the ballot, it forbade "preferential treatment" on the basis of "race, sex, color, ethnicity, or national origin" and nothing else.

On Election Day, November 5, 1996, Proposition 209 won 54 percent of the vote and became part of the California Constitution. At the time, women- and minority-owned businesses were receiving about 20 percent of state contracts—African Americans 1.8 percent ($50.6 million), Latinos 4.8 percent ($134.5 million), Pacific Asians and Asian Indians 2.2 percent ($62.2 million), and Native Americans 0.6 percent ($16.9 million).[49]

The impact of this sort of affirmative action was epitomized by Connerly himself: listing his business as minority owned had helped him land more than $1 million in state contracts between 1989 and 1994, and he sought new contracts as a minority owner during that period. He acknowledged taking advantage of a "repugnant" program, checking the box to indicate that he was a minority owner starting in 1988.[50] No fewer than fifteen of those who had hired one of Connerly's companies reported that they met affirmative action goals by doing so. But Connerly insisted it was not really affirmative action, since he had been forced to claim minority status in order to keep 100 percent of the contracts he otherwise would have been required to share with non-white-owned firms.[51] Ironically, even as Connerly campaigned to pull the minority contract ladder up behind him, the *Los Angeles Times* was reporting on a reality Connerly was intimately familiar with: "minorities and women remain largely shut out of the billions of dollars in public contracts awarded each year by California's three biggest government entities," in part because "contracting programs are highly vulnerable to exploitation by 'fronts'—white-male controlled businesses that fraudulently claim ownership by minorities and women."[52]

Unlike Connerly, not everyone who voted for Proposition 209 realized what it meant. One poll found that 60 percent of respondents did not realize that 209 would end affirmative action. An exit poll found that "when voters were asked whether they supported affirmative action 'to help women and minorities get better jobs and educations' 54% said yes, while 46% said no, exactly the opposite [of the] results on 209 that day."[53] In the end, 209's triumph reduced Black educational attainment and cut the career earnings of Latinos who were turned away from (or too discouraged to apply to) top schools, according to economist Zachary Bleemer. Bleemer did not analyze 209's impact on women but found that whites and Asians gained no significant bump in admissions or postgraduate earnings from the end of affirmative action.[54] These findings contradict Connerley's view that affirmative action's main products are minority self-doubt and the theft of opportunity from top students. But Connerly was soon scheming to replicate his victory in other states, and after opponents went to court to block Proposition 209 and lost, organizations like the Pacific Legal Foundation went to work in San Francisco, Sacramento, and elsewhere to root out anything that resembled affirmative action.[55]

19

ENTER EDWARD BLUM

In 1993, at the age of forty-one, a Paine Webber stockbroker named Edward Blum found his calling and, by his own lights, affirmed the values he learned from his parents: a father who had served in World War II and, as a Yiddish speaker, was tapped to help resettle Holocaust survivors at the conflict's end, and a mother who adored Franklin Delano Roosevelt and worked at a government job during the war. After the war, his father established himself as a traveling salesman and settled in Michigan, where Blum was born in 1952. He spoke Yiddish with his parents and still turns to it for favorite words like *emes* (truth). In 1961 the family moved to Texas, where his parents, who leaned left, supported the civil rights movement and protested segregation at a Woolworth store. Blum joked that he was probably the first Republican his mother ever met. He attended the University of Texas at Austin, where he became an activist for affirmative action, quotas included. Inspired by an African professor, Blum applied to and got into graduate school, with the goal of earning a Ph.D. in African literature. In part because of money troubles, he dropped out after a year and spent two and a half years teaching at a mostly Black elementary school. Next, feeling he was less effective as a teacher than he wished to be, he opened one of those neighborhood bookstores where part of the ambience is the conversation between the owner and the customers. Discussions with one regular, a University of Houston professor named Allan Stone, led to a close friendship and eventually to a conversion experience in which *Commentary* magazine played the part of holy book for Blum. He began to devour the magazine, which ran essays by superstar opponents of affirmative action such as Nathan Glazer and Charles Murray.[1]

Like many converts, Blum pulled his new belief system down over his soul. After behemoth bookstores like B. Dalton moved in and made his shop unsustainable, he became a successful stockbroker, but he held tight to his new beliefs and eventually decided to use them to change the world. The first thing he decided to fix was the electoral system in Texas. After he moved into the Eighteenth Congressional District in Houston, Blum discovered that its boundaries had been drawn to concentrate enough Black voters to elect a Black representative. The resulting district was so dominated by the Democratic-leaning African American vote that Republicans did not bother to field a candidate. "That pissed me off," Blum told journalist Tim Fleck. Blum's anger was intensified by positions taken by incumbent congressman Craig Washington. Blum, who is a staunch supporter of Israel, saw some of Washington's positions as bad for the Jewish state. In addition, Blum was troubled by the number of House votes Washington missed and by what Blum considered "wacky votes" against things like a supercollider for subatomic research.

In 1992 Blum jumped into the race, determined to unseat Washington. But he found that "business is not so great when you're in a primary running against Craig Washington. People asked, 'Who is this fool?'" Blum was happy to be Quixote, but he balked at the sort of windmill he was battling—the gerrymandered Eighteenth District. He found it easier going house to house in white neighborhoods, "where you could say, 'I'm running against Craig Washington' and you're a hero. I could have been a skinhead, and it wouldn't have mattered." In Black neighborhoods, Blum sometimes found himself at a loss. "You knock on a door, and a 38-year-old woman opens it with a baby on her hip. You introduce yourself as Edward Blum running for Congress, and she asks you what you can do to help her grandbaby. I was speechless. I had no idea what to say to her."

The fact that it is the job of members of Congress to have ideas about what to do for someone's grandchild seems not to have occurred to Blum. His description of the woman as a typical Black neighborhood resident resonates strongly with accounts published in *Commentary*, such as one Charles Murray wrote in 1985. Having been a *Commentary* reader since 1980, Blum's inability to respond to the woman may have been due to the presence of thoughts like Murray's in his head: that the best thing the government could do for the woman's grandchild was nothing at all. In "Helping the Poor: A Few Modest Proposals," a reply to critics of his hugely successful book *Losing Ground*, Murray points to an epidemic of out-of-wedlock births in poor communities, especially poor, Black, inner-city communities. "As the babies grow up," Murray alleges, "they not only continue to have problems; they also add to other people's problems. They tend to make schools hard to learn in and neighborhoods hard to live in. . . . They commit a disproportionate share of crimes and are disproportionately addicted to drugs." In other words, these out-of-wedlock births are a threat to society, and Murray blames Lyndon Johnson's social welfare programs for the growing number of these problem children. Ticking through a series of possible solutions—including the morally unsavory (for Murray) "carrot" of paying women not to have babies and the "sticks" of institutionalized stigmatization and denial of the right to vote—Murray lands on what he presents as a more modest albeit politically impossible solution: "Take away all governmentally-sponsored subsidies for irresponsible behavior, and the natural system will produce the historically natural results [fewer out-of-wedlock births and less poverty]. The residual problem, infinitesimal compared to the present one, can safely be left to the equally natural responses of relatives helping relatives, friends helping friends, and communities protecting communities."[2] Murray made similar arguments in "The Legacy of the '60s," published in *Commentary* in 1992, the year of Blum's run for Congress.[3]

So, Blum's speechlessness may have been attributable to the idea that a grandmother caring for her grandchild is just what the doctor—Dr. Murray—ordered, but candidate Blum could not bring himself to say so to an actual Black person, rather than the theoretical Black people who inhabit writings like Murray's.

In any case, the great lesson Blum learned from his congressional race, which he handily lost, was that the Eighteenth District was an abomination. While campaigning, he and his volunteers had a hard time figuring out which doors to knock on because the district had been generated by computer, with race playing a key role in which residences were in and which were out. When he later saw a *New York Times* article about the Supreme Court questioning a North Carolina district drawn to favor the election of a Black candidate, Blum said to himself: "Here's your calling, are you going to grab it?"

Blum reached out to right-wing think tanks and, eventually, to former Reagan administration official William Bradford Reynolds to gauge the feasibility of contesting the gerrymander in court. Reynolds estimated that his firm would require $1 million to guide the case through the courts, so Blum found a cheaper lawyer and acquired some coplaintiffs. His case, bundled with similar ones, rose all the way to the Supreme Court as *Bush v. Vera.* Blum won—with the aid of friend-of-the-court briefs from the Pacific Legal Foundation and from Clint Bolick and others at the Institute for Justice (founded in 1991 by Bolick and William H. "Chip" Mellor and maintained with money from the Bradley, Olin, and Scaife Foundations, among others).[4]

In the plurality opinion that handed Blum his victory, Sandra Day O'Connor applied strict scrutiny to the tailoring of the Eighteenth District, which, admittedly, resembled an illustration in a book of fractal geometry or perhaps a sunfish splattered by a meteor. O'Connor explained that the district had been drawn with the help of a new computer program called REDAPPL, which crunched data from the 1990 census about the racial composition of Houston neighborhoods and streets. Based on the census results, Texas was entitled to three new congressional seats—largely due to a rise in its minority population—so the legislature had decided to create two new Latino districts and reinforce a Black district. The redrawn Eighteenth District was a puzzle piece that fit perfectly with the new Latino Twenty-Ninth District. It was probably in the interlocking teeth of these two districts that Blum's campaign got chewed up.

The focus on race, O'Connor argued, had sidelined traditional race-neutral district-drawing criteria such as a compact and nonbizarre shape, protection of incumbents, and conformity to the twists and turns of county lines. She reasoned, "To the extent that race is used as a proxy for political characteristics [such as voting Democratic], a racial stereotype requiring strict scrutiny is in operation." Stressing the bizarreness of the two districts, O'Connor concluded that they had "caused a severe disruption of traditional forms of political activity" and had managed to "misuse race and foster harmful and divisive stereotypes without a compelling justification." John Paul Stevens, assuming the Thurgood Marshall role in this instance, penned a long dissent expressing extreme discombobulation over O'Connor's reasoning. First, he noted, districts like the Eighteenth had no monopoly on bizarre configurations. (He offered in an appendix some equally outlandishly drawn majority-Anglo districts.) Second, O'Connor's opinion had led the court "into a jurisprudential wilderness that lacks a definable constitutional core and threatens to create harms more significant than any suffered by [Blum and the other] individual plaintiffs challenging districts."[5]

After all, the only harm to Blum had been that he and his volunteers had to pore over maps while campaigning. The harm to residents of the Eighteenth District if its African American vote were diluted might be a change in representation from someone who knew how to communicate with a Black grandmother to someone like Blum, who seemed to see her through the condescending neoconservative lens of *Commentary* magazine.[6] And it was no small matter that the 1965 Voting Rights Act had put Texas and other states under federal supervision because of their history of defying the Fifteenth Amendment and denying Blacks and other minorities their voting rights.

Stevens went on to argue that taking race into account was actually a good way to protect incumbents, a time-honored practice favored by both parties that resulted in a 97 percent success rate for both incumbents and incumbents-in-waiting for whom districts were drawn. "It is not easy," Stevens wrote, "for the State to achieve these results while simultaneously guaranteeing that each district enclosed the residence of its incumbent, contained the same number of people, and complied with other federal and state districting requirements." Furthermore, because minority community leaders had pressured the legislature to create majority-minority districts, the claim that the new districts perpetuated damaging stereotypes made no sense.[7]

In short, "Blacks usually vote Democratic" is not the same type of stereotype as a Murray-style "Black children born out of wedlock are enough of a threat to society that depriving their parents of the vote might be worth considering." It is not even the sort of stereotype Blum voiced when he said that the key to solving the problems of poor Blacks in the inner city was to have people like himself "inculcate middle-class virtues and values that will eventually get them out of the ghetto." (Many living in the ghetto already have "middle-class" virtues and values.)

Blum, who could easily leave the Eighteenth District if he chose, unlike many of its poorer residents, nevertheless defeated Texas governor George W. Bush and others who appealed *Bush v. Vera* to the Supreme Court. Decades later, Stevens was still unable to fathom what O'Connor and the rest of the plurality—including Marshall's replacement, Clarence Thomas, who thought O'Connor hadn't gone far enough—were thinking. "How a state's decision to provide better representation of minority groups in the legislature can be treated as a violation of the Equal Protection Clause remains one of the most puzzling questions that I confronted during my tenure on the Court," he wrote in 2019.[8]

For Blum, the victory was sweet vindication of his view that affirmative action in the drawing of congressional districts, or just about anywhere else, was racial discrimination plain and simple. As icing on the cake, the $100,000 he had invested in the case was returned to him in the wake of the Supreme Court decision.

Looking for new worlds to conquer and advice on how to conquer them, Blum reached out to Ward Connerly and even made a pilgrimage, together with some friends, to sit at Connerly's feet in the wake of the Proposition 209 victory. Although Blum's long, thoughtful face and even-toned voice might seem designed to project Vulcan rationality, he had tears in his eyes after the meeting and said, according to one of his friends, "I feel about meeting Connerly the same way I felt after finishing my bar mitzvah with my rabbi."[9]

By then, Blum had founded the Campaign for a Color-Blind America. Seeking to pull off a Connerly-like coup in Texas, Blum and his organization gathered the twenty thousand signatures needed to launch Proposition A, a ballot measure to end affirmative action in Houston contracting. But unlike Connerly, Blum was up against a canny, popular adversary who was well aware of events in California: Houston mayor Bob Lanier, a former real estate tycoon. Lanier had set a goal of awarding contracts for 17 percent of city construction, 24 percent of professional services, and 11 percent of purchasing to minority-owned firms. He warned Houstonians that "a group from California" was trying to wreck their city and its cosmopolitan future and told them, "Let's not turn back the clock to the days when guys like me got all the city's business."[10]

Lanier did more than that. He convinced the Houston City Council to revise the language submitted by Blum's group so that the proposition referred explicitly to affirmative action. Instead of posing a question about racial preferences, as Blum wanted, the proposition asked, "Shall the Charter of the City of Houston be amended to end the use of affirmative action for women and minorities in the operation of the City of Houston employment and contracting, including ending the current program and any similar programs in the future?"

Connerly traveled to Houston more than once to champion Proposition A, but in the majority-minority city, he was no match for Lanier—or for the Black community, which he perceived as somewhat threatening: "Whenever I made a public appearance the city's minority employees showed up and stood in the back of the room glowering with their arms crossed over their chests, looking like members of Louis Farrakhan's praetorian guard, the Fruit of Islam."[11] Although Connerly helped convince many whites, most Houston minorities voted against Proposition A, and the measure was defeated 54 to 46 percent. "We were swindled," Blum concluded.[12] Insertion of the term "affirmative action" and other deviations from his original wording amounted, he said, to asking the voters, "Should the city drown young children and puppies?" Sheila Jackson Lee, the Black, no-nonsense Yale and University of Virginia Law School graduate who had defeated Craig Washington (in part because of his chronic absenteeism) and now represented the Eighteenth District, told the *New York Times*, "This vote will affirm to the rest of the country and the entire world that Houston will remain a city of opportunity."[13]

Meanwhile, Blum had other problems. Paine Webber informed him that his public speeches, op-eds, and other activism, some of it carried out in the company's offices, might negatively affect its business. Therefore, Paine Webber would no longer clear his anti–affirmative action op-eds for publication.[14] Blum resigned, not without bitterness, and reportedly not without a hefty settlement.[15]

By then, Ward Connerly had launched (on Martin Luther King's birthday, no less) the American Civil Rights Institute (ACRI), an effort to replicate the results of Proposition 209 in every state in the nation. Connerly took the conservative seizure of the civil rights vocabulary to new heights, vowing that if King were to come back from the dead and issue a cease-and-desist order to Connerly and his supporters, they would correct King and explain what he actually meant to say in 1963.[16]

It is true that King's dream went beyond the African American community and included poor whites in a contemplated Bill of Rights for the Disadvantaged, but he made no demand for color blindness.[17] King held up African Americans' quest for equal rights as an example to other disadvantaged Americans, not as an object of their resentment, and, as noted earlier, he called for affirmative action–like measures. Indeed, King called on the federal government to, in effect, join the civil rights movement, and Lyndon Johnson responded. Yet Johnson's—and, in a different way, the Ford Foundation's—answering of King's call became an abomination for Connerly and the rest of the anti–civil rights movement. Apparently unaware that Johnson was paraphrasing King, Connerly writes in his autobiography that "civil rights professionals" have substituted for King's vision "the notion of blacks as hobbled runners, in Lyndon Johnson's unfortunate metaphor."[18]

Connerly's ACRI, created in 1997, quickly became a major force with the help, in 1998 alone, of $475,000 from the Bradley Foundation, $225,000 from the Olin Foundation, and $275,000 from the Sarah Scaife Foundation, among other donors.[19] The starkness of the resulting contradictions is plain when one recalls that the Bradley and Olin Foundations were major backers of Richard J. Herrnstein and Charles Murray's *The Bell Curve*, a 1994 book that sought to demonstrate the intellectual inferiority of African Americans. Their argument was so controversial that the Manhattan Institute, where Murray wrote *Losing Ground* with $25,000 of support from the Olin Foundation and $75,000 from the Scaife Foundation, fired Murray, lest *The Bell Curve*'s connections to the deepest mythology of racism taint the institute.[20] But Michael Joyce, the man behind the $25,000 Olin grant, left Olin to run the Bradley Institute just in time to catch the project dropped by the Manhattan Institute. Piping in about $1 million in grants, Joyce made sure Murray had no financial concerns during the writing of *The Bell Curve.*

In the completed book, old stereotypes are made young again, and the case against affirmative action is made in language that, despite key similarities to Connerly's pronouncements, is the opposite of discourse that might clear the way for Connerly's color-blind America. "Affirmative action is part of this book," Herrnstein and Murray explain, "because it has been based on the explicit assumption that ethnic groups do not differ in the abilities that contribute to success in school and the workplace. . . . Much of this book has been given over to the many ways in which that assumption is wrong." By the time they arrive at this sentence, they have already divided Americans up by IQ scores and argued that the answer to each of the following questions is yes: "Could low intelligence possibly be a cause of irresponsible childbearing and parenting behavior? . . . Could low intelligence possibly be a cause of unemployment and poverty?" Education can do only so much for the poor, the authors conclude.[21]

"Diversity," the thread from which Justice Powell suspended affirmative action, is a dangerous canard for Herrnstein and Murray because, "given the differences in cognitive abilities of the students in different groups, diversity has other consequences." A typical student (who, in the authors' formulation, is almost certainly white) would be able to distinguish students ranking in the top 10 percent of IQ scores from those in the bottom 10 percent on the basis of classroom discussion, lab work, and behavior in the library. This typical student could not help but see that 52 percent of those in the bottom 10 percent are Black. Said student would be justifiably resentful because it would be clear who was "getting a large edge in the admissions process." This justifiable resentment was at the root of campus clashes in the news while Herrnstein and Murray were working on the book.[22] Conclusions they draw from gaps between Black and white students' SAT scores are equally fantastical and unscientifically oblivious to alternative explanations.

Nevertheless, just as *Losing Ground* had become the reigning gospel of welfare reform with the help of a massively well-funded campaign (including payment to influential media figures to attend a two-day seminar on the book), *The Bell Curve* was dropped like an expensive bomb into the poverty alleviation and affirmative action discussion.[23] The American Enterprise Institute sent advance copies to likely supporters and kept the book from those who were likely to write negative reviews. Sympathetic pundits were brought to Washington to be briefed on the book by Murray himself (Herrnstein died of lung cancer the same year the book appeared). This "strategy paid off when the book was released and the publicity machine put into action, long before the scientific establishment could garner a look and form any coherent judgments."[24] When experts in the fields it purported to contribute to did get ahold of it, the authors' claims were ripped to shreds. But by then, *The Bell Curve* had served its purpose by breathing new life into politically useful stereotypes about Black intellectual inferiority, hypersexuality, and compulsive criminality and by casting doubt on the quest for deep equality in general and affirmative action in particular.[25]

Of course, it may be unfair to hold Connerly guilty by association with the foundations that made *The Bell Curve* possible. After all, the anti–affirmative action argument is a bit like the three-card monte con game, where the mark is shown two black cards and one red card that are then turned facedown and moved around at lightning speed while the con man chants, "always the red, never the black." The mark wagers cash that he will be able to follow the cards and pick the red one. To challenge the anti–affirmative action argument, one must identify the "these folks are inferior" card as it is shuffled around with the "equality" and "fairness" cards. But in a skillful anti–affirmative action argument, this is very hard to do. Although stereotypes anchor the entire discourse, those stereotypes tend to be subliminal—so much so that calling attention to them can lead to accusations of playing the "race card." After all, even *The Bell Curve*'s authors claim to be fighting racism: "That bigotry exists is incontestable," they write. "But that does not mean that bigotry would prevail in the American job market as of the end of the twentieth century if the vast machinery of antidiscrimination law did not exist. Much of what we have presented . . . suggests the opposite."[26]

Faced with this sort of con game, is it possible that Connerly (and his disciples like Blum) simply cannot see the red card? This seems unlikely, since they all play three-card monte so adeptly themselves. Connerly, for instance, is in rare form when he responds in his autobiography to William G. Bowen and Derek Bok's *The Shape of the River*, an epic 1998 pro–affirmative action analysis of data compiled by the Andrew W. Mellon Foundation on the experiences of more than one hundred thousand students at selective colleges. Dismissing stereotypes of Black cognitive inferiority, Bowen (who was head of the Mellon Foundation at the time) and Bok question Herrnstein and Murray's reliance on test scores, noting that SAT-style "objective" criteria cannot measure "resilience, creativity, and the ability to benefit from criticism," which are ultimately more important than tests in determining success in college.[27]

This caused Connerly to reach for his revolver, so to speak. "The black success stories Bok and Bowen boasted about were for the most part, people who received preferences every step of the way: getting into college, then into graduate and professional school, then into a job, and then promotion within the job."[28] This is not far from Rush Limbaugh's 2010 claim that Barack Obama was failing as president because for "the first time in his life there's not a professor around to turn his C into an A, or to write the law review article for him he can't write. He is totally exposed."[29]

Nevertheless, insisting that he was trying to end stereotypes and create justice, Connerly launched an anti–affirmative action ballot initiative in Washington State that passed by a margin of 58.3 to 41.7 percent.[30] In Florida, Governor Jeb Bush, feeling Connerly's breath on his neck, ended affirmative action by executive order.[31] True to form, Connerly was not happy. He complained that Bush's top 20 percent *race-neutral* admissions order posed a threat to the *second* 20 percent of students at Florida's most competitive schools. He refused to acknowledge the door it opened for those at high schools with less stellar reputations and, in all likelihood, fewer resources.[32] Nevertheless, in the three-card monte blur of the national debate, Connerly's ACRI was, for a time, the hottest ticket in the anti–affirmative action arena. In the year 2000 Blum shut down his own organization and moved to ACRI's Washington, DC, headquarters to become Connerly's director of legal affairs. Blum looked forward to benefiting from Connerly's bigger budget, deeper infrastructure, and, in all likelihood, greater ability to make governors tremble in their boots.

20

CONSERVATIVE THREE-CARD MONTE

By the time Edward Blum joined forces with Ward Connerly, the conservative counterforce was casting a shadow from California to Florida. Clarence Thomas had been on the Supreme Court for nine years, participating at every opportunity in the dismantling of Thurgood Marshall's legal legacy. Right-wing talk radio was in full cry, espousing grievance, racial resentment, and distrust of other sources of information. Fox News was on its way to number one in the ratings, driving a never-ending message about government overreach, threats to viewers' safety and freedom, and, most importantly, the mainstream media's dishonesty. The result, historian Brian Rosenwald explains, was the discrediting and removal of mainstream media as "an arbiter of truth" and the freeing of political extremists to "make outlandish claims that no one could effectively dispute."[1] By 2021, these forces, working in tandem with Republican Congresses and White Houses, had split the American mind in two. That year, close to a majority of those who responded to a University of Virginia poll agreed that it would be best if Republican-voting states and Democratic-voting states divided into two separate countries.[2]

A key factor in this divide has been the renewal or manufacture of stereotypes—the red cards in games of three-card monte—connected with affirmative action in particular and race in general. Perhaps the only issues in American life that have stirred more passion are abortion and, for a critical period, drugs. All three issues are promoted by the counterintelligentsia as indicia of the liberal attack on American family and religious values, but no issue carries more psychological and historical weight than race.

One memorable three-card monte game in the 1970s caused ripple effects that still mesmerize the nation. This game grew out of a battle between the IRS and Bob Jones University. The segregated university had admitted a few Black students but prohibited interracial dating, claiming it was contrary to the Bible. The IRS revoked the university's tax-exempt status and, after some back-and-forth, demanded back taxes in the amount of $489,675. This enraged evangelicals, and Paul Weyrich's strategic antennae picked up that rage. He began to organize and, with Jerry Falwell, grew the concept of the Moral Majority around the idea that the IRS had violated religious liberty. Already, Weyrich and Falwell were playing a masterful game of three-card monte: "Although Bob Jones, Jr., the school's founder, argued that racial segregation was mandated by the Bible, Falwell and Weyrich quickly sought to shift the grounds of the debate, framing their opposition in terms of religious freedom rather than in defense of racial segregation," historian Randall Balmer explains.[3]

Adopting the Falwell-Weyrich line, the Reagan Justice Department took the side of the university. But university president Bob Jones III waved the red card like a flag, lambasting the Supreme Court's eight-to-one decision that his school's racial rules were not biblical as he claimed but were contrary to the public good that a charitable, tax-exempt entity was supposed to advance.[4] Speaking from the pulpit, he said: "We're in a bad fix in America when eight evil old men and one vain and foolish woman can speak a verdict on American liberties. Our nation from this day forward is no better than Russia insofar as expecting the blessings of God is concerned."[5] Keeping the red card out of sight, Falwell called the *Bob Jones* decision a "blow against religious liberty." Ronald Reagan, like a monte dealer spying the police approaching, responded to the *Bob Jones* decision with a terse, "I will obey the law."

Living in the midst of such shenanigans affects the psyche. Claude M. Steele, a Black psychologist who became provost of Columbia University, identifies a phenomenon he calls "stereotype threat," which he experienced himself in graduate school:

> [It] was a place where intellectual ability was just about the most prized human characteristic, and it wasn't wasted on me that, in the American consciousness, this was precisely the characteristic my group was stereotyped as lacking. Lest I forget that, the science of psychology itself [of which Herrnstein was a practitioner], like a child picking a scab, keeps raising the question of whether blacks and whites have the same genetic intellectual capacity. In those days Arthur Jensen [one of Murray and Herrnstein's sources] raised doubts in his paper entitled "How Much Can We Boost IQ and Scholastic Achievement?" Later it would be Richard Herrnstein and Charles Murray in *The Bell Curve*. Psychology poses this question with seasonal regularity. And there I was, a specimen of the group in question. . . . [The resulting anxiety—the "stereotype threat"] could cause a paralysis of personality, especially around faculty, even in informal settings like program picnics.[6]

In 1991, in a precursor to the Herrnstein-Murray uproar that affected Steele, the Center for Individual Rights successfully defended the free speech privileges of National Association of Scholars member and City University of New York professor Michael Levin. Levin was being investigated by the university because of his published belief that the intellectual inferiority of Blacks made them prone to criminality and worthy of harassment by the police.[7] Though Levin was an outlier in the pride he took in being a sort of faceup red card, the conservative monte game was having a wide impact in the post-Reagan era. It drove attitudes and policies that accelerated the incarceration of African Americans and Latinos that had ramped up during the Nixon administration but exploded during the Reagan and George H. W. Bush presidencies as a result of the so-called war on drugs.[8]

Thus, even as affirmative action opened doors for middle-class and some poor African Americans and Latinos (as well as Native Americans, Asians, and white women), the political three-card monte game, alive on the airwaves and in the netherworlds of criminology, psychology, and politics, was sending many poor and some middle-class African Americans and Latinos into increasingly crowded and dehumanizing prisons. By 1990, the number of Black men in prison had surpassed the number of Black men in college.[9] By 1995, one in three Black men between the ages of twenty and twenty-nine was in some sort of incarceration. By 1999, there were a total of 604,200 African Americans enrolled in institutions of higher learning and about 757,000 Black men in prison—285,000 of them incarcerated for drug-related crimes. Driving this phenomenon was the ultimate in anti–affirmative action activity: a frenzy of new drug laws and harsh sentencing requirements that landed devastating blows on Black and Latino communities. The powerful role of mythology in this expansion of incarceration is clear when one considers scholar David Garland's observation that, during the 1990s, there were "widespread and sustained reductions in American crime rates."[10]

If John Ehrlichman is to be believed, Richard Nixon, the expander of affirmative action, also threw down a devastating red card:

> [The] Nixon campaign in 1968, and the Nixon White House after that, had two enemies: the antiwar left and black people. . . . We knew we couldn't make it illegal to be either against the war or black, but by getting the public to associate the hippies with marijuana and blacks with heroin, and then criminalizing both heavily, we could disrupt those communities. We could arrest their leaders, raid their homes, break up their meetings, and vilify them night after night on the evening news.[11]

Where the Nixon administration went, the white supremacist faction of the anti–civil rights movement was sure to follow. In 2002, when Ward Connerly was still barnstorming the country and proclaiming that the only remaining source of racial animus was affirmative action, Jared Taylor, president of the white supremacist New Century Foundation, and coauthor Glayde Whitney were endorsing the racial profiling of Blacks and citing "the philosopher Michael Levin" as a key source in an essay for *Mankind Quarterly*.[12] Like so much theorizing about Black intellectual and moral inferiority, their article is not an example of good scholarship. Michael J. Lynch, in an article that also appeared in *Mankind Quarterly*, details the many ways in which Taylor and Whitney maul the rules of statistical analysis to reach their conclusions.[13] In trying to prove that too little attention has been paid to Black-on-white crime, for instance, they overlook the fact that whites far outnumber Blacks in the United States. When corrections are made for this and other errors, the conclusions they reach "are reversed" because "the disproportionate ratio[s] . . . of Black-on-White violent crime . . . that appear to 'shock' Taylor and Whitney are actually a function of their method for calculating odds."[14]

None of this neutralized the contribution of such men to the production of anti-Black stereotypes and Black misery. Roger Ailes's Fox News certainly got the message about Black-on-white crime. "Black on white" was the most prominent phrase in a word cloud built from Fox News crime coverage. The result of this racialization of crime coverage, according to economists Elliott Ash and Michael Poyker, was that elected judges in areas with high Fox viewership doled out harsher sentences to appeal to voters who had been hopped up on Fox. And those harsher sentences were likelier to fall on Blacks, who were arrested more frequently than whites committing the same drug-related offenses. Ash and Poyker reason that since "Blacks are disproportionately arrested for non-violent drug-related offences, the effect could be driven by racial bias in media messag[ing]." This inference is bolstered by their finding that higher Fox viewership resulted in more Google searches for a certain racial slur.[15]

Even for those who were not arrested or sentenced, what law professor Charles Ogletree calls "the presumption of guilt" had an effect. In Los Angeles between 2003 and 2004, Blacks were stopped and frisked 3,400 times more often than whites, and Hispanics were stopped 360 times more often. Yet, Ogletree reports, Blacks were 42.3 percent less likely than whites to be found with weapons and 23.7 percent less likely to be found with drugs. Hispanics were 32.8 percent less likely than whites to be found with weapons and 34.3 percent less likely to be found with drugs.[16] The difference between the likelihood of being frisked and the likelihood of being found with incriminating or dangerous possessions is a rough measure of the power of stereotypes. And as journalist Greg Palast discovered, this can have electoral consequences. He concluded that many thousands of African Americans in Florida were barred from voting in 2000 because, in defiance of state law, they were wrongfully placed on lists of felons who could not vote because their civil rights had not yet been restored.[17] Palast convincingly argues that this swung the 2000 presidential election from Al Gore to George W. Bush. Furthermore, since Bush appointed the avidly anti–affirmative action Samuel Alito to the Supreme Court and made the harder-to-predict but reliable restrictor of voting rights John Roberts chief justice, this purging of Black voters in Florida is a rough measure of the effects of the fast-moving red card.

The constant revivification of negative stereotypes by Herrnstein, Murray, Levin, the war on drugs, Fox News, and—extrapolating from Ash and Poyker—Limbaugh and the rest of conservative talk radio lengthened prison sentences for some Blacks and—again extrapolating from Ash and Poyker—probably Latinos as well (one of the words in the Fox word cloud but not in those for CNN and MSNBC is "deportable"). Native Americans fared no better.[18]

The presumptions of guilt and echoes of civil death resonating in antiminority stereotypes were a fungible currency in the anti–affirmative action movement because they connote a general unworthiness—a general state of being nothing more than a Patrick Chavis in waiting, regardless of how exalted one's position might be. All this contributes to the sense that whites (and Asians) are victimized by the admission of Blacks (as well as Latinos and Native Americans) to competitive universities.

21

THE CENTER FOR INDIVIDUAL RIGHTS VERSUS THE UNIVERSITY OF MICHIGAN

Working, perhaps inadvertently, in a kind of pincer movement with Connerly's ballot initiatives, the Center for Individual Rights (CIR) helped nationalize the trope of Blacks as "guilty by admission."[1] Not long after the appearance of Bowen and Bok's *The Shape of the River*, CIR placed full-page advertisements in fourteen major college newspapers, calling on students to dig for information on reverse discrimination at their schools and offering a handbook on how to start a lawsuit. CIR cofounder Michael Greve, always a master of the catchy statement, set the stage for the campaign with a *Weekly Standard* essay in which he proclaimed that if university presidents were forced to open the books on their diversity policies, "they'd all be in jail." Along with a National Press Club event that kicked it off, this effort "quickly converted CIR from a relatively unknown public litigator to a national poster boy for racial conservatives," according to Theodore Cross, then editor of the *Journal of Blacks in Higher Education*. Cross argued that CIR's newspaper ads "had the clear purpose of increasing racial animosities and fears on college campuses." Furthermore, they aimed to trigger "the racial stereotypes and biases of university alumni in order to persuade them to place financial pressures on their admissions officers, administrators, and trustees."[2] CIR even threatened individual trustees with legal action. The prestigious University of Virginia was sufficiently cowed to alter its admissions policies.[3]

Meanwhile, in Michigan, philosophy professor Carl Cohen submitted a Freedom of Information Act (FOIA) request for details about the admissions criteria at the University of Michigan at Ann Arbor, where he taught. Cohen was a leader of the local chapter of the American Civil Liberties Union and a regular contributor to the NAACP Legal Defense Fund, and although he contributed anti–affirmative action essays to *Commentary* magazine, he was no Charles Murray. An article in the *Journal of Blacks in Higher Education* celebrating reports that Blacks were admitted at a higher rate than whites at a number of top schools made Cohen suspicious and prompted his FOIA request. The documents he received intensified his suspicions. Admissions grids showing acceptable and unacceptable combinations of grades and test scores revealed that acceptable tests scores and GPAs for underrepresented minorities—in both the undergraduate college and the law school—were lower than those of whites. He pressured the university's president and regents to end this "shocking" situation, and when he got no response, he wrote a raging (but rigorously reasoned) *Commentary* article to make the case that affirmative action was indefensible (a conclusion he had reached in previous *Commentary* essays on *Wygant* and other cases).[4]

Within a relatively short time, law school head Lee Bollinger took over as president of the university and set about revising its approach to affirmative action.[5] But by then, the waves Cohen made had reached the state legislature, and he was summoned to testify about his findings.[6] At a March 1, 1996, subcommittee hearing, Cohen, whose deep-set eyes and sharp facial angles gave him an aura of authority, gave lawmakers a stark warning: "Racial tension in our country today grows ever more pronounced; since the early 1970s, when racial preferences began in earnest, race relations have been going downhill." About the era of Jim Crow laws, lynchings, assassinations of civil rights workers and leaders, and the near-total absence of Blacks and Latinos at the University of Michigan, Cohen offered a kind of shrug: "we cannot right the wrongs of times past by engaging now in the same invidious practices that engendered these wrongs."[7] At the same time, he was careful to stress his benevolent intentions. He was there not to call attention to "constitutional issues" but to arrest "the *damage* race preferences do *to the minority preferred* and to race relations generally."[8]

Gloria Woods, president of the Michigan chapter of the National Organization for Women, told the same subcommittee that Cohen did not know what he was talking about. "Routinely being denied a job because of one's gender or race is humiliating," she said. "This man," she added, "comes from a position of privilege. I don't think people in positions of privilege can make decisions for others on how those others are humiliated [or] are benefited by programs that help them become middle class."[9]

But Cohen saw his position as one of almost absolute moral and constitutional purity.[10] And he was not alone. Two of the people who heard his testimony—state representatives Deborah Whyman and David Jaye—had followed the *Hopwood* case closely and longed to achieve its results in Michigan. So they called the Center for Individual Rights and offered to make a deal with Michael Greve: they would round up plaintiffs for CIR to choose from if CIR would come to Michigan and replicate its achievement in Texas. Greve and his partner, Michael McDonald, traveled to Michigan and met with Cohen—one sitting on either side of him on a couch in his office—to examine his report.[11]

The next step was critical: find a charismatic plaintiff. Whyman and three others sent out a press release calling on anyone who felt victimized by the university's "discriminatory racial preference policies" to contact them. The press picked up the story, and calls poured into the representatives' offices. The four lawmakers whittled the would-be plaintiffs down from about one hundred to a dozen or so. Among that dozen, CIR found what the *Detroit News and Free Press* called "the perfect poster child" for a case: Jennifer Gratz. The daughter of a policeman and a lab technician in the 94 percent white Detroit suburb of Southgate, Gratz achieved a 3.8 GPA at her high school and an 83 percent on the ACT, while organizing blood drives, performing athletic stunts on the cheerleading team, tutoring other students in math, and serving as student body vice president, baseball team statistician, and homecoming queen.[12] It did not hurt that Gratz was blonde and photogenic, with "all American" good looks. Convinced that people with less impressive records had been accepted to Ann Arbor, she was so certain of being admitted that she applied to no other school. When she was wait-listed and then rejected, the devastation and shame were so great that she did not tell anyone outside her family, not even her boyfriend.

From CIR's point of view, Gratz was a walking rebuttal of the claim that resentment of affirmative action was a disease of angry white males and conservative zealots. In the words of one newspaper headline, she had suffered a shattered dream that her every move in high school had been designed to achieve. That being said, she was in fact very angry. After reading her rejection letter, the first thing she said was, "Dad, can we sue them?"[13] In 1997 she got in touch with Whyman's group.[14]

Ironically, in picking Gratz, CIR was taking a page from the playbook written by Thurgood Marshall and the NAACP Legal Defense Fund. Greve and McDonald quite consciously appropriated the NAACP strategy of using "the courts instead of the legislatures, to change the law." But unlike Marshall, Greve wanted to eject the government from almost all aspects of private life. Before the presidency of Franklin Roosevelt, "most things in life and the economy were none of the government's business," Greve observed. "Then we had six decades of everything is the government's business." It was absurd for government to micromanage race at a time when "being black was not a disadvantage and being white was not an advantage," Greve insisted.[15]

In the bottomless pit of ironies that statements like Greve's open up is the fact that his entire life was made possible by various kinds of government micromanagement, starting with the Marshall Plan, a massive welfare and recovery program implemented by the US government to rebuild Germany (where Greve was from) and the rest of Europe after World War II. A tax consultant's son, Greve took a dislike to the largesse the German welfare state doled out while he was studying at the tuition-free University of Hamburg. He was particularly offended by—but apparently did not refuse—government stipends to students who, Greve assumed, "simply pocketed the money while doing essentially no academic work." Greve considered entering German politics but, feeling like an outsider, decided he would not be allowed to burrow into the German political system deeply enough to change it.[16] Offering a theory of what was wrong with the system, Greve lamented in 1985:

> The success of liberal capitalism coincided with the development of the welfare state. Hard as it is to roll back the latest entitlement program even in the United States, Americans can easily distinguish the Great Society from liberal capitalism. . . . When today's Christian Democrats [the dominant party in Germany at the time] ask themselves why their predecessors were able to construct a remarkably stable democracy on the ruins of Nazism, the answer is mass prosperity. To them, that means the welfare state.[17]

With the hindsight of the 2020s—when economic inequality and the poisoning of political wells by the anti–civil rights movement have left US society balanced uncertainly like a crystal glass on the edge of a table—it seems clear that Greve might have found something to celebrate in the bargain the German government struck with its people. But in 1985 the Reagan administration was in full cry, and the welfare state was a monster that had to be destroyed.

Greve had not only the luxury but also the glory of using the intellectual capital from the welfare state in one country to attack the welfare state in another. This sort of transnational three-card monte exemplifies what German philosopher Jürgen Habermas identifies as a side effect of the welfare state's own success: "In times of crisis the upwardly mobile groups of voters who have received the greatest direct benefits from the welfare state development can develop a mentality concerned with maintaining their standard of living and may ally themselves with . . . the strata concerned with 'productivity,' to form a decisive coalition opposing underprivileged or marginalized groups."[18] The upwardly mobile Greve traveled to the United States on a Fulbright fellowship—a US government program whose core purpose is to foster "the acquisition of empathy—the ability to see the world as others see it, and to allow for the possibility that others may see something we have failed to see, or may see it more accurately."[19]

Empathy and seeing others' point of view may have been among Greve's concerns in 1981 when he settled in at Cornell University to earn a Ph.D. in political science.[20] But by the time he and CIR launched their campaign against the University of Michigan, he seemed more interested in lacerating the opposition than in understanding it. Commenting on the "Michigan Mandate," a program to increase the university's number of minority students, faculty, and staff, Greve was withering: The "'Michigan Mandate' is a thing of beauty," he wrote. "It's a plan, a strategy, a manifesto. It's diversity-speak, Newt Gingrich on acid, and TQM [total quality management] gobbledygook. Enacted and periodically updated by Kaiser Duderstadt [university president when the mandate was adopted], the Mandate committed U of M to do anything and everything to help nice minorities."[21] Here, Greve, who spoke English with a shadow of a German accent that Cohen found charming, can be heard exulting in his mastery of American zinger vocabulary ("gobbledygook," "diversity-speak," "on acid," and "Kaiser" as a reference to Teutonic iron-fistedness). But there is no nod to the self-interested humanitarianism of the Marshall Plan or to the fact that the Fulbright fellowship that brought him to the United States was itself justified by a species of diversity-speak.

Of course, this divide between the Fulbright-style pursuit of international diversity and the rejection of Michigan's mini–Marshall Plan for "nice minorities" echoed some of Senator J. William Fulbright's own attitudes.[22] An opponent of desegregation and the Civil Rights Act of 1964, Fulbright, as Charles King explains, "occupied a zone inhabited by so many white leaders of the [post–World War II] era, especially if they took an interest in global affairs. It was a position whose evil lay in its sheer banality. With the great questions of war and peace clamoring for attention, they felt full citizenship for Black Americans just wasn't that important."[23]

My guess is that Greve, arriving in the United States in 1981 and focused on the rigors of graduate study and the dawning of the Reagan revolution, knew little about Fulbright's Mr. Hyde side. But knowingly or not, Greve was steeped in a version of political science that had never sought to explain the massive resistance to the civil rights movement that Fulbright took part in.[24] Thus, while still a graduate student, Greve lamented in an article for the American Enterprise Institute's house organ, the *Public Interest*, that the Reagan revolution did not entirely fulfill its promise to "defund the Left" and pull the plug on the tax exemptions, grants, and Great Society creations, such as the Legal

Services Corporation, that liberals had used (with the help of people like Ed Steinman) to revise American law.[25]

Unable to defund the Left, Greve apparently decided to join it, at least strategically, by cofounding CIR as a tax-exempt, 501(c)(3) outfit using legal techniques perfected by the NAACP Legal Defense Fund.[26] It is true that CIR sometimes took on Black clients and even sued a historically Black college that offered diversity scholarships to whites, but its marquee cases featured white plaintiffs whom it championed as the final victims of racial discrimination. In the Michigan cases, the American faces of the racially oppressed belonged to Jennifer Gratz and another white woman, Barbara Grutter, who had applied to the University of Michigan Law School at age forty-three and been rejected because "her racial ancestry was not correct," according to CIR's newsletter.[27]

CIR senior counsel Terry Pell, who became the organization's public face after Greve abruptly left for the American Enterprise Institute in 2000, took a slightly softer line. During a 1999 appearance on the TV show *Frontline*, Pell went so far as to agree with a major point pressed by supporters of affirmative action: that the SAT might not be the last word in the measurement of academic merit. But because schools used their students' scores as a metric of their own status as institutions, those that hoped to measure up to the Harvards and Yales of the world had to continue to place heavy weight on test scores.[28] The one thing schools were absolutely forbidden to do, Pell said, was to use affirmative action to compensate for the gap between the scores of Black and Latino students and the scores of white and Asian students. Unlike Greve and Connerly, Pell acknowledged that American society had not become race blind. But, he insisted, the question is "whether the government, in making official decisions and handing out benefits—like admission to institutions— . . . should be color blind."[29]

Responding to this line of argument during the same broadcast, Derek Bok called it a "supreme irony" that the past use of racial classifications to destroy opportunity should become the reason for banning the present use of racial classifications to create opportunity. In any case, the role of race in admissions had been blown out of proportion by the enemies of affirmative action, Bok added. "I don't think people realize [that] a lot of whites are being admitted with lower board scores and grades than blacks who were excluded. 43% of all black applicants in our sample who finished in the top 5% of their high school classes were denied admission. 25% of black students with 1400 board scores were denied admission. Now why was that? Because the admissions officers were not just looking at grades and scores."[30] To this, Claude Steele added in a *Frontline* interview that Black students who believed they were taking a standardized test as part of garden-variety research did as well as white students, while those who were told the tests measured intellectual ability did much worse. But none of this affected the core arguments put forward by Pell, Greve, and their colleagues.

In the *Gratz* case, CIR brooked no nuance, even when it came from district judge Patrick Duggan, who ruled that even though the pre-1999 system that had denied Gratz admission was not constitutional, *Bakke* meant that weighing race for diversity's sake still was. When the Sixth Circuit Court of Appeals reversed the lower court's ruling and upheld the University of Michigan Law School's admissions process, CIR published an unsigned essay full of Greve-style sarcasm. It hooted at Duggan's distinction between the pre-1999 and post-1999 admissions systems, condemned the appeals court's action, and declared that "anyone who has been on one of these college campuses recently will have a bitter laugh—most of those institutions are enclaves of carefully enforced political correctness and liberal orthodoxy. The only kind of diversity they welcome is the most superficial kind—a variety of skin tones."[31]

Pell, a bespectacled, brown-eyed blond with a pleasant tenor voice, was much less diplomatic than he had been on *Frontline* at a CIR press conference held the day before Supreme Court oral arguments in the *Gratz* and *Grutter* cases. He called the higher dropout rate among minority and especially Black admittees to the University of Michigan clear evidence of what has become known as the "mismatch theory": "Michigan may boost the number of minority students who get into its system, but this kind of admissions system makes it hard to keep minority students at the university. . . . These individuals are told that they are being accepted according to the same standard as everybody else, only to show up in Ann Arbor and find out that that is clearly not the case."[32]

Rebutting a version of this reasoning promulgated years later by Richard Sanders and Stuart Taylor in their 2012 book *Mismatch: How Affirmative Action Hurts Students It's Intended to Help, and Why Universities Won't Admit It*, Jeff Strohl, director of research at the Georgetown Center on Education and the Workforce, told me that mismatch theorists have the story "exactly backwards [when] they state we do a disservice by enrolling students with relatively lower SAT scores (compared to the school's median). The data shows us that disadvantaged students actually do better (graduate more) when attending selective schools whose median scores are higher." According to Strohl, these students "end up demonstrating that they have what it takes. Because the university actually puts the resources into them. They are getting much more than they pay in tuition in [terms] of educational services, support, mentoring, cohort effects. . . . So this is where the Sanders hypothesis falls apart."[33] In fact, Strohl, Carnevale, and a coauthor reported in 2016 that "three times more students are qualified to attend the top 468 universities than actually go to them. These qualified students, particularly minorities, are being held back under the false assumption that they cannot succeed, when in reality, they can."[34]

Strohl suggests something that Pell conveniently overlooks: students drop out for economic as well as academic reasons. (Edward Blum dropped out of graduate school partly for economic reasons.) It is unscientific to look at dropout percentages and say, "Aha! Unqualified!" But CIR, of course, was all about the "aha!" It received an assist in its University of Michigan cases from the like-minded National Association of Scholars in the person of proven affirmative action killer Thomas Wood himself. This closing of the CIR and Proposition 209 halves of the anti–affirmative action pincer is taken up in the next chapter.

22

THE MEANING OF 20 POINTS

At a CIR news conference the day before the Supreme Court heard oral arguments in the Michigan cases, Terry Pell declared that part of CIR's mission had already been accomplished. "As a result of the publicity surrounding our cases," he said, citing a *Washington Post* poll, "Americans of all outlooks now are opposed to race even being a factor in admissions. . . . This astounding shift in public opinion is a clear repudiation of the University of Michigan's public relations strategy in these cases, which has been to flatly acknowledge that it discriminates on the basis of race."[1] Although this was not exactly the university's position, Pell was right that he was winning the contest for what A. Philip Randolph called the most powerful weapon in America: public opinion.

The other part of CIR's mission was to knock down the strongest of the remaining pillars supporting affirmative action—Lewis Powell's notion that diversity has educational and workplace value. Thus, as the *Gratz* and *Grutter* cases worked their way through the legal system, University of Michigan administrators scrambled to prove that diversity is indeed a rare element worth mining applications for. The university called out one of its big guns: professor of psychology and women's studies Patricia Gurin, who sat on the Russell Sage Foundation's Committee on Race, Culture, and Contact. Gurin had been researching diversity at the university since 1991, and in 1998, the year after the *Gratz* and *Grutter* cases were filed, she had become interim dean of the College of Literature, Sciences, and the Arts—the immediate target of Gratz's lawsuit. So, as the National Association of Scholars later insisted, she indeed had a stake in the outcome.

Nevertheless, the study Gurin produced was widely acknowledged to be rigorous and convincing in its demonstration that diversity is a precious educational commodity. Drawing on survey data about students at the University of Michigan and elsewhere, Gurin showed that experience in diverse classroom and campus environments is especially beneficial to whites, who are the group least likely to have grappled with the complexities of race and ethnicity. Engagement with diversity raised these students' "scores on measures of complex thinking and social/historical thinking," Gurin reported.[2]

Students of all races and ethnicities who had been challenged by diversity, whether inside or outside the classroom, were better equipped to thrive after graduation in an increasingly multiethnic, multiracial, and multicultural society, she added. Such graduates' secret weapon was what might be called democratic knowledge—something the SAT does not test for.[3] Being educated in diversity, Gurin found, raised students' democratic IQ because it helped them (1) learn "a more complex, less automatic mode of thought"; (2) "understand and consider the multiple perspectives that are inherent in a diverse environment"; and (3) practice dealing with the "conflicts that different perspectives sometimes entail."[4] The case Gurin made was so convincing that Judge Duggan affirmed the legitimacy of Michigan's undergraduate admissions procedure (revised repeatedly, starting in 1996), even as he declared that Gratz had been wronged.[5]

For CIR and its allies, this meant that Gurin's methodology and results had to be discredited. To that end, the National Association of Scholars commissioned Thomas Wood to critique Gurin's work. Wood and mathematician Malcolm Sherman teamed up to write a 212-page report that showed why, in the words of their subtitle, *Justice Powell's Diversity Rationale for Racial Preferences in Higher Education Must Be Rejected.*

This was the first shot in a mini-war during which Gurin responded to Wood and Sherman's claim that she had ignored key findings about diversity and had made fundamental methodological errors.[6] Coming to Gurin's defense, and responding to a National Association of Scholars amicus brief that relied on Wood and Sherman's work, the Stanford Institute for Higher Education Research affirmed Gurin's findings.[7] As a non–social scientist, I make no attempt to analyze the scientific details, but historically, the negative effects of an *absence* of diversity at the University of Michigan have been painfully obvious. In the 1980s racist jokes were broadcast over the university radio station and racist flyers were distributed around campus. And although the climate had improved by the mid-1990s, racist incidents continued to occur right through the time the *Gratz* and *Grutter* cases were filed.[8]

In an effort to turn all this gloomy history around, university president James Duderstadt instituted the Michigan Mandate to both increase diversity and make the campus more inclined to welcome it.[9] He spent $27 million beefing up programs for minority students and established scholarships for Black, Latino, and Native American students. He also blessed the infamous admissions grid that weighted the test score–GPA combinations of minorities differently from those of other applicants.[10] Although it is hard to justify this weighting system, it is important to remember that the university's goal, under both the grid system and its successor, was to avoid simply ranking test score–GPA combinations from lowest to highest. Instead, it sought to recognize not only diverse perspectives but also special talents that might electrify the educational space in Ann Arbor.[11]

Starting in 1998, applicants were evaluated on a 150-point scale. Each applicant could get up to 80 points for a strong GPA, up to 10 points for attending a highly competitive high school, 8 points for completing difficult course work, and up to 12 points for high ACT or SAT scores.[12] A student who achieved perfect scores across these academic categories would earn 110 points. The remaining 40 points were awarded based on nonacademic factors. For example, an applicant could receive 10 points for being a Michigan resident, another 6 points for being from a geographically underrepresented part of Michigan, and 4 points for being a close relative of an alumna or alumnus. Applicants could also earn points for meeting criteria in a "miscellaneous" category: 20 points for being socioeconomically disadvantaged or a graduate of a disadvantaged high school, 20 points for being an underrepresented racial or ethnic minority, 20 points for being a student-athlete, 5 points for being a man applying to nursing school, or 20 points awarded at the discretion of the provost. All these nonacademic points represented a species of affirmative action.

Importantly, a minority applicant who was from an underrepresented Michigan county could earn 36 out of 40 points; this could be increased to 40 points if the applicant was among the small minority of underrepresented students who were relatives of alumni. But a white socioeconomically disadvantaged applicant from an underrepresented Michigan county could also earn 36 points, increased to 40 points if related to a Michigan alum. So by 1998, the Sturm und Drang whipped up by the *Gratz* case was a fight over 0 points.[13] As we weigh the cries of injustice, dishonesty, arrogance, and racism from Michael Greve, Thomas Wood, and Jennifer Gratz herself, it is important to keep this in mind, and it is worth considering that a white student-athlete or a white beneficiary of the provost's largesse was more likely to have alumni parents and earn the extra 4 points to raise the student's nonacademic total to 40.

The intensity of those cries is yet another indication that affirmative action is a battle over getting and keeping agenda-setting power rather than a battle over "preferences." In the anti–affirmative action narrative, the awarding of 20 points for being an underrepresented minority amounted to a shameful and stigmatizing preference, whereas 20 points for being favored by the provost, 16 points for coming from an underrepresented county, or 10 points for residing anywhere in Michigan were perfectly red, white, and blue reasons for preferential treatment.

I dwell on this because it brings us back to the issue of status as agenda-setting power. Someone who is admitted to a selective university is granted high status that can have lifelong social and financial consequences and provide access to agenda-setting power or at least access to agenda-setting powers that be like the provost. Although it was later clothed in the language of equality and fairness, Gratz's first reaction to her rejection letter was humiliation at her sudden loss of status. Feeling thrust out of her own future, deprived of the transcendental merit she assumed she had, she gave up her dream of becoming a doctor: "If I'm not qualified to go to the University of Michigan," she asked herself, "am I really qualified to be a doctor?"[14] Well in advance of the call for plaintiffs from Whyman and the other politicians, Gratz had settled on affirmative action as the cause of her lost future.[15]

Gratz was so committed to showing that her rejection was illegitimate that, years later, she not only condemned the grid system but also misrepresented its 150-point replacement by asserting (in an essay published by the Heritage Foundation) that it was a 100-point system that awarded 20 points to "select minorities" and only 12 points for a perfect SAT score, neglecting to mention the 10 points for Michigan residency or the 16 points for residing in an underrepresented county.[16] Nor did she exhibit any of the uncertainty expressed by Pell when a *Washington Post* reporter asked him how Gratz knew that her spot at Michigan had been taken by a minority. Pell replied, "She doesn't."[17]

Gratz was not alone in discounting such inconvenient nuances. When her case reached the Supreme Court, the six–three majority determined that Gratz's and fellow plaintiff Patrick Hamacher's Fourteenth Amendment and Title VI rights had been violated. Chief Justice William Rehnquist, writing for the majority, found that "unlike Justice Powell's example, where the race of a 'particular black applicant' could be considered without being decisive . . . the LSA's [College of Literature, Science, and the Arts'] automatic distribution of 20 points has the effect of making 'the factor of race . . . decisive' for virtually every minimally qualified underrepresented minority applicant."[18]

Justice David Souter had been appointed by President George H. W. Bush in 1990, but his performance on the court scandalized conservatives. He stressed in a dissent that the 20 points for underrepresented minorities "does not set race apart from other weighted considerations." He then ticked through the points awarded for "athletic ability, socioeconomic disadvantage, attendance at a socioeconomically disadvantaged or predominantly minority high school, or at the provost's discretion." He concluded that, since "admission is not left entirely to inarticulate intuition, it is hard to see what is inappropriate in assigning some stated value to a relevant characteristic."[19]

Ruth Bader Ginsburg, the tiny, mighty-spirited Bill Clinton appointee who was already building the portfolio of dissents that would earn her the moniker the "Notorious RBG," cited legal scholars Stephen Carter and Goodwin Liu in an attempt to bring the hammer down on the majority opinion. From Carter she quoted an eloquent observation: "To say that two centuries of struggle for the most basic civil rights have been mostly about freedom from racial categorization [the trigger for strict scrutiny] rather than freedom from racial oppression is to trivialize the lives and deaths of those who have suffered under racism"[20] From Liu, Ginsburg took the insight that underrepresented minorities are *so* underrepresented that giving them some small edge in the admissions competition has almost no impact on the much larger pool of white applicants.[21]

Some shrewd observers have pointed out that people like Gratz also suffer from the law of supply and demand—which is perhaps the most important law in a capitalist country. In effect, the plenitude of applicants similar to Gratz lowers their value, and the scarcity of applicants from underrepresented groups raises their value—according to Michigan, by 20 points. In that sense, there is nothing more all-American than affirmative action.

AFFIRMATIVE ACTION AS NATIONAL SECURITY

Gratz's victory was not the end of affirmative action in Michigan. On the same day the decision in her case was announced, the court ruled in *Grutter* that the law school's affirmative action plan was constitutional. Interestingly, the decisive evidence for Sandra Day O'Connor, who wrote the majority opinion, came not from Gurin or from Bok and Bowen (whom she cited) but from high-ranking retired US military officers who had filed a brief stressing that the US war effort in Vietnam was hurt by the fact that an overwhelmingly white officers corps commanded soldiers who were disproportionately minority. The lack of minority officers "seriously threatened the military's ability to function effectively and fulfill its mission to defend the nation," according to one general quoted by the officers. In an effort to shore up the national defense, the officers reported, the military instituted a vigorous affirmative action program in its service academies and ROTC (taking care to conform to the *Bakke* guidelines).[22] Justice O'Connor appeared to recognize that this kind of military cohesion was inseparable from the sort of national cohesion that, according to the University of Michigan, affirmative action policies contribute to.[23] With the caveat that she expected affirmative action to no longer be necessary in twenty-five years, O'Connor and the majority let the law school's admissions policy stand.

Derrick Bell might have seen this as an example of interest convergence. But O'Connor's fellow justice Clarence Thomas—whose views on race sometimes read like a through-the-looking-glass version of Bell's—called her majority opinion "benighted."[24] In doing so, Thomas no doubt burnished the hero status he had been building among conservatives since his days in the Reagan administration. Nominated to the Supreme Court by George H. W. Bush, prepped for his nomination hearings by Clint Bolick (among others), and supported by much of the anti–civil rights movement through what turned out to be a traumatic confirmation process (after his former subordinate Anita Hill accused him of sexual harassment), Thomas has emerged as an accomplished thrower of intellectual thunderbolts. David Brock, a square-jawed, closeted gay conservative, was in the midst of the pro-Thomas (and therefore anti-Hill) behind-the-scenes strategizing and opposition researching that occurred during the Senate confirmation hearings. Years later, after he had come out of the closet and broken with the increasingly antigay conservative movement, he recalled the power of Thomas's Black face. Except for the Gulf War, Brock observed, "nominating Clarence Thomas to the Supreme Court was the only worthwhile thing George Bush did in office, so far as most conservatives were concerned. Thomas . . . was a prized symbol whose presence in the GOP legitimized conservative attacks on civil rights policies."[25]

Thomas's career is in some ways a creation of the anti–civil rights movement. According to Brock, two lawyers in the presidential orbit advised Bush to nominate Thomas: Ichabod Crane lookalike C. Boyden Gray and Lee Lieberman, "a diminutive woman in Coke-bottle glasses who was known as 'Rasputin' for her immense, behind-the-scenes influence over Bush's judicial picks." Gray, Lieberman, and Thomas himself, Brock writes, decided that the "only way to slide a hard-right conservative through the Senate was to choose a 'black Bork.'" Conservatives had never forgiven the Left for torpedoing Ronald Reagan's nomination of Robert Bork to the Supreme Court, and now they pulled out all the stops. Paul Weyrich deployed a nationwide network of "antiabortion, antipornography, and pro–school prayer activists" to support Thomas and set up a Washington, DC, war room to swat down any allegations against him.[26]

Lieberman, at the tip of the spear, was not only a Bush whisperer but also a founder of the Federalist Society (which coached Thomas on confirmation strategy) and a crafter of the Federalist mission to, in Brock's words, "roll back decades of liberal jurisprudence in areas such as civil rights, property rights, due process rights, and reproductive freedom."[27] When Thomas emerged from his confirmation battle bloodied but with a lifetime claim to Thurgood Marshall's vacated seat, the anti–civil rights movement had reason to be pleased.

Thomas, however, did not see himself as a character in someone else's plot. His "benighted" remark was no doubt heartfelt and fully thought out—a repurposing of an insult once directed at Africa and Africans. Blacks, he asserted, "can achieve in every avenue of American life without the meddling of university administrators." Giving a nod to the friend-of-the-court brief from the retired military leaders, Thomas conceded that only national security considerations can justify "racial discrimination," but no such considerations were involved in the comparatively "trivial" arena of law school admissions. As for diversity, it had marginal educational value at best. And why, Thomas wanted to know, did Michigan need an elite law school anyway? Putting his own spin on an established anti–civil rights movement line, Thomas wrote that the desire for elite status was at the root of the evil of both requiring high LSAT scores and easing that requirement for selected minorities. The easing of this requirement stained affirmative action beneficiaries with an indelible stigma, Thomas wrote. But Thomas contradicted his vote of confidence in Black students and piled on the stigma by going all in on the mismatch theory and describing minorities at elite schools as inevitably "overmatched" and unable to "succeed in the cauldron of competition."[28]

Writing such passages, sometimes wearing his own hurts on his sleeve, and speaking in a deep, rumbling voice heavy with authority, Thomas can be an especially complicated alloy of contradictions, high ideals, and low vengefulness. At times, his thinking comes close not only to Derrick Bell's but also to that of his one-time Yale Law School classmate Lani Guinier. When Clint Bolick caricatured her as a "quota queen," Guinier responded by noting that her father had been a "quota of one" at Harvard in 1929, when he was barred from the segregated dormitories and "denied any financial aid on the ground that one black student had already been awarded a full scholarship."[29] During the *Grutter* case, Guinier pointed to Thomas himself as an embodiment of how affirmative action is supposed to work.

Thomas's admission to Yale was only one of the benefits he received from affirmative action, Guinier points out. His path to Yale was cleared years earlier by admission to the selective College of the Holy Cross and by the careful mentoring he received there from Father John Brooks. Brooks believed that the Black students in Thomas's cohort "may not have been fully prepared for Holy Cross," but it was up to Holy Cross to help them close the gap between themselves and those who were better prepared. In Guinier's telling, Thomas turned out to be a perfect example of the sort of student Jeff Strohl and Anthony Carnevale describe—one who rises to the level of better-credentialed classmates.[30] Guinier's point seems to be that affirmative action is not a "badge of inferiority," as Thomas (echoing an opinion in *Plessy v. Ferguson*) put it, but a badge of opportunity.

Perhaps the unkindest cut of all in Thomas's defection to the anti–civil rights movement was, from Guinier's point of view, the fact that she herself mentored him, helping him win a summer fellowship at a civil rights law firm during his years at Yale.[31] In the Gratz–CIR–National Association of Scholars camp, all these contradictions were like unheard overtones of Thomas's "trumpet blast" against affirmative action.[32]

AFTERMATH

The trumpet blast did not suffice for the anti–civil rights movement or for the victorious Gratz. She was doubled over psychologically from the "gut punch" delivered by the defeat of Barbara Grutter.[33] But she found a new purpose. "Over breakfast in New York City, the day after the Supreme Court decision," Gratz recalled in an article for the journal of the National Association of Scholars, "Terry Pell suggested I contact Ward Connerly. . . . That afternoon I was on the phone with Ward, and within a few weeks we had launched what initially was the Michigan Civil Rights Initiative"—modeled almost word for word on the California Civil Rights Initiative.[34]

This was actually Connerly's second bite at the anti–affirmative action apple in Michigan. His first came in 1998, when he flew to Michigan to testify in favor of a bill (ultimately unsuccessful) intended to prohibit affirmative action in the state. While Connerly was still on the ground, the bespectacled, big-haired Deborah Whyman announced a Connerly-style ballot initiative in an effort to avoid a long journey through the courts.[35] Her initiative did not succeed. Attacking not only affirmative action but also an effort to include gays in a hate crimes bill, and facing a defamation suit brought by a gay rights group she had accused of promoting pedophilia, Whyman lost a 1998 bid for election to the state senate.[36]

Five years later, it was up to Gratz and Connerly to pick up the ball. By then, Gratz had been married for six months and had moved to California. But after her tête-à-tête with Connerly, she laid down the law to her husband: "I'm quitting my job, and I'm moving back to Michigan. And I know you can't move to Michigan, so we're going to have to figure out how we can make this work."[37] Her husband got with the program and drove her back to her home state. For the next three years, with Connerly's counsel, Gratz's Michigan Civil Rights Initiative collected signatures and finally got Proposal 2—with language almost identical to Proposition 209—on the Michigan ballot.

23

SHANTA DRIVER TAKES ON THE ANTI–CIVIL RIGHTS MOVEMENT

In 1995 a determined activist lawyer named Shanta Driver moved to block Ward Connerly's effort to end affirmative action at University of California campuses by cofounding the Coalition to Defend Affirmative Action by Any Means Necessary (BAMN). When Connerly turned his eyes toward Michigan, BAMN moved its operation there.[1]

A striking biracial woman who earned an undergraduate degree in psychology and social relations from Harvard in 1975, Driver is an almost compulsive activist. She has been among those trying to protect an abortion clinic from pro-life supporters by forming a human chain and shouting, at allegedly ear-splitting volume, "Keep your rosaries off my ovaries!"[2] She has both run for election to a school board and provoked school board members to seek an injunction against her because of her disruptive behavior at meetings to protest layoffs.[3] In 1994 she was thrown out of the funeral of a youth shot by a police officer after she grabbed a microphone and called the mayor a hypocrite for coming to the funeral after doing nothing to discipline the officer.[4] She has run at various time for leadership of a union local, for the Detroit City Council, and for mayor of Detroit.[5] Long before the idea became a gift for opponents of her causes, she called for abolition of the police.[6]

Finally, perhaps seeking the extra quantum of agenda-setting power that attorney status brings, Driver entered law school at Wayne State University when she was in her forties and earned her J.D. in 2002. Wasting no time, she became part of a legal team that intervened in the

Grutter case on behalf of BAMN and other groups.[7] Determined to fuse law and activism to jump-start a new civil rights movement, she and BAMN made moves that discomfited the university and some students who believed that BAMN's penchant for theatrical militancy did not represent them. At the same time, university administrators capitalized on BAMN's "successful mobilization of mass demonstrations," according to Ellen Barry.[8] BAMN also had some success in court. In 2004, Driver, as the head of BAMN, contributed to a district court setback for Gratz and Connerly's effort to end Michigan affirmative action. When Connerly and Gratz pressed on, Driver had a resistance infrastructure in place, ready to deploy against them.[9]

Nevertheless, the Connerly-Gratz Michigan Civil Rights Initiative (MCRI) gathered more signatures than it needed to get the proposition on the 2006 ballot. But BAMN and another group, Operation King's Dream, appealed to the State Board of Canvassers, offering evidence that MCRI representatives had bamboozled some individuals by telling them they were signing a petition that *endorsed* affirmative action. In the subsequent legal wrangling, the Board of Canvassers was found to lack the authority to investigate allegations of fraud. The case was brought before district court judge Arthur J. Tarrow, with Driver arguing that the issue was one of "systematic, unrelenting, pervasive, racially-motivated voter fraud." Tarrow agreed about the fraud, but he found that because MCRI did not target minority voters alone—rather, it defrauded Michiganders without regard to race—the action was color blind and therefore unstoppable: "Because the Voting Rights Act is not a general anti-fraud statute, but rather prohibits practices which result in unequal access to the political process because of race, the Court must conclude that the defendants' conduct, though unprincipled, did not violate the Act."[10]

In the end, the Michigan Court of Appeals ordered that the signatures be certified, and the Connerly-Gratz measure, Proposal 2, was approved by 58 percent of those who cast ballots. "Voters under the age of 40 were the only group to oppose the measure in significant numbers," one poll found. "Men overwhelmingly supported the ban; women narrowly opposed it. Democrats opposed it while Republicans and independents favored it. Black voters strongly opposed the proposal but it was passing among white voters."[11] The interest-divergence work done by CIR and the rest of the anti–civil rights movement had succeeded.

Driver and her organization immediately went to work to undo the codification of Proposal 2 as article 1, section 26 of the Michigan Constitution. Eventually, BAMN's case reached the US Supreme Court as *Schuette v. Coalition to Defend Affirmative Action*, and Driver decided to face the justices herself. But before entering the court, she raised a bullhorn, surveyed the crowd of twenty-five hundred young supporters through her stylish shades, led them in a chant of "They say Jim Crow—we say, 'Hell, no!'" and declared she wanted to be a voice for a new civil rights movement.[12]

Driver had coauthored briefs that played a part in an appeals court victory over the new provision in the Michigan Constitution, but this was her first appearance before the Supreme Court. During oral arguments, she had some noticeable stumbles in comparison to her colleague Mark Rosenbaum, who was making his fourth appearance before the Supreme Court and representing a group of students, faculty, and prospective applicants to the University of Michigan who had joined the effort to invalidate section 26. Driver was also a novice in comparison to her and Rosenbaum's opponent, the boyish Michigan solicitor general John J. Bursch, who was making his sixth Supreme Court appearance.

Driver wasted little time in challenging the race-neutral preferences of the conservative justices. She called for the court to "bring the 14th Amendment back to its original purpose and meaning, which is to protect minority rights against a white majority." When Justice Scalia asked her whether there was "any case of ours" that viewed the Fourteenth Amendment as she did, she admitted, "No case of yours."[13] But Justices Sotomayor and Ginsburg thought Driver was on solid ground when she pointed to cases that forbade any restructuring of the political process in a way that placed a special burden on minorities seeking to preserve their rights under the new system. Since the changes to the Michigan Constitution excluded efforts to lobby the university to consider race—but did not exclude efforts to lobby for modifications of other admissions criteria—pro–affirmative action minorities would have to change the state constitution to reintroduce race as a consideration, while alumni parents would not have to go to such lengths if they wished to increase the advantages enjoyed by their children.

Sotomayor, whose nomination to the Supreme Court had been bitterly challenged by the anti–civil rights movement because she once called herself a "wise Latina," agreed with Driver.[14] In fact, she came to Driver's rescue when a question from Justice Alito about this burden on minorities threw Driver off balance and caused her to stumble through an answer. Not every burden on minorities could trigger prohibition of a restructuring of the political process, Sotomayor noted. But restructuring could be barred when the "political process has changed specifically and only for race."[15] Accepting Sotomayor's formulation, Driver regained her balance. In light of the fact that the Supreme Court upheld affirmative action in the *Grutter* case, she suggested, it was not unreasonable for minorities to expect diversity to be a factor in admissions decisions. Scalia accused her of conveniently changing an earlier claim she had made to Justice Roberts that the case turned on whether affirmative action truly benefited minorities. Driver offered an effective riposte. The two answers, she said, were two halves of a test that section 26 failed to pass. The passage of Proposal 2 not only eliminated a policy beneficial to minorities but also restructured the political process to make it almost impossible for them to restore the lost policy. Furthermore, Proposal 2 changed the constitution to prohibit consideration of race while ignoring the advantages related to legacy status and other nonacademic factors. To change the Michigan Constitution back to its previous form, minorities would have to mount an expensive campaign, while those lobbying and bending the ears of agenda setters in an effort to expand other nonacademic considerations would have to do no such thing.

Six months later, the Supreme Court handed down its ruling. Writing the plurality opinion, Justice Kennedy carefully demolished the precedents established by the cases Driver relied on when she argued that a special burden had been placed on resource-poor minorities. Kennedy insisted that earlier embodiments of the Supreme Court had gone too far in a key busing case, *Washington v. Seattle School District*, which the court of appeals had relied on in the case won by BAMN and Driver, and that Rosenbaum had relied on as well. Making the Seattle case and its characterization of what counts as an excessive burden a precedent would clear the way, Kennedy avowed, for greater racial tension and for maneuvers designed to frustrate the will of the voters.[16]

Sotomayor responded with a lengthy Thurgood Marshall–esque dissent that journalists felt obliged to cover, in part because Sotomayor broke her own precedent and read a portion of it from the bench when the decision was announced. Like Marshall, she offered a capsule history of race in America, including passages about the visceral experience of being nonwhite in environments where that made one suspect. She cited Marshall himself, as well as Ginsburg, Breyer, Brennan, Blackmun, White, and Stevens in defending the appeals court's use of the Seattle case and another key precedent: "nothing the Court has said in the last 32 years undermines the principles announced in [those two cases]." Sotomayor emphasized, "Race matters. Race matters in part because of the long history of racial minorities being denied access to the political process."[17]

As Joan Biskupic notes, the issues involved in *Schuette* hit close to home for Sotomayor.[18] A self-described "affirmative action baby," Sotomayor fits the paradigm of the minority student who does not have the highest test scores but thrives in an elite school. In her autobiography, she stresses that she feels no need to apologize for the "look wider, search-more affirmative action that [at] Princeton and Yale had opened doors for me." Making it clear that she brooks no mismatch theories, she adds:

> I had been admitted to the Ivy League through a special door, and I had more ground to make up before I was competing with my classmates on an equal footing. But I worked relentlessly to reach that point, and distinctions such as the Pyne Prize, Phi Beta Kappa, summa cum laude, and a spot on the *Yale Law Journal* were not given out like so many pats on the back to encourage mediocre students.

The shaming of affirmative action beneficiaries, she observes, is "another face of the prejudice that would deny them a chance even to try."[19]

Sotomayor's fellow Yale Law School graduate Clarence Thomas joined a concurrence in which Scalia lamented the dragging of the court into a "twilight zone" where it had to answer "the frighteningly bizarre question: Does the Equal Protection Clause of the Fourteenth Amendment *forbid* what its text plainly *requires*?" Sotomayor, both in her main text and in thrusting and parrying footnotes, crossed sabers with Scalia and the rest of the plurality. Answering Scalia's insistence that equal protection applies to individuals and not groups, Sotomayor wrote, "This criticism ignores the obvious: Discrimination against an individual occurs because of that individual's membership in a particular group. Yes, equal protection is a personal right, but there can be no equal protection violation unless the injured individual is a member of a protected group of individuals. It is membership in the group—here the racial minority—that gives rise to an equal protection violation." "Today's decision," she concluded, "eviscerates an important strand of our equal protection jurisprudence."[20]

Debating Shanta Driver about a year later on *Fox News Sunday*, Jennifer Gratz opined that Sotomayor's dissent "took the discourse to a level that was beyond what we've seen, and I think her behavior, quite frankly, was unbecoming of a Supreme Court Justice."[21] The *National Review*, which had been very much present at the creation of the anti–civil rights movement, proclaimed Sotomayor's dissent "legally illiterate." Margaret Burnham of Northeastern University Law School, however, called Sotomayor "our new great dissenter" and "Thurgood Marshall's rightful heir."[22]

24
BLUM TAKES OVER

By the time *Schuette* concluded, Edward Blum had left Ward Connerly's organization, spent a few years at Linda Chavez's Center for Equal Opportunity, and finally landed at the American Enterprise Institute.[1] He then proceeded to single-handedly replace CIR as the prime mover of high-profile anti–affirmative action cases. Thanks to funding from major anti–civil rights organizations, Blum was able to steadily expand his impact on American law. Through DonorsTrust, which collects money from benefactors it allows to remain anonymous, Blum's Project on Fair Representation received $1.5 million between 2006 and 2011 and a total of $3 million between 2008 and 2015.[2] DonorsTrust also gave Blum administrative support.

The year before *Schuette*, Blum orchestrated a case on behalf of Abigail Fisher, the daughter of one of his friends. Like Jennifer Gratz, Fisher was devastated when she was rejected by her dream school, the University of Texas at Austin. Like Gratz, she blamed affirmative action because the university had restored the policy after the *Grutter* decision overruled *Hopwood*. *Fisher v. University of Texas at Austin* reached the Supreme Court in 2013, and the seven–one majority, concluding that the Fifth Circuit Court of Appeals had given too much deference to the university, sent the case back to the Fifth Circuit, instructing the lower court to "verify" that UT–Austin's use of affirmative action could survive strict scrutiny. In 2016 *Fisher* boomeranged back to the Supreme Court, which had been left short-handed by the unexpected death of Antonin Scalia and the recusal of Elena Kagan.

The remaining majority let UT–Austin's affirmative action plan stand, over bitter objections from Clarence Thomas and Samuel Alito. Salvaging what he could, Alito sent a signal to future litigants by stressing that Texas's admissions policies were unfair to Asian applicants. In doing so, he ignored a friend-of-the-court brief from the Asian American Legal Defense and Education Fund asserting that claims the university discriminated against Asians are "entirely unsupported by evidence."[3] Blum had already spun off a new organization from Project on Fair Representation called Students for Fair Admissions, and in 2014 he filed suit against the University of North Carolina and Harvard University, accusing both of racial discrimination in general and Harvard of discrimination against Asians in particular.[4]

While he awaited the outcomes of the new cases and contemplated the defeat in *Fisher*, Blum was not idle. In 2013, the year the *Fisher* case first arrived at the Supreme Court, Blum completed the other half of his anti–civil rights pincer movement and struck a tremendous blow against voting rights that still has the American electoral system reeling. In doing so, he put into practice theories worked out in part by one of his anti–civil rights movement colleagues, Abigail Thernstrom, whose parents had been even further left than Blum's.

In her 1987 book *Whose Votes Count? Affirmative Action and Minority Voting Rights*, Thernstrom argues that, although it was once a necessary counter to the South's massive resistance to African American suffrage, section 5 of the Voting Rights Act (VRA)—which required federal preclearance of voting law changes in nine formerly Jim Crow states and in parts of six others—led to excessive race-consciousness in the electoral process.[5] In 2009, convinced that the election of Barack Obama meant the old civil rights movement had reached both its zenith and its conclusion, Thernstrom wrote:

> Integration was the aim of the civil rights movement in the 1950s and much of the 1960s, and, by the ultimate test, American politics is now integrated. Obama's victory contradicted everything most black voters had long been led to believe. . . . America in black and white, separate and unequal—that was still the conventional wisdom, particularly in African American circles. By any meaningful

measure, it was no longer true—and had not been for many years. Yet civil rights spokesmen, the mainstream media, and politicians in both parties continued to poison the racial climate by feeding the deep distrust and alienation that remained ubiquitous among blacks.[6]

Who knew that it was civil rights spokesmen and the rest who gave rise to Rush Limbaugh's ditty about "Barack the Magic Negro," Tea Party rallies (supported by anti–civil rights movement superfunders the Koch brothers) portraying Obama as a witch doctor, and Donald Trump's path to the presidency paved by the relentless questioning of the authenticity of Obama's birth certificate and boosted by heavy investment from anti–civil rights movement bankroller Robert Mercer?[7] Of course, acknowledging some of this would have required Thernstrom to see into the future. But by 2009, when her new book, *Voting Rights—and Wrongs*, appeared, the writing (including some of her own) was already on the wall.

In *Voting Rights—and Wrongs*, Thernstrom defended herself against critics of *Whose Votes Count?* by claiming, "I came to a greater appreciation of the benefits of race-conscious districting in the South" and by insisting that the surviving lions of the original civil rights movement were not in touch with the new realities of race. Even the legendary John Lewis, beaten to within an inch of his life during a 1965 march for voting rights (depicted on the cover of this book), was just too close to the issue. According to Thernstrom, "It cannot be said too strongly or too often: the skepticism [about scrapping section 5 of the VRA] of those, like Georgia representative John Lewis, who cannot forget the brutality of those years, is understandable. But the South they remember is gone."[8]

In a passage that must have been music to Blum's ears (assuming that he read the book, which was published by his own American Enterprise Institute), Thernstrom writes, "Majority-minority legislative districts . . . protect minority voters' 'candidates of choice' from electoral defeat, giving these voters a sheltered status enjoyed by members of no other groups." Invoking *Gratz* and *Grutter* later in the book, she asks a key question: "What principle separated acceptable from unacceptable racial classification? The Court has had no answer to that question—in voting rights cases, or in those involving education, employment, or contracting."[9] Indeed, the Supreme Court, running cold in *Gratz* and hot in *Grutter*, had given the nation no clear answer. Thernstrom, Blum, and their sponsors set out to engineer one.

Thus, as Congress prepared to debate reauthorizing the full Voting Rights Act in 2005, Blum used funds from the American Enterprise Institute, the Searle Freedom Trust, and elsewhere to commission a scholarly study of Black voting rights in the states covered by section 5.[10] Not waiting for the study's authors to publish their book, Blum collaborated with Thernstrom (who was serving as George W. Bush's vice chair of the US Commission on Civil Rights at the time) on an executive summary of the portion of the report covering Louisiana. The two shared the happy news that the "initial goals of the Voting Rights Act have long since been achieved in Louisiana."[11]

Next, Blum weaponized the Texas section of the report to defend the partisan redrawing of that state's electoral map after Republicans gained control of the Texas legislature and, without waiting for the usual trigger of the decennial census, rushed into a gerrymander that they claimed replicated what the Democrats had done when they held power. The gerrymander ended up in court when the League of United Latin American Citizens challenged the map in general and the contours of District 23 near Austin in particular. The new district was drawn in such a way as to make it impossible for the booming Latino population to oust the Republican incumbent. The case was consolidated with others and eventually reached the Supreme Court. Texas solicitor general and future senator Ted Cruz defended the map before the justices, and future Texas governor Greg Abbott worked with Cruz and five others on the state's briefs. Blum filed a friend-of-the-court brief on behalf of himself and Roger Clegg, a Reagan administration alumnus who became head of the Federalist Society's Civil Rights Practice Group in 2001 and, at the time the brief was filed, was head of the Scaife- and Olin-funded Center for Equal Opportunity.[12]

Their brief in the 2006 case included a kind of mission statement: "Blum and Clegg have worked to advance race-neutral principles in the areas of education, public contracting, public employment, and voting.

They have a substantial interest in limiting or eliminating the use of race as a factor in redistricting." Bringing the carefully crafted pieces of Blum's work together, they cited the study he had commissioned as evidence that scrapping the GOP map would "inject further partisanship into the redistricting process, exceed the clear language and intent of the VRA, and violate the Equal Protection clause by favoring the preferred outcome of some voters and politicians over others on the basis of race."[13]

Blum and Clegg got half of what they wanted. The court allowed the Texas electoral map as a whole to stand but invalidated the redrawn District 23 because it worked against the voting rights of Hispanics. Blum, true to his mission statement, already had two other cases in the works. He was also engineering evidence that he deployed in congressional testimony and in a slim volume, published by the American Enterprise Institute in 2007, that characterized the 2006 renewal of the VRA, section 5 and all, as "ignoble." Condemning the way the reauthorization had sailed through Congress and been signed into law by President Bush as the chairman of the NAACP and other civil rights leaders looked on, Blum lamented that the truths he had uncovered had been overlooked: "According to a massive study conducted for the Project on Fair Representation at the American Enterprise Institute, which was made part of the Congressional record and widely cited during the debate . . . the data in 2006 make clear that there is no quantifiable difference in minority voting rights in covered [by section 5] jurisdictions versus noncovered jurisdictions. . . . In other words, the VRA has accomplished exactly what it was designed to accomplish."[14]

Two years later, a case Blum had launched to free a municipal utility district (MUD) near Austin, Texas, from federal supervision under section 5 reached the Supreme Court. As was becoming his habit, Blum won. In an opinion joined by all the justices except Thomas (who concurred in part and dissented in part), Chief Justice John Roberts cited a 2006 study coauthored by Blum and released through the American Enterprise Institute in granting the MUD's desire to bail out of section 5.[15] Roberts carefully avoided passing judgment on section 5 itself, but in his concurring opinion, Thomas wrote that it was time for section 5 to be ruled unconstitutional.

Blum claimed that the purpose of the MUD case was not to strike down section 5.[16] However, he took direct aim at that section in the next case he engineered—this time on behalf of Shelby County, Alabama. As had become his practice, Blum (who has compared himself to "Yenta the matchmaker") brought plaintiffs and lawyers together and arranged the necessary financing, which, by the time a case completed its journey to the Supreme Court, was about $2 million in 2012.[17]

Since his first campaign in Houston's Eighteenth Congressional District, Blum had been working with the high-powered Washington, DC, firm Wiley Rein to knock down Democratic racial gerrymanders. (His donors would brook no such campaigns against Republican map drawing.)[18] In 2013 Blum's matchmaking skills brought Bert Rein, a founding partner of Wiley Rein who was "certainly not known as a Supreme Court lawyer," before the Supreme Court twice in one term. One of those appearances climaxed a final attack on section 5 that Blum had dreamed up during the MUD case when he learned of the Justice Department's refusal to approve an electoral map submitted by a city in Shelby County, Alabama. Wasting no time, Blum cold-called Frank "Butch" Ellis, the Shelby County attorney, and asked if Ellis would like to go to court to end the requirement for the county to preclear changes to its election laws.[19]

Ellis had served as Shelby County attorney since the year before the Voting Rights Act was passed, when there was no doubt about the county's intent to bar Blacks from voting.[20] But afterward, Ellis began to chafe under the preclearance requirements: "We were spending thousands of dollars [on preclearance] even though it was clear to us that the coverage formula [spelled out in section 4b of the VRA] was unconstitutional," Ellis later said. "Mr. Blum basically reached out to us and asked if we'd be willing to pursue it in court"—and for free. Ellis signed up after the MUD case left section 5 standing and Blum contacted him again.[21]

And so, on February 27, 2013, craggy-faced Bert Rein stood up in front of the justices of the Supreme Court to argue Shelby County's case in careful cadences, his heavy voice giving each phrase a bit of vibrato. He did not get far before Justice Sonia Sotomayor interrupted him to ask, in effect, what had possessed him to bring such an action: "Assuming

I accept your premise, and there's some question about that, that some portions of the South have changed, your county pretty much hasn't," she said. In fact, she added, it had tried to enact 240 "discriminatory voting laws that were blocked by Section 5 objections. . . . And why would we vote in favor of a county whose record is the epitome of what caused the passage of the law to start with?"[22]

Rein cited the MUD case (decided four months before Sotomayor took her seat on the court), in which eight justices admitted that the South *had* changed. Justice Ruth Bader Ginsburg, who had joined the majority in the MUD case, jumped in at this point, saying that of course the South had changed, but not enough. (On its way to the Supreme Court, the Shelby County case had passed through an appeals court, where one judge noted that section 5 still mattered in three states: "Mississippi, Louisiana, and Alabama, those states have the worst records, and application of Section 5 to them might be okay."[23]) Next, Obama-appointee Kagan weighed in, dismissing Rein's objection to the boxes that had to be checked in the current section 4 formula to avoid section 5 supervision: "under any formula that Congress could devise," she said, "it would capture Alabama."[24]

Rein weathered the barrage until the more conservative justices came to his aid. Alito offered a helpful hypothetical: "Suppose Congress passed a law that said, everyone whose last name begins with A shall pay a special tax of $1000 a year. And let's say that tax is challenged by somebody whose last name begins with A. Would it be a defense to that challenge that for some reason this particular person really should pay a $1000 penalty that people with a different last name do not pay?" Rein said it would not and noted that trying to make it a defense would amount to inventing a new statute. Here, Scalia offered a hypothetical intended to tip the scales in Rein's favor: "If someone is acquitted of a Federal crime . . . would the prosecution be able to say, well, okay, he didn't commit this crime, but Congress could have enacted a different statute which he would have violated in this case? Of course, you wouldn't listen to that, would you?" All Rein had to say was, "I agree with you."[25]

Fed up, Sotomayor turned her fire on Alito and Scalia:

> The problem with those hypotheticals is obviously that it starts from a predicate that the application [of section 5 in Shelby County] has no basis in any record, but there's no question that Alabama was rightly-included in the original Voting Rights Act. . . . The only question [before us] is whether a formula should be applied today. . . . It's a real record as to what Alabama has done to earn its place on our list.[26]

When Rein pointed out that forty-five years had passed since Alabama's placement on the list, Bill Clinton appointee Stephen Breyer offered his own analogy: "Imagine a state has a plant disease and in 1965 you can recognize the presence of the disease. . . . Now it's evolved. So by now, when we use that same formula [to identify the disease], all we're doing is picking out that State. But we know one thing: The disease is still there in the State." So, Breyer concluded, if the disease is still present, is it rational to continue to require preclearance as a sort of booster shot to at least some of the original section 5 states?[27]

Again, Rein invoked the MUD case, noting that Breyer himself had joined that opinion and had therefore signed on to its assertion that only *current* needs could justify retaining section 5. Current healthy Black voter registration and turnout meant that the problems of 1965 no longer existed. Sotomayor countered by saying that discrimination, that protean entity, had simply changed its form, which is why Congress reauthorized the act in the first place: "And what Congress said is it continues, not in terms of voter numbers, but in terms of examples of other ways to disenfranchise voters, like moving a voting booth from a convenient location for all voters to a place that historically has been known for discrimination." She then added, as an attempted knockout punch, that the moving-of-the-voting-booth analogy was "taken from one of the Section 2 and 5 cases from Alabama."[28]

Rein was able to keep his footing. Even after Kagan pointed to fifteen thousand pages of evidence of ongoing voting discrimination gathered by Congress, he argued that preclearance was no longer the right remedy. Scalia was with him: "I thought it's sort of extraordinary to say Congress can just pick out, we want to hit these eight States, it doesn't matter what formula we use; so long as we want to hit these eight states, that's good enough and that makes it constitutional."[29]

And so it went. The liberal justices invoked Shelby County's and Alabama's preclearance failures, and the conservatives invoked the specter of arbitrary federal power. Arguing for the Obama administration, solicitor general Donald Verrilli Jr. said that any progress Shelby County had made was "a result of the deterrence and the constraint Section 5 imposes on States and subjurisdictions." Now Chief Justice Roberts pounced, noting that of the thirty-seven hundred preclearance submissions the Justice Department received in 2005, it objected to only one.[30]

"You can always say," Scalia concluded, "oh, there's been improvement, but the only reason there has been improvement are these extraordinary procedures that deny the States' sovereign powers which the Constitution preserves to them. So, since the only reason it's improved is because of these procedures, we must continue these procedures in perpetuity."[31] Going for his own knockout punch a bit later, Scalia pointed out that the overwhelming congressional support for renewal of the Voting Rights Act in 2006 was due not to any real evidence of discrimination but to "a phenomenon that is called perpetuation of racial entitlement."

Four months later, the Supreme Court announced its opinion. Writing for a five–four majority, and relying partly on the intellectual edifice built by the MUD case, Chief Justice Roberts struck down section 4b of the Voting Rights Act, which contained the formula for deciding whether states should be subject to section 5 supervision. Section 5 was left in place, like the keystone of an arch that improbably hangs in the air after the rest of the structure has been removed. Roberts declared that by treating the states differently, depending on whether they met the formula's criteria or not, section 4b infringed on state sovereignty and forced states to "beseech the Federal Government for permission to implement laws that they would otherwise have the right to enact and execute on their own." Ultimately, Congress was to blame for not updating the original formula to match current conditions, as the court had admonished it to do in the MUD case, Roberts concluded.

Now it was Justice Ginsburg's turn to write an epic dissent, arguing that the agenda-setting power of minorities was still being diminished in new and creative ways in states that the majority had just freed from section 5. She invoked the fifteen thousand pages of evidence compiled by Congress and stated that the systematic and "intentional racial discrimination in voting remains so serious and widespread in covered jurisdictions that section 5 preclearance is still needed." After all, she added, actions brought under section 2 of the Voting Rights Act (allowing lawsuits to be filed after the fact against voting rules that discriminate on the basis of race) had a higher success rate in the states covered by section 5 than in those that were not. To counter Roberts's argument about infringing on state sovereignty, she stressed that the stated purpose of the Fourteenth and Fifteenth Amendments was "to arm Congress with the power and authority to protect all persons within the Nation from violations of their rights by the States. . . . Until today, in considering the constitutionality of the VRA, the Court has accorded Congress the full measure of respect its judgments in this domain should garner."[32]

Blum's dogged campaign, in short, had diminished the agenda-setting power of Congress (which had voted almost unanimously to reauthorize the VRA) and enhanced the power of the Supreme Court's conservative majority. The sheer volume of Blum's efforts against race-conscious policy proved so lucrative and prestigious that in 2014 a pair of Wiley Rein lawyers broke away to form what one blog dubbed "The Ed Blum Law Firm"—an outfit that advertised itself as offering "Supreme Court level representation" and that, like Wiley Rein before it, was paid on Blum's behalf by DonorsTrust.[33] Meanwhile, the *Shelby County* decision set off a wave of new laws in formerly supervised states—laws that likely would have triggered section 5. North Carolina, for example, enacted a law so discriminatory that parts of it were struck down by the Fourth Circuit Court of Appeals on the grounds that, as one of the judges put it, "the State's very justification for the challenged statute hinges explicitly on race—specifically its concern that African Americans, who had overwhelmingly voted for Democrats, had too much access to the franchise."[34] Looking back on *Shelby County* ten years later, the Biden Justice Department ticked off the types of laws in various states—including statutes moving or shutting down polling places or restricting early voting—that probably would have triggered section 5 if section 4b had not been struck down.[35]

Even Blum was a little chastened at first. He told the *Guardian* in 2016, "I agonize over" the new voting rights restrictions. "It may be that one or two of the states that used to be covered by Section 5 has gone too far."[36] But Blum did not agonize so much that he seriously questioned his attempt to make race disappear from American law, even though it continues to saturate American life. He still had enough faith in the other half of his pincer that, even before his case against the University of Texas ended, he continued his reverse-engineering of civil rights organizing by launching Students for Fair Admissions (SFFA) in 2014 as a membership organization to counter the NAACP and ACLU. He immediately advertised to rejected and aggrieved university applicants. "Membership organizations have a source of energy that think tanks and legal advocacy groups just simply don't have," he explained in a 2017 deposition.[37]

Among other things, SFFA's formation, with Abigail Fisher and her father as officers, gave Fisher a place from which to continue her battle for vindication. SFFA launched new cases against UT–Austin in 2017 and 2020, arguing that the university was engaging in "intentional discrimination against disfavored racial groups, including Whites and Asians."[38] When the 2017 suit was dismissed in district court, SFFA refiled in 2019 and again in 2020.[39] The plaintiffs in 2020 were white, but the highlighting of Asian applicants in all three iterations of the case suggests that Blum had heard Alito loud and clear. Blum told me in 2016 that Fisher was an "ideal" plaintiff, but in fact, she wasn't. She ranked outside the top 10 percent in the rigorous high school she attended in the affluent city of Sugar Land, Texas. She lacked the working-class bona fides of a Gratz or the difficult circumstances of a Hopwood. Her academic record (3.59 GPA, 1180 on the SATs) was strong but not preeminent. When I interviewed Gregory J. Vincent, the University of Texas vice president for diversity, in 2016, he told me that Fisher was wrong to believe "her spot was taken by a minority student, despite the fact that there were white students admitted with lower grades, and there were black and Latino students with higher grades who were denied admission."[40]

Now, building his new cases, Blum added Asians to SFFA's board for two-year terms. Blum's interest in using these new board members as symbols is clear. One of them, Eva Guo, did not even have college-age children but feared that when her young children grew up, compiling stellar academic records along the way, and applied to top colleges, "they will suffer racial discrimination in the admissions process."[41] Clearly, Blum was strategizing on the basis of the long-standing conservative argument that affirmative action harms not only whites but also an overachieving model minority—Asians—whose successes prove that discrimination in America is not so severe as to hold back hardworking, clever people.

THE MODEL MINORITY ARGUMENT

For conservatives, reports of comparatively high test scores and GPAs among Asian applicants to elite universities were like mother's milk. As Dana Y. Takagi explains, conservatives highlight differences between Asian and Black academic achievement, linking Black admissions with "diversity and affirmative action, nonmeritocratic admissions, anticompetitiveness, and equality of outcomes [as opposed to equality of achievement]," while linking Asian admissions with transcendental merit and everything that affirms "the ideal of individual equal access."[42]

In 1984 Ling-Chi Wang, then chair of UC–Berkeley's Ethnic Studies Department, inadvertently added to the conservatives' ammunition when he heard disparaging remarks about Asian students in campus-wide faculty meetings. At one meeting, Wang recalled, "Some English Department professor said that we should do something about these Asian students who are really deficient in the English language, [and] just because they are good in math and science doesn't mean they make good undergraduate students." At the time, Asians accounted for 80 percent of Berkeley's immigrant students. But Wang heard through the grapevine that the university might limit the number of ESL students it admitted. He decided to see whether this was indeed the case. He reviewed admissions statistics and was floored when he discovered that the number of matriculating Asian students, which had risen steeply between 1978 and 1983, had dropped by 21 percent between 1983 and 1984.[43]

Ever the organizer, Wang formed a task force consisting of Bay Area judges, academics, community leaders, and lawyers. The group, which christened itself the Asian American Task Force on University Admissions, devoted half a year to uncovering the reasons for the 21 percent drop in Asian students. It discovered that the university had cut the number of Asians by requiring a minimum score of 400 on the verbal part of the SAT and directing Asians who were poor enough to qualify for financial aid to campuses other than Berkeley, on the grounds that Asians were not underrepresented minorities at Berkeley.[44]

Wang's task force found that the university was planning to tighten the screws even further: admissions criteria set to take effect in 1985 added factors (such as four years of English or knowledge of European languages) that discriminated against recent immigrants whose "foreign" language happened to be English. Equally objectionable to the task force was the fact that the university made these changes in the admissions policy behind closed doors, without including any Asians among the decision makers.[45]

Wang's task force recommended that the policy of redirecting poor Asians to campuses other than Berkeley be terminated. It also demanded an end to cutoffs based on "unreliable" tests such as the SAT and insisted on the addition of Asian language tests as well as a consideration of the diversity within the "Asian" category.[46] The university balked at making these changes, and there was another drop in Asian enrollment in 1986. Wang kept pushing. Finally, remarks he made about admissions at a conference on anti-Asian violence (another issue that, unfortunately, resonates strongly in 2023) caught the attention of the media.

It also caught the attention of the Reagan Justice Department, which announced an investigation of the university. The controversy went into orbit. The *Washington Post*, *New York Times*, *Los Angeles Times*, and *Chronicle of Higher Education* ran stories. Wang suddenly had a national platform and a rare agenda-setting opportunity. "As soon as admissions of Asian students began reaching 10 or 12 percent," he told the *New York Times*, "suddenly a red light went on" not only at Berkeley but also at "Stanford, MIT, Yale, in fact all the Ivy League schools."[47]

Firing back in a letter to the *New York Times*, William Kami, editor of the *Status Report of the Association for California Education*, argued that "enrollments from 1982 to 1986 have decreased for only the two largest Asian groups: Chinese and Japanese. All other Asian enrollments have increased."[48] Nevertheless, the fact-finding doggedness and activism of Wang's task force (combined with pressure from the Justice Department) achieved a major victory in 1989 when Berkeley chancellor Ira Heyman apologized to the Asian community for the university's mishandling of the whole affair and vowed to "bring more Asians into key positions in his administration."[49]

It was not long before Blum's precursors in the anti–civil rights movement scented political opportunity in the dispute. In 1989, for instance, a bearded surfer-congressman named Dana Rohrabacher introduced a resolution against anti-Asian discrimination, but he failed to achieve the warm feelings and political support he expected. Instead, the *Orange County Register* reported that Wang, Henry Der, and other Asian American leaders saw Rohrabacher as attempting a hostile takeover of their cause in pursuit of goals that were not their own. "Facially, this resolution sounds beneficial," Paul Igasaki of the Japanese American Citizen League told the *Register*. "But at the Heritage Foundation, Rohrabacher said this was a vehicle, or a first step, for defeating affirmative-action programs in general, and we don't want to be used in a beginning barrage against affirmative action. In a lot of places, affirmative action has been beneficial to Asian-Americans." Robert Matsui, a Democratic congressman from Sacramento, said, "Rep. Rohrabacher's apparent sudden conversion to civil rights advocate is both disturbing and puzzling. Prior to being elected to Congress, he worked as a speech writer and special assistant under President Reagan, whose administration worked long and hard toward unraveling civil-rights gains, including affirmative action." All would be forgiven, Matsui told Rohrabacher, if he amended his resolution with a pledge of congressional support for affirmative action. Rohrabacher refused at first but finally offered a compromise: a new resolution affirming support for affirmative action programs that complied with current Supreme Court decisions.[50]

One of the remarkable aspects of this story is that Wang, Der, and other Asian American leaders took great care to avoid defecting from their coalition with African Americans, Latinos, and other minorities. This care was reciprocated by the irrepressible Willie Brown, speaker of the California Assembly and future African American mayor of San Francisco. Brown appointed Der to the California Postsecondary Education Committee and gave him a no-nonsense assignment: "I want my appointees to be offensive. I want the other board members not to want to drink coffee with them. Because I want them to be twisting the tail of the donkey to meet the needs of Asian Americans."[51]

Another element of this story is that minorities struggling for space in a society saturated with stereotypes are always in a prisoner's dilemma–like situation. The pattern of cooperation that can emerge—as theorists such as Anatol Rapoport and Robert Axelrod have shown[52]—when the same individuals play the game indefinitely is always fragile, always subject to disruption by maneuvers from Rohrabacher-like conflict entrepreneurs or from figures within the coalition who, for one reason or another, do not remember the previous games and behave like prisoners in the one-shot game, where defection is the only thing that makes sense.[53]

Affirmative action, after all, is a Rube Goldberg–like contraption, pure legal and political bricolage built out of tight budgets, painful history, political tricks, and compromises. Its categories are born from the minds of bureaucrats, from clarion calls for justice and empathy, from court battles over levels of scrutiny, from status hunger, and from impossible choices among qualified applicants. Hugh Davis Graham sketches a map of the machine and its peculiar fragilities in his book *Collision Course: The Strange Convergence of Affirmative Action and Immigration Policy in America*. He reminds us that affirmative action was developed with the removal of barriers to African American mobility in mind. But other groups—Latinos and Asians—wanted in, having already lobbied to be listed on government forms designating official minorities. Native Americans did not lobby but were included on the forms as well. When the Civil Rights Act of 1964 gave birth to the EEOC and then Executive Order 11246, minority interests were more or less fully convergent: "The spread of affirmative action programs to other racial and ethnic groups was seen as broadening and strengthening the civil rights coalition," Graham writes. But, he adds, "at the same time it weakened the logic of affirmative action's original, black-centered rationale."[54] Put another way, as more groups were added, it took more hermeneutic work to find the points where their interests converged, and it became easier for conflict entrepreneurs to lure them into hermeneutic traps.[55]

Hermeneutic difficulties increased as a result of another civil rights breakthrough—the Immigration and Nationality Act of 1965, which scrapped draconian restrictions on the number of immigrants allowed into the United States from non-European countries. This transformed the ratios of minorities eligible for affirmative action, as 26 million immigrants came from Asia and Latin America.[56] Crucially, the 1965 immigration law favoring people with "exceptional ability in the sciences" drew large numbers of immigrants from India, China, and Korea who were disproportionately equipped with academic and professional qualifications and familiar with test-centric school systems.[57] This gave them and their children an instant advantage in the long-running effort to diversify US classrooms and workplaces.[58] Inevitably, this academic difference born of immigration law was translated into a *racial* difference that reinforced the nation's habit of looking down on African Americans, Latinos, and Native Americans.[59] The new immigration reality increased competition for three scarce resources: university admissions, economic opportunities, and social advancement. It became an inevitable weakness in the minority coalition that Blum, Rufo, and others were only too happy to exploit: the Rube Goldberg machine of affirmative action began to rattle.

Rufo and company take advantage of the fact that race is a political mythology rather than a biological reality, something that is rooted in rhetoric, not genetics.[60] Affirmative action and related policies are built on that endlessly manipulable mythology in ways that few fully understand or even think about.[61] Early affirmative action policy flew under the radar because there was no real public debate about which groups should be added to the credit line created by the African American civil rights movement.[62] As Graham shows, decisions about which groups to include or exclude were improvised like back-of-the-envelope calculations by government bureaucrats in dialogue with civil rights groups and with each other. In the process, like so many Americans, they dodged all the tricky issues and questions. In other words:

> With inherited notions of race that were being abandoned in science and social science, government officials drew up questionnaires that reflected assumptions they took for granted. . . . What was race? Were Spanish-Americans a race? . . . Were Portuguese-Americans a race? Were persons from the Middle East or North Africa "white"? . . . Not having to answer questions like this in public made it easier for government officials to adjust their lists.[63]

One cannot put all the blame on the bureaucrats because the American myth of race, despite its seemingly eternal Black-white axis, is always in flux: Negro becomes Black (and proud) and then African American; Spanish American becomes Hispanic then Latino then (controversially) Latinx; Chinese, Japanese, Filipino, and others become Asian American; Indian becomes Native American or American Indian or Alaska Native, depending on the current census form and community or individual preferences. And this says nothing about the once despised non–Anglo-Saxon Protestant immigrants from Europe becoming white. Pity the poor bureaucrat who has to sort all this out while putting together a complicated Rube Goldberg machine that can dig for deep equality.

And the dilemma of whether to defect or not created by conflict entrepreneurs—or the raw thirst to gain agenda-setting power—became more intense as members of the same groups sometimes took advantage of affirmative action in one arena while raging against it in another. For example, in 1973, after the Small Business Administration began directing resources toward culturally disadvantaged groups (defined as small-business owners who were Black, Hispanic, Asian American, or American Indian), non-Black affirmative action eclipsed affirmative action for African Americans in California, the land of Proposition 209.[64] In the 1990s, Graham notes, "Asian-Americans sped past Latinos to become the top beneficiaries in California of the [Small Business Administration's] $6 billion minority business enterprise program. Nationwide, the share of contract dollars for Asians had risen to

28 percent while the Hispanic share had fallen to 26 percent and the black share to 34 percent" by 1996.[65]

In Minnesota, where Allan Bakke practices and where whites are 84 percent of the population, Blacks are 7.4 percent, Asians are 5.4 percent, and Hispanics are 5.8 percent, a push to increase lending to minority-owned firms resulted in $30.1 million in Small Business Administration–backed loans to Black businesses, $74.9 million to Asian and Pacific Islander businesses, and $22 million to Hispanic-owned businesses in fiscal year 2022.[66]

THE CUPERTINO BLUES

This numbers game played out in dramatic fashion in San Francisco, where Henry Der, Ling-Chi Wang, and their associates worked hard to hold the old affirmative action coalition together. In the San Francisco Unified School District, the perceived value of that coalition shifted due to massive demographic changes. As Der explains in a 2004 essay, when the NAACP secured a consent decree requiring that no student body in the San Francisco schools consist of more than 45 percent of any one "racial" group—defined as African American, Latino, white, Chinese, Japanese, Korean, Filipino, American Indian, and other non-white—African Americans were the largest minority in the city. But by 2003, the number of African American students had dropped by 40 percent (due to departures resulting from gentrification and a spike in housing prices, Der told me).[67] At the same time, white flight from desegregation led to a 20 percent drop in white students in SFUSD, while the number of Latino students spiked by 20 percent and "that of Chinese students, exclusive of other Asian groups, by 55%." Thus, "Asian students—Chinese, Japanese, Korean, and Filipinos—comprise 50% of the total SFUSD student population."[68] Meanwhile, Latinos accounted for 22 percent of students, African Americans 15 percent, and whites 10 percent.

This demographic metamorphosis shifted the perceived value of a multiethnic coalition so much that the Chinese American Democratic Club (CADC) of San Francisco initiated an anti–affirmative action lawsuit, *Ho v. SFUSD*, in 1994. Although Ho was in elementary school, the heart of the case was an allegation by an older student that the school district discriminated against high school–age Chinese students by requiring them to have test scores higher than other applicants to get into Lowell High School, the district's elite campus. Der, in another essay, accused the parents associated with CADC of selfish hypocrisy and allowing themselves to be used in an attack on multiracial democracy. He offered the example of a Chinese firefighter who opposed the fire department consent decree that Chinese for Affirmative Action helped secure but then asked CAA for help in challenging an exam he had to pass to get a promotion.[69] This sort of hypocrisy—and maybe even hypocrisy itself—is a classic cave-in to prisoner's dilemma pressure, which can make short-term payoffs eclipse everything else.

Unsurprisingly, the political scent of the *Ho* case reached all the way to Washington, DC, and the Center for Individual Rights joined the case on the side of the Chinese parents. Other anti–civil rights movement luminaries such as Pete Wilson (who rode into the California governor's office on the back of an anti-immigration proposition) weighed in, and Stephan Thernstrom, husband of Abigail Thernstrom, served as an expert for the plaintiffs.

Der explains that those who brought the *Ho* case "initially recruited several elementary students," but those plaintiffs dropped out and a high school student named Patrick Wong became the primary plaintiff. Der's insider analysis of the situation is so illuminating that it is worth quoting at length:

> Lowell selects its freshman students based on their middle school grades and test scores. Chinese student applicants had to hit at least 56 points; whites and other Asians, 54 points; and Blacks and Latinos, 52 points. I have to look at the record but I think the differential was like that.
>
> These selection criteria were for the purpose of integrating Lowell High School. . . . CAA took the position that these selection criteria placed a burden on Chinese students. We asked, "Why doesn't Lowell High School establish a minimum score that would demonstrate that anyone who at least hits the minimum score has a

> likelihood of benefiting and succeeding from Lowell High School?" And if they were to hit that minimum score, then put everyone in a pool, and you select the students by lottery.

But this solution was rejected. "Chinese American parents, who are my contemporaries," Der said, "wanted to have it strictly based on points ranking with the highest getting in, and then going down from there." He tried to reason with them:

> I said, "If you don't want to have a lottery and there is high demand for seats at Lowell, why not establish another high school where you would have a very similar program where you would have AP [advanced placement] courses and other academic offerings." Lowell alumni and parents vehemently objected to my proposal because they did not want to compete with another high school to have the so-called best and the brightest. Their opposition was just ultimate selfishness and arrogance on their part because they wanted to limit the supply and jack up the demand. By limiting the supply, you are necessarily disadvantaging those who are the most marginalized.

The resulting testocratic academic utopia was not a happy one, Der says:

> Students may be academically proficient but end up hating it because it's so cut-throat and everyone is worried about class rank. A lot of these parents, tiger moms, put a lot of pressure on their kids to get into Lowell. Even immigrant parents, who may not know that much about the school system, hear other parents talking and think, "Oh, my kid has to go to Lowell in order to get into a UC." Truth be told, not every Lowell graduate gets into UC–Berkeley or UCLA. The data would show that a fair number end up going to SF City College or they go to UC–Davis, but not [the high-status] Berkeley or UCLA.

This craving for Lowell seems to be part of a larger quest for agenda-setting power in the United States. As Der explains:

> The Chinese American obsession toward Lowell is the same as the obsession that some Chinese American parents have for their students to get into Harvard or Yale, as if those are the only universities that matter. I find this obsession tragic. There is a significant number of Chinese parents who feel that if their student doesn't get into Lowell, their kid will be a failure. We parents shouldn't be placing this pressure and playing these psychological games on our children.[70]

Der's deep knowledge of Lowell is informed by his wife, who graduated from the school and found it to be a testocratic hell. Der offers as an alternative the example of his own children, who thrived outside the deep fryer of Lowell competition after attending San Francisco's George Washington High School:

> My first daughter was an okay student, but she only did what she had to do, nothing more. She may have taken at most one or two AP courses. She had decent scores but not spectacular, like in the 1500s or high 1400s, something like that. I had told her, "I'm not sure if you are going to get into UCLA, looking at your grades and test scores." To my surprise she got into UCLA. She proved me wrong. My second daughter was the more stereotypical Asian student, often doing more than what was necessary for a high school class. She got into UCLA and Berkeley and wisely chose UCLA to get away from home and experience a different environment. My first daughter ended up being quite a good student at UCLA, better than she was in high school. She ended up double majoring. We need to recognize that students who are not straight A (or near straight A) students or do not receive very high SAT scores can benefit and thrive at a university like UCLA, Berkeley, Harvard.

This supports the findings of Carnevale and Strohl. But the paradoxes created by those who refuse to accept such findings are profound. Der points out that if late-blooming high schoolers do not show their full potential, middle schoolers cannot be expected to grow the equivalent of a "Lowell material" tattoo on their foreheads. A school district violates its obligation to provide equal opportunity to all, Der concludes, if it "pours resources into and/or designates one or two high schools as 'academic' or superior schools. Parents will necessarily be obsessed about having their students attend these one or two high schools. . . . It is harmful for the other high schools to be perceived as a remainder high school or a school of last resort."

As for Patrick Wong, although he was "angry and depressed about his nonadmission to Lowell," according to his mother, he went to the perfectly fine Lincoln High School on the west side of San Francisco. He "got a pretty good education there," she admitted, according to Der. Wong took AP courses and got into the University of California at Irvine. He is now "a senior physician assistant taking care of children going through brain surgery. His life was not over because he did not get admitted to Lowell High School," Der concludes. "He was not damaged by not attending Lowell."

Der told the parents behind the *Ho* case to their faces that their obsession with Lowell was "all about middle-class angst" and double standards because CADC "was the biggest proponent of affirmative action in business contracts for Asian Americans. You guys are a bunch of hypocrites! How can you argue that it should be 'merit-based,' and that race should not be considered when it comes to Lowell High School admissions. And yet you want special consideration because of your race when it comes to government contracts?"

The prisoner's dilemma is working overtime here, in part because affirmative action in admissions is well known, thoroughly demonized, and seemingly profitable to defect from, while affirmative action in contracts flies under the radar. There is little stigma attached to the latter, while stigma has been pumped into the former for decades. Thus the "payoff" for resisting affirmative action in school admissions, where status is a function of the scarcity of seats, is high, while the status cost of seeking affirmative action in business is low. It makes strategic sense to game the system by defecting from one kind of affirmative action while clinging to the other, despite the fact that someone like Patrick Wong suffers no permanent harm from affirmative action in the school system and the whole Bay Area would be better off if more people could more easily access the up-escalator to opportunity provided by a good education.

Edward Blum and Ward Connerly's exploits as leaders of the anti–civil rights movement depend on ignoring voices like Henry Der's. Connerly inadvertently underscored the point in 2020, when he re-emerged to oppose a proposition to restore affirmative action in California. The current leadership of CAA campaigned for the proposition, but the measure went down to defeat, leaving Connerly and a new wing person, Wenyuan Wu, to crow in an op-ed that *Wall Street Journal* lauded them as "The Duo that Defeated the 'Diversity Industry.'" Tellingly, Wu, an immigrant from China, was thirty-three at the time, and the article describes her as someone who "recently become an activist opposed to anti-Asian discrimination in higher education."[71] Wu had not been born yet when *Lau v. Nichols* was decided or when Der and Wang and others at CAA used affirmative action to push Asians through the doors of the San Francisco Police and Fire Departments and the Bay Area media.

During my interview with him, I asked Der how pervasive this lack of awareness is among the anti–affirmative action cohort in the Chinese American community, and his answer was informed by the fact that he grew up in a mixed neighborhood in Stockton, California, and, despite a stellar record and musical talent, did not even consider applying to Stanford, his eventual alma mater, until a mentor who knew about the university's effort to diversify suggested that he should. He pointed to the new American plague of disinformation as part of the problem:

> I attended a high school that was racially mixed—whites, Blacks, Chicanos, and a handful of Asians. It was a good learning and life experience that went beyond the course work. I blame myself and others that we've not done a good job of educating newly arrived immigrant parents. During my time at Chinese for Affirmative Action, we assumed if we talk about racial discrimination in general, and discrimination specific to Chinese Americans, immigrants in the community would get it. We made a mistake in not being more conscientious, deliberate, and intentional in reaching out and educating immigrant parents. . . . What's worse today is the amount of misinformation on the internet. It's much more challenging be-

> cause there are far-right elements intent on driving wedges among racial minority groups.

Of course, misinformation has long been a part of the anti–civil rights toolbox. Back in 1994, Der recalls:

> State senator Edward Hernandez introduced SCA 5, which if approved by California voters, would have pulled back Proposition 209 and its ban on the use of race in education and public contracting. Many college-educated Chinese immigrant parents, especially from Taiwan and Hong Kong, living in suburbs like Cupertino and Fremont and [elsewhere] in Southern California, strongly opposed SCA 5. . . .
>
> That year Ling-Chi Wang and I participated in a town-hall meeting about SCA 5, held in Cupertino, whose audience was comprised of overwhelmingly college-educated Chinese immigrant parents. California state senate minority leader Bob Huff was one of the speakers. . . . He argued California should not reinstitute affirmative action, in a calculated move to deepen the wedge between Chinese and Blacks and Latinos.
>
> Ling-Chi and I countered that the problem with UC freshman admissions lies with the university enrolling more and more out-of-state students for budgetary reasons (because out-of-state students pay full tuition), at the expense of UC-eligible California high school graduates.
>
> UC pointed out it had to do so because the California state legislature and governor had provided an inadequate budget for UC to enroll all UC-eligible California high school graduates who accepted their UC admission, per the California Master Plan for Higher Education.[72]

This is in line with Anthony Carnevale's view that, for all the high-minded talk of merit and excellence, admissions directors just want to make the budget. And it underscores the fact that, in the United States, money becomes merit if the amount is large enough.

BLUM TAKES THE KILL SHOT

Once Blum settled on Asians as the ideal plaintiffs in the college admissions wing of his crusade, he picked up where people like Rohrabacher left off. Long obsessed with the SAT as an indicator of merit, Blum advertised for Asian plaintiffs as he mounted lawsuits against the admissions policies at Harvard, Yale, and the University of North Carolina. The Harvard and North Carolina cases eventually reached the Supreme Court. The Harvard case focused on the claim that Asians were not being admitted in the numbers commensurate with their academic records because the "personal ratings" assigned to applicants discriminated against them.

Handing down an earthquake of an opinion on June 29, 2023, Chief Justice John Roberts raised, in effect, a legal laurel crown and set it on Blum's color-blind head. Roberts affirmed the "transcendent aims of the Equal Protection Clause" of the Fourteenth Amendment and accused predecessors who had upheld affirmative action of failing to live up to the clause's "core commitments"—much as those who had permitted segregation had failed. Without mentioning Blum, Roberts confirmed his interpretation of the meaning of *Brown v. Board of Education*: that "the right of public education must be made available to all on equal terms," and any exception must survive strict scrutiny.[73]

Turning to *Bakke* and Lewis Powell's designation of diversity as the only justification for affirmative action, Roberts took out his axe, polishing Sandra Day O'Connor's optimistic twenty-five-year limit on the policy as if it were the axe's blade. "Twenty years later, no end is in sight" for affirmative action, Roberts lamented. He then sliced away at O'Connor's major reason for upholding affirmative action nationwide in *Grutter*: the manifest national security value of affirmative action that former military leaders testified to in their *Grutter* amicus brief.

Roberts did show some restraint: Blum had not thought to sue a military academy, so although affirmative action had to fall at state schools and private colleges, Roberts passed no judgment on affirmative action at the nation's officer factories. That might have to wait for Blum's next lawsuit. Having skirted the obvious positive impact of affirmative action on national security, Roberts was free declare

Harvard's affirmative action goals, such as "training future leaders in the public and private sectors," too vague and incoherent "for purposes of strict scrutiny." Like someone questioning why vaccines that might save an unspecified number of people during an epidemic should be distributed, Roberts asked, "Even if these goals could somehow be measured, how is a court to know when they have been reached, and when the perilous remedy of racial preferences may cease?"

Turning to SFFA's argument that Harvard robbed Asians of admissions opportunities, Roberts both affirmed that Asians had been discriminated against and called Harvard's use of that category too blunt an instrument because it did not distinguish between East Asians and South Asians. The key distinction among Asian applicants—the differences between educated or high-skilled immigrants and less fortunate refugees and their children—did not rate a mention in Roberts's opinion. Nor did the differences pro–affirmative action Asian scholars have identified between the conservative-leaning Chinese immigrants who arrived after 1990 and those who arrived earlier.[74]

University of California–Davis Medical School professor Michelle J. Ko told me in a July 21, 2023, interview that the widening differences between immigrants from China and India and other Asian Americans gave Blum something to exploit. Citing the scholarship of OiYan Poon, Ko explained, "Twenty years ago is when we really start to see the emergence of a really strong Chinese nationalism effort within China itself that carries over to immigrants here. . . . Then we see that [carrying] over into the social media environment"—particularly the platform WeChat, which is popular in China and among Chinese immigrants and some Chinese Americans. Indeed, the big-bang moment for Blum's Students for Fair Admissions came after he spoke to the Silicon Valley Chinese Association and members of that group went on WeChat to spread the color-blind gospel.[75] Perhaps he found fertile ground there, Ko explains, because for years there has been "a targeted effort" on WeChat to attack affirmative action and illegal immigration, in part by using misinformation and appealing to the seductive idea of East Asian superiority.

Poon herself told *Mother Jones* that reliance on test scores as measures of merit also played a role:

> Many of the folks that are leading the anti–affirmative action movements here in the US came here as graduate students, after going to elite colleges in China. They have a belief that high-stakes testing is the only fair way to get into the best colleges. . . . Many of them, because of their class status, end up in relatively white and upper middle class communities. And that allows for the kind of development and perpetuation of stereotypes of other people.[76]

Ko told me that among people from India, feelings of caste superiority can play into anti–affirmative action attitudes.

In fact, in India itself, where everyone is "Asian" and affirmative action appears in the constitution under the name "reservations," the policy has stirred bitter, sometimes fatal, protest.[77] In America, even Steve Bannon has joined other US ethnonationalists in buying space in the Asian media to push an anti–affirmative action message. One result, Ko suggests, is the small, well-funded cohort of conservative Asian groups that were available to converge with Blum and the Supreme Court supermajority led by Roberts and to be platformed by the controversy-hungry, deadline-bound US media.[78]

Ignored in the lengthy opinion and concurrences of the SFFA supermajority is a crucial reality: the aforementioned transformation of the affirmative action debate by post-1965 immigration. A significant number of SFFA's twenty-one thousand members are "immigrant Chinese"—many of them recruited in places like Cupertino, California—as Blum notes in a 2017 deposition.[79] In other words, many of them likely have no knowledge of the history this book chronicles. Making race and its history invisible (however real the effects of race remain)—not eliminating race as a perpetuator of unequal opportunity—is Blum's goal. His dream was for the Supreme Court to use the Harvard and North Carolina cases to ban all acknowledgment of the role of race not only in education but also in voting, contracting, employment, and beyond.[80]

He is of course not alone. The opportunity to file amicus briefs with the Supreme Court for the SFFA cases brought members of the old anti–civil rights band back together. Reagan Attorney General Edwin Meese—father of the originalism that shapes the thinking of a powerful cohort on the current Supreme Court—filed a brief. So did the Pacific

Legal Foundation, the Southwestern Legal Foundation, the Center for Equal Opportunity, and similar organizations.[81] The Claremont Institute's Center for Constitutional Jurisprudence, headed by John Eastman (infamous for his efforts to nullify the 2020 presidential election), filed a brief too.

Closing the circle with Christopher Rufo's CRT panic, Parents Defending Freedom filed a brief consisting of cherry-picked (albeit sometimes truly misguided) discussions of white privilege in K–12 texts assigned in various schools. The group demanded that Blum's organization be granted the right to use Title VI to cut down the poisoned tree of *Grutter*, which, of course, has nothing to do with whatever someone might write in an effort to teach children about the impossibly tangled subject of race.

In the midst of such irrationalities and non sequiturs and their consequences, it seems fitting to end this account of SFFA's triumph over Harvard with a final non sequitur from Blum himself. While fishing for Asian plaintiffs in Houston, Blum was asked what would happen if race-conscious admissions were eliminated but there were demands for special consideration of sexuality or some other element of identity. "Race in America is very unique," he said:

> Legally, race is a world unto itself. If Harvard said—if the admissions committee sat down and said . . . we are only going to admit people that are really swell dancers . . . we just want great dancers here at Harvard, to hell with anything else. It's stupid, it's foolish, but they can do that. The law when it pertains to race is very unique. So if Harvard said, well, hey we want more disabled people, or we want additional gays, or we want some additional heterosexuals, as long as race isn't part of that equation, that's something that, you know, they can pursue.[82]

This answer, which, despite its humorous grace notes, seems to be quite earnest, collapses the notion that Blum's goal is to establish a world of "fair admissions." Here, his pursuit of color blindness has more in common with Ahab's pursuit of the unkillable white whale than it does with a pursuit of justice. His education lawsuits, after all, inevitably call attention to gaps in "merit," which he analyzes like a lepidopterist and classifies by race. Most ironically, Blum—the champion of color-blind individual achievement—has used a stereotype about a model minority to unravel the holistic, "whole person" review of every applicant for admission to a place like Harvard. This unraveling likely reduces the chances of not only many multifaceted Black, Latino, and Native American students but also many Asian students whose own idiosyncratic ways of grappling with the world's bottomless problems might be hard to capture on a test.[83]

CONCLUSION: ESCAPING OPPORTUNITY DESERTS

On July 10, 2023, the Association of American Medical Colleges (AAMC) held a webinar on the meaning of the Supreme Court's *SFFA* decisions. Participants went out of their way to make their remarks precise and unemotional, even optimistic. But the session had the feel of a lesson on how to live in a minefield without getting blown up. Front and center explaining the "perplexing" new legal world the Supreme Court had created were Heather Alarcon and Frank Trinity, two of the authors of an amicus brief that tried to convince the court that diversity among medical practitioners saves lives—including the lives of at-risk newborns, whose importance the court had stressed the year before when it overturned abortion rights.[1]

Alarcon, a strawberry-blond forty-something with frank, widely spaced eyes, warned that the Roberts court saw "college admissions as a zero sum game with absolute winners and losers for every spot. So even if a school could show that no person was actually harmed by the consideration of race, which UNC and Harvard both did show in the lower courts, the current Supreme Court is going to infer that harm."[2] The potentially lifesaving results of considering race were sealed off, except for the narrow window left for the discussion of race in an applicant's essay and the exception for military academies. Picking up a few additional bread crumbs dropped by Roberts, Alarcon noted that admissions offices now knew that efforts to diversify had to be "specific, measurable and time-bound." She added:

> Medicine is full of specific, measurable interests that relate to human safety. But hold on. Because even if a school were to articulate the best goals, and I believe that every medical school could do that today, I wouldn't count on a future determination before *this* Court turning on how compelling or measurable a goal is. Because I think the real reason, the main reason the Court didn't uphold Harvard's and UNC's admissions processes is because a controlling majority of this Court sees any distinctions made on the basis of race in admissions as inherently discriminatory.[3]

Roberts's argument, in short, might be a hermeneutic trap that leads schools into enormously expensive, reputation-damaging lawsuits that the Supreme Court will make sure they lose.

One way out of the trap that received a flurry of press coverage in the wake of the *SFFA* decision is epitomized by the University of California–Davis Medical School, which has built remarkably diverse classes in the land of Proposition 209 in part by measuring applicants against a socioeconomic disadvantage scale. But Michelle Ko, a professor in the Department of Public Health Sciences at the medical school, told me that the Davis model cannot repair the damage done by the Roberts court:

> Part of what makes UC–Davis successful is the ability to create missions-based programming and admissions serving very specific populations. . . . We have a new program that is dedicated towards serving tribal communities in northern California and southern Oregon. We have a program dedicated toward serving agricultural and rural communities within our state. And so then the students are selected on their ability to understand the needs of those communities and their potential for practicing in them.[4]

But not all education can target services to meet the needs of specific communities. Thus, the Davis model is not a universal solution, and the loss of race-conscious admissions will make it harder to replicate Davis's diversity nationwide, Ko said. Another hard-to-match Davis feature is its small size, which allowed it to waive application fees for 40 percent of the 133 matriculants in 2023. This sort of generosity would probably break the bank at bigger programs, to say nothing of whole institutions.[5]

In the environment Blum has shaped, it is a challenge to get the message out that the Davis approach is not a substitute for affirmative action and that affirmative action still has a role to play. The challenge both motivates and deeply frustrates Ko. The daughter of Taiwanese immigrants, she was inspired to research race- and ethnicity-based medical care after she saw her "mother and other women of color receive uninformed, culturally-inappropriate care."[6] The SFFA cases' transit through the courts inspired Ko to do her part to craft a counternarrative. Thus, she describes her own choice to train in a program designed for students "who are committed to practicing in underserved communities." That program, a partnership between UCLA and Drew Hospital (located in the underserved Black community of Watts), kept Ko shuttling between the tony UCLA campus, where people asked her why an Asian was participating in a program alongside presumptively unworthy Blacks and Latinos, and Watts. It taught her "that there is no way that our health care systems will care about black, brown, or other marginalized minority lives until we change who enters the profession."[7]

In another part of her counternarrative, Ko led a team that analyzed the experience in the "advancement of diversity, equity and inclusion" of thirty-nine deans and admissions directors from thirty-seven medical schools. She and her coauthors concluded that, despite "decades of diversity initiatives in US medical schools . . . only affirmative action has brought substantive change."[8] Striving to shift the medical world's attention to this reality and away from an overemphasis on MCAT scores (which, she agrees with other critics, measure a school's desire for prestige more than an applicant's potential as a physician), Ko had a moment of real distress when I asked her how she intended to get her message out in the current political environment. "I feel like I'm just trying, pushing away to get at the people who don't really know what happens in admissions," she said. "We're doing our best to help people understand and journalists understand as well. . . . It's hard." At least in the short run, Ko knows that her and her colleagues' efforts to restructure medicine in the direction of diversity and inclusion are no match for the anti–civil rights movement's anger-seeking rhetorical missiles as they enter the brains of ratings-hungry news executives and ambitious politicians.

RUFO'S NEW PANIC

Indeed, by 2022, the tireless Chris Rufo had launched a sequel to the CRT panic by targeting "radical gender theory"—his self-described "catch-all for queer theory, trans ideology, neo-pronouns, and gender identity activism."[9] Focusing the new panic on protecting children from any affirmation of feelings of gender fluidity or of being in the wrong body, Rufo and his fellow travelers—including the National Association of Scholars, the Goldwater Institute (where Clint Bolick was employed when he got his scorpion tattoo), and GOP politicians—once more trapped the American mind, or at least the part of it that was heard shouting in 2022 and 2023 at school board meetings, on cable shows, and, increasingly, on the political campaign trail.[10]

To institutionalize the panic, Rufo coauthored model legislation published as part of a Manhattan Institute issue brief titled "Abolish DEI Bureaucracies and Restore Colorblind Equality in Public Universities." It targets everything from the very idea of "transgenderism" to the "promulgating and enforcing of Critical Race Theory" to any use of the principles of diversity, equity, and inclusion (DEI) to "manipulate or otherwise influence the composition of the faculty or student body with reference to race, color or ethnicity."[11] This legislation would all but outlaw Ko's intellectual tools, or at least stain and discredit her argument as critical race theory or her promotion of DEI (zombified by Rufo's definitions as dangerous). Politicians in Florida, Texas, and elsewhere have made laws based on Rufo's model.[12]

Nevertheless, Ko and others press on. Indeed, anticipating the anti–civil rights triumph over Harvard and UNC, some had been formulating strategies to keep a route to deep equality open in a post–affirmative action world. One strategy is to craft or sharpen tools to measure disadvantage—although, as Alarcon suggests, the Supreme Court may beat those tools too into metal blindfolds.

In June 2023 Anthony Carnevale, Peter Schmidt, and Jeff Strohl published a study that highlights an instrument devised by the Educational Testing Service (a subcontractor of the College Board, where Carnevale used to work) called "Landscape." This new tool processes "extensive information about the applicant's high school and neighborhood," including poverty rates, likelihood of being a crime victim, scholastic success in comparison to others in the same high school, and the percentage of students in a school who qualify for free or reduced-price lunch.[13] Similarly, the Davis Medical School's Landscape-like socioeconomic disadvantage scale rates applicants from 0 to 99, based on, among other things, family income and parents' educational attainment. But the difficulty in replicating the program, or following through on the implications of Landscape likely lie, as already noted, in the cost of funding disadvantaged but deserving students. And this difficulty may increase because, post *SFFA*, there may be fewer underrepresented minority applicants to medical schools, and it may be harder to direct scholarships to such students.[14]

Furthermore, because traditional indicia such as test scores and grades remain part of the Davis evaluation, any replication of it will have to consider findings like those reported in 2019 by Sean F. Reardon, Demetra Kalogrides, and Kenneth Shores. Crunching numbers from the thousands of US high schools where 92 to 93 percent of Black and Latino students are educated, they found that minority students' relatively lower scores were attributable to patterns of residential and educational segregation and other "symptoms of underlying racial inequalities."[15] They note that more data mining and ethnographic study are needed to fully account for the social machinery that turns segregation (and resegregation) into achievement gaps that vary from school district to school district and sometimes even within a single school. In other words, they call for a more complete map of American opportunity. Detailed opportunity maps in education and beyond (including in credit markets and health care) need to be drawn, integrated with one another, and used to direct opportunities to those candidates who have achieved the most relative to their circumstances.

BLUM'S NEW THREATS

Unfortunately, the drawing of such opportunity maps, much less their use, is under threat from Blum. Hours after his *SFFA* victory, he marched to the microphones, flanked by the two lead lawyers who benefited from the millions of dollars in billable hours the anti–civil rights movement poured into his Harvard and UNC cases.

The one nonwhite person on Blum's stage was Calvin Yang, a rejected Harvard applicant from Canada whose desire to attend the school originated in his ambition to follow in the political footsteps of Pierre Trudeau, Canada's prime minister from 1968 to 1983 and a Harvard alumnus. Yang made no mention of Canada, but he confirmed Ko's worry by presenting himself as the embodiment of Asian Americans who were finally free to pursue "the grand American dream."[16] The son of Chinese immigrants who were likely selected by Canada's competitive immigration system for their educational or professional attainments, Yang went to high school at a prestigious private academy in New York City and has secured a green card.[17] But in his moment of triumph, he presented himself as an American who, through SFFA, would help realize "the potential of our nation's youth."[18]

As for Blum, he presented himself as the leader of a new panoptic branch of government, vowing to monitor admissions procedures around the country and "initiate litigation should universities defiantly flout this clear ruling"—of which he was the prime interpreter.[19] "Flouting" would include any introduction of proxies for race that Blum and his organization deemed in violation of the equal protection clause or Title VI. It would also include race-targeted scholarships—independent of fair or unfair admissions practices and independent of the financial chasm such scholarships are intended to bridge.

Never mind that researchers have shown that a true opportunity map must reckon with race, not only because color-blind warriors like Blum always invoke it in the most stereotype-affirming ways but also because color-blind proxies for race are fatally flawed, not least because conservative commitments to budget cutting tend to conflict with commitments to fund deserving but economically struggling students. What is more, race-neutral tools for identifying the racially disadvantaged are blunt instruments.[20] One effort to use neighborhood as a proxy for race in a poor Latino area in post–Proposition 209 California, for instance, lifted up not the Latinos mired in poverty but the children of people *passing through* poverty: children of "immigrants from Asia whose parents temporarily had low income but have advanced education."[21]

Asked whether he would go after the superficially race-neutral tool of legacy admissions, Blum said that, as far as he knew, it was not actionable; if it were, organizations such as the NAACP, the Mexican American Legal Defense and Education Fund, or the ACLU would have targeted it long ago. Perhaps. But some observers suggest that there has been a serendipitous bargain that allowed legacy preferences to be balanced by the far smaller diversity credit permitted under affirmative action.[22] With that serendipitous and unspoken bargain ruptured, organizations associated with the Leadership Conference on Civil Rights filed a July 2023 complaint with the US Department of Education against legacy admissions at Harvard, and the department opened an investigation.[23] Whatever comes of the probe, the complaint opens a much-needed counternarrative to decades of attacks on affirmative action because it highlights the unearned opportunities of the Jared Kushners of the world.

The crux of the complaint is that legacy admissions overwhelmingly benefit whites—by a rate of 70 percent versus 30 percent at Harvard. Since an estimated 25 percent of whites would not have been admitted to Harvard without the legacy benefit, the elimination of this silver spoon is expected to increase Black, Latino, and Native American matriculation.[24] But it is unlikely to be a full substitute for affirmative action, since Blum is likely to cast a litigious gaze over any rise in Black, Latino, and Native American access to slots that might have gone to whites or Asians.

Thus, the question remains: who has access to enough credit—in the form of loans, AP classes, other school resourses, unchallenged voting rights, or freedom from criminalization in advance of committing any crime—to break out of opportunity deserts? The answer lies partly in taking a closer look at, rather than turning a blind eye to, the nuances of race in the United States. And such a look is best taken with the aid of an opportunity map. Sociologist Natasha Warikoo suggests that Asian immigrants who are educationally and economically poised to thrive in test-centric environments and move into neighborhoods traditionally barred to Blacks and Latinos do not need affirmative action—or any substitute for it. But those who arrive as refugees do.[25] Someone like Ling-Chi Wang might disagree because, as Warikoo admits, Asians face racial discrimination and sometimes outright violence. Yet she notes that "model minority" is a less confining stereotype than "intellectual inferior," particularly in the academic admissions sweepstakes. What is certain is that, given all this racial complexity, one needs a map.

THE DEEPEST INEQUALITY

In the America that Rufo and Blum envision, complexity will be difficult to acknowledge, and good opportunity maps will be difficult to draw. The ultimate cause of this is not any Rufo or Blum but the fact that their power rests not just on the anti–civil rights networks I have sketched but also on another reality that Rufo's proposed legislation would banish from public discussion: structural inequity.

Pretending that structural inequity does not exist may be the ultimate three-card Monte game, for the supermajority that struck down affirmative action is the result of structural inequity in the US Senate (which confirms nominations to the Supreme Court). The court's supermajority began with the 2016 decision by then–Senate majority leader Mitch McConnell to not even hold hearings on Barack Obama's nomination of Merrick Garland to replace Justice Antonin Scalia, who died in his sleep eleven months before the 2016 presidential election.[26] McConnell had the power to stick his finger in the president's eye because he had the votes of fifty-four Republican senators, thanks to a profound, democracy-warping structural inequity that has given white-dominated states outsized power since the era of slavery. As political scientists Richard Johnson and Lisa L. Miller explain:

> Three quarters of the U.S. Latino population (75.4%) and almost two thirds of Black Americans (64.3%) live in the 12 most popu-

> lated states. The 25 least populous states are 71.5% white, well above the 60.1% national average. The population distribution of African Americans and Hispanics means that a winning Senate coalition can be constructed without needing to secure the support of any of the states that have sizeable Latino and Black populations. . . . [The Senate] vastly underrepresents two underserved minority groups (i.e., Blacks and Hispanics), who tend to live in high-population states.[27]

This is why the views of a white conservative numerical minority often prevail over the views of a diverse majority in American politics. It is the profoundest sort of affirmative action for whites, a level of agenda-setting power that civil rights activists could never dream of. It allows people like Rufo to pick any given civil rights achievement and redefine it against itself.

After all, Black support for affirmative action is in the 77 percent range, according to an April 2023 NBC News poll.[28] About half of Asians favor affirmative action, though only 21 percent favor it in college admissions, according to a recent Pew poll.[29] Another Pew poll found that Latinos are split down the middle on affirmative action in school admissions (their views on other types of affirmative action were not reported). White respondents disapproved of affirmative action by a margin of 57 percent to 29 percent. However, a thin majority of Democrats approved of affirmative action in college admissions, while 74 percent of Republicans disapproved.[30]

Thus, the Democratic coalition, such as it is, slightly favors affirmative action in college admissions and favors it more robustly elsewhere (if it is aware of the "elsewhere"). But because the white conservative minority handed Donald Trump and Mitch McConnell a color-blind blunderbuss during a critical period when two Supreme Court justices died, the wishes of supporters of affirmative action count for little. Although Pew does not comment on this, my guess is that decades of demonization and the daily resetting of hermeneutic traps in the conservative media (and sometimes in the mainstream media, as it bends over backward to show no "liberal bias") have kept the nation focused on the usual two-dimensional Black-white (or Black–model minority) affirmative action debate—a debate during which some conservatives wrapped Obama and his nomination of a new justice in a foreign flag. McConnell was able to use a massive white advantage to ignore Obama's nominee, offering the eye roll of an explanation that the 2016 election and the end of Obama's presidency were only eleven months away. And yet, eight days after Ruth Bader Ginsburg died of cancer in 2020, McConnell led a house-on-fire rush to confirm conservative judge Amy Coney Barrett to the Supreme Court less than a month before the 2020 election, in which, as he may have anticipated, he lost the majority and thus the power to control the confirmation process.[31]

By contrast, Biden nominee Ketanji Brown Jackson ascended to the high court only because Democrats had cobbled together a photo-finish majority (fifty seats plus the tie-breaking vice president) by winning 40 million more votes in the 2022 midterms than the fifty GOP senators.[32] Of the many indicia of white conservative agenda-setting power, this ability to create a Supreme Court supermajority with millions fewer votes is among the most consequential. It is a perfect example of a structural inequity that Rufo, Blum, and the rest are working to make impossible to acknowledge, much less repair.

Still, a glimmer of hope lies in the fact that even the new supermajority is not a guarantee of wall-to-wall anti–civil rights victories. On June 8, 2023, for instance, the Supreme Court handed Blum and company a rare defeat and shocked liberals, who had been cringing as if they were about to be beaten, when it handed down its decision in an Alabama voting rights case, *Allen v. Milligan*. The case consolidated several challenges to the GOP-dominated state's decision to respond to population growth by drawing a sort of anti-opportunity map: a new electoral map that kept the number of Black-majority districts at one, when it made sense to create two and let the state's African Americans elect an extra representative.[33]

Blum's Project on Fair Representation had no role in litigating the case, but it weighed in with an amicus brief that demanded absolute color blindness in tones closer to those of a religious revival meeting than a legal brief: "the colorblind constitution is like the charred stake that Odysseus drove into the eye of Cyclops to escape that monster's man-eating tyranny," the brief's authors wrote. "The prohibitions in the Reconstruction Amendments require a complete and fundamental destruction of the government's ability to use—and even to perceive—racial categories."[34]

Needless to say, the brief's cyclops metaphor does not acknowledge what happens in the actual story after the cyclops, Polyphemus, is blinded by Greek tactician Odysseus: Polyphemus prays to his father, the god of the sea, asking that the homeward voyage of Odysseus be thwarted. As a result, Odysseus is forced to battle the sea for a weary decade. Similarly, the Reconstruction amendments may have blinded slavery, but the urges and ideas that made slavery possible persisted, preventing African Americans and others touched by civil death from reaching their long-sought home—equal citizenship—for 159 years and counting.

Still, Chief Justice John Roberts, who handed Blum his victory in *Shelby County v. Holder*, shocked the world by striking down the Alabama map, joining a coalition of not only the court's three liberals but also Brett Kavanaugh—all but stamped with the Federalist Society's seal of approval. Against an epic dissent from Clarence Thomas, Roberts provided a Thurgood Marshall–esque history of attacks on Black voting rights, quoted Congress's declaration that the Voting Rights Act is "the most successful civil rights statute in the history of the nation," clung to Supreme Court precedent allowing the limited consideration of race under section 2 of the Voting Rights Act, endorsed a lower court's view that the "totality of circumstances" in Alabama included the state's "extensive history of repugnant racial and voting-related discrimination," and relied on a majority opinion written by Marshall to make a key point.[35]

During a joyous discussion of the decision on the podcast *Amicus*, Roberts was credited with using footnotes to deliver some "sick burns" to Thomas. But the sickest burn of all had to be the quotation from Marshall, the man whose legacy Thomas has worked for decades to undo. Still, *Amicus* host Dahlia Lithwick and her partner in crimes against obtuseness, Mark Joseph Stern, were quick to caution that Roberts and Kavanaugh might have simply been rejecting bad lawyering on Alabama's part. Or the two conservatives might have been trying to defend the court against the charge that it has become another political arm of the American Right, given not only the public outrage over some supermajority decisions but also the price tags hanging from the robes of Federalist Society picks and especially from the robe of Thomas, who has been bankrolled for years by an über-rich conservative supporter.[36] The *Amicus* pair speculated that Roberts might have been looking ahead and trying to inoculate the court against the uproar that might follow the supermajority's upcoming decisions on affirmative action, LGBTQ rights, and other American dilemmas.[37]

The anti–civil rights movement, in short, is not an infallible progress-reversing machine, free to implement even the most brazen of anti-opportunity maps. It is more like a many-headed sea god, not all of whose heads agree all the time. Still, it will continue to throw obstacles like the *SFFA* decision onto the path leading to equal citizenship for those whose "totality of circumstances" Blum, Rufo, and the rest want to remove from the American mind.

Blum, king of the long game, has already formed a new Alliance for Fair Board Recruitment to target efforts to diversify corporate governance, and with the Supreme Court supermajority in place, he has a real shot at dispensing color blindness like white spray paint over the eyes of powerful people interested in seeing the realities of race in America. Already, the decades of anti–civil rights messaging on affirmative action, including the eclipsing of the entire policy by its educational component and the Asian-centric framing of the *SFFA* decision itself, have won majority public support.[38]

But the civil rights movement's inheritors can still muster enough electoral strength to, for instance, send Ketanji Brown Jackson to combine with Sonia Sotomayor (as well as Elena Kagan) and maintain a critical quantum of diversity on a lopsided Supreme Court. Both during oral arguments and in her dissent in the *SFFA v. UNC* case, Jackson offered a memorable burst of light in the form of a thought experiment: Two applicants with North Carolina roots dating to 1789 apply to UNC. The white applicant can discuss to the tiniest tendril his roots in the soil where the University of North Carolina is built. But under Blum-style absolutist color blindness, the Black student can say nothing about ancestors enslaved between 1789 and 1863. The white student's centuries of advantage continue in his mysteriously more fully developed and authentic essay.[39] *Amicus* regular Stern speculates convincingly that Jackson's point, together with similar ones made in the lead dissent penned by Sotomayor, extracted Roberts's grudging concession that allows applicants to discuss their racial experiences in essays.[40]

Blum will surely attack the Roberts loophole if universities start pulling too many Black, Latino, and Native American students through it. But forcing Roberts to create the loophole in the first place is testament to minority agenda setters' power to steer America away from complete disaster. In this way, concession by extracted concession, the civil rights movement continues.

NOTES

INTRODUCTION: HUG-GATE AND OTHER HERMENEUTIC TRAPS

1. Meg Vaillancourt, "Derrick Bell Threatens to Leave Harvard," WGBH 10:00 News, April 24, 1990, http://bostonlocaltv.org/catalog/V_UDAMVZGA4JEY06N; Derrick Bell, *Ethical Ambition: Living a Life of Meaning and Worth* (New York: Bloomsbury, 2002), 169–170.

2. "(Extended) Barack Obama Speaks at Harvard Law in 1990," 9:33–10:15, LeakSourceArchive, https://www.youtube.com/watch?v=_DNEgvjdM1k.

3. In a more nuanced manner than Bell's caricature suggests, Kennedy calls for the management of racial reputation in a way that, "without sacrificing rights or dignity, elicits respect and sympathy rather than fear and anger . . . from other races." Randall Kennedy, *Race, Crime and the Law* (New York: Vintage Books, 1998), 21. One of the findings of the present book, however, is that this kind of reputation management is probably doomed to fail for those who do not control the means of producing information.

4. Derrick Bell, "The Strange Career of Randall Kennedy," *New Politics* 7, 1 (Summer 1998), https://archive.newpol.org/issue25/bell25.htm.

5. Erik Wemple, "Breitbart.com and the Obama Footage: Showmanship Prevails," *Washington Post*, March 8, 2012, https://www.washingtonpost.com/blogs/erik-wemple/post/breitbartcom-and-the-obama-footage-showmanship-prevails/2012/03/08/gIQABFzqzR_blog.html; Peter Dreier, "The Right-Wing Firestorm that Rages On," *Dissent*, July 27, 2018, https://www.dissentmagazine.org/online_articles/acorn-firestorm-documentary-breitbart-vs-grassroots.

6. Christopher Beam, "Breitbart's Back: The Man behind the Shirley Sherrod Shakeup," Slate, July 22, 2010, https://slate.com/news-and-politics/2010/07/a-slate-profile-of-andrew-breitbart.html.

7. Joshua Green, *Devil's Bargain: Steve Bannon, Donald Trump, and the Nationalist Uprising* (New York: Penguin Books, 2018), 199–200, Kindle.

8. Tommy Christopher, "Late Prof. Derrick Bell's Widow Defends Him against Sarah Palin and Co. 'Racist' Smear," Mediaite, March 13, 2012, https://

www.mediaite.com/tv/late-prof-derrick-bells-widow-defends-him-against-sarah-palin-and-co-racist-smear.

9. Jake Tapper, "Did Professor Derrick Bell Visit the White House?" ABC News, March 2012, https://abcnews.go.com/blogs/politics/2012/03/did-professor-derrick-bell-visit-the-white-house.

10. Green, *Devil's Bargain*, 130–134.

11. Bryan Metzger and Jake Lahut, "Trump Issued an Executive Order on Critical Race Theory after Seeing a Segment about It on Tucker Carlson's Show," *Business Insider*, December 7, 2021, https://www.google.com/amp/s/www.businessinsider.com/trump-critical-race-theory-found-out-from-tucker-carlson-book-2021-12%3famp.

12. See, for instance, Alan David Freeman, "Legitimizing Racial Discrimination through Antidiscrimination Law: A Critical Review of Supreme Court Doctrine," *Minnesota Law Review* 62 (1978): 1049–1119. See also Richard Delgado and Jean Stefanic, *Critical Race Theory* (Philadelphia: Temple University Press, 2013); Patricia J. Williams, *The Alchemy of Race and Rights* (Cambridge, MA: Harvard University Press, 1991).

13. Derrick Bell, *And We Are Not Saved: The Elusive Quest for Racial Justice* (New York: Basic Books, 1989), 45.

14. Sylvia Eisner Danovich, ed., *Making a Right a Reality: An Oral History of the Early Years of the EEOC, 1965–1972; in Celebration of the Twenty-Fifth Anniversary, July 2, 1990* (Washington, DC: EEOC, 1990), 14.

15. William J. Collins and Marianne H. Wanamaker, "Up from Slavery? African American Intergenerational Economic Mobility since 1880," NBER Working Paper 23395, May 2017, 3, 5, http://www.nber.org/papers/w23395.

16. Warren Fiske, "Schools Still See Segregated Students," *Houston Chronicle*, June 20, 2022, A3, A5.

17. Derrick A. Bell Jr., *Race, Racism and American Law*, 6th ed. (New York: Aspen, 2008), xx.

18. Christopher F. Rufo (@realchrisrufo), "Replying to @realchrisrufo and @ConceptualJames," Twitter, March 15, 2021, 2:14 p.m., https://twitter.com/realchrisrufo/status/1271540368714428416?/lang=en. See also David Brock, *The Republican Noise Machine: Right Wing Media and How It Corrupts Democracy* (New York: Crown, 2004).

19. Mark R. Levin, *American Marxism* (New York: Threshold Editions, 2021), 111.

20. Richard J. Herrnstein and Charles Murray, *The Bell Curve: Intelligence and Class Structure in American Life* (New York: Free Press, 1994), 470, 476, 484.

21. Derrick A. Bell, "Who's Afraid of Critical Race Theory," *University of Illinois Law Review* 1995, 4 (1995): 894.

22. Levin, *American Marxism*, 99.

23. The executive order is available at https://trumpwhitehouse.archives.gov/presidential-actions/executive-order-combating-race-sex-stereotyping/.

24. It forbade, for instance, the idea that "an individual should be discriminated against or receive adverse treatment solely or partly because of his or her race or sex."

25. Hailey Fuchs, "Trump Attack on Diversity Training Has a Quick and Chilling Effect," *New York Times*, October 13, 2020, https://www.nytimes.com/2020/10/13/us/politics/trump-diversity-training-race.html.

26. Ina Fried, "Labor Department Probes Microsoft's Diversity Policy," Axios, October 6, 2020, https://www.axios.com/2020/10/06/labor-department-probes-microsofts-diversity-policy.

27. Regarding white men and affirmative action, see Jonathan Zimmerman, "Who's Benefiting from Affirmative Action? White Men," *Washington Post*, August 11, 2017, https://www.washingtonpost.com/opinions/who-benefits-from-affirmative-action-white-men/2017/08/11/4b56907e-7eab-11e7-a669. See also Charlotte West, "An Unnoticed Result of the Decline of Men in College: It's Harder for Women to Get In," *Hechinger Report*, October 27, 2021, https://hechingerreport.org/an-unnoticed-result-of-the-decline-of-men-in-college-its-harder-for-women-to-get-in/. According to West, "Seeking gender balance, some selective schools are giving men a leg up in admission." Although that would theoretically benefit all men, the large percentage of white men at these selective schools are among those who benefit from what a law school lecturer told West was something resembling "quotas . . . based on race."

28. Melvin I. Urofsky, *The Affirmative Action Puzzle: A Living History from Reconstruction to Today* (New York: Pantheon Books, 2020).

29. William Shakespeare, *Four Great Tragedies: Hamlet, Othello, King Lear, Macbeth* (New York: Signet Classic, 1998), 70–71, 91.

30. J. Scott Carter and Cameron D. Lippard, *The Death of Affirmative Action? Racialized Framing and the Fight against Racial Preference in College Admissions* (Bristol, UK: Bristol University Press, 2021), 8–10.

31. Sol Stern, "Think Tank in the Tank," *Democracy: A Journal of Ideas*, July 7, 2020, https://democracyjournal.org/arguments/think-tank-in-the-tank/.

32. Carter and Lippard, *Death of Affirmative Action?* 8–9.

33. Ellen Messer-Davidow, *The Making of Reverse Discrimination: How* DeFunis *and* Bakke *Bleached Racism from Equal Protection* (Lawrence: University Press of Kansas, 2021), 21–22.

34. "Jewish philanthropy and the long, ardent, direct Jewish participation in the Civil Rights Movement were critically important factors contributing to the degree of success the civil rights movement enjoyed." C. Eric Lincoln, *Race, Religion, and the Continuing American Dilemma* (New York: Hill & Wang, 1999), 182.

35. Messer-Davidow, *Making of Reverse Discrimination*, 25–26.

36. Greenberg's "no-nonsense manner" is noted by Richard Kluger in *Simple Justice: The History of* Brown v. Board of Education *and Black America's Struggle for Equality* (New York: Alfred A. Knopf, 2004), 273.

37. Jack Greenberg, *Crusaders in the Courts: How a Dedicated Band of Lawyers Fought for the Civil Rights Revolution* (New York: Basic Books, 1994), 467–469.

38. Daniel Kahneman and Amos Tversky, "Conflict Resolution: A Cognitive Perspective," in *Barriers to Conflict Resolution*, ed. Kenneth Arrow,

Robert H. Mnookin, Lee Ross, Amos Tversky, and Robert Wilson (New York: W. W. Norton, 1995), 54.

39. Greenberg, *Crusaders in the Courts*, 52, 461–469.

40. The prisoner's dilemma has been used to model everything from the choice governments make between free trade and protectionism to the choice Supreme Court majorities make between affirming or discarding precedent to the "tragedy of the commons," which occurs when resources are exhausted because no one takes responsibility for protecting them. See Geoffrey Garrett, "International Cooperation and Institutional Choice: The European Community's Internal Market," in *Multilateralism Matters: The Theory and Practice of an International Form*, ed. John Gerard Ruggie (New York: Columbia University Press, 1993), 365–398; Neil S. Siegel, "State Sovereign Immunity and Stare Decisis: Solving the Prisoner's Dilemma within the Court," *California Law Review* 89 (2001): 1165–1197; Anatol Rapoport, "Prisoner's Dilemma," in *Game Theory*, ed. John Eatwell, Murray Milgate, and Peter Newman (New York: Macmillan, 1989), 199–204.

41. Tom Burns and Walter Buckley, "The Prisoners' Dilemma Game as a System of Social Dominance," *Journal of Peace Research* 11, 3 (1974): 223–224.

42. My term is inspired in part by mathematical psychologist Anatol Rapoport's "social trap." Rapoport defines a social trap as "a situation in which each of two or more participants acts 'rationally' in pursuit of [his or her] own interest but nevertheless the outcome is bad for everyone concerned. Arms races, runs on banks and other varieties of panics are well known examples. The Prisoner's Dilemma game is the best known formal model of a social trap." Anatol Rapoport, *Certainties and Doubts: A Philosophy of Life* (Montreal: Black Rose Books, 2000), 150.

43. On the importance of the long run and perspective shifts, see W. G. Runciman and Amartya Sen, "Games, Justice and the General Will," *Mind* 74, 296 (October 1965): 554–562.

44. Roger Boesche, "Homeless? Hungry? It's All Your Fault: The Gingrich Era Means Class-Based Politics, 'Us' vs. 'Them' in a War on the Poor," *Los Angeles Times*, December 1, 1994, https://www.latimes.com/archives/la-xpm-1994-12-01-me-3357-story.html.

45. "Conflict entrepreneur" is Amanda Ripley's term for people who deliberately create or inflame conflict. See Amanda Ripley, *High Conflict: Why We Get Trapped and How We Get Out* (New York: Simon & Schuster, 2021), 117, 136, Kindle.

46. Bell, *And We Are Not Saved*, 3.

47. Rufo, Twitter, March 15, 2021.

48. One of the reasons I use the prisoner's dilemma as my guide through certain mysteries rather than, say, King and Smith's "white supremacist" and "egalitarian transformative" orders is that the prisoner's dilemma story, but not necessarily the mathematical game itself, emphasizes the central role of manipulation in the making and breaking of alliances. The game also emphasizes the boundedness of human knowledge and decision-making power and the seeming unboundedness, at times, of impulse and greed. Finally,

discrimination is not always the result of conscious racism; sometimes it originates in something more like nepotism or embezzlement. The prisoner's dilemma explains that better than a term like "white supremacy."

49. Derrick Bell, "*Brown* and the Interest-Convergence Dilemma," in *Shades of* Brown: *New Perspectives on School Desegregation*, ed. Derrick Bell (New York: Teachers College Press, 1980), 95.

50. According to Bell, poor whites, confronted by the command to desegregate classrooms, "feared loss of control over their public schools and other facilities"—they feared the loss of agenda-setting power in education and beyond. Of course, they also feared the loss of old-fashioned social superiority. "There is evidence," Bell observes, "that segregated schools and facilities were initially established by legislatures at the insistence of the white working class." Bell, "*Brown* and the Interest-Convergence Dilemma," 97. See also Michèle Lamont, Bo Yun Park, and Elena Ayala-Hurtado, "Trump's Electoral Speeches and His Appeal to the American White Working Class," *British Journal of Sociology* 68, S1 (November 2017): S153–S180.

51. "Biden Thinks 'White Supremacy' Is the Greatest Threat to US," *The Five*, https://www.youtube.com/watch?v=mwUyMny7Mt4.

52. Fox's ability to police viewers' minds is discussed in Philip Bump, "The Unique, Damaging Role Fox News Plays in American Media," *Washington Post*, April 4, 2022, https://www.washingtonpost.com/politics/2022/04/04/unique-damaging-role-fox-news-plays-american-media. Fox's token liberals—losing argument after argument, or at least unable to change anyone's mind—actually reinforce the conservative message, as Alexis Sobel Fitts explains in "And from the Left . . . Fox News: There's More to Fox News Strategy of Hiring Liberals than Creating a Public Boxing Match," *Columbia Journalism Review*, March–April 2014, https://archives.cjr.org/feature/and_from_the_left_fox_news.php.

53. Bell joins political scientist Jennifer Hochschild in questioning Myrdal's optimism about the prospects for a racism-free America. He notes that, unlike Myrdal, Hochschild suggests that racism may not be merely a removable stain on the American claim that all people are created equal; it may be a symbiont feeding on America's brain—a symbiont America cannot live without. See Bell, *Race, Racism and American Law*, 67.

54. Gunnar Myrdal, *An American Dilemma*, vol. 1, *The Negro Problem and Modern Democracy* (New Brunswick, NJ: Transaction, 2009), lxx.

55. Ibid., lxxi. Racist thought and totalitarian thought coevolved, combining murderously in Nazi Germany and elsewhere. See Hannah Arendt, *The Origins of Totalitarianism* (Orlando, FL: Harcourt, 1985), 221; Aime Cesaire, *Discourse on Colonialism* (New York: Monthly Review Press, 2000).

56. Hermeneutics originated in interpretations of the Bible. But hermeneutic pursuits can become full-blown religions or all-encompassing political doctrines. This is clear when philosopher Hans-Georg Gadamer asks, which "is the right interpretation of [the Old Testament], the Jewish one or the Christian one in light of the New Testament? . . . But what would a Marxist, who understands religious utterances only as the reflections of class interests, say?"

Hans-Georg Gadamer, *Truth and Method*, trans. Joel Weinsheimer and Donald G. Marshall (New York: Continuum, 2000), 331–332.

57. On conspicuous consumption, see Thorsten Veblen, *The Theory of the Leisure Class: An Economic Study of Institutions* (New York: New American Library, 1953), 65.

58. Nicholas Confessore, "How Tucker Carlson Stoked White Fear to Conquer Cable," *New York Times*, April 30, 2022, https://www.nytimes.com/2022/04/30/us/tucker-carlson-gop-republican-party.html?smid=tw-nytimes&smtyp=cur.

59. "Buffalo Shooter's Weapons Covered in White Supremacist Messaging," ADL, May 15, 2022, https://www.adl.org/resources/blog/buffalo-shooters-weapons-covered-white-supremacist-messaging. On the demonization of Black Lives Matter, see Tyler Cherry, "How Fox News' Primetime Lineup Demonized Black Lives Matter in 2015," Media Matters for America, December 29, 2015, https://www.mediamatters.org/sean-hannity/how-fox-news-primetime-lineup-demonized-black-lives-matter-2015.

60. Bell, *And We Are Not Saved*, 26–50.

61. For a balanced assessment of the democratic upside and the racist downside of the Enlightenment, see Glenn C. Loury, *The Anatomy of Racial Inequality* (Cambridge, MA: Harvard University Press, 2002), 116–121. For more on the downside, see Robert A. Williams Jr., "Documents of Barbarism: The Contemporary Legacy of European Racism and Colonialism in the Narrative Traditions of Federal Indian Law," in Delgado and Stefanic, *Critical Race Theory*, 129–131. See also John P. Diggins, "Slavery, Race, and Equality: Jefferson and the Pathos of Enlightenment," *American Quarterly* 28, 2 (Summer 1976): 206–228.

62. Amy Coney Barrett, "Precedent and Jurisprudential Disagreement," *Texas Law Review* 91 (2013): 1714–1715.

63. Pushing back against one such overturning in one of his last dissents, Thurgood Marshall accused his colleagues of banishing reason. See *Payne v. Tennessee*, 501 U.S. 808 (1991), 844. For an account of Marshall as one pole in an ongoing internal Supreme Court dialectic about the role of precedent, see Colin Starger, "The Dialectic of Stare Decisis Doctrine," *in Precedent in the United States Supreme Court*, ed. Christopher J. Peters (Dordrecht, Netherlands: Springer, 2013), 19–45.

64. Garrett Epps, "The Littlest Rebel: James J. Kilpatrick and the Second Civil War," *Constitutional Commentary* 10, 19 (1993): 24. See also Numan V. Bartley, *The Rise of Massive Resistance: Race and Politics in the South during the 1950s* (Baton Rouge: Louisiana State University Press, 1999), 67, 80.

65. Barry M. Goldwater, *The Conscience of a Conservative* (Eastford, CT: Martino Fine Books, 2011), 31–37; Alfred Regnery, "Goldwater's 'The Conscience of a Conservative' Transformed American Politics," *Washington Times*, November 17, 2014, https://www.washingtontimes.com/news/2014/nov/17/goldwaters-the-conscience-of-a-conservative-transf/; John Micklethwait and Adrian Woolridge, *The Right Nation: Conservative Power in America* (New York: Penguin Press, 2004), 54.

66. Desmond S. King and Rogers M. Smith argue in "Racial Orders in

American Political Development," *American Political Science Review* 99, 1 (2005): 76–79, that US society has been shaped by two competing racial institutional orders: a white supremacist one and an "egalitarian transformative" one. "To accomplish much at all," they explain, "American political actors have generally felt compelled to join either their current form of white supremacist order or its more egalitarian opponent." The temptation to defect from one order to some (perhaps disguised) version of the other is very real because "most political actors possess partly conflicting identities and interests."

67. Matthew Avery Sutton, *Jerry Falwell and the Rise of the Religious Right: A Brief History with Documents* (Boston: Bedford/St. Martin's, 2013), 12, 58; Randall Balmer, *Bad Faith: Race and the Rise of the Religious Right* (Grand Rapids, MI: William B. Erdmans, 2021), 64, Kindle.

68. Liliana Garces and Daniel Woofter, Brief of 1,241 Social Scientists and Scholars on College Access, Asian American Studies, and Race as Amici Curiae in Support of Respondent, Students for Fair Admissions, Petitioner, v. President & Fellows of Harvard College, Respondent, 2–9.

69. Jack Bricksilver, review of *Tearing down the Color Bar: A Documentary History and Analysis of the Brotherhood of Sleeping Car Porters*, by Joseph Wilson, *Journal of Economic History* 51, 1 (March 1991): 248–249.

70. Eileen Boris, "Fair Employment and the Origins of Affirmative Action," *NWSA Journal* 10, 3 (Autumn 1998): 142.

71. Bruce J. Dierenfield, *The Civil Rights Movement* (Harlow, UK: Pearson Education, 2004), 14, 17, 84–85.

72. Bricksilver, review of *Tearing down the Color Bar*, 248. Title VI eliminated the need for the Powell amendments, which the congressman was famous for adding to bills in an effort to prevent the federal government from financing discrimination. See Civil Rights Division, US Department of Justice, *Title VI Legal Manual*, 1–2, last modified April 22, 2022, https://www.justice.gov/crt/book/file/1364106/download.

73. Hugh Davis Graham, *The Civil Rights Movement: Origins and Development of National Policy* (New York: Oxford University Press, 1990), 97–99.

74. Greenberg, *Crusaders in the Courts*, 294–295; Thurgood Marshall, "Remarks at the Annual Conference of the Second Circuit [The Future of Civil Rights] (September 8, 1989)," in *Thurgood Marshall: His Speeches, Writings, Arguments, Opinions, and Reminiscences*, ed. Mark V. Tushnet (Chicago: Lawrence Hill Books, 2001), 216.

75. Sarah H. Brown, "The Role of Elite Leadership in the Southern Defense of Segregation, 1954–1964," *Journal of Southern History* 77, 4 (November 2011): 846–858, 859.

76. Epps points this out in "Littlest Rebel," 20.

77. One early blackface troupe seemed "characteristically Negrolike" to a reviewer because one of its members' "white eyes rolled in a curious frenzy." Hans Nathan, "The Performance of the Virginia Minstrels," in *Inside the Minstrel Mask: Readings in Nineteenth-Century Blackface Minstrelsy*, ed. Annemarie Bean, James V. Hatch, and Brooks McNamara (Middletown, CT: Wesleyan University Press, 1996), 35–36.

78. James Kilpatrick, "Court Endorses Race Discrimination," *Richmond (IN) Palladium-Item*, July 3, 1979, 4.

79. James J. Kilpatrick, "Half Circle on Race: Discrimination Again," *Lancaster (PA) New Era*, September 2, 1981, 18.

80. Ta-Nehisi Coates, "Kilpatrickism," *Atlantic*, August 17, 2010, https://www.theatlantic.com/entertainment/archive/2010/08/kilpatrickism/61611/.

81. The term "anti–civil rights movement" has been used previously. Samuel L. Myers Jr. observed that some of the conservatives wrapping themselves in the flag of civil rights are actually part of "an *anti–civil rights* undertaking." Samuel L. Myers Jr., preface to *Civil Rights and Race Relations in the Post Reagan-Bush Era*, ed. Samuel L. Myers Jr. (Westport, CT: Praeger, 1997), vii. The movement has also been mapped by other scholars, such as Lee Cokorinos, *The Assault on Diversity: An Organized Challenge to Racial and Gender Justice* (Lanham, MD: Rowman & Littlefield, 2003), and Richard Delgado and Jean Stefancic, *No Mercy: How Conservative Think Tanks and Foundations Changed America's Social Agenda* (Philadelphia: Temple University Press, 1996). Here, I flesh out those mappings with the stories and ideas behind them and try to achieve a little of the verve of Jane Mayer's cartographic masterpiece *Dark Money: The Hidden History of the Billionaires behind the Rise of the Radical Right* (New York: Anchor Books, 2016).

82. Michelle Alexander, *The New Jim Crow: Mass Incarceration in the Age of Colorblindness* (New York: New Press, 2012), 9–10, 248.

83. "Plans relying on racial balance [of school populations] to foreclose evasion [of desegregation orders] have not eliminated the need for further orders protecting black children against discriminatory policies, including resegregation within desegregated schools, the loss of black faculty and administrators, suspensions and expulsions at much higher rates than white students, and varying forms of racial harassment ranging from exclusion from extracurricular activities to physical violence," Bell writes. "The educational benefits that have resulted from the mandatory assignment of black and white children to the same schools are also debatable. . . . A preferable method is to focus on obtaining real educational effectiveness, which may entail . . . the creation or preservation of model black schools." Bell, "*Brown* and the Interest-Convergence Dilemma," 100–101.

84. Bell, *Ethical Ambition*, 156–157.

85. Bell's second thoughts about integration were too pessimistic. Seema Metha and Michael Finnegan reported in 2019 that, according to some studies, children attending integrated schools "are more likely to graduate high school and attend college, and they get jobs with higher incomes." Seema Metha and Michael Finnegan, "Segregation Has Soared in America's Schools as Federal Leaders Largely Looked Away," *Los Angeles Times*, July 8, 2019, https://www.latimes.com/politics/la-na-pol-2020-school-segregation-busing-harris-biden-20190708-story.html. Bell explains his resignation from the deanship at the University of Oregon in *Ethical Ambition*, 3.

86. Bell sometimes questioned himself as fiercely as he questioned American society. He confessed in his book *Confronting Authority* that "those of us

who speak out are moved by a deep sense of the fragility of our self-worth"—and by a deep need to defend that self-worth. He reveals in *Ethical Ambition* that when he gave Harvard his ultimatum about awarding tenure to a woman of color, "friends were aware of [his wife] Jewel's failing health, and I fear some of them have never fully forgiven me for going ahead with the protest. . . . Those two questions—Why does it always have to be you? and Who do you think you are?—are the kernels of the themes with which I have wrestled in this book." Derrick Bell, *Confronting Authority: Reflections of an Ardent Protestor* (Boston: Beacon Press, 1994), ix; Bell, *Ethical Ambition*, 170.

87. Bell, *Ethical Ambition*, 31.

88. "Badge of inferiority" appears in both the plaintiff's appeal and the majority opinion in *Plessy v. Ferguson* (1896), and it has been quoted, infused with a different meaning, by Supreme Court justice Clarence Thomas.

89. Affirmative action is, of course, practiced and debated in other countries, but space constraints require that this book focus on the United States.

90. A characteristic manifesto is Anthony Kinnett and Daniel Buck's "Conservatives, Take Back the Education Field," *National Review*, September 20, 2021. A characteristic development is the appointment of Chris Rufo to the board of Florida's New College as part of Governor Ron DeSantis's mission to eradicate "social justice orthodoxy" from the state. See Zac Anderson, "New Era at New College Kicks off with Contentious Meetings, Report of Death Threat," *Herald-Tribune*, January 25, 2023, https://www.heraldtribune.com/story/news/politics/2023/01/25/new-college-of-florida-trustee-appointed-by-ron-desantis-reports-death-threat/69838694007/.

91. Evan Thomas, *First: Sandra Day O'Connor* (New York: Random House, 2019), 259.

92. Ibid.

93. Cheryl I. Harris, "Whiteness as Property," *Harvard Law Review* 106, 8 (June 1993): 1715, 1770, 1773.

94. Brice R. Wachterhauser, "Prejudice, Reason and Force," *Philosophy* 63, 244 (April 1988): 231–232. See also Daniel Kahneman, *Thinking, Fast and Slow* (New York: Farrar, Straus & Giroux, 2013), 30–86, 103–105, 127–128, 202–208.

95. Second Amendment decisions are not the only ones in which interpretation of the Constitution is a life-and-death matter—or "deadly hermeneutics," in the words of Terence Ball, "Constitutional Interpretation and Conceptual Change," in *Legal Hermeneutics: History, Theory, and Practice*, ed. Gregory Leyh (Berkeley: University of California Press, 1992), 129.

96. Gadamer, *Truth and Method*, 164–169, 298–299. Gadamer's term *Vorurteil* is usually translated as "prejudice" rather than "prejudgment." But as Wachterhauser points out, "Vor-urteil" literally means "pre-judgment." The English "prejudice" has similar roots but is more heavily freighted with negative connotations. Wachterhauser, "Prejudice, Reason and Force," 232.

97. Gadamer, *Truth and Method*, 299.

98. About a week after I sent the completed manuscript of this book to the copy editor, the renowned journalist Nikole Hannah-Jones published "The 'Colorblindness' Trap: How a Civil Rights Ideal Got Hijacked." Like this book,

her *New York Times Magazine* article explores the heroic legacy of Thurgood Marshall, the significance of Marshall's defeat in the 1973 case of *Bakke v. University of California at Davis*, and the impact of the anti–affirmative action campaigns of Edward Blum. My book goes further, however, in insisting that affirmative action cannot be fully understood—nor can replacements for it be fully conceptualized—without counting the ways in which the policy has benefited not only the much-scapegoated Black, Latino, and Native American communities, but also many in the Asian American community that Blum claimed to champion in his celebrated 2023 defeat of Harvard University. This book also follows to their sources the many millions of dollars that irrigate not only successes like Blum's but also the successes—against everything from LGBTQ rights to the United States' very ability to reason—that have been racked up by the organizational and conceptual network that I call the anti–civil rights movement.

1. RUNNING THURGOOD RAGGED

1. Richard Kluger, *Simple Justice: The History of* Brown v. Board of Education *and Black America's Struggle for Equality* (New York: Knopf, 2004), 732–749.

2. Ibid., 750. See also J. Harvie Wilkinson III, *From* Brown *to* Bakke*: The Supreme Court and School Integration: 1954–1978* (Oxford: Oxford University Press, 1981), 63–64.

3. Harry Golden, *Mr. Kennedy and the Negroes* (New York: Crest Books, 1964), 85.

4. Transcript, Thurgood Marshall Oral History Interview I, July 10, 1969, by T. H. Baker, LBJ Library, http://www.lbjlibrary.net/assets/documents/archives/oral_histories/marshall_t/marshall.pdf.

5. Judge Tom P. Brady, A *Review of Black Monday: In an Address Made to the Indianola Citizens' Council, October 28th, 1954* (Winona: Association of Citizens Councils of Mississippi, 1954), https://archive.org/details/1954Brady/mode/2up.

6. Ibid., 8.

7. Ibid.

8. The points in this paragraph are drawn from Kurt T. Lash, "Federalism and the Original Fourteenth Amendment," *Harvard Journal of Law and Public Policy* 42, 1 (2014): 69–79.

9. Scholars trace the idea of civil death to the Middle Ages, when a person sentenced to death was treated like a walking corpse from the moment of his conviction. See Valena E. Beety, Judge Michael Aloi, and Evan Johns, "Emergence from Civil Death: The Evolution of Expungement in West Virginia," *West Virginia Law Review Online* 117 (2014): 65; Gabriel J. Chin, "The New Civil Death: Rethinking Punishment in the Era of Mass Conviction," *University of Pennsylvania Law Review* 160 (2012): 1794; Henry David Saunders, "Civil Death—A New Look at an Ancient Doctrine," *William and Mary Law Review* 11, 4 (1970): 989.

10. Forrest G. Wood, *Black Scare: The Racist Response to Emancipation and Reconstruction* (Berkeley: University of California Press, 1968), 104.

11. Johnson's full veto message can be found at Andrew Johnson, "Veto Message, March 27, 1866," *The American Presidency Project*, http://www.presidency.ucsb.edu/documents/veto-message-438.

12. Ibid., 288; Dr. Rayford Logan, *The Betrayal of the Negro: From Rutherford B. Hayes to Woodrow Wilson* (New York: Collier Books 1965), 20. See also Robert J. Kaczorowski, "Revolutionary Constitutionalism in the Era of Civil War and Reconstruction," *New York University Law Review* 61 (November 1986): 884.

13. Richard L. Aynes, "The 39th Congress (1865–1867) and the 14th Amendment: Some Preliminary Perspectives," *Akron Law Review* 42 (2009): 1035–1037. See also Kurt T. Lash, "The Origins of the Privileges or Immunities Clause, Part III: Andrew Johnson and the Constitutional Referendum of 1866," *Georgetown Law Journal* 101 (2013): 1327–1329; Richard L. Aynes, "Constricting the Law of Freedom: Justice Miller, the Fourteenth Amendment, and the Slaughter-House Cases—Freedom: Constitutional Law," *Chicago-Kent Law Review* 70, 2 (December 1994): 629–630.

14. Scott Yenor, ed., *Reconstruction: Core Documents* (Ashland, OH: Ashbrook Press, 2018), 98, 99.

15. August H. Garland, "The Court a Century Ago," in *Yearbook 1976: Supreme Court Historical Society* (1975), 38.

16. See Robert A. Ferguson, *Law and Letters in American Culture* (Cambridge, MA: Harvard University Press, 1984), 19–20, 291–295.

17. Eve-Marie Becker and Jacob Mortensen, eds., *Paul as Homo Novus* (Göttingen, Germany: Vandenhoeck & Ruprecht, 2018), 22.

18. Senator Carl Schurz, "Plea for Amnesty," January 30, 1872, in Yenor, *Reconstruction: Core Documents*, 130.

19. *Ex parte Garland*, 71 U.S. (4 Wall.) 333 (1867), 387, https://www.loc.gov/item/usrep071333/.

20. Ibid., 353.

21. "An exanimation of Miller's background suggests that Miller was hostile to the Fourteenth Amendment and the Congress which proposed it." Aynes, "Constricting the Law of Freedom," 686.

22. For more on this case, see James Pope, "Snubbed Landmark: Why *United States v. Cruikshank* (1876) Belongs at the Heart of the American Constitutional Canon," *Harvard Civil Rights–Civil Liberties Law Review* 49 (2014): 389. See also *United States v. Cruikshank et al.*, 92 U.S. 542 (1876), 554; Lash, "Origins of the Privileges or Immunities Clause," 1290–1293, 1327–1329.

23. Brady, *Review of Black Monday*, 14–16.

24. In his oral history interview, Brady claims he gave the Citizens Councils the copyright to *Black Monday*, his book that grew out of more than six hundred speeches promoting his cause: "I understand they printed around 375,000 to 380,000 copies of it, . . . [and] it enabled the Citizens' Council to operate, it gave them funds." Oral history with Thomas P. Brady, part 1, 1972, Digital Collections at the University of Southern Mississippi, https://usm.access

.preservica.com/uncategorized/IO_bd53df99-c595-47ae-a3af-11f41759eca8/. *Black Monday* sold for $1 per copy "in drugstores and other places across the South." John Bartlow Martin, *The Deep South Says "Never"* (New York: Ballantine Books, 1957), 16.

25. Joan Hoff, *Nixon Reconsidered* (New York: Basic Books, 1994), 79.

26. Kevin P. Phillips, *Post-Conservative America: People, Politics & Ideology in a Time of Crisis* (New York: Vintage Books, 1983), 23.

27. Gerard Robinson and Elizabeth English, "The South's School Choice Scars: The Legacy of School Integration Battles over Today's Education Reform Debate," *U.S. News and World Report*, March 8, 2016, https://www.usnews.com/opinion/knowledge-bank/articles/2016-03-08/the-southern-manifesto-still-impacts-school-choice-after-60-years.

28. Justin Driver, "60 Years Later, the Southern Manifesto Is as Alive as Ever," *Los Angeles Times*, March 11, 2006, https://www.latimes.com/opinion/op-ed/la-oe-0311-driver-southern-manifesto-anniversary-20160311-story.html.

29. Governor J. Strom Thurmond, "Accepting the States' Rights Democratic Nomination as President of the United States," 1948, in Strom Thurmond Collection, ms. 100.366, https://tigerprints.clemson.edu/strom/366.

30. *Nomination of Thurgood Marshall: Hearings before the Committee on the Judiciary, United States Senate, Ninetieth Congress, First Session on Nomination of Thurgood Marshall, of New York, to Be an Associate Justice of the Supreme Court of the United States, July 13, 14, 18, 19, and 24, 1967* (Washington, DC: US Government Printing Office, 1967), 168.

31. Ibid., 166, 172–174.

32. Transcript, Marshall Oral History Interview I.

2. THE SEARCH FOR DEEP EQUALITY

1. Mark Brilliant, *The Color of America Has Changed: How Racial Diversity Shaped Civil Rights Reform in California, 1941–1978* (Oxford: Oxford University Press, 2010), 221.

2. Associated Press, "Reagan Opposes Rumford Act, Proposition 14 Too," *Fresno Bee*, April 22, 1966, 5-A. Other outlets, including the *Los Angeles Times*, reported that Reagan supported Proposition 14. See also UPI, "Reagan's Stand on Birchers Shocks Brown," *Sacramento Bee*, August 6, 1966, A3.

3. Vic Pollard, "Speaks to 200 in Redlands: Ronald Reagan Seeks Help on Big Government Issue," *Redlands Daily Facts*, May 18, 1966.

4. Matthew Fleischer, "How the L.A. Times Helped Write Segregation into California's Constitution," *Los Angeles Times*, October 21, 2020, http://www.latimes.com/opinion/story/2020-10-21/prop-14-ronld-reagan-la-times-vote-segregation-californias-constitution. See also Brilliant, *Color of America*, 222–226; Michael C. Dawson and Lawrence D. Bobo, "The Reagan Legacy and the Racial Divide in the George W. Bush Era," *Du Bois Review* 1, 2 (2004): 209; United Press International, "State Officials at Odds on Proposition 14," *Desert Sun*, May 12, 1966.

5. Thomas A. Delaney, "Fighting Housing Discrimination in Orange County," *Daily Journal*, December 5, 2017, https://www.dailyjournal.com/articles/345077-fighting-housing-discrimination-in-orange county.

6. See "Memories of Migration: Dorothy Mulkey," Santa Ana Oral History Project, https://www.youtube.com/watch?v=Bf3Mye5eBU; "Witness History: Dorothy Mulkey—US Fair Housing Campaigner," May 26, 2015, https://www.bbc.co.uk/sounds/play/p02rq84x.

7. David B. Oppenheimer, "California's Anti-Discrimination Legislation, Proposition 14, and the Constitutional Protection of Minority Rights: The Fiftieth Anniversary of the California Fair Employment and Housing Act," *Golden Gate University Law Review* 40 (2010): 125.

8. The California Supreme Court had combined the Mulkey-Reitman case with another, *Prendergast v. Snyder*, and the US Supreme Court also considered these cases in tandem. *Reitman v. Mulkey*, 387 U.S. 369 (1967), 372.

9. Juan Williams, *Thurgood Marshall: American Revolutionary* (New York: Times Books, 1998), 314–317.

10. For example:

Marshall: I say this provision is an absolute bar to a court taking any action against racial discrimination in housing.

Warren: And it would at least, it seems to me, be a discouragement to . . . any agency of the State of California from ever cooperating with the Federal government in any such statute.

Marshall: That's right.

11. Oppenheimer, "California's Anti-Discrimination Legislation," 124; Brilliant, *Color of America*, 191–192.

12. William French Smith, one of the deep pockets that pressed Reagan to run for governor in the first place, stepped forward in his capacity as a lawyer to file a brief intended to sway the Supreme Court in Reitman's direction. Peter P. F. Radkowski III, "Managing the Invisible Hand of the California Housing Market, 1942–1967," *California Legal History Journal* (2006): 69, http://www.law.berkeley.edu/files/radkowski-paper.pdf; University of Virginia Miller Center, "William French Smith (1981–1985)," https://millercenter.org/president/reagan/essays/smith-1981-attorney-general.

13. Lou Cannon, *Governor Reagan: His Rise to Power* (New York: Public Affairs, 2003), 6, 274.

14. Oppenheimer, "California's Anti-Discrimination Legislation," 124–125.

15. Robert Cohen, *Freedom's Orator: Mario Savio and the Radical Legacy of the 1960s* (Oxford: Oxford University Press, 2009), 99.

16. Meg Jacobs and Julian E. Zelizer, *Conservatives in Power: The Reagan Years, 1981–1989: A Brief History with Documents* (Boston: Bedford/St. Martin's, 2011), 168, Kindle.

17. Seth Rosenfeld, *Subversives: The FBI's War on Student Radicals* (New York: Farrar, Straus & Giroux, 2012), 344.

18. See John J. Goldman, "Pollsters Call Backlash Big Factor in Election:

Opinion Analysts Say Resistance to Negro Demands Is at All-Time High across U.S.," *Los Angeles Times*, November 6, 1966, A-2. See also Fleischer, "How the L.A. Times Helped Write Segregation"; John A. McCone et al., *A Report by the Governor's Commission on the Los Angeles Riots: Violence in the City—An End or a Beginning?* December 2, 1965, 4, 75–79; Jeanne Theoharis, "Alabama on Avalon: Rethinking the Watts Uprising and the Character of Black Protest in Los Angeles," in *The Black Power Movement: Rethinking the Civil Rights–Black Power Era*, ed. Peniel E. Joseph (London: Routledge, 2006), 48.

19. Kurt Schuparra, *Triumph of the Right: The Rise of the California Conservative Movement, 1945–1966* (Armonk, NY: M. E. Sharpe, 1998), 120.

20. African Americans fleeing the Jim Crow South in the early twentieth century were greeted in many places by restrictive covenants that barred them from renting in entire neighborhoods. See LaDal C. Winling and Todd M. Michney, "The Roots of Redlining: Academic, Governmental, and Professional Networks in the Making of the New Deal Leading Regime," *Journal of American History* 108, 1 (June 2021): 42–69; Richard Rothstein, *The Color of Law: A Forgotten History of How Our Government Segregated America* (New York: Liveright, 2018), viii.

21. Rothstein, *Color of Law*, vii, 37, 44–56, 153–171. See also Eduardo Bonilla-Silva, *Racism without Racists: Color-Blind Racism and the Persistence of Racial Inequality in America* (Lanham, MD: Rowman & Littlefield, 2018), 1–4.

22. Aaron J. Leonard and Conor A. Gallagher, "The Case of Richard Aoki: Berkeley Radical, Black Panther, FBI Informant," *Jacobin*, August 2018, https://www.jacobinmag.com/2018/08/richard-aoki-fbi-informant-leonard-gallagher. See also Seth Rosenfeld, "New FBI Files Show Wide Range of Black Panther Informant's Activities," Reveal, June 9, 2015, https://revealnews.org/article/news-fbi-files-show-wide-range-of-black-panther-informants-activities/.

23. K. Connie Kang, "Activist for a New Era of Civil Rights," *Los Angeles Times*, July 6, 2001, https://www.latimes.com/archives/la-xpm-2001-jul-06-me-19283-story.html; Michael Collins, interview with L. Ling-Chi Wang, June 1, 2021 (unless otherwise noted, subsequent quotes are from this interview).

24. L. Ling-Chi Wang, "UC Berkeley's Asian American Studies: 50 Years of Growing Pains & Gains," in *Mountain Movers: Student Activism & the Emergence of Asian American Studies*, ed. Russell Jeung, Karen Umemoto, Harvey Dong, Eric Mar, Lisa Hirai Tsuchitani, and Arnold Pan (Los Angeles: UCLA Asian American Studies Press, 2019), 98.

25. The next step at Berkeley was the creation of an "experimental class" on Asian American history sponsored by criminology professor Paul Takagi and team-taught by Wang, Richard Aoki, future architecture superstar Bing Thom, and anthropology graduate student Alan Fong.

26. Associated Press, "Construction Boycott on Chinese Told," *Eureka Times Standard*, July 12, 1970.

27. Rachel F. Moran, "The Story of *Lau v. Nichols*: Breaking the Silence in Chinatown," in *Education Law Stories*, ed. Michael A. Olivas and Ronna Greff Schneider (New York: Foundation Press, 2008), 116–117.

28. Quoted in Edward H. Steinman, "*Lau v. Nichols*: Implications for Bilingual Education," in *Bilingual-Bicultural Education: Conference Papers*, ed. Charles D. Moody Sr. and Mary B. Davis (Ann Arbor: Program for Educational Opportunity, University of Michigan, 1977), 32.

29. Ibid., 32, 118–119; *Lau v. Nichols*, 483 F.2d 791 (9th Cir. 1973), https://casetext.com/case/lau-v-nichols/case-details?PHONE_ NUMBER _GROUP=P.

30. Moran, "Story of *Lau v. Nichols*," 119.

31. *Hearings before the Select Committee on Equal Education Opportunity of the United States Senate, Ninety-Second Congress, First Session on Equal Educational Opportunity, Part 9B—San Francisco and Berkeley, Calif.—Appendix* (Washington, DC: US Government Printing Office, 1971), 4733.

32. Moran, "Story of *Lau v. Nichols*," 122. See also *In re Certain Chinese Family Benevolent & District Ass'n*, 19 F.R.D. 97 (1956), https://cite.case.law/frd/19/97/.

33. According to Moran, Steinman "thinks that the Nixon administration was receptive because it saw the growing number of Latinos in the United States as likely to become a Republican constituency." Moran, "Story of *Lau v. Nichols*," 125.

34. *Lau v. Nichols*, 483 F.2d 791 (9th Cir. 1973), https://openjurist.org/483/f2d/791/lau-v-h-nichols.

35. *Lau v. Nichols*, 414 U.S. 563 (1974), 566–567, 569.

36. Edward H. Steinman, "Kinney Kinmon Lau, et al., Appellants, v. Alan H. Nichols, et al., Appellees, No. 26155: Appellants' Opening Brief on Appeal for the Ninth Circuit," in *Hearings before the Select Committee on Equal Educational Opportunity*, 4718.

37. The Jack Greenberg–driven *Griggs v. Duke Power Company* (1971) used Title VII to forbid seemingly neutral job requirements that had disparate impacts on different groups. As for *Lau*, J. D. Hsin observes that it was the first case in which the Supreme Court implied that section 60 of Title VI "outlawed policies with discriminatory effects, irrespective of their motivating intent—a form of discrimination now commonly known as *disparate impact*. . . . However, just four years after the *Lau* decision, the Court seemed to walk its reading of Title VI back, ruling in *Regents of the University of California v. Bakke* that a Title VI violation 'must involve more than just a racially disparate impact, but a provable discriminatory intent as well.'" J. D. Hsin, "Civil Rights at School: Agency Enforcement of Title VI of the Civil Rights Act of 1964," Congressional Research Service, April 4, 2019, 9. See also Jared P. Cole, "Civil Rights at School: Agency Enforcement of Title VI in the Civil Rights Act of 1964," Congressional Research Service, April 4, 2019. For more on disparate impact, see Rachel Moran, "Undone by Law: The Uncertain Legacy of *Lau v. Nichols*," *Berkeley La Raza Law Journal* 16, 1 (2005): 1–10.

38. Kevin L. Yuill, *Richard Nixon and the Rise of Affirmative Action: The Pursuit of Racial Equality in an Era of Limits* (Lanham, MD: Rowman & Littlefield, 2006), 93–94. Nixon "wanted to assemble a more diverse 'New Republican Majority,' which led to him supporting several liberal policies, including

bilingual education," according to Jerry Sisneros, "California's Bilingual Education Battle: From 'Great Society' to 'Save Our State,'" *Perspectives: A Journal of Historical Inquiry* 47 (Spring 2020): 101.

39. Thomas J. Sugrue, "Affirmative Action from Below: Civil Rights, the Building Trades, and the Politics of Racial Equality in the Urban North, 1945–1969," *Journal of American History* 91, 1 (June 2004): 146–149, 154, 164.

40. Rick Perlstein, *Nixonland: The Rise of a President and the Fracturing of America* (New York: Scribner, 2008), 515; Donald Janson, "U.S. Judge Upholds Controversial Philadelphia Plan to Increase Hiring of Minorities in Building Industry," *New York Times*, March 15, 1970, 30.

41. Perlstein, *Nixonland*, 515; Jo Ann Ooiman Robinson, ed., *Affirmative Action: A Documentary History* (Westport, CT: Greenwood Press, 2001), 133.

42. Interview with John Ehrlichman and J. Stanley Pottinger, May 29, 1986, by William Stueck, UGA Special Collections Libraries Oral Histories, https://georgiahistory.libs.uga.edu/RBRL1750HD-014.

43. Ibid.

44. Unprompted during the 1986 interview, Pottinger contrasted the national furor over the killing of four students by National Guardsmen at Kent State University and the relative silence that greeted similar killings at Black universities: "You must remember that at Jackson State, which is a black college, and Southern University, which is a black college, more kids were killed than at Kent State," he said. "No one ever remembers that, because in white America that doesn't count."

45. Joseph Crespino, *Strom Thurmond's America* (New York: Hill & Wang, 2013), 8, 215, 221.

46. Hugh Davis Graham, *Collision Course: The Strange Convergence of Affirmative Action and Immigration Policy in America* (Oxford: Oxford University Press, 2002), 83, 84; "Administration Denies Intent to Scrap the Philadelphia Plan," *New York Times*, September 5, 1972, 14.

47. Graham, *Collision Course*, 83, 84.

48. Caroline Lazo, *Gloria Steinem: Feminist Extraordinaire* (Minneapolis: Lerner Publications, 1998), 87; Carol Iannone, "Enough Is [Never?] Enough," *Academic Questions* (Fall 2021), https://www.nas.org/academic-questions/34/3/enough-is-never-enough.

3. THE RISE OF CHINESE FOR AFFIRMATIVE ACTION

1. L. Ling-Chi Wang, "*Lau v. Nichols*: History of a Struggle for Equal and Quality Education," in *Counterpoint: Perspectives on Asian America*, ed. Emma Gee (Los Angeles: Regents of the University of California, 1978), 247.

2. Ibid., 247–249.

3. Dexter Waugh and Bruce Koon, "Breakthrough for Bilingual Education: *Lau v. Nichols* and the San Francisco School System," *Civil Rights Digest* 6, 4 (Summer 1974): 20.

4. Ibid., 20, 24, 26.

5. Ibid., 24.

6. Doris R. Fine, *When Leadership Fails: Desegregation and Demoralization in the San Francisco Public Schools* (New Brunswick, NJ: Transaction, 1986), 123, 122, Google Books.

7. Ibid., 93, 109.

8. Ibid., 109, 110.

9. Steven P. Morena, Superintendent of Schools, "To All District Staff Members," *San Francisco Unified School District Newsletter* 46, 20 (June 9, 1975): 2.

10. Charlie Euchner, "Languages, Law, and San Francisco," *Education Week*, January 25, 1984, https://www.edweek.org/education/languages-law-and-san-francisco/1984/01.

11. Michael Collins, interview with L. Ling-Chi Wang, June 1, 2021. Starting in 1981, a Newcomer High School was opened for students who did not speak English.

12. Of course, Der knows how to raise his voice when necessary. His 1982 shouting match with famed attorney Melvin Belli made the newspapers. Complaining about personal injury damage awards, the seventy-five-year-old Belli said, "The goddamn Chinese won't give you a short noodle on a verdict." Der and about forty others responded by picketing Belli's office, and Der confronted the lawyer when he came out to talk to the protesters. Belli commented, "I love every Chinaman in town," and Der informed him that he was using a racist slur. Belli eventually apologized. UPI, "Lawyer Belli Sorry about Racial Slurs," July 29, 1982, https://www.upi.com/Archives/1982/07/29/Lawyer-Belli-sorry-about-racial-slurs/6332396763200/.

13. "Presentation of Henry Der, Executive Director, Chinese for Affirmative Action, San Francisco, California," in *Civil Rights Issues of Asian Pacific Americans: Myths and Realities, May 8–9, 1979, Washington D.C. A Consultation Sponsored by the United States Commission on Civil Rights*, ed. Laura Chin, Arthur S. Fleming, et al. (US Commission on Civil Rights, 1979), 406.

14. Associated Press, "Justice Department Says S.F. Police Apply Discrimination," *Times Standard*, November 18, 1977, 7.

15. Associated Press, "Chinatown Gang Leader Was Target," *Santa Cruz Sentinel*, September 7, 1977, 1, 12; "Tape Details Planning for Chinatown Raid," *Santa Cruz Sentinel*, May 4, 1978, 6.

16. Wang interview.

17. Jim Herron Zamora, "Fred Lau Overcame Height Restrictions to Fulfill Dream of Joining Force," *San Francisco Examiner*, January 10, 1996, https://www.sfgate.com/news/article/Fred-Lau-overcame-height-restrictions-to-fulfill-3153484.php.

18. Kevin J. Mullen, "The Golden Dragon Restaurant Massacre: Historical Essay," Found SF, n.d., https://www.foundsf.org/index.php?titles+The_Golden_Dragon_Restrurant_Massacre.

19. Jim Herron Zamora and Cicero Estrella, "A Low-Profile Chief/Heather Fong May Serve behind the Scenes, but She's Tough and Reform-Minded," SFGATE, May 2, 2004, https://www.sfgate.com/news/article/A-low-profile-chief-Heather-Fong-may-serve-2762691.php.

20. Der also outlined CAA's overall strategy: "Chinese for Affirmative Action firmly is convinced that the protection of the civil rights of Chinese Americans is dependent on several ingredients. One, vigorous and vigilant enforcement of civil rights and affirmative action laws by appropriate Federal agencies. Two, substantial community interest and support. . . . Three, coalition efforts with other ethnic minority and women's groups. Four, persistency by civil rights groups to implement and monitor, whenever possible, court decisions, consent decrees, and other judgments and agreements affecting employment opportunities." "Presentation of Henry Der," 405–406. Regarding the plaintiffs in the case, see *Officers for Justice v. Civil Service Commission of San Francisco*, 473 F. Supp. 809 (1979), https://www.anylaw.com/case/officers-for-justice-v-civil-serv-commn-of-san/n-d-california/03-29-1979/3Jh4RGYBTITomsSBCCJL.

21. *Officers for Justice*, 371 F. Supp. 1328 (1973).

22. In *Griggs*, the Supreme Court ruled that requiring a job applicant to have a high school diploma or to pass an intelligence test when "neither standard is shown to be significantly related to successful job performance" disadvantages Blacks, in violation of Title VII of the Civil Rights Act of 1964. *Griggs v. Duke Power Co.*, 401 U.S. 424 (1971), 425–426, https:/www.loc.gov/item/usrep401424/. Judge Peckham struck down the height requirement on the grounds that the "statistical data before this court is sufficient to establish a prima facie case of employment discrimination where, as here, the selection device . . . has an a priori foreseeably exclusionary effect." *Officers for Justice*, 395 F. Supp. 378 (N.D. Cal., 1975).

23. *Officers for Justice*, 473 F. Supp. 801 (N.D. Cal. 1979); *Officers for Justice*, 395 F. Supp. 378 (N.D. Cal. 1975).

24. "Police Quotas Set in San Francisco: Minority Groups Win Suit—Present Exams Barred," *New York Times*, December 2, 1973, 29.

25. Prentice Earl Sanders and Bennett Cohen, *The Zebra Murders: A Season of Killing, Racial Madness, and Civil Rights* (New York: Arcade, 2006), 11.

26. Anthony J. Balzer, "Quotas and the San Francisco Police: A Sergeant's Dilemma," *Public Administration Review* (May–June 1977): 277, 278, 280.

27. Ibid., 280–282, 283.

28. In 1970, 14.4 percent of white males and 8.4 percent of white females had completed four or more years of college, compared with only 4.2 percent of Black males and 4.6 percent of Black females and 7.8 percent of Hispanic males and 4.3 percent of Hispanic females. No 1970 statistics are available for Asian Americans, perhaps because Wang and his associates had just invented the category. *Statistical Abstract of the United States: 1999*, 169, https://www.census.gov/library/publications/1999/compendia/statab/119ed.html.

29. The Katzenbach Commission called for higher-quality policing, explaining that "'quality' is used here in a comprehensive sense. One thing it means is a high standard of education for policemen. Police work always will demand quick reflexes, law enforcement know-how and devotion to duty, but modern police work demands much more than that. . . . A policeman today is poorly equipped for his job if he does not understand the legal issues involved in his everyday work. . . . 'Quality' also means personnel who represent all sectors

of the community that the police serve. It scarcely needs stating that a college education does not guarantee that its recipient will be able to deal successfully with people whose ways of thought and action are unfamiliar to him. . . . [A] lack of understanding of the problems and behavior of minority groups is common to most police departments and is a serious deterrent to effective police work." Nicholas Katzenbach, chairman, *The Challenge of Crime in a Free Society: A Report by the President's Commission on Law Enforcement and Administration of Justice* (Washington, DC: US Government Printing Office, 1967), 107.

30. Balzer, "Quotas and the San Francisco Police," 280.

31. Sanders and Cohen, *Zebra Murders*, 168.

32. Ibid., 169.

33. Balzer, "Quotas and the San Francisco Police," 4. The answer to Balzer's question might be that a minority group member belongs to a community touched by civil death that requires some form of affirmative action to overcome.

34. Sanders and Cohen, *Zebra Murders*, 4.

35. Ibid., 37.

36. See Dick Nolan, "Real Story of the Zebra Tipster: Police Fear Too Much Talk Blew the Case," *San Francisco Examiner*, May 7, 1974, 1. See also *People v. Cooks* (1983), Crim. No. 15402, Court of Appeals of California, First Appellate District, Division 2, https://caselaw.indlaw.com/court/ca-court-of-appeal/1838717.html.

37. Sanders and Cohen, *Zebra Murders*, 86, 90. Decades later, the racial subtext emerged when Sanders was on a book tour for *The Zebra Murders*. Former fellow officer Louis Calabro showed up at a reading and accused Sanders of playing down the level of Black-on-white crime at the time of the Zebra murders. Calabro's anger is rooted in a typical anti–civil rights movement grievance: "African Americans, Asians, Hispanics, women, etc. have their own organizations" within the police department, he wrote in a 1989 opinion piece published in the POA newspaper. "Additionally, these groups have the CONSENT DECREE and the FEDERAL COURT trying to gain benefits for them to the exclusion of white males. . . . If I am your BROTHER how can you stand by and allow 'THE SYSTEM' to injure me on the basis of race and sex[?]" Lou Calabro, "Ain't I Your Brother???" *Police Officers Association Notebook* 21, 11 (November 1989): 6. Less interested in brotherhood than he claimed, Calabro was distressed by the first TV commercials depicting interracial couples. See Ron Russell, "Earl's Last Laugh," *SF Weekly*, February, 21, 2007, https://www.sfweekly.com/news/earls-last-laugh/; Thomas Ginsberg, "Taboos Tumbling in Ad Portrayals: Bureau of Census Data, Advertisers Plan to Feature More Diversity," *Wisconsin State Journal*, October 22, 2000, 14A.

38. Sanders and Cohen, *Zebra Murders*, 201.

39. "S.F. Appeals Federal Injunction Halting Zebra Dragnet," *ACLU News* 40, 7 (February 1975): 3.

40. Balzer, "Quotas and the San Francisco Police," 282.

41. See Jeffrey Toobin, "Fajita Justice: How a Fight over Takeout Led to a

Citywide Police Scandal," *New Yorker*, July 6, 2003, https://www.newyorker.com/magazine/2003/07/14/fajita-justice. It also emerged that, before he became chief, Sanders and a partner suppressed evidence and sent an innocent man to jail. The conspiracy charge against Sanders—driven by lurid *San Francisco Chronicle* coverage—was eventually dismissed by a judge who asked, "Where was the nod? Where was the wink?" For Sanders, the accusation might have been well-earned bad karma, but Black officers saw it as an outrageous attempt to bring a man who had opened doors for them to his knees. Russell, "Earl's Last Laugh."

42. Balzer, "Quotas and the San Francisco Police," 282, 284.

43. Scholarship on overcoming inequity—or scholarship on equity—considers the value of these and other measures and explores the reasons for persistent inequities, including many of those I discuss in this book. According to a 2018 essay, equity "emerged as an alternative and prominent construct linked to social justice, especially in the fields of health and education. Equity invokes a search for the social, economic, and political causes of inequality, and for remedies that consider the context and circumstances of disparate outcomes. . . . [If one runner in a race is set far behind the starting line, equity] moves the disadvantaged . . . to the same starting point as the advantaged runner." David T. Takeuchi, Tiziana C. Dearing, Melissa W. Bartholomew, and Ruth G. McRoy, "Equality and Equity: Expanding Opportunities to Remedy Disadvantage," *Generations: Journal of the American Society on Aging* 42, 2 (Summer 2018): 14. In this book, to underscore how this sort of difference flies under the radar until something like the *Lau* case makes it visible, I refer to the inequality faced by the disadvantaged runner as deep inequality.

44. Sanders and Cohen, *Zebra Murders*, 14.

45. *Officers for Justice*, 371 F. Supp. 1328 (1973).

46. Henry Der told me that CAA helped the fire department lawsuit in a similar way by recruiting community members to apply and that then CAA leader Owyang Turner took part in meetings where details of the consent decree were worked out.

47. "Presentation of Henry Der," 523.

4. THE COALITION SPLITS

1. Weigel delayed deciding the *Johnson* case for eight months so that he could align himself with the Supreme Court's ruling in *Swann v. Charlotte-Mecklenburg Board of Education*, decided April 20, 1971. Doris R. Fine explains the reason for Weigel's delay in *When Leadership Fails: Desegregation and Demoralization in the San Francisco Public Schools* (New Brunswick, NJ: Transaction, 1986).

2. *Johnson v. San Francisco Unified School District*, 339 F. Supp. 1315 (N.D. Cal. 1971).

3. Robert Strand, "Many Determined to Protest until Order Changed: Busing Program Leaves San Francisco Residents Angry," *Lubbock Avalanche-Journal*, September 10, 1971.

4. The trope turned up again, in the form of whites' right to freedom of association, in an effort by Los Angeles County assemblyman Floyd Wakefield to block school integration. See Daniel Martinez HoSang, *Racial Propositions: Ballot Initiatives and the Making of Postwar California* (Berkeley: University of California Press, 2010), 91–96. Wakefield claimed that integration was being shoved down the throats of innocent white Angelenos. But of course, much of the Los Angeles area had been deliberately segregated, in the most guilty ways imaginable, for the benefit of such "innocents." See Richard Rothstein, *The Color of Law: A Forgotten History of How Government Segregated America* (New York: Liveright, 2017), 81.

5. "It turns out that the average white person views racism as a zero-sum game. If things are getting better for black people, it must be at the expense of white people." Quoted in Heather McGhee, *The Sum of Us: What Racism Costs Everyone and How We Can Prosper Together* (New York: One World, 2021), 6.

6. Ibid.

7. United Press International, "Alioto, SF Board of Education Head Hit Superintendent Attack," *Appeal-Democrat*, February 9, 1972; Nanette Asimov, "Dr. Zuretti Goosby of S.F.—Longtime Education Leader," SFGATE, February 3, 2000, https://www.sfgate.com/news/article/Dr-Zuretti-Goosby-of-S-F-Longtime-Education-2779064.php.

8. Joseph Alsop, "Busing to Be Major Issue of '72," *Syracuse Post-Standard*, December 6, 1971.

9. Oral History Interview with Quentin L. Kopp, August 18 and 19, October 6, 8, 11, 18, and 25, November 17 and 29, December 3 and 30, 2001, by Donald B. Seay, California State Archives, State Government Oral History Program, 159, https://archive.org/stream/oh2003-03-kopp/oh2003-kopp-djvu.txt.

10. Associated Press, "Bid to Exclude Chinese Schoolchildren Filed," *Press Telegram*, July 15, 1971; United Press International, "Chinese Parents File US Appeal," *Appeal-Democrat*, October 7, 1971.

11. The enrollment numbers for the various schools appear in Nicholas Appleton's *Multiculturalism and the Courts*, Bilingual Education Paper Series 2, no. 4 (HEW, November 1978).

12. "San Francisco: The School Busing Furor Goes On," *This World: A Section of the S.F. Sunday Examiner & Chronicle*, August 8, 1971, 5.

13. "Pleas to Supreme Court, Reagan on S.F. Busing," *San Francisco Examiner*, August 15, 1971, 13.

14. Oral History Interview with Kopp, 161.

15. Martin Meeker, "Quentin Kopp: Minority Politics in San Francisco, 1964–1996," 2007, 33, Regional Oral History Office, Bancroft Library, University of California–Berkeley.

16. In *Swann*, the court sought to break massive resistance to the *Brown* desegregation requirements by giving district courts the authority to impose remedies that included busing and, as a "starting point," the "very limited" setting of goals for the percentage of Black students in a student body. *Swann v. Charlotte-Mecklenburg Board of Education*, 402 U.S. 1 (1971), 25.

17. *Guey Heung Lee et al. v. Johnson et al.*, 404 U.S. 1215 (1971), 1216–1217.

18. Ibid., 1217.

19. Associated Press, "Douglas Refuses Busing Halt," *Daily Review*, August 30, 1971.

20. United Press International, "Chinese to Continue Bus Fight Despite Ruling," *Daily Review*, September 1, 1971, 1.

21. UPI, "SF Boycott 'Invited' by Court Ruling," *Martinez (CA) Morning News-Gazette*, September 2, 1971, 3.

22. "Attorney to Run for S.F. Board," *Oakland Tribune*, August 18, 1971.

23. UPI, "SF Boycott 'Invited' by Court Ruling."

24. Robert Strand, "Boycott Continues: Chinatown Steadfastly Resists Busing Attempt," *Lubbock Avalanche-Journal*, September 23, 1971.

25. Edith Lederer, "Threat to Culture: S.F.'s Chinese United in Opposition to Busing," *Press-Telegram*, August 11, 1971.

26. Strand, "Boycott Continues."

27. Ibid.

28. UPI, "Alioto, SF Board of Education Head Hit Superintendent Attack."

29. "News of the Week: San Francisco; the Storm over Busing," *San Francisco Examiner*, August 1, 1971.

30. Wing S. Wong, "Editor's Mailbox: The Shaheen Episode," *San Francisco Examiner*, February 15, 1972.

31. Michael Collins, interview with Ling-Chi Wang, June 1, 2021. See also Mike Silverman, "Chinese Open Neighborhood Schools as Protest to Court-Ordered Busing," *Nashua Telegraph*, September 22, 1971.

32. After Wang successfully lobbied for the creation of a Chinese immersion program in the public schools, he told me in 2021, "Every year the school that had the immersion program—you know there are about fifty elementary schools in San Francisco—always ranked at the top, the very top—especially in verbal and math tests, standardized tests, which is a requirement for the state. . . . There are now five or six elementary schools in San Francisco that have Chinese immersion programs, some in Cantonese and some in Mandarin." The small miracle this represents is clear if one considers the intensity of the mutual resentment sparked in some parts of the Black, Chinese, and Latino communities by the clash between bilingualism and integration. Ronald Reagan cannily exploited these resentments as part of the "Southwestern strategy" he pursued in his runs for governor and, in 1980, for president. See Mark Brilliant, *The Color of America Has Changed: How Racial Diversity Shaped Civil Rights Reform in California, 1941–1978* (Oxford: Oxford University Press, 2010), 237–241.

33. Associated Press, "Nixon Loses Vote of Chinese-American," *Auburn (NY) Citizen Advertiser*, October 29, 1971, 22.

34. Philip A. Lum, "The Creation and Demise of San Francisco Chinatown Freedom Schools: One Response to Desegregation," *Amerasia* 5, 1 (1978): 67.

35. HoSang, *Racial Propositions*, 103–104.

36. Lum, "Creation and Demise of San Francisco Chinatown Freedom Schools," 63.

37. Wang interview.

38. Lum, "Creation and Demise of San Francisco Chinatown Freedom Schools," 62.

39. Douglas Martin, "Willis Carto, Far-Right Figure and Holocaust Denier, Dies at 89," *New York Times*, November 1, 2015.

40. Lum, "Creation and Demise of San Francisco Chinatown Freedom Schools," 62.

41. George Michael, *Willis Carto and the American Far Right* (Gainesville: University Press of Florida, 2008), 34.

42. HoSang, *Racial Propositions*, 130–135.

43. Jay Patterson, registrar of voters, *San Francisco Voter Information Pamphlet: Municipal Election, November 8, 1983*, 71, 72.

44. Ibid., 75–76.

45. William Endicott, "After Years of Inaction, S.F. Chinese Flex Political Muscles: Ouster of Voter Registrar over Slur Dramatizes Growing Power," *Los Angeles Times*, February 13, 1980, 3.

46. John Jacobs, "Supporters Spread Word on English-Only Ballot," *Washington Post*, November 12, 1983, https://www.washingtonpost.com/archive/politics/1983/11/12/supporters-spread-word-on-english-only-ballot/0d02ca04-8bb9-494f-bc34-062ccf64fec8.

47. Ibid.; Carly Goodman, "The Shadowy Network Shaping Trump's Anti-Immigration Policies," *Washington Post*, September 27, 2018, https://washingtonpost.com/outlook/2018/09/27/shadowy-network-shaping-trumps-anti-immigration-policies/.

48. Heidi Beirich, *The Nativist Lobby: Three Faces of Intolerance; a Report from the Southern Poverty Law Center* (Montgomery, AL: Southern Poverty Law Center, 2009), 20.

49. Angela Saini, *Superior: The Return of Race Science* (Boston: Beacon Press, 2019), 75–76. On the other side of the ledger, some proponents of Black inferiority maintained that East Asians have higher IQs than whites. Barry Sautman, "Theories of East Asian Superiority," in *The Bell Curve Debate: History, Documents, Opinions*, ed. Russell Jacoby and Naomi Glauberman (New York: Times Books, 1995), 209.

50. Sautman, "Theories of East Asian Superiority," 209–210.

51. Much of the information on Pearson is from William H. Tucker, *The Funding of Scientific Racism: Wickliffe Draper and the Pioneer Fund* (Urbana: University of Illinois Press, 2002). See also Southern Poverty Law Center, "John Tanton," https://splcenter.org/fighting-hate/extremist-files/indiviual/john-tanton; Southern Poverty Law Center, "Pioneer Fund," https://www.splcenter.org/fighting-hate/extremist-files/group/pioneer-fund.

52. Nicholas Kulish and Mie McIntire, "The New Nativists: Why an Heiress Spent Her Fortune Trying to Keep Immigrants Out," *New York Times*, August 14, 2019, https://www.nytimes.com/2019/08/14/us/anti-immigration

-cordelia-scaife-may-html; Brendan O'Connor, *Blood Red Lines: How Nativism Fuels the Right* (Chicago: Haymarket Books, 2021), 43, Kindle.

53. Saini, *Superior*, 77.

5. BACKLASH INC.

1. L. Ling-Chi Wang, "Chinatown and the Chinese," SF State College Strike Collection, https://diva.edu/collections/strike/bundles/187935.

2. Jason Stahl, *Right Moves: The Conservative Think Tank in American Political Culture since 1945* (Chapel Hill: University of North Carolina Press, 2016), 24–68, 40.

3. Ibid., 55.

4. Robert G. Kaiser and Ira Chinoy, "How Scaife's Money Powered a Movement," *Washington Post*, May 2, 1999, https://www.washingtonpost.com/archive/politics/1999/05/02/how-scaife's-money-powered-a-movement/a7e219bf-2b5c-4efa-92fd-eb30431fcaa1/.

5. Scaife's total contribution "was so large that in 1974 AEI had to get the donations classified as 'excludable unusual grants' in order to maintain its tax-exempt status." Stahl, *Right Moves*, 55.

6. Richard Starnes of the Scripps-Howard news service described Weyrich as "a pink-cheeked, earnest political activist who looks like a choirboy and thinks like a computer" in "Right-Wing Voice Avoids 'Lunatic' Label," *Knoxville News-Sentinel*, November 7, 1977, C-1.

7. In a CSPAN interview, Weyrich refers to a meeting of the Civil Rights Coalition, but contextual cues suggest that it was the Leadership Conference on Civil Rights.

8. Q&A with Paul Weyrich, CSPAN, March 27, 2005, 24:31–34:17.

9. See Lee Edwards, "Chapter One: The Power of Ideas; the Heritage Foundation at 25 Years," *New York Times Book Review*, https://archive.nytimes.com/www.nytimes.com/books/98/05/10/reviews/980510.10greenbt.html; Joseph Crespino, *Strom Thurmond's America* (New York: Hill & Wang, 2013), 254–258. Crespino points out that Thurmond seemed more centrist not only because he softened his rhetoric but also because the whole country was shifting right. Organizations like Heritage contributed to this shift.

10. Frederick L. Berns, "Once a Kenosha Broadcaster: State Man Leads with His Right," *Kenosha News*, October 28, 1980, 4. Weyrich harbored views not far removed from Thurmond's, according to David Brock, who reports that Weyrich "had ties to the most exteme groups of the American right wing, dating back to his involvement in [segregationist] George Wallace's American Independent Party. Weyrich and his organizations have had associations with the John Birch Society and the anti-Semitic Liberty Lobby and to Christian reconstructionist Rousas John Rushdoony, a right-wing theologian who taught that 'biblical law' allowed segregation and slavery and required the death penalty for homosexuals." David Brock, *The Republican Noise Machine: Right-Wing Media and How It Corrupts Democracy* (New York: Crown, 2004), 44.

11. Elaine Woo, "Paul Weyrich, Religious Conservative and Ex-President of the Heritage Foundation, Dies at 66," *Los Angeles Times*, December 12, 2008.

12. Matthew Avery Sutton, *Jerry Falwell and the Rise of the Religious Right: A Brief History with Documents* (Boston: Bedford/St. Martin's, 2013), 22.

13. Anne Nelson, *Shadow Network: Media, Money, and the Secret Hub of the Radical Right* (New York: Bloomsbury, 2019), 19.

14. Ibid., xiv–xvi; Lee Cokorinos, *The Assault on Diversity: An Organized Challenge to Racial and Gender Justice* (Lanham, MD: Rowman & Littlefield, 2003), 22.

15. David D. Kilpatrick, "The 2004 Campaign: The Conservatives; Club of the Most Powerful Gathers in Strictest Privacy," *New York Times*, August 28, 2004, https://www.nytimes.com/2004/02u2004-campaign-conservatives-club-most-powerful-gathers-strictest-privacy.html.

6. *BAKKE*: THE MAKING OF A DAGGER

1. Quoted in Eric Malnic, "Doctor in Landmark Anti-Bias Case Slain," *Los Angeles Times*, August 13, 2002. See also Associated Press, "Patrick Chavis, Landmark Affirmative Action Figure," *Morning Call* (Allentown, PA), August 16, 2002.

2. Mark Lasswell, "The Fall of an Affirmative Action Hero," *Wall Street Journal*, August 27, 1997, https://www.wsj.com/articles/SB872642722185174000.

3. Michelle Malkin, "Fallen Affirmative Action 'Hero,'" *Indianapolis Star*, August 7, 2002, A16.

4. Malnic, "Doctor in Landmark Anti-Bias Case Slain."

5. Nicholas Lemann, "Taking Affirmative Action Apart," *New York Times Magazine*, June 11, 1995, 62, 66. In the same article, however, Lemann gives a full summary of the anti–affirmative action arguments and profiles the pair of intellectuals (more about them later) who were crafting a ballot measure to end affirmative action in California.

6. Julie Marquis, "Liposuction Doctor Has License Revoked," *Los Angeles Times*, August 26, 1988; William McGowan, *Coloring the News: How Crusading for Diversity Has Corrupted American Journalism* (San Francisco: Encounter Books, 2001), 3.

7. Marquis, "Liposuction Doctor Has License Revoked."

8. Ward Connerly, *Creating Equal: My Fight against Race Preferences* (New York: Encounter Books, 2007), 125.

9. The information about Chavis in this paragraph is from Lasswell, "Fall of an Affirmative Action Hero," and Julie Marquis, "State Probe of Lynwood Doctor in Liposuction Death Assailed," *Los Angeles Times*, June 6, 1997, A28.

10. Jackie Shearer, interview with Dr. Toni Johnson-Chavis, conducted by Blackside Inc. on March 2, 1989, for *Eyes on the Prize II: America at the Racial Crossroads, 1965–Mid-1980s*, Henry Hampton Collection, Film and Media Archive, Washington University Libraries, http://repository.wustl.edu/concern/videos/x633f4934.

11. Ibid.

12. Lou Cannon and Joel Kotkin, "The Students," *Clarion-Ledger Jackson Daily News*, October 9, 1977, 1C, 2C.

13. Ronald W. Powell, "Sacramento's First Test-Tube Baby Born at Sutter Memorial," *Sacramento Bee*, April 27, 1984, 1; Norris Burkes, "Mother's Love for Child Greater than Life," *Californian*, March 11, 2006, 3F.

14. Vernon Jarrett, "Minorities Burned up over Bakke-Case Misinformation," *Miami Herald*, August 22, 1978, 7-A.

15. Cannon and Kotkin, "Students," 1C, 2C.

16. Fred Mann, "The Records of Those Who Beat Bakke," *Philadelphia Inquirer*, November 7, 1977, 6-A.

17. Elizabeth Fernandez and Lance Williams, "If (Liposuction) Were a Drug, It Would Have Been Pulled from the Market," *San Francisco Examiner*, September 13, 1998, https://www.sfgate.com/news/article/if-liposuction-were-a-drug-it-would-have-been-3070689.php.

18. "The Rationale of Some Racial Conservatives: One Bad Apple Spoils the Whole Bunch," *Journal of Blacks in Higher Education* 18 (Winter 1997–98): 69.

19. Jonathan Haidt, *The Righteous Mind: Why Good People Are Divided by Politics and Religion* (New York: Vintage Books, 2012), 105.

20. Robert C. Davidson and Ernest L. Lewis, "Affirmative Action and Other Special Consideration Admissions at the University of California, Davis, School of Medicine," *JAMA* 278, 14 (October 8, 1997): 1153.

21. For further evidence, see Tim McNeese, *Regents of the University of California v. Bakke: American Education and Affirmative Action* (New York: Chelsea House, 2007), 76.

22. White affirmative action is the subject of Ira Katznelson's *When Affirmative Action Was White: An Untold History of Racial Inequality in Twentieth-Century America* (New York: W. W. Norton, 2005).

23. Joel Dreyfuss and Charles Lawrence III, *The Bakke Case: The Politics of Equality* (New York: Harcourt Brace Jovanovich, 1979).

24. Linda Robertson, "How a Black Quarterback in a White School Led His Team to Glory and Racial Harmony," *Miami Herald*, February 23, 2017, https://www.miamiherald.com/news/local/community/miami-dade/coral-gables/article134406584.html.

25. Information in this paragraph is from Robert Lindsey, "White/Caucasian—and Rejected," *New York Times Magazine*, April 3, 1977, 43, and Robert Lindsey, "Focus of Historic Battle in Civil Rights Law: Allan Paul Bakke," *New York Times*, June 29, 1978.

26. Some material in this paragraph is derived from McNeese, *Regents of the University of California v. Bakke*.

27. The information in this paragraph is from Alfred A. Slocum, ed., *Allan Bakke versus Regents of the University of California* (Dobbs Ferry, NY: Oceana Publications, 1978), 80–82.

28. "In 1973 Plaintiff's [Bakke's] file was not received and processed in the normal course until after the March 14, 1973 mailing of acceptances, at which

time 123 of the 160 acceptances had already been mailed." "Points of Authorities," in Slocum, *Allan Bakke versus Regents*, 101.

29. Ibid.

30. Dreyfuss and Lawrence, *Bakke Case*, 12.

31. Slocum, *Allan Bakke versus Regents*, vol. 2, 269.

32. The Labor Department issued the order partly in response to feminists' demands that women of all races be included in affirmative action programs. See Terry H. Anderson, *The Pursuit of Fairness: A History of Affirmative Action* (New York: Oxford University Press, 2002), 133.

33. Paul Seabury, "HEW & the Universities," *Commentary*, February 1972, https://www.commentarymagazine.com/articles/hew-the-universities/.

34. Susan Welch and John Gruhl, *Affirmative Action and Minority Enrollments in Medical and Law Schools* (Ann Arbor: University of Michigan Press, 2001), 54; Herbert M. Morais, *The History of the Negro in Medicine* (New York: Publishers Company, Inc., under the auspices of The Association for the Study of Negro Life and History, 1969), 208.

35. *History of the Negro in Medicine*, 200.

36. *Report of the National Advisory Commission on Civil Disorders* (New York: New York Times, 1968), 253, 250, 255.

37. Dreyfuss and Lawrence note that the Association of American Medical Colleges (AAMC) recommended in 1969 that by 1975–76, 12 percent of all entering medical classes should be Black. Dreyfuss and Lawrence, *Bakke Case*, 19. See also Anderson, *Pursuit of Fairness*, 151.

38. Slocum, *Allan Bakke versus Regents*, vol. 2, 273.

39. According to Katherine Puddifoot, almost instinctive implicit biases are more likely to affect clinical decisions when, as is the case in modern hospitals, physicians are stressed by heavy workloads. Katherine Puddifoot, "Stereotyping Patients," *Journal of Social Philosophy* 50, 1 (Spring 2019): 72, 77.

40. See Slocum, *Allan Bakke versus Regents*, vol. 2, 274–275. See also Dreyfuss and Lawrence, *Bakke Case*, 26–27.

41. According to Howard Ball, in December 1973 Bakke wrote to Storandt to let him know, "I have heard from Mr. DeFunis, and expect to receive some helpful information from him." Dreyfuss and Lawrence, *Bakke Case*, 57.

42. Ibid., 51; McNeese, *Regents of the University of California v. Bakke*, 74.

43. *Bakke Case*, 51; Lindsey, "White/Caucasian—and Rejected," 46.

44. He did so after first filing a racial discrimination complaint with the San Francisco office of the Department of Health, Education, and Welfare, which went unanswered for five months.

45. Bernard Schwartz, *Behind Bakke: Affirmative Action and the Supreme Court* (New York: New York University Press, 1988), 17–18.

46. Worried about the age issue, in 1971 Bakke wrote to ask how it might affect his chances at Davis. He was told that since applicants older than thirty were expected to have careers ten years shorter than average, the admissions committee "believes that an older applicant must be unusually highly qualified." Dreyfuss and Lawrence, *Bakke Case*, 13.

47. Goodwin Liu, "The Causation Fallacy: Bakke and the Basic Arithmetic of Selective Admissions," *Michigan Law Review* 100, 5 (2002): 1053.

48. Lou Cannon and Joel Kotkin, "Bakke Also Vied with the Well-to-do," *Washington Post*, October 2, 1977, https://www.washingtonpost.com/archive/politics/1977/10/02/bakke-also-vied-with-children-of-the-well-to-do/72f4829f-f-e7-47be-b73d-fb840aad42ad/.

7. THE STIPULATION

1. Charles R. Lawrence III and Nathaniel S. Colley Inc., "Brief Amicus Curiae on Behalf of the National Association for the Advancement of Colored People," in *Allan Bakke versus Regents of the University of California*, ed. Alfred A. Slocum (Dobbs Ferry, NY: Oceana Publications, 1978), vol. 1, 487–489.

2. Douglas Martin, "William Coblentz, California Power Broker, Dies at 88," *New York Times*, September 19, 2010, https://www.nytimes.com/2010/09/20/us/politics/20coblentz.html.

3. William K. Coblentz, "San Francisco Lawyer, California Higher Education, and Democratic Politics: 1947–1988," oral history, conducted 1997–98 by Leah McGarrigle, Regional Oral History Office, Bancroft Library, University of California–Berkeley, 2002, https://archive.org/stream/lawyersanfranwil00coblrich/lawyersanfranwill00coblrich_djvu.txt.

4. "UC Lawyer Who Leaped off Bridge Tells of His Despair in Suicide Note," *Los Angeles Times*, December 21, 1985, https://www.latimes.com/archives/la-xpm-1985-12-21-fi-3166-story.html.

5. Dreyfuss and Lawrence argue that the university regents picked Cox as a signal that the *Bakke* appeal was about the rights of the university, not the rights of minorities. Joel Dreyfuss and Charles Lawrence III, *The Bakke Case: The Politics of Equality* (New York: Harcourt Brace Jovanovich, 1979), 177.

6. See "Bakke: Wrong Case, Wrong Place," *Washington Post*, October 16, 1977, https://www.washingtonpost.com/archive/opinions/1977/10/16/bakke-wrong-case-place/ccd34b35-b70c-4ad6-a2c1-f2bd5dde6555; "A Ramrod Lawyer: Archibald Cox," *New York Times*, May 19, 1973, 19.

7. When I spoke with Anthony Carnevale and his colleague Jeff Strohl by telephone on June 24, 2020, Carnevale was eloquent on the economics of college admissions and even raised the issue of whether dropping the SAT as a requirement was guaranteed to eliminate structural antiminority bias. "When you take away the SAT, it's not clear who you're going to let in—Jared [Kushner] or the person from the underserved neighborhood," he said. He added that economic pressure on colleges will only "grow over the next several years because the size of the college age population is going down, so there's going to be more and more competition for bodies, and the other thing is the population will be made up of more and more low-income and minority students. . . . At the same time, there will be more and more rich kids. . . . So if you're an elite school, the population you feed on, the ones with the high test scores and big checking accounts, that's going to grow." Money, in short, may be more of a plus in competitive college admissions than race ever could be.

8. See Dreyfuss and Lawrence, *Bakke Case*, 19–20. See also Slocum, *Allan Bakke versus Regents*, vol. 2, appendix B, 187, 278.

9. Donald L. Reidhaar, Gary Morrison, Paul Mishkin, and Jack B. Owens, "Petition for a Writ of Cetriorari to the Supreme Court of California" (December 6, 1976), in Slocum, *Allan Bakke versus Regents*, vol. 2, 194–198.

8. CERTIORARI

1. "Bakke: Wrong Case, Wrong Place," *Washington Post*, October 16, 1977, https://www.washingtonpost.com/archive/opinions/1977/10/16/bakke-wrong-case-place/ccd34b35-b70c-4ad6-a2c1-f2bd5dde6555.

2. *Regents of the University of California v. Bakke*, Oral Argument, October 12, 1997, https://apps.oyez.org/player/#/burger6/oral_argument_audio/16983. Unless otherwise noted, subsequent quotes are from this source.

3. Joel Dreyfuss and Charles Lawrence III, *The Bakke Case: The Politics of Equality* (New York: Harcourt Brace Jovanovich, 1979), 180, 183.

4. Dreyfuss and Lawrence report that during the 1975–76 school year, a dean overruled the admissions committee and admitted "one white student whose grade point average was 2.19, well below the 2.5 cutoff for regular admissions." Ibid., 93. The average GPA of task force admittees was 2.62 in 1973 and 2.42 in 1974.

5. Title 42, section 2000d, of the US Code on federally assisted programs holds that "no person in the United States shall, on the ground of race, color, or national origin, be excluded from participation in, be denied the benefits of, or be subjected to discrimination under any program or activity receiving Federal financial assistance."

9. THE CONTEST INSIDE THE COURT

1. Bernard Schwartz, *Behind Bakke: Affirmative Action and the Supreme Court* (New York: New York University Press, 1988), 59.

2. Reynold H. Colvin and Robert D. Links, "Supplemental Brief of Respondent Regarding Application of Title VI of the Civil Rights Act of 1964," in *Allan Bakke versus Regents of the University of California*, ed. Alfred A. Slocum (Dobbs Ferry, NY: Oceana Publications, 1978), vol. 6, 197, 161.

3. Archibald Cox, Donald Reidhaar, Paul J. Mishkin, and Jack B. Owens, "Supplemental Brief for the Petitioner," in Slocum, *Allan Bakke versus Regents*, vol. 6, 207.

4. Griffin Bell, Wade H. McCree Jr., Drew S. Days III, Lawrence G. Wallace, Frank H. Easterbrook, Brian K. Landsberg, Jessica Dunsay Silver, Miriam R. Eisenstein, and Vincent F. O'Rourke, "Supplemental Brief for the United States as Amicus Curiae," in Slocum, *Allan Bakke versus Regents*, vol. 6, 135–136.

5. Howard Ball, *The Bakke Case: Race, Education & Affirmative Action* (Lawrence: University Press of Kansas, 2000), 87–88.

6. Justice Thurgood Marshall, Draft Opinion No. 78-811, *Regents of the University of California v. Bakke*, circulated to the other justices June 23,

1978, Lewis F. Powell Jr. Archives, Washington and Lee University School of Law Scholarly Commons, https://scholarlycommons.law.wlu.edu/cgi/view content.cgi?filename=21&article=1113&context=casefiles&type=additional.

7. Ibid.

8. Juan Williams, *Thurgood Marshall: American Revolutionary* (New York: Times Books, 1998), 362. There is likely some overstatement in Williams's view, given the consternation caused by Marshall's retirement (and not only among African Americans).

9. Corey Robin, *The Enigma of Clarence Thomas* (New York: Metropolitan Books, 2019), 11.

10. Juan Williams, *Thurgood Marshall*, 365–366.

11. Bob Woodward and Scott Armstrong, *The Brethren: Inside the Supreme Court* (New York: Simon & Schuster, 1979), 258. Cecelia Ridgeway explains that beliefs about a person's status influence judgments about whether a person should or is able to fill certain roles. Cecilia Ridgeway, "Why Status Matters for Inequality," *American Sociological Review* 79, 1 (February 2014): 5.

12. Schwartz, *Behind Bakke*, 129.

13. Stevens strove to make his finding as narrow as possible, arguing that *Bakke* should be decided strictly on a Title VI basis and the Fourteenth Amendment should be left out completely. In addition, he wanted the decision to apply only to Bakke's case, without affecting "the legal status of any admissions program other than the [one at UC–Davis]." *Regents of the University of California v. Bakke*, 439 U.S. 256 (1978), 408, 418.

14. John Paul Stevens, *The Making of a Justice: Reflections on My First 94 Years* (New York: Little, Brown, 2019), 161. It is doubtful that Marshall's opinion could be taught in some states today.

15. Lewis F. Powell Jr., "Statement on Behalf of the School Board Supporting Construction of the New High Schools without Delay," 7–8, https://scholarly commons.law.wlu.edu/powellspeeches.

16. Andres Walker, "A Lawyer Looks at Civil Disobedience: How Lewis F. Powell, Jr. Reframed the Civil Rights Revolution," *University of Colorado Law Review* (October 21, 2014): 6.

17. Powell was unmoved by King's memorable definition of an unjust law: A "law is unjust if it is inflicted on a minority that, as a result of being denied the right to vote, had no part in enacting or devising the law. Who can say that the legislature of Alabama [or the legislature in Powell's Virginia, for that matter] which set up the state's segregation laws was democratically elected?" Martin Luther King Jr., *Why We Can't Wait* (New York: Signet Classics, 2000), 93–95.

18. Lewis F. Powell Jr., "A Lawyer Looks at Civil Disobedience," *Washington and Lee Law Review* 23, 2 (Fall 1966): 210.

19. Some of Marshall's resentment bubbles through his praise for King in an oral history interview. See Mark V. Tushnet, ed., *Thurgood Marshall: His Speeches, Writings, Arguments, Opinions, and Reminiscences* (Chicago: Lawrence Hill Books, 2001), xxiii, 471, 479, 503–504.

20. Walker, "Lawyer Looks at Civil Disobedience," 18, 4.

21. *Bakke*, 439 U.S. 256 (1978), 327, 315, 294.

22. Ibid., 294. Whiteness is a status category more than a biological one. As the social opposite of whiteness, Blackness has been a writ of partial or complete civil death. Thus, as Powell surely knew, there is a difference in degree and kind between white ethnic status and Black "racial" status. For more on this, see Nell Irving Painter, "What Is Whiteness?" *New York Times*, June 21, 2015, SR8.

23. *Bakke*, 439 U.S. 256 (1978), 5.

24. Ball, *Bakke Case*, 126–133.

25. *Bakke*, 439 U.S. 256 (1978), 372.

26. Ibid., 272, 326–328. Eric A. Tilles argues that "*Bakke* became the logical foundation to the development of the Supreme Court's approach to affirmative action in employment. This can be seen in cases such as *Weber*, *Wygant* and *Johnson*." Eric A. Tilles, "Lessons from Bakke: The Effect of Grutter on Affirmative Action in Employment," *University of Pennsylvania Journal of Labor and Employment Law* 6, 2 (2004): 454.

27. *Bakke*, 439 U.S. 256 (1978), 395–396.

28. Joel Dreyfuss and Charles Lawrence III, *The Bakke Case: The Politics of Equality* (New York: Harcourt Brace Jovanovich, 1979), 223.

29. "Bakke Wins, Quotas Lose: But the Divided Supreme Court Endorses Affirmative Action Based on Race," *Time*, July 10, 1978, 9, 11.

30. Allan Bakke, Twitter, October 14 and 15, 2015, https://twitter.com/bakke_allan.

10. THE AMERICAN MIND AFTER *BAKKE*

1. See "The Bakke Decision," *Washington Post*, June 29, 1978, https://www.washingtonpost.com/archive/politics/1978/06/29/the-bakke-decision/c80dadfc-4d6c-448d-82b8-f64e639200a0/; "Bakke Wins, Quotas Lose: But the Divided Supreme Court Endorses Affirmative Action Based on Race," *Time*, July 10, 1978, 11.

2. Transcript of "The Bakke Decision," CBS News Special Report, June 28, 1978, https://danratherjournalist.org/ground/crises-and-conflicts/civil-rights-movement/document-bakke-decision-transcript.

3. Ralph Smith, "Only One Thing Counts: Allan Bakke Won Case," *Paducah Sun*, June 29, 1978, 4-D.

4. "Bakke Ruling Evokes Sigh of Relief in Many Quarters," *Sacramento Bee*, June 29, 1978, A20; Associated Press, "Future for U.S. Race Relations Uncertain after Bakke Ruling," *Santa Cruz Sentinel*, June 29, 1978, 1.

5. Tom Wicker, "The 'Powell Test,'" *New York Times*, July 21, 1978, A25.

6. "Bakke Ruling Evokes Sigh of Relief."

7. Transcript, "Bakke Decision."

8. See Charlotte Steeh and Maria Krysan, "Trends: Affirmative Action and the Public, 1970–1995," *Public Opinion Quarterly* 60, 1 (Spring 1996): 130–131.

9. Lester A. Sobel, ed., *Quotas & Affirmative Action* (New York: Facts on File, 1980), 144.

10. Lawrence D. Bobo, Camille Z. Charles, Maria Krysan, and Alicia D.

Simmons, "The *Real* Record of Racial Attitudes," in *Social Trends in American Life: Findings from the General Social Survey since 1972*, ed. Peter V. Marsden (Princeton, NJ: Princeton University Press, 2012), 47, 46.

11. Lawrence Bobo, "Group Conflict, Prejudice, and the Paradox of Contemporary Racial Attitudes," in *Eliminating Racism: Profiles in Controversy*, ed. Phyllis A. Katz (New York: Plenum, 1988), 90, 91–92. Economist Gary S. Becker and coauthor George J. Stigler formulate a rather stark interest-divergence theory of their own: "distinction is a scarce resource and is to a large extent simply redistributed among persons: an increase in one person's distinction generally requires a reduction in that of other person's." George J. Stigler and Gary S. Becker, "De Gustibus Non Est Disputandum," in *The Essence of Becker*, ed. Ramon Febrero and Pedro S. Schwartz (Stanford, CA: Hoover Institution Press, 1995), 202–203.

12. Bobo, "Group Conflict," 94–95, 97–98, 100.

13. John Kifner, "White Pupils' Rolls Drop a Third in Boston Busing," *New York Times*, December 15, 1975, 1.

14. Matthew O. Hunt, "African American, Hispanic, and White Beliefs about Black/White Inequality, 1977–2004," *American Sociological Review* 72, 3 (June 2007): 400.

15. Steeh and Krysan, "Trends: Affirmative Action and the Public," 144.

16. Howard Schuman and Maria Krysan, "A Historical Note on Whites' Beliefs about Racial Inequality," *American Sociological Review* 64, 6 (December 1999).

17. "Eyes on the Prize: Interview with David Vann," American Archive of Public Broadcasting, https://americanarchive.org/catalog/cpb-aacip_151-6t0gt5g44p.

18. Schuman and Krysan, "Historical Note on Whites' Beliefs," 852; Michelle Alexander, *The New Jim Crow: Mass Incarceration in the Age of Colorblindness* (New York: New Press, 2012), 44.

19. Schuman and Krysan note that "by 1967 the picture of peaceful black protestors being assaulted by brutal southern whites had disappeared from the media, soon to be replaced by images of black ghetto inhabitants looting and burning." Schuman and Krysan, "Historical Note on Whites' Beliefs," 854. See also Clay Risen, *A Nation on Fire: America in the Wake of the King Assassination* (Hoboken, NJ: John Wiley & Sons, 2009), 4–8.

20. David Welky, *Marching across the Color Line: A. Philip Randolph and Civil Rights in the World War II Era* (Oxford: Oxford University Press, 2014), 160.

21. Lawrence Bobo, "Race, Public Opinion, and the Social Sphere," *Public Opinion Quarterly* 61, 1 (Spring 1997): 8.

22. Steeh and Krysan, "Trends: Affirmative Action and the Public," 130.

23. Jesse Jackson, "Myths in the Bakke Case," *Modesto Bee*, May 28, 1978, A-13.

24. Thomas W. Jones, *From Willard Straight to Wall Street: A Memoir* (Ithaca, NY: Cornell University Press, 2019), 25.

25. Allan Bloom, *The Closing of the American Mind* (New York: Simon & Schuster, 1987), 94–95.

26. John J. Miller, *A Gift of Freedom: How the John M. Olin Foundation Changed America* (San Francisco: Encounter Books, 2006), 18–22, 30–32.

27. John M. Crewdson, "Worldwide Propaganda Network Built by the C.I.A.," *New York Times*, December 26, 1977, 1, 37.

28. See Miller, *Gift of Freedom*, 26–27, 32; Steven M. Teles, *The Rise of the Conservative Legal Movement: The Battle for Control of the Law* (Princeton, NJ: Princeton University Press, 2008), 183–186. See also Crewdson, "Worldwide Propaganda Network Built by C.I.A.," 1, 37.

29. Miller, *Gift of Freedom*, 152–153.

11. THE EQUALITY MATRIX

1. Robert Belton, "Discrimination and Affirmative Action: An Analysis of Competing Theories of Equality and *Weber*," *North Carolina Law Review* 59, 3 (1981): 531–598.

2. *McDonald v. Santa Fe Trail Transportation Company*, 427 U.S. 273 (1976), 280.

3. *United Steelworkers of America v. Weber*, 443 U.S. 193 (1979), 221.

4. Ibid. Marshall's footnote observes that "Santa Fe disclaims that the actions challenged here were any part of an affirmative action program, see Brief for Respondent Santa Fe 19 n. 5, and we emphasize that we do not consider here the permissibility of such a program, whether judicially required or otherwise prompted." *McDonald v. Santa Fe Trail*, 427 U.S. 273 (1976), 281.

5. Shelly J. Venick and Ronald A. Lane, "Doubling the Price of Past Discrimination: The Employers' Burden after *McDonald v. Santa Fe Trail Transportation Co.*," *Loyola University Chicago Law Journal* 8, 4 (1977): 811.

6. *Metro Broadcasting Inc. v. Federal Communications Commission*, 497 U.S. 547 (1990), 568.

7. Even if only a person's ability to contribute to diversity is considered, people from less represented groups will be favored.

8. Jo Ann Ooiman Robinson, *Affirmative Action: A Documentary History* (Westport, CT: Greenwood Press, 2001), 212.

9. Ira Katznelson, *When Affirmative Action Was White: The Untold History of Racial Inequality in Twentieth-Century America* (New York: W. W. Norton, 2005), 164–166.

12. SEA CHANGE

1. Nina Totenberg, "O'Connor, Rehnquist and a Supreme Marriage Proposal," NPR, October 31, 2018, https://www.npr.org/2018/10/31/662293127/a-supreme-marriage-proposal/.

2. Peter J. Wallison, *Ronald Reagan: The Power of Conviction and the Success of His Presidency* (Boulder, CO: Westview Books, 2003), 151.

3. See Lee Cokorinos, *The Assault on Diversity* (Lanham, MD: Rowman & Littlefield, 2003), 86. Meese played various roles in Reagan's gubernatorial administration, eventually rising to the position of chief of staff. Smith was among the first to back Reagan's run for governor. See also John J. Miller, *Strategic Investment in Ideas: How Two Top Foundations Reshaped America* (Washington, DC: Philanthropy Roundtable, 2003), 32; John J. Miller, *A Gift of Freedom: How the John M. Olin Foundation Changed America* (San Francisco: Encounter Books, 2006), 98; Mark Tushnet, *A Court Divided: The Rehnquist Court and the Future of Constitutional Law* (New York: W. W. Norton, 2005), 39–40; Steven M. Teles, *The Rise of the Conservative Legal Movement: The Battle for Control of the Law* (Princeton, NJ: Princeton University Press, 2008), 60–61; Lee Edwards, ed., *Bringing Justice to the People: The Story of the Freedom-Based Public Interest Law Movement* (Washington, DC: Heritage Books, 2004), 9–13.

4. Ronald Reagan, "The Tan Riffle Shell Case," *The Modesto Bee*, October 9, 1977, C-3.

5. Philip Hager, "Public Interest Law Firms Seek to Help Those Who Need a 'Voice' against Powerful Opponents," *Morning Call*, March 26, 1978; Ronald Reagan, "The Tan Riffle Shell Case."

6. Though not every brief submitted influences the justices, the sheer volume of conservative friend-of-the-court submissions claiming to speak for the true America likely had an impact here. Perhaps for that reason, and out of a desire to shape every hermeneutic aspect of a case, what Senator Sheldon Whitehouse calls the "armada of amichi" has only grown in the post–Marshall years. See Sheldon Whitehouse with Jennifer Mueller, *The Scheme: How the Right Wing Used Dark Money to Capture the Supreme Court* (New York: New Press, 2022), 127–134.

7. Dan Morgan, "Conservatives: A Well-Financed Network," *Washington Post*, January 4, 1981, https://washingtonpost.com/politics/1981/01/04/conservatives-well-financed-network/.

8. *City of Richmond v. J. A. Croson Company*, 488 U.S. 469 (1989).

9. *Fullilove v. Klutznick*, 448 U.S. 448 (1980), 457.

10. Ronald A. Zumbrun and John H. Findley, City of Richmond, Virginia, Appellant, v. J. A. Croson Company, Appellee: Brief Amicus Curiae of Pacific Legal Foundation in Support of Appellee, 3.

11. Walter H. Ryland, City of Richmond, Appellant, v. J. A. Croson Company, Appellee: Brief on Behalf of the Appellee, 5, 4, 19.

12. Official transcript, *Proceedings before the Supreme Court of the United States: City of Richmond, Appellant v. J. A. Croson Company: Case No. 87-998* (Washington, DC: Alderson Reporting Company, 1988), 21, 8.

13. *City of Richmond v. J. A. Croson Company*, Oral Argument, October 5, 1988, https://apps.oyez.org/player/#/rehnquist3/oral_argument_audio/17986.

14. Charles Fried, Wm. Bradford Reynolds, Donald B. Ayer, Roger Clegg, Glen D. Nager, David K. Flyn, and Michael P. Socarras, Brief for the United States as Amicus Curiae Supporting Appellee, *Richmond v. Croson* (1987), 1–2.

15. Zumbrun and Findley brief, 4.

16. Mountain States Legal Foundation, City of Richmond, Appellant, v. J. A. Croson, Appellee: Brief Amicus Curiae, June 8, 1988, 8–9.

17. Edwards, *Bringing Justice to the People*, 99–100.

18. *Richmond v. Croson*, 488 U.S. 469 (1989), 490–491.

19. Ibid., 531–532.

20. Ibid., 534–535, 481, 499.

21. Ibid., 529.

22. Ibid., 540, 546.

23. Juan Williams, *Thurgood Marshall: American Revolutionary* (New York: Times Books, 1998), 388–389.

24. *Richmond v. Croson*, 488 U.S. 469 (1989), 524.

25. Ibid., 559.

26. Ibid., 520.

27. Wiping people and neighborhoods clean of credit can take many forms, but it always involves the denial of equal access to credit. For instance, as Francesca Lina Procaccini explains, "In the early 1980's, the old practice of refusing credit to low-income, minority communities—which the ECOA [Equal Credit Opportunity Act] expressly prohibited—was replaced by the equally devastating practice of targeting these same communities for high-risk, high-interest loans." Francesca Lina Procaccini, "Stemming the Rising Risk of Credit Inequality: The Fair and Faithful Interpretation of the Equal Credit Opportunity Act's Disparate Impact Prohibition," *Harvard Law and Policy Review* 9 (2015): S45, S48. Although the ECOA's mission was to end such inequity, there has been much resistance from the anti–civil rights movement, including a full-on "campaign to completely eliminate the disparate impact theory of discrimination"—a key battering ram that has been used to knock down discrimination in everything from *Griggs*-style workplaces to housing discrimination to unfair credit practices—"from American jurisprudence," according to Procaccini.

28. *Korematsu v. United States*, 323 U.S. 214 (1944), 216.

29. *Oregon v. Mitchell*, 400 U.S. 112 (1970), 117. Richard H. Fallon Jr. uses the term "modern strict scrutiny test" in "Strict Judicial Scrutiny," *UCLA Law Review* 54 (2007): 1335. See also Gerald Gunther, "Foreword: In Search of Evolving Doctrine on a Changing Court; a Model for a Newer Equal Protection," *Harvard Law Review* 86, 1 (November 1972): 8.

30. *Weber v. Aetna Casualty & Surety Co. et al.*, 406 U.S. 164 (1972), 173.

31. *Regents of the University of California v. Bakke*, 438 U.S. 265 (1978), 264–265, 287.

32. The set-aside was created under the Public Works Employment Act of 1977.

33. *Fullilove v. Klutznick*, 448 U.S. 448 (1980), 496.

34. The PLF relied on Marshall's majority opinion in *Dunn v. Blumstein*, 405 U.S. 330 (1972), and also cited the four-person Stevens-led opinion in *Bakke*, but it ignored both Marshall's solo dissent and the opinion he joined in *Bakke* that took the opposite view of the Stevens opinion See Sandra M. Robertson, Ronald A. Zumbrun, and John H. Findley, H. Earl Fullilove, et al. v. Juanita

Kreps: Brief Amicus Curiae of Pacific Legal Foundation in Support of Petitioners H. Earl Fullilove, et al., 6.

35. *Fullilove v. Klutznick*, 448 U.S. 448 (1980), 518–519.

36. Ibid., 522.

13. REAGAN JUSTICE

1. Admittedly, like something out of quantum mechanics, strict scrutiny was born, established itself, and still like a virtual particle exists in a state of uncertainty. Richard H. Fallon Jr. identifies three forms of it: catastrophe strict scrutiny, which permits the abridgment of fundamental rights only when the alternative is catastrophe; alarm bell strict scrutiny, which rings when a law or policy has been made with "illicit motivation"; and tightrope strict scrutiny (favored by Marshall), which is "the difficult process of balancing individual and state interests that the Court must embark upon when faced with a classification touching fundamental right." Fallon also notes, however, that since "the modern [strict scrutiny] test emerged during the 1960s under the Warren Court, the narrowly-tailored-to-a-compelling-interest formula [has] continued . . . under the Burger, Rehnquist, and Roberts Courts." Richard H. Fallon Jr., "Strict Judicial Scrutiny," *UCLA Law Review* 54 (2007): 1271, 1297, 1306.

2. John A. Jenkins, "The Partisan: A Talk with Justice Rehnquist," *New York Times Magazine*, March 3, 1985, 33, 34.

3. Terry Eastland, *Energy in the Executive: The Case for the Strong Presidency* (New York: Maxwell Macmillan International, 1994), 167.

4. *City of Richmond v. J. A. Croson Company*, 488 U.S. 469 (1989), 527–528. See also Alan David Freeman, "Legitimizing Racial Discrimination through Antidiscrimination Law: A Critical Review of Supreme Court Doctrine," *Minnesota Law Review* 62 (1978): 1054.

5. *Wygant v. Jackson Board of Education*, 467 U.S. 267 (1986), Joint Appendix, 13.

6. Charles Fried, William Bradford Reynolds, Charles J. Cooper, Samuel Alito Jr., Walter W. Barnett, David K. Flynn, and Michael Carvin, Wendy Wygant v. Jackson Board of Education: Brief for the United States as Amicus Curiae Supporting Petitioners, 10.

7. *Wygant*, 467 U.S. 267 (1986), 273.

8. "So where do the Justices find information that enables them to decide factual questions about the world? . . . If a fact is important to a case's resolution, then the parties (and the amici) can provide the Court with enough information to address it through testimony (at the trial level) and briefing (on appeal). . . . The idea, however, that courts depend only on the adversary system to inform their decisions—even for fact finding—is 'more myth than reality.' . . . It is not uncommon for [Justice Breyer] to quiz an advocate at oral argument with extra-record statistics." Allison Orr Larsen, "Confronting Supreme Court Fact Finding," *Virginia Law Review* 98 (2012): 1257–1261.

9. Marshall, Powell wrote, was violating "the heretofore unquestioned rule that the Court decides cases based on the record before it." *Wygant*, 278–279.

But this rule was made to be (very carefully) broken. See Larsen, "Confronting Supreme Court Fact Finding," 1257–1261.

10. *Wygant*, 298–299.

11. Ibid., 301–302.

12. Frederick A. O. Schwartz Jr., Lorna B. Goodman, Laura J. Blankfein, Lin B. Saberski, Robert Abrams, Robert Herman, O. Peter Sherwood, Rosmarie Rhodes, Lawrence S. Kahn, Alan D. Aviles, and Martha J. Olson, Sheet Metal Workers v. Equal Employment Opportunity Commission: Respondents' Brief in Opposition to Petition for Writ of Certiorari, 3; *Local 28, Sheet Metal Workers v. EEOC*, 478 U.S. 421 (1986), 426–440; Sheet Metal Workers v. Equal Employment Opportunity Commission: Brief for Respondent the City of New York, 2.

13. *Local 28 Sheet Metal Workers*, 478 U.S. 421 (1986), 480.

14. Ibid., 482.

15. *Local Number 93, International Association of Firefighters, AFL-CIO, C.L.C. v. City of Cleveland et al.*, 478 U.S. 501 (1986).

16. Dean J. Kotlowski, *Nixon's Civil Rights: Politics, Principle, and Policy* (Cambridge, MA: Harvard University Press, 2001), 117–118.

17. Carrrie N. Baker, *The Women's Movement against Sexual Harassment* (Cambridge: Cambridge University Press, 2008), 140.

18. AT&T agreed to "develop goals for increasing the utilization of women and Minorities in each job classification" and to assess all female college graduates hired in basic supervisory jobs between 1964 and 1971 for possible service in upper management. EEOC press release, "Major EEO Agreement Reached by Government and Bell Telephone Companies," January 18, 1973, 2. See also *The Story of the United States Equal Employment Opportunity Commission: Ensuring the Promise of Opportunity for 35 Years, 1965–2000* (Washington, DC: US Equal Employment Opportunity Commission, 2000), 10.

19. Kotlowski, *Nixon's Civil Rights*, 120.

20. *Nomination of William Bradford Reynolds to Be Associate Attorney General of the United States: Hearings before the Committee on the Judiciary, United States Senate, Ninety-Ninth Congress, First Session, on the Confirmation of William Bradford Reynolds to Be Associate Attorney General of the United States, June 4, 5 and 18, 1985* (Washington, DC: US Government Printing Office, 1986), 5.

21. Ibid., 32.

22. William B. Reynolds, "The Reagan Administration's Civil Rights Policy: The Challenge for the Future," *Vanderbilt Law Review* 42, 4 (1989): 994.

23. Ibid., 996.

24. Ibid.

25. Charles Fried, William Bradford Reynolds, Carolyn B. Kuhl, Samuel A. Alito Jr., Brian K. Landsberg, Michael Carvin, and Dennis J. Dimsey, Brief of the Equal Employment Opportunity Commission, Local 28 v. EEOC, 84-1656, 10–11.

26. Reynolds, "Reagan Administration's Civil Rights Policy," 997–998.

14. ORIGINALISM FROM STROM THURMOND TO EDWIN MEESE

1. Associated Press, "Affirmative Action Is Backed," *New York Times*, September 19, 1985, A23.

2. "Testimony of Benjamin L. Hooks, Executive Director of the National Association for the Advancement of Colored People on the Nomination of Clarence Thomas for the Supreme Court of the United States before the Committee on the Judiciary, United States Senate, September 20, 1991," in *Hearings before the Committee on the Judiciary United States Senate, One Hundred Second Congress, First Session on the Nomination of Clarence Thomas to Be Associate Justice of the Supreme Court of the United States, September 20, 1991, Part 3 of 4 Parts* (Washington, DC: US Government Printing Office, 1992), 39.

3. According to US District Court judge Sam Sparks of the Western District of Texas, "During the early 1980s, the OCR [Office of Civil Rights] and Texas officials engaged in considerable negotiations regarding efforts to bring Texas into compliance with Title VI. Texas . . . attempted to address OCR concerns through submission of the Texas Equal Education Opportunity Plan for Higher Education (Texas Plan), which included a commitment to the goal of equal educational opportunity and student body desegregation for both black and Hispanic students. . . . [But in] 1982, Assistant Secretary of Education Clarence Thomas informed Governor Clements that the Texas Plan was deficient because the numeric goals of black and Hispanic enrollment in graduate and professional programs were insufficient to meet Texas's commitment to enroll those minority students in proportion to the representation among graduates of the state's undergraduate institutions. . . . Texas revised its plan and resubmitted it to the OCR; the OCR found the modified plan to be deficient because it did not set targets for increasing minority enrollment in each institution, instead of on a statewide basis, and it did not project achievement dates for the targeted goals." "Memorandum Opinion," *Hopwood v. Texas*, 861 F. Supp. 551 (1994), https://law.justia.com/cases/federal/district-courts/FSupp/861/551/2261859.

4. Ronald Suresh Roberts, *Clarence Thomas and the Tough Love Crowd: Counterfeit Heroes and Unhappy Truths* (New York: New York University Press, 1995), 122. See also Drew S. Days III, "The Court's Response to the Reagan Civil Rights Agenda," *Vanderbilt Law Review* 42, 4 (1989): 1008; Drew S. Days III, "Turning Back the Clock: The Reagan Administration and Civil Rights," *Harvard Civil Rights–Civil Liberties Law Review* 19 (1984): 318.

5. *Hearings on the Nomination of Clarence Thomas*, 19.

6. "Prepared Statement of the Alliance for Justice on the Nomination of Clarence Thomas to the U.S. Court of Appeals for the District of Columbia," February 16, 1990, in *Hearings before the Committee on the Judiciary, United States Senate, One Hundred First Congress, Second Session on Confirmation Hearings on Appointments to the Federal Judiciary, February 6, 21, and 27, 1990, Part 4* (Washington, DC: US Government Printing Office, 1990), 392.

7. Clarence Thomas, "Affirmative Action Goals and Timetables: Too Tough? Not Tough Enough!" *Yale Law and Policy Review* 4 (1987): 404. In a

long dissent, Justice Antonin Scalia heaped contempt on the use of statistical imbalances as evidence of unequal opportunity. *Johnson v. Santa Clara Transportation Agency*, 480 U.S. 616 (1987), 676.

8. Merrill Hartsons, "Business Group Opposes Overhaul of Executive Order," Associated Press, September 12, 1985, https://apnews.com/article/25f471e525d50634a92c3bc78c23c3e2.

9. Nicholas Laham, *The Reagan Presidency and the Politics of Race: In Pursuit of Colorblind Justice and Limited Government* (Westport, CT: Praeger, 1998), 89. See also Associated Press, "Affirmative Action Is Backed."

10. Thomas, "Affirmative Action Goals and Timetables," 406.

11. Under Sylvester, the OFCCP put the Bethlehem Steel Corporation on notice that its federal contracts were at risk after a probe found that although 38 percent of the Bethlehem blue-collar labor force was Black, only 3 percent of blue-collar supervisors were Black. Blue-collar workers were paid significantly less than their white peers. Associated Press, "5 Firms on Race Spot," *Muenster (IN) Times*, May 26, 1968, 7C; Matt Schudel, "Labor, Hill Official Edward Sylvester Dies," *Washington Post*, February 18, 2005, https://www.washigtonpost.com//archive/local/2005/02/18/labor-hill-official-edward-sylvester-dies/4c3d8b/cf8a-4078-98d9-4bee4a93eb8b/.

12. Journalist Roger Wilkins remarked on Sylvester's character in Schudel, "Labor, Hill Official Edward Sylvester Dies."

13. For more on the development of affirmative action under Kennedy, see Frank Dobbin, *Inventing Equal Opportunity* (Princeton, NJ: Princeton University Press, 2009), 41–50.

14. "Testimony of Edward C. Sylvester, Jr., Former Director of the Office of Federal Contract Compliance," in *Hearings before the Subcommittee on Administrative Practice and Procedure of the Committee on the Judiciary, United States Senate, Ninety-First Congress, First Session, Pursuant to S. Res. 39, on the Practice and Procedures Involved in the Implementation of Executive Order 11246 and Related Laws, Regulations, and Constitutional Provisions Concerning Equal Employment Opportunity in Federal and Federally Assisted Contracts, March 27 and 28, 1969* (Washington, DC: US Government Printing Office, 1969), 25.

15. See Richard Rothstein, *The Color of Law: A Forgotten History of How Our Government Segregated America* (New York: Liveright, 2017), 153–175; Susan Faludi, *Backlash: The Undeclared War against American Women* (New York: Doubleday, 1991), 363–399.

16. Hartsons, "Business Group Opposes Overhaul of Executive Order."

17. Lena Williams, "Leadership Conference on Civil Rights: An Administrator of Many Hats and Colors," *New York Times*, August 17, 1987, A12.

18. Frank Dobbin, *Inventing Inequality* (Princeton, NJ: Princeton University Press, 2009), 138–140. At my own university, the political wave that began to rise in the 1980s crested and crashed in 2023, washing away the hiring of distinguished African American journalist Kathleen McElroy, in part because of the opposition of the Claremont Institute, a prominent anti–civil rights organization (discussed later in this book), and in part because of the opposition of

conservative regents, alumni, and Texas politicians who were nakedly continuing the Olin-Powell mission to twist American thought to the right. One regent, Jay Graham, complained in a text that university president Kathy Banks "told us multiple times the reason we were going to combine [the colleges of] arts and sciences together was to control the liberal nature that those professors brought to campus. We were going to start a journalism department to get high-quality conservative Aggie students into the journalism world to help direct our message. This won't happen with this type of hire." Kate McGee, "Top Texas A&M Officials Were Involved in Botched Recruiting of Journalism Professor, Who Will Receive $1 Million Settlement," *Texas Tribune*, August 3, 2023, https://texastribune.org/2023/08/03/texas-am-regents=kathleen-mcelroy/.

19. Dobbin, *Inventing Inequality*, 141–142.

20. Laham, *Reagan Presidency*, xiii, 3.

21. Objecting to Neas's vocabulary, one Reagan administration official complained to the *New York Times* that Neas portrayed "anyone and everyone" who opposed Leadership Conference positions as "anti–civil rights." But another said that Neas "doesn't play dirty pool. And he's not totally blinded by the objective. As a result he has entrée to people at the highest levels of the White House." Williams, "Leadership Conference on Civil Rights." For more on Reagan administration efforts to change the government's approach to equal opportunity, see William Wines, "Title VII Interpretation and Enforcement in the Reagan Years (1980–89): The Winding Road of the Civil Rights Act of 1991," *Marquette Law Review* 77, 4 (1994): 645–718. See also Theodore Y. Blumoff and Harold S. Lewis Jr., "The Reagan Court and Title VII: A Common-Law Outlook on a Statutory Task," *North Carolina Law Review* 69, 1 (1990): 1–86.

22. Edwin Meese III, "Address before the D.C. Chapter of the Federalist Society Lawyers' Division," in Stanford Levinson and Steven Mailloux, *Interpreting Law and Literature: A Hermeneutic Reader* (Evanston, IL: Northwestern University Press, 1988), 29, 30, 27, 29.

23. William Brennan Jr., "The Constitution of the United States: Contemporary Ratification," in Levinson and Mailloux, *Interpreting Law and Literature*, 15.

24. Ibid., 19.

25. Edwin Meese III, "The Law of the Constitution: A Bicentennial Lecture," 1986, 12–13, https://eric.ed.gov/?id=ED278586.

26. Ibid., 11.

27. Since Meese, originalism has evolved and branched so much and has been used as the basis of such divergent lines of reasoning that two law professors contended in 2009 that it suffers "from the very flaws that its proponents have identified in its alternatives." Thomas B. Colby and Peter J. Smith, "Living Originalism," *Duke Law Journal* 59 (2009): 240.

28. Raymond T. Diamond, "Confrontation as Rejoinder to Compromise: Reflections on the Little Rock Desegregation Crisis," *National Black Law Journal* 11, 2 (1989): 176.

29. C. M. A. McCauliff, "Originalism: Privileges v. Fundamental Values," *Hofstra Law Review* 47, 4 (2019): 1289.

30. Harry V. Jaffa, "What Were the 'Original Intentions' of the Framers of the Constitution of the United States?" *University of Puget Sound Law Review* 10 (1987): 351–352.

31. Chief Justice Roger Brooke Taney, "Opinion of the Court in *Dred Scott, Plaintiff in Error v. John F. A. Sandford*, March 6, 1857," in Paul Finkleman, *Dred Scott v. Sandford: A Brief History with Documents*, 2nd ed. (Boston: Bedford/St. Martin's, 2017).

32. What might be called racist originalism has been a longtime element of American politics, as Jared A. Goldstein shows in *Real Americans: National Identity, Violence, and the Constitution* (Lawrence: University Press of Kansas, 2022), 58–110.

33. Edwin Meese, "Dickinson College Constitution Day Speech," September 17, 1985, 17, 19, https://www.justice.gov. Jaffa concludes that Taney's reading is wrong; he takes Meese's side in condemning Brennan for reading his own sentiments into the Constitution and even offers his own version of originalism; and he is sympathetic to Meese's condemnation of affirmative action. However, Jaffa finds Meese's reasoning to be similar to Taney's without seeming to know it. Jaffa, "What Were the 'Original Intentions' of the Framers," 353, 355, 362–366, 368–369, 403–409.

34. Strom Thurmond, "Declaration of Constitutional Principles," 1956, Strom Thurmond Collection, ms. 100.1379, https://www.tigerprints.clemson.edu/strom/1379. In a sense, Thurmond gentrified a long line of racist originalism. See Goldstein, *Real Americans*, 29–140. The exact paternity of the Southern Manifesto is disputed, but Thurmond biographer Joseph Crespino confirms that the senator had a strong claim. Joseph Crespino, *Strom Thurmond's America* (New York: Hill & Wang, 2012), 105–106.

35. Logan E. Sawyer III, "Originalism from the Soft Southern Strategy to the New Right: The Constitutional Politics of Sam Ervin, Jr.," *Journal of Policy History* 33, 1 (January 2021): 32–59; "Sam Ervin: A Featured Biography," https://www.senate.gov/senators/FeaturedBios/Featured_Bio_ErvinSam.htm. See also Hugh Davis Graham, *The Civil Rights Era: Origins and Development of National Policy* (New York: Oxford University Press, 1990), 151; E. W. Kenworthy, "Senate Invokes Cloture on Rights Bill, 71 to 29, Ending 75-Day Filibuster," *New York Times*, June 11, 1964, 1.

36. Sawyer, "Originalism from the Soft Southern Strategy to the New Right," 33–34.

15. WORLD MAKING, ORIGINALIST STYLE

1. William B. Reynolds, "The Reagan Administration's Civil Rights Policy: The Challenge for the Future," *Vanderbilt Law Review* 42, 4 (1989): 1001.

2. The Texaco case is described in Bari-Ellen Roberts with Jack E. White, *Roberts vs. Texaco: A True Story of Race and Corporate America* (New York: Avon Books, 1998), 162–163.

3. Adam Bryant, "How Much Has Texaco Changed? A Mixed Report Card

on Anti-Bias Efforts," *New York Times*, November 2, 1997, Money and Business, 16.

4. "Testimony of Edward C. Sylvester, Jr., Former Director of the Office of Federal Contract Compliance," in *Hearings before the Subcommittee on Administrative Practice and Procedure of the Committee on the Judiciary, United States Senate, Ninety-First Congress, First Session, Pursuant to S. Res. 39, on the Practice and Procedures Involved in the Implementation of Executive Order 11246 and Related Laws, Regulations, and Constitutional Provisions Concerning Equal Employment Opportunity in Federal and Federally Assisted Contracts, March 27 and 28, 1969* (Washington, DC: US Government Printing Office, 1969), 29.

5. Mark R. Levin, *Men in Black: How the Supreme Court Is Destroying America* (Washington, DC: Regnery, 2005), 9.

6. Ibid., 8–9.

7. See Richard Beeman, *The Penguin Guide to the United States Constitution* (New York: Penguin Books, 2010), 35.

8. Mark V. Tushnet, ed., *Thurgood Marshall: His Speeches, Writings, Arguments, Opinions, and Reminiscences* (Chicago: Lawrence Hill Books, 2001), 284–285.

9. *Men in Black* "was virtually ignored by traditional Supreme Court media and the legal academy," Jamal Greene observes. "It was not reviewed in the *New York Times* or the *Washington Post*, and in the week it reached its peak on the best-seller list, David Garrow was quoted as saying, 'The fascinating thing is that it's a bestseller on a subject where 100 percent of us who present ourselves as experts haven't read it.' . . . [It] was marketed on talk radio and over the Internet." Jamal Greene, "Selling Originalism," *Georgetown Law Journal* 97 (2009): 703–704.

10. Meese also convened a regular Heritage Foundation roundtable where conservative lawyers could compare notes, resolve disputes, and coordinate strategies. In addition, the Heritage Foundation hosted biannual gatherings where conservative lawyers could coordinate their efforts to combat Brennan- and Marshall-style visions of America. Mark Tushnet, *A Court Divided* (New York: W. W. Norton, 2005), 45.

11. John J. Miller, *A Gift of Freedom: How the John M. Olin Foundation Changed America* (San Francisco: Encounter Books, 2006), 88.

12. Ibid., 90.

13. Jerry Landry, "The Federalist Society: The Conservative Cabal That's Transforming American Law," *Washington Monthly*, March 2000, https://web.archive.org/web/20150221015400/www.washingtonmonthly.com/features/2000/0003.landay.html.

14. Michael Avery and Danielle McLaughlin, *The Federalist Society: How Conservatives Took the Law Back from Liberals* (Nashville: Vanderbilt University Press, 2013), 26.

15. Quoted in ibid., 8.

16. Commenting on remarks Ronald Reagan made during the investiture of Antonin Scalia as a Supreme Court justice and William Rehnquist as chief

justice, Federalist Society founder Steve Calabresi endorsed a perspective that he says Reagan borrowed from Daniel Webster: "our written Constitution is the Ark of the Covenant of the New Israel that is America." Steven G. Calabresi, ed., introduction to *Originalism: A Quarter-Century of Debate* (Washington, DC: Regnery, 2007), 15, 17–18.

17. Sam Ervin, "The United States Congress and Civil Rights Legislation," *North Carolina Law Review* 42, 1 (1963): 9–10. Bork argued that the Civil Rights Act would have to be paid for in lost freedom. But this cost, as Derrick Bell would surely point out, can only be a cost to whites, not to Blacks and other excluded persons whose freedom the act was intended to expand.

18. "Michael Avery: Co-author, *The Federalist Society: How Conservatives Took the Law Back from Liberals*," https://www.pbs.org/wgbh/frontline/interview-collection/supreme-revenge/.

19. Nina J. Easton, *Gang of Five: Leaders at the Center of the Conservative Crusade* (New York: Simon & Schuster, 2000), 196.

20. Ibid., 105–108.

21. Ibid., 107–110; Stanley O. Wilford, "Duane E. Bennett: He Has the Evidence," *CCC E-Newsletter*, June 2019, https://www.faithdome.org/cccenewsletter/june19/pews.html.

22. Easton, *Gang of Five*, 100; Felicia Campbell, "Know Your Rights: The Fight for Social Change," UC–San Diego: Extended Studies, September 25, 2020, https://extendedstudies.ucsd.edu/division-of-extended-studies-blog/September-2020/Know-Your-Rights-The-Fight-For-Social-Change.

23. Duane E. Bennett, LinkedIn, https://linkedin.com/in/duaneebennett.

24. Lee Cokorinos, *The Assault on Diversity* (Lanham, MD: Rowman & Littlefield, 2003), 70, 74–75.

25. Easton, *Gang of Five*, 194.

26. Clint Bolick, *Changing Course: Civil Rights at the Crossroads* (New Brunswick, NJ: Transaction Books, 1988), 94.

16. CLINT BOLICK GOES TO WAR

1. "A Tattooed Libertarian on the Arizona Supreme Court: Clint Bolick's Long Fight for Freedom," *Reason TV*, https://www.youtube.com/watch?v=hGVT03700dM; Steven A. Holmes, "Political Right's Man on Race: G.O.P. Lawyer Has Shaped the Debate on Affirmative Action," *New York Times*, November 16, 1977, 24.

2. *Board of Education of Oklahoma City Public Schools, Independent School District No. 89, Oklahoma County, Oklahoma v. Dowell et al.*, 498 U.S. 237 (1991), 247.

3. Gary Orfield and Chungmei Lee, *New Faces, Old Patterns? Segregation in the Multiracial South* (Cambridge, MA: Civil Rights Project at Harvard University, 2005), 4, 6; Gary Orfield, "Turning Back to Segregation," in Gary Orfield and Susan E. Eaton, *Dismantling Desegregation: The Quiet Reversal of* Brown v. Board of Education (New York: New Press, 1996), 1–4. Another turning point came in 2007 in the "resegregation cases" discussed in Justice

Stephen Breyer's *Breaking the Promise of Brown: The Resegregation of America's Schools* (Washington, DC: Brookings Institution Press, 2022).

4. *Oklahoma v. Dowell*, 498 U.S. 237 (1991), 237, 257, 268.

5. Clint Bolick, *Changing Course: Civil Rights at the Crossroads* (New Brunswick, NJ: Transaction Books, 1988), 60.

6. Ibid., 65.

7. "Diane Joyce," https://www.legacy.com/us/obituaries/mercurynews/name/diane-joyce-obituary?pid=148351011.

8. Susan Faludi, *Backlash: The Undeclared War against American Women* (New York: Doubleday, 1992), 392.

9. Michael I. Urovsky, *Affirmative Action on Trial: Sex Discrimination in* Johnson v. Santa Clara (Lawrence: University Press of Kansas, 1997), 91–93.

10. *Johnson v. Transportation Agency, Santa Clara County, California*, 480 U.S. 616 (1987), 640–642.

11. Faludi, *Backlash*, 393.

12. Bolick, *Changing Course*, 73–74.

13. Richard Rothstein explains how this works: While "many *de jure* segregation policies aimed to keep African Americans far from white residential areas, public officials also shifted African American populations away from downtown business districts. . . . 'Slum clearance' was the way to accomplish this. By the mid-twentieth century, 'slums' and 'blight' were widely understood as euphemisms for African American neighborhoods." Richard Rothstein, *The Color of Law: A Forgotten History of How Our Government Segregated America* (New York: Liveright, 2017), 126–127.

14. Noel Ignatiev, *How the Irish Became White* (New York: Routledge, 1995), 1.

15. Melvin I. Urofsky points out that, "starting in the mid-1970s, when record-keeping became more sophisticated . . . one could find clear gains in white collar jobs going to white, Asian American, Hispanic, and black women, with white women gaining the most." Melvin I. Urofsky, *The Affirmative Action Puzzle: A Living History from Reconstruction to Today* (New York: Pantheon Books, 2020), 127.

16. Kimberlé W. Crenshaw, "Framing Affirmative Action," *Michigan Law Review First Impressions* 105 (2006): 129.

17. Bolick, *Changing Course*, 117–118.

18. Ibid., 85–86.

19. Ibid., 114.

20. According to Michael K. Brown, Lyndon Johnson's Great Society programs, which were often narrowly tailored to meet the needs of poor Blacks, were slashed and diluted during the Nixon and Reagan administrations, largely for political benefit: "George Wallace's racially coded incantations about lazy welfare recipients convinced many people that the Great Society undermined the work ethic. Such attitudes were exploited by conservative politicians willing to play the race card." Michael K. Brown, *Race, Money, and the American Welfare State* (Ithaca, NY: Cornell University Press, 1999), 323–326.

21. Ibid. See also Martin Gilens, *Why Americans Hate Welfare: Race, Media,*

and the Politics of Antipoverty Policy (Chicago: University of Chicago Press, 1999), 3, 181–184.

22. Bolick, *Changing Course*, 75.

23. Ronald Reagan Presidential Library Digital Collection, Barr, William, files, [Affirmative Action Studies] folder (1 of 7), box 1, 3–9.

24. Jonathan S. Leonard, "Employment and Occupational Advance under Affirmative Action," *Review of Economics and Statistics* 66, 3 (August 1984): 382–383.

25. Jonathan S. Leonard, "The Impact of Affirmative Action on Employment," *Journal of Labor Economics* 2, 4 (October 1983): 459.

26. Bernice Resnick Sandler, "Title IX: How We Got It and What a Difference It Made," *Cleveland State Law Review* 55, 4 (2007): 475.

27. Ibid., 476.

28. Ibid., 477–479, 487.

29. US Department of Health, Education, and Welfare, Office of the Secretary, Office for Civil Rights, *Higher Education Guidelines for Executive Order 11246* (October 1972), 4, 14.

30. Mariam K. Chamberlain, *Women in Academe: Progress and Prospects* (New York: Russell Sage Foundation, 1988), 186.

31. Kul B. Rai and John W. Critzer, *Affirmative Action and the University: Race, Ethnicity, and Gender in Higher Education Employment* (Lincoln: University of Nebraska Press, 2000), 135.

32. Fidan Ana Kurtulus, "Affirmative Action and the Occupational Advancement of Minorities and Women during 1973–2003," *Industrial Relations* 51, 2 (April 2012): 240–241.

33. Bolick, *Changing Course*, 112–113.

17. THE 10 PERCENT SOLUTION

1. Quoted in David Brock, *The Conservative Noise Machine: Right-Wing Media and How It Corrupts Democracy* (New York: Crown, 2004), 49.

2. Frank R. Baumgartner and Bryan D. Jones, *Agendas and Instability in American Politics* (Chicago: University of Chicago Press, 2009), xxiii.

3. Ibid., 148.

4. Among Democrats, as of 2008 there was "a large split on the issue of affirmative action, with 46 percent of white Democrats opposed compared to just 12 percent of nonwhites." D. Sunshine Hillygus and Todd G. Shields, *The Persuadable Voter: Wedge Issues in Presidential Campaigns* (Princeton, NJ: Princeton University Press, 2008), 76.

5. Ibid., 138. See also Rick Perlstein, "Exclusive: Lee Atwater's Infamous 1981 Interview on the Southern Strategy," *Nation*, November 13, 2012, https://www.thenation.com/article/archive/exclusive-lee-atwaters-infamous-1981-interview-southern-strategy=.

6. Joseph Crespino, *Strom Thurmond's America: A History* (New York: Hill & Wang, 2012), 312–313.

7. The anti–civil rights movement did not object, for instance, to the billions

spent on the arms and influence race with Russia, of which the disastrous Vietnam War was a part. The War on Poverty was another matter.

8. Clint Bolick, *Changing Course: Civil Rights at the Crossroads* (New Brunswick, NJ: Transaction Books, 1988), 90, 94.

9. Desmond S. King and Rogers M. Smith, *Still a House Divided: Race and Politics in Obama's America* (Princeton, NJ: Princeton University Press, 2011), 21–22.

10. John J. Miller, *A Gift of Freedom: How the John M. Olin Foundation Changed America* (San Francisco: Encounter Books, 2006), 160.

11. "Chairman of the CIR Board of Directors: Professor Jeremy Rabkin," *Docket Report*, Fall 2002, 14, https://www.cir-usa.org/wp-content/uploads/2021/02/Docket-Report_Fall-02.pdf.

12. "History," https://www.cir-usa.org/about/history/.

13. Lee Cokorinos, *The Assault on Diversity* (Lanham, MD: Rowman & Littlefield, 2003), 60, 66; James J. Miller and Karl Zinsmeister, with Ashley May, *Agenda Setting: A Wise Giver's Guide to Influencing Public Policy* (Washington, DC: Philanthropy Roundtable, 2015), 111.

14. Sam Howe Verhovek, "For 4 Whites Who Sued University, Race Is the Common Thread," *New York Times*, March 23, 1996, 6.

15. Lyle Denniston and David Folkenflik, "Colleges Watching *Texas vs. Hopwood*: High Court Has a Chance to Further Define Limits on Affirmative Action," *Baltimore Sun*, June 23, 1996, 10A2.

16. Ibid.; Robert Bryce, "Naked City: The GOP's Far Right-Hand Man," *Austin Chronicle*, November 24, 2000, https://www.austinchronicle.com/news/2000-11-24/79550/.

17. *Cheryl J. Hopwood, et al. v. State of Texas, et al.*, 78 F.3d 932 (1996), http://www.clearinghouse.net/detail.php?id=11840.

18. Ibid.

19. Linda P. Campbell, "Cheryl Hopwood Moving on with Her Life, but Fight Continues," *Monitor*, May 9, 1998, 23.

20. Michael S. Greve, "Hopwood and Its Consequences," *Pace Law Review* 17 (1996): 2, 4.

21. Ibid., 11, 20.

22. Ibid., 10.

23. Lani Guinier, *Lift Every Voice: Turning a Civil Rights Setback into a New Vision of Social Justice* (New York: Simon & Schuster, 2003), 295–296.

24. Greve, "Hopwood and Its Consequences," 23–24.

25. Anna M. Tinsley, "Despite Cancer, Rangel Remains an Education Advocate," *Brownsville Herald*, April 29, 2001, C9.

26. Lisa Morgan, "Women in Texas," *Duncanville Suburban*, February 26, 1986, 8.

27. Shelby Hodge, "Attorney Seeks Acceptance," *Corpus Christi Caller-Times*, June 20, 1971, 6D.

28. Steve Ray, "Upbringing Shaped Rangel's Career: Kingsville Lawmaker Enters Hall of Fame," *Corpus Christi Caller-Times*, January 30, 1994, A12.

29. Tinsley, "Despite Cancer, Rangel Remains an Education Advocate," C10.

30. "Irma Rangel for State Representative," advertisement, *Valley Morning Star*, June 3, 1976, D4.

31. Eduardo Martinez, "Women Are Learning to 'Call the Shots,'" *Brownsville Herald*, June 2, 1980.

32. Ray, "Upbringing Shaped Rangel's Career."

33. Guinier, *Lift Every Voice*, 295–296.

34. Irma Rangel, "Legislators' Perspectives on *Hopwood*: The Honorable Irma Rangel, Texas State House of Representatives," in *The Hopwood Effect: Problems, Prospects, and Impact on Minorities in Higher Education: Proceedings of the Conference Held February 12–13, 1988 at the George Bush Presidential Conference Center, Hosted by the Office of the President and the Race and Ethnic Studies Institute, Texas A&M University, College Station, Texas*, ed. Mitchell F. Rice (College Station, TX: Race and Ethnic Studies Institute, 1998), 52.

35. Ibid.

36. Tinsley, "Despite Cancer, Rangel Remains an Education Advocate," C9.

37. H.S. No. 588, https://capitol.texas.gov/tlodocs/75R/billtext/html/HB005881.htm.

38. Irma Rangel, remarks during question-and-answer session, in Rice, *Hopwood Effect*, 61–62.

39. Quoted in Michael S. Collins, "A Matter of Degrees: America's Long Struggle with Affirmative Action," *Harper's Magazine*, September 2017, 74.

40. Neely Tucker, "He Got His Way, Then He Got a Mess," *Washington Post*, January 7, 2016, https://www.washingtonpost.com/sf/national/2016/01/07/decidersbush/.

18. PROPOSITION 209

1. John J. Miller, *A Gift of Freedom: How the John M. Olin Foundation Changed America* (San Francisco: Encounter Books, 2006), 160.

2. Ibid., 161; Lydia Chávez, *The Color Bind: California's Battle to End Affirmative Action* (Berkeley: University of California Press, 1998), 11.

3. Chávez, *Color Bind*, 5–7.

4. M. Ali Raza, A. Janell Anderson, and Harry Glynn Custred Jr., *The Ups and Downs of Affirmative Action Preferences* (Westport, CT: Praeger, 1999), 143.

5. Luke Dormehl, *Apple Revolution: Steve Jobs, the Counter Culture and How the Crazy Ones Took over the World* (London: Virgin Books, 2013), 8, 44–46.

6. Raza, Anderson, and Custred, *Ups and Downs of Affirmative Action Preferences*, 143–144.

7. Chávez, *Color Bind*, 14.

8. Ibid., 16–17.

9. Ward Connerly, *Creating Equal: My Fight against Race Preferences* (New York: Encounter Books, 2007), 161.

10. S. I. Hayakawa, J. William Orozco, and Stanley Diamond, "Argument in Favor of Proposition 63," Voter Information Guide for 1986, General Election (1986), 46, https://repository.uchastings.edu/cgi/viewcontent.cgi?article+1970&context=ca_ballot_props.

11. Paul Burka, "What's Black and White and Red-faced All Over?" *Texas Monthly*, December 1997, https://www.texasmonthly.com/articles/whats-black-and-white-and-red-faced-all -over/.

12. Katharine T. Bartlett, "Affirmative Action and Social Discord: Why Is Race More Controversial than Sex?" *University of California, Davis Law Review* 52 (June 2019): 2333.

13. Chávez, *Color Bind*, 21–22.

14. Ibid., 22.

15. Patrick J. Buchanan, "The Quota Busters from Berkeley," *San Francisco Examiner*, February 3, 1994, A-17.

16. Chávez, *Color Bind*, 21, 40–41.

17. Quoted in Lee Cokorinos, *The Assault on Diversity: An Organized Challenge to Racial and Gender Justice* (Lanham, MD: Rowman & Littlefield, 2003), 46.

18. Chávez, *Color Bind*, 44.

19. Ibid., 74–75; Connerly, *Creating Equal*, 164–167.

20. Carl Rowan, "Ward Connerly's Powerful Black Face," *Buffalo News*, October 26, 1998, https://buffalonews.com/news/ward-connerlys-powerful-black-face/article_a138012c-be5b-5d23-82c7-0babc811f7f1.html.

21. Chávez, *Color Bind*, 31, 49.

22. On the genealogy of Obama's success, see Deborah F. Atwater, "Senator Barak Obama: The Rhetoric of Hope and the American Dream," *Journal of Black Studies* 38, 2 (November 2007): 121–129.

23. Chávez, *Color Bind*, 58–67.

24. Ibid., 73.

25. Raza, Anderson, and Custred, *Ups and Downs of Affirmative Action Preferences*, 148, 153.

26. Harry Bearak, "Questions of Race Run Deep for Foe of Preferences," *New York Times*, July 27, 1997, 20.

27. "In 10 to 15 years," he told the *Times* in 1997, "intermarriage will make this entire debate a moot one, anyhow, and we'll wonder why we didn't see it coming." Ibid.

28. Ibid.

29. Chávez, *Color Bind*, 114–116.

30. Ibid., 212–215.

31. Connerly, *Creating Equal*, 167–168.

32. Ronald Brownstein, "Kemp Now Backs Immigration Curbs, End to Preferences," *Los Angeles Times*, August 14, 1996; Ronald Brownstein and Gebe Martinez, "Dole 'Betting the Campaign' on California," *Los Angeles Times*, October 22, 1996; Chávez, *Color Bind*, 130.

33. Zev Chafets, *Roger Ailes: Off Camera* (New York: Sentinel, 2013), 70.

34. Gabriel Sherman, *The Loudest Voice in the Room: How the Brilliant, Bombastic Roger Ailes Built Fox News—and Divided a Country* (New York: Random House, 2014), 14; David Brock, *The Republican Noise Machine: Right-Wing Media and How It Corrupts Democracy* (New York: Crown, 2004), 231.

35. David Brock writes: "The time for FOX was ripe. 'Liberal media bias'—first branded into the national consciousness by Ailes' political mentor [and, to some extent, his creation], Richard Nixon, decades before . . . had taken hold in the public mind. . . . The $1 billion think tank network, and the billions in subsidies being poured into [conservative publications such as] the *Washington Times/New York Post* [owned by Murdoch]/*American Spectator/National Review*/NewsMax distribution channels, had harnessed this powerful backlash [to Great Society–style government] into a wildly successful political campaign against 'Big Government,' against 'political correctness,' against unions, against the United Nations, and against affirmative action." Brock, *Republican Noise Machine*, 315.

36. See Fairleigh Dickinson University's Public Mind Poll, "What You Know Depends on What You Watch: Current Events Knowledge across Popular News Sources," http://publicmind.fdu.edu/2012/confirmed/final.pdf. See also Deena A. Isom, Hunter M. Boehme, Toniqua C. Mikell, Stephen Chicoine, and Marion Renner, "Status Threat, Social Concerns, and Conservative Media: A Look at White America and the Alt-Right," https://mdpi-res-com/d_attachment/societies/societies-11-00072/article_deploy/societies-11-00072.pdf?version=1625220495.

37. Cokorinos, *Assault on Diversity*, 35.

38. "Fox News Republicans are more likely to say that Christians and white people, rather than racial and ethnic minorities, face a lot of discrimination in the USA today," according to the nonpartisan Public Religion Research Institute. PRRI, "Trumpism after Trump? How Fox News Structures Republican Attitudes," https://www.prri.org/wp-content/uploads/2020/11/PRRI-Nov-2020-Fox-News-1.pdf.

39. Chávez, *Color Bind*, 216–217.

40. Connerly, *Creating Equal*, 241.

41. Chávez, *Color Bind*, 217.

42. Martin Luther King, "I Have a Dream," in *Martin Luther King: I Have a Dream; Writings and Speeches that Changed the World* (San Francisco: HarperSanFrancisco, 1992), 105.

43. Daniel Martinez HoSang, *Racial Propositions:Ballot Initiatives and the Making of Postwar California* (Berkeley: University of California Press, 2010), 226.

44. Connerly, *Creating Equal*, 195.

45. Katherine Seligman, "Connerly Lashes out at Civil Rights Leader," SFGATE, February 2, 1997, https://www.sfgate.com/bayarea/article/Connerly-lashes-out-at-civil-rights-leader-3137257.php.

46. Connerly, *Creating Equal*, 195–196.

47. Martin Luther King, *Why We Can't Wait* (New York: Signet Classics, 2000), 165.

48. Chávez, *Color Bind*, 127, 211–214.

49. Marilyn Kalfus, "Proposition 209," *Orange County Register*, October 19, 1996, 18.

50. Ann Bancroft, "UC Regent Accused of Hypocritical Viewpoint: Connerly's Use of His Ethnicity Questioned," *University of California–Santa Barbara Daily Nexus*, May 9, 1995, 1.

51. Suzanne Espinosa Solis, "Affirmative Action Critic Used His Minority Status/UC Regent Got No-Bid State Contracts," SFGATE, May 8, 1995, https://www.sfgate.com/news/article/Affirmative-Action-Critic-Used-His-Minority-3034207.php; Suzanne Espinosa Solis, "UC Regent Fights Law that Helped Him/Minority Contract Program at Issue," SFGATE, May 18, 1995, https://www.sfgate.com/news/article/UC-Regent-Fights-Law-That-Helped-Him-Minority-3032307.php.

52. Virginia Ellis and John Hurst, "Women, Minorities Still Lag in Government Contracting," *Los Angeles Times*, September 11, 1995, https://www.latimes.com/archives/la-xpm-1995-09-11-mn-44605-story.html. Connerly was well aware of this problem, having served on an advisory committee for a 1993 report on the best way to spend the $4 billion California paid to contractors each year. The report documented the difficulties faced by minorities trying to break into the contracting loop, noting that in their fifth year, the "Minority Business Enterprise/Women Business Enterprise/Disabled Veteran Business Enterprise" failed to meet their goals owing to a lack of enforcement mechanisms and fragmented administration and, in some cases, because "the law has simply been ignored." Little Hoover Commission, *California's $4 Billion Bottom Line: Getting the Best Value out of the Procurement Process* (Sacramento: Little Hoover Commission, 1993), vii, 155.

53. Tim Wise, "Is Sisterhood Conditional?" *NWSA Journal* (Fall 1998): 22, quoted in Jo Ann Ooiman Robinson, *Affirmative Action: A Documentary History* (Westport, CT: Greenwood Press, 2001), 341. Custred insists that the Proposition 209 crew did not intend any deception and refused to use the term "affirmative action" because *it* is deceptive. Performing some remarkable logical gymnastics, he and his coauthors assert that after decades of use by government agencies, lawyers, and courts of law, affirmative action "was what George Orwell called a 'meaningless word.'" Raza, Anderson, and Custred, *Ups and Downs of Affirmative Action Preferences*, 150.

54. Zachary Bleemer, "Proposition 209 and Affirmative Action at the University of California," UC-CHP Policy Brief 2020.4, August 2020, 2–3. Bleemer explains that Asians at the top of the University of California's "academic index" saw a slight increase in their admission chances, but that was dwarfed by the 40 percent drop in admissions among Black and Latino applicants. And there was no difference in white and Asian earnings after graduation.

55. Dan Walters, "Racial Quotas Taking a Beating," *Barstow (CA) Desert Dispatch*, December 6, 2000, A4.

19. ENTER EDWARD BLUM

1. The biographical information about Blum and subsequent quotations from him (unless otherwise noted) are from Tim Fleck, "The Great Decolorizer," *Houston Press*, June 19, 1997, https://www.houstonpress.com/news/the-great-decolorizer-6570856. The *emes* anecdote is from Joan Biskupic, "Special Report: Behind U.S. Race Cases, a Little-Known Recruiter," Reuters, December 4, 2012, https://www.reuters/com/article/idUSBRE8B30V9/.

2. Charles Murray, "Helping the Poor: A Few Modest Proposals," *Commentary*, May 1995, https://www.commentary.org/articles/charles-murray/helping-the-poor-a-few-modest-proposals. Murray's title alludes to Jonathan Swift's famous satirical essay "A Modest Proposal," but Murray seems to be unaware that his reference to Swift and his remarks about the pernicious effects of the poor giving birth to too many out-of-wedlock children cause his essay to satirize itself. It is precisely these kinds of arguments that Swift was attacking when he wrote that infants born to poor Irish people should be sold and eaten as a way to "lessen *the Number of Papists*, with whom we are yearly overrun, being the principal breeders of the nation, as well as our most dangerous enemies." Jonathan Swift, "A Modest Proposal," in *A Modest Proposal and Other Writings*, ed. Carole Fabricant (London: Penguin Group, 2009), 235.

3. Here is an example of Murray's 1992 argument: "In 1960, it was extremely punishing, financially and socially, to have a baby without a husband. The reforms made the behavior less punishing on both counts. In 1960, the odds of being caught and going to jail if you committed crimes were high. The reforms lowered the odds of both getting caught and going to jail. . . . [Social effects of 1960s reforms interact in] numerous feedback loops and, among other things, tear apart the web of status and rewards that govern behavior in any community." Charles Murray, "The Legacy of the '60s," *Commentary*, July 1992, https://www.commentary.org/articles/charles-murray/the-legacy-of-the-60s. While I cannot mount a full rebuttal of these points here, it is worth noting that the term "civil rights" is never mentioned in Murray's essay; nor is the Civil Rights Act of 1964.

4. Lee Cokorinos, *The Assault on Diversity: An Organized Challenge to Racial and Gender Justice* (Lanham, MD: Rowman & Littlefield, 2003), 73.

5. *Bush v. Vera*, 517 U.S. 952 (1996), 1005.

6. Dismissing the dilution argument as not enough of a demonstration of racial discrimination, O'Connor cited *Wygant* as well as previous voting rights cases to support her assertion that stronger evidence of a need for remedial measures must be found before any affirmative action could be taken. Ibid., 982.

7. Ibid., 1006, 1007, 1011.

8. John Paul Stevens, *The Making of a Justice: Reflections on My First 94 Years* (New York: Little, Brown, 2019), 317.

9. Fleck, "Great Decolorizer."

10. "Affirmative Action Isn't Dead Yet," *Atlanta Business Chronicle*, November 17, 1997, https://www.bizjournals.com/atlanta/stories/1997/11/17

/editorial1.html; William Schneider, "Affirmative Action Still Lives," *National Journal*, November 15, 1997, https://www.aei.org/articles/affirmative-action-still-lives/; "Affirmative Proaction," editorial, *Houston Business Journal*, August 24, 1997, https:www.bizjournals.com/houston/stories/1997/08/25/editorial1.html.

11. Ward Connerly, *Creating Equal: My Fight against Race Preferences* (New York: Encounter Books, 2007), 216. The reference to Farrakhan is intended to suggest that the African Americans at Connerly's events were motivated by a racial animus akin to that of Farrakhan, who was known for making anti-Semitic remarks that received heavy coverage in the mainstream media.

12. Rochelle Sharp and G. Pascal Zachary, "Support of Affirmative Action in Houston May Pose Trouble," *Wall Street Journal*, November 6, 1997, https://www.wsj.com/articles/SB878777396655955500.

13. Sam Howe Verhovek, "Referendum in Houston Shows Complexity of Preference Issue," *New York Times*, November 6, 1997, A1.

14. Steven A. Holmes, "Broker Asserts Political Views Drew Pressure," *New York Times*, July 10, 1998, A10.

15. Tim Fleck, "Mr. Blum Goes to Washington," *Houston Press*, September 14, 2000, https://www.houstonpress.com/news/mr-blum-goes-to-washington-6564043.

16. B. Drummond Ayres Jr., "Foes of Affirmative Action Form a National Group," *New York Times*, January 16, 1997, A16.

17. Martin Luther King, *Why We Can't Wait* (New York: Signet Classics, 2000), 170.

18. Connerly, *Creating Equal*, 21. Connerly does distinguish those he dismisses as "civil rights professionals" from President Johnson, arguing that Johnson's intentions for affirmative action were perverted by the professionals, just as King's were. Ibid., 193.

19. Cokorinos, *Assault on Diversity*, 32.

20. John J. Miller, *A Gift of Freedom: How the John M. Olin Foundation Changed America* (San Francisco: Encounter Books, 2006), 137–139; Jayne Mayer, *Dark Money: The Hidden History of the Billionaires behind the Rise of the Radical Right* (New York: Anchor Books, 2017), 138–139; Jean Stefancic and Richard Delgado, *No Mercy: How Conservative Think Tanks and Foundations Changed America's Social Agenda* (Philadelphia: Temple University Press, 1996), 58.

21. Richard J. Herrnstein and Charles Murray, *The Bell Curve: Intelligence and Class Structure in American Life* (New York: Free Press, 1994), 449, 117–118, 449, 476.

22. Ibid., 472–473.

23. "Poor college performance has many causes . . . black and Latino students faced more such 'causes' than their white and Asian counterparts. They were less likely to come from a two-parent home; their families were more likely to experience a distracting level of violence and trauma while the student was in college; these students were more likely to come from segregated backgrounds that gave them less access to cultural knowledge and know-how

that go into good college performance; the money they needed for college was a higher percentage of their family income; they were less likely to have gone to a high school with Advanced Placement courses; their precollege friendship networks were less likely to have been focused on college achievement, and so on." Claude M. Steele, *Whistling Vivaldi: How Stereotypes Affect Us and What We Can Do* (New York: W. W. Norton, 2010), 149.

24. Ibid., 151.

25. Leon J. Kamin, "Lies, Damned Lies, and Statistics," in *The Bell Curve Debate: History, Documents, Opinions*, ed. Russell Jacoby and Naomi Glauberman (New York: Times Books, 1995), 98.

26. Herrnstein and Murray, *Bell Curve*, 506–507.

27. William G. Bowen and Derek Bok, *The Shape of the River: Long-Term Consequences of Considering Race in College and University Admissions* (Princeton, NJ: Princeton University Press, 1998), 75–76.

28. Connerly, *Creating Equal*, 237.

29. John K. Wilson, "Rush Limbaugh's False Smears about Obama's Harvard Record," *Academe* blog, August 2, 2012, https://academeblog.org.2012/08/02/rush-limbaughs-false-smears-about-obamas-harvard-record/.

30. Connerly, *Creating Equal*, 244.

31. As the Florida campaign got under way, Connerly met with Bush, and for a time, they had an open line of communication. But Connerly alleges that "some of Florida's black legislators" pressured Bush, and "Jeb tried to stigmatize me as a 'carpetbagger.'" Connerly, *Creating Equal*, 257.

32. Connerly, *Creating Equal*, 259.

33. Fleck, "Mr. Blum Goes to Washington." California, meanwhile, instituted a top 4 percent rule, as Barbara A. Perry reminds us in *The Michigan Affirmative Action Cases* (Lawrence: University Press of Kansas, 2007), 40.

20. CONSERVATIVE THREE-CARD MONTE

1. Brian Rosenwald, *Talk Radio's America: How An Industry Took over a Political Party that Took over the United States* (Cambridge, MA: Harvard University Press, 2019), 5.

2. UVA Center for Politics, "New Initiative Explores Deep, Persistent Divides between Biden and Trump Voters," September 20, 2021, https://centerforpolitics.org/crystalball/articles/new-initiative-explores-deep-persistent-divides-between-biden-and-trump-voters/.

3. Randall Balmer, "The Real Origins of the Religious Right," *Politico*, May 27, 2014, https://www.politico.com/magazine/story/2014/05/religious-right-real-origins-107133/.

4. *Bob Jones University v. United States*, 461 U.S. 574 (1983), 591–598.

5. Phil Gailey, "Bob Jones, in Sermon, Assails Supreme Court," *New York Times*, May 25, 1983, A23.

6. Claude M. Steele, *Whistling Vivaldi: How Stereotypes Affect Us and What We Can Do* (New York: W. W. Norton, 2010), 153–154.

7. Jean Stefanic and Richard Delgado, *No Mercy: How Conservative Think*

Tanks and Foundations Changed America's Social Agenda (Philadelphia: Temple University Press, 1996), 39; Alex Michelini, "Court Backs CCNY's Levin," *New York Daily News*, June 9, 1992. Levin did not neglect to denigrate high-achieving African Americans. During a contentious appearance at a California college, he cried, "The presence of blacks in high-prestige jobs doesn't prove that they can make it on their own. It proves the opposite." Associated Press, "Pickets Greet Speaker at FCC," *Hanford Sentinel*, April 6, 1992.

8. See Michelle Alexander, *The New Jim Crow: Mass Incarceration in the Age of Colorblindness* (New York: New Press, 2012), 74–78, 107–114.

9. "More Black Men Are in Jail than Are Enrolled in Higher Education," *Journal of Blacks in Higher Education* 41 (Autumn 2003): 62.

10. David Garland, "Introduction: The Meaning of Mass Imprisonment," in *Mass Imprisonment: Social Causes and Consequence*, ed. David Garland (London: Sage, 2001), 2, 1.

11. Dan Brown, "Legaize It All: How to Win the War on Drugs," *Harper's Magazine*, April 2016, 22.

12. Jared Taylor and Glayde Whitney, "Racial Profiling: Is There an Empirical Basis?" in *Taking Sides: Clashing Views in Crime and Criminology*, ed. Thomas Hickey (Dubuque, IA: McGraw-Hill, 2006), 125.

13. The balance here is deceiving. *Mankind Quarterly* gave significant space to articles purporting to prove Black inferiority. See Stefanic and Delgado, *No Mercy*, 43.

14. Michael J. Lynch, "Misleading 'Evidence' and the Misguided Attempt to Generate Racial Profiles of Criminals: Correcting Fallacies and Calculations Concerning Race and Crime in Taylor and Whitney's Analysis of Racial Profiling," in Hickey, *Taking Sides*, 134–135.

15. Elliott Ash and Michael Poyker, "Conservative News Media and Criminal Justice: Evidence from Exposure to Fox News Channel" (Columbia Business School research paper, December 8, 2021), 6, 5, 18, https://papers.ssrn.com/sol3/papers.cfm?abstract_id=3381827.

16. Charles Ogletree, *The Presumption of Guilt: The Arrest of Henry Louis Gates Jr. and Race, Class, and Crime in America* (New York: Palgrave Macmillan, 2010), 110–111.

17. Greg Palast, *The Best Democracy Money Can Buy* (New York: Plume, 2003), 30–59. In May 2000 Florida's secretary of state—using a flawed list compiled by a contractor—ordered eight thousand voters purged from the rolls because they were allegedly felons. But in fact, "none of the group was charged with anything more than a misdemeanor, a mistake caught but never fully reversed." Ibid., 38, 43. Since the margin of victory in Florida was five hundred votes, the purging of thousands mattered.

18. Leah Wang, "The U.S. Criminal Justice System Disproportionately Hurts Native People: The Data, Visualized," Prison Policy Initiative, October 8, 2021, https://www.prisonpolicy.org/blog/2021/10/08/indigenouspeoplesday.

21. THE CENTER FOR INDIVIDUAL RIGHTS VERSUS THE UNIVERSITY OF MICHIGAN

1. The phrase is from an illustration in Theodore Cross, "African-American Opportunities in Higher Education: What Are the Racial Goals of the Center for Individual Rights?" *Journal of Blacks in Higher Education* (Spring 1999): 95.

2. Ibid., 99, 96, 99.

3. Barbara A. Perry, *The Michigan Affirmative Action Cases* (Lawrence: University Press of Kansas, 2007), 40–41.

4. Greg Stohr, *A Black and White Case: How Affirmative Action Survived Its Greatest Legal Challenge* (Princeton, NJ: Bloomberg Press, 2004), 9–18; Carl Cohen, *A Conflict of Principles: The Battle over Affirmative Action at the University of Michigan* (Lawrence: University Press of Kansas, 2014), 27–77.

5. Stohr, *Black and White Case*, 34.

6. Cohen, *Conflict of Principles*, 70–77.

7. Judy Daubenmier, "Affirmative Action Takes Heat at Hearing," *Herald-Palladium*, March 1, 1996, 4A.

8. Cohen, *Conflict of Principles*, 77.

9. Daubenmier, "Affirmative Action Takes Heat at Hearing."

10. See Carl Cohen and James P. Sterba, *Affirmative Action and Racial Preference: A Debate* (Oxford: Oxford University Press, 2003), 23–106.

11. Cohen, *Conflict of Principles*, 85.

12. Stohr, *Black and White Case*, 1–2; Jodi S. Cohen, "Denial Shatters Dream: Southgate Woman Key Figure in University Bias Suit," *Detroit News and Free Press*, November 12, 2000, 8A. See also James Taranto, "The Woman Who Fought Racial Preference," *Wall Street Journal*, June 28, 2013, https://www.waj.com/articles/SB10001424127887323419604578570041957165544.

13. Cohen, "Denial Shatters Dream."

14. The eventual lawsuit was filed on behalf of Gratz and Patrick Hamacher, but he was obviously in no position to neutralize the "angry white male" charge.

15. Peggy Walsh-Sarnecki, "The Men Who Would End Affirmative Action," *Detroit Free Press*, August 25, 1998, 3A.

16. Ibid.

17. Michael Greve, "Germany: The Untouchable Welfare State," *Public Interest* 80 (Summer 1985): 107–108.

18. Jürgen Habermas, "The Crisis of the Welfare State and the Exhaustion of Utopian Energies," in *Jürgen Habermas on Society and Politics: A Reader*, ed. Steven Seidman (Boston: Beacon Press, 2005), 290–291.

19. "J. William Fulbright Quotes," https://eca.state.gov/fulbright/about-fulbright/history/j-william-fulbright/j-william-fulbright-quote.

20. Cohen, *Conflict of Principles*, 83.

21. Stohr, *Black and White Case*, 73–75.

22. Martin Luther King called for a Marshall Plan at home to match "the Marshall Plan and technical assistance to handicapped peoples around the world." Martin Luther King, *Why We Can't Wait* (New York: Signet Classics, 2000), 168.

23. Charles King, "The Fulbright Paradox: Race and the Road to a New American Internationalism," *Foreign Affairs*, July–August 2021, https://www.foreignaffairs.com/articles/united-states/2021-06-18/fulbright-paradox.

24. Ernest J. Wilson III and Lorrie A. Frasure explain that the discipline of political science was born in the segregation era. It has traditionally looked the other way where racial issues are concerned and has viewed research into racial politics as a low-status activity. Ernest J. Wilson III and Lorrie A. Frasure, "Still at the Margins: The Persistent Neglect of African American Issues in Political Science, 1986–2003," in *African American Perspectives on Political Science*, ed. Wilbur C. Rich (Philadelphia: Temple University Press, 2007), 21.

25. Michael S. Greve, "Why 'Defunding the Left' Failed," *National Affairs* 49 (Fall 2021): 95–96.

26. Cindy Vreeland explains that the NAACP's victory in *Brown v. Board of Education* launched both a desegregation revolution and a legal revolution involving public law litigation—defined by law professor Abram Chayes as lawsuits brought not on behalf of individuals involved in private disputes but on behalf of individuals representing the larger public in cases meant to "vindicate important social values that affect numerous individuals and entities." Cindy Vreeland, "Public Interest Groups, Public Law Litigation, and Federal Rule 24(a)," *University of Chicago Law Review* 57, 1 (1990): 279.

27. "CIR Will Appeal UM's Racial Preferences—All the Way," *CIR Docket Report*, Fall 2002, 2, 3.

28. While I was making final corrections before this book went to press, the news broke that Yale and Dartmouth have returned to requiring the SAT (or an equivalent test) after making it optional during the COVID-19 pandemic. Both schools explained that dropping the SAT might actually harm low-income and minority applicants who fear that scores that would actually get them admitted in a holistic evaluation were too low. However, Columbia, Harvard, and 80 percent of other schools did not restore the SAT. At the University of Michigan, source of the *Gratz* and *Grutter* cases, the test is optional. In short, the country is running a real-time experiment on the value of the SAT, but it is unlikely to return to its status as a pure measure of transcendental merit. Stephenie Saul, "Yale to Require Standardized Test Scores for Admissions," *New York Times*, February 22, 2024, https://www.nytimes.com/2024/02/22/us/yale-standardized-testing-sat-act.html.

29. "Interview: Terrence Pell," in "Secrets of the SAT: Why the National Obsession with the SAT Test? And How Fair, Reliable, and Democratic Is It?" *FRONTLINE*, https://www.pbs.org/wgbh/pages/frontline/shows/sats/interviews/pell.html.

30. "Interview: Derek Bok," in "Secrets of the SAT: Why the National Obsession with the SAT Test? And How Fair, Reliable, and Democratic Is It?" *FRONTLINE*, https://www.pbs.org/wgbh/pages/frontline/shows/sats/interviews/bok.html.

31. "CIR Goes to Trial against Racial Preferences at UM," *CIR Docket Report*, Fall 2002, 2.

32. "Supreme Court Affirmative Action Cases," https://www.c-span.org/video/?175842-1/supeme-court-affirmative-action-cases.

33. Anthony Carnevale and Jeff Strohl, interview with the author, June 23, 2020.

34. Anthony P. Carnevale, Jeff Strohl, and Martin Van Der Werf, "The Concept of 'Mismatch' at Play in the Supreme Court Fisher Decision Is Empirically Unsound," 2016, https://cew.georgetown.edu/wp-content/uploads/Mismatch-Paper_62016.pdf.

22. THE MEANING OF 20 POINTS

1. "Supreme Court Affirmative Cases: Center for Individual Rights News Conference, March 31, 2003," *C-SPAN*, https://www.c-span.org/video/?175842-1/supreme-court-affirmaive-action-cases

2. Patricia Gurin, "Expert Report of Patricia Gurin," *Michigan Journal of Race and Law* 5 (1999): 389.

3. Ibid., 367. Law professor Lani Guinier has argued that "democratic merit" should replace standardized "testocratic" merit in American education: "when we redefine merit by those characteristics that indicate a student's potential for future success in our democracy . . . then we might be able to make use of actions that prioritize such traits." Lani Guinier, *The Tyranny of the Meritocracy: Democratizing Higher Education in America* (Boston: Beacon Press, 2015), 33.

4. Gurin, "Expert Report," 383.

5. Greg Stohr, *A Black and White Case: How Affirmative Action Survived Its Greatest Legal Challenge* (Princeton, NJ: Bloomberg Press, 2004), 50.

6. Wood blogs about his campaign against Gurin's report in "Just Say No to Racial Preferences," posted on the National Association of Scholars website on April 28, 2008, https://www.nas.org/blogs/article/just_say_no_to_racial_preferences. For one of her responses to her critics, see Patricia Gurin, "Evidence for the Educational Benefits of Diversity in Higher Education: Response to the Continuing Critique by the National Association of Scholars of the Expert Witness Report of Patricia Gurin in Gratz, et al. v. Bollinger, et. al. and Grutter v. Bollinger, et al.," May 20, 2003, https://diversity.umich.edu/admissions/research/pgurin-nas-html.

7. Jeffrey F. Liss, James J. Halpert, and Elizabeth R. Dewey, Brief for Amicus Curiae Stanford Institute for Higher Education Research in Support of Affirmance in Nos. 01-1333, 01-1418. "The brief of the National Association of Scholars in Gratz v. Bollinger relies primarily on analyses by Thomas E. Wood and Malcolm J. Sherman," another amicus confirms. See Angelo N. Ancheta and Christopher F. Edley Jr., Brief of the American Educational Research Association, the Association of American Colleges and Universities, and the American Association for Higher Education as Amici Curiae in Support of Respondents in *Grutter v. Bollinger*, March 3, 2003, 8.

8. The information in this paragraph comes from Barbara A. Perry, *The Michigan Affirmative Action Cases* (Lawrence: University Press of Kansas, 2007), 52–53.

9. *Gratz et al. v. Bollinger et al.*, 135 F. Supp. 2d 790 (E.D. Mich. 2001).

10. Perry, *Michigan Affirmative Action Cases*, 53. Duderstadt, like previous University of Michigan presidents, was also influenced by student protests led by the Black Action Movement, which had been demanding a greater African American presence on campus since the 1970s. In 1987 another organization, the United Coalition against Racism, had responded to racist incidents on campus by demanding a "mandatory workshop on racism and diversity." Keith A. Owens, "Blacks Say U-M's Reply Inadequate," *Ann Arbor News*, March 19, 1987, A4.

11. "1998 Guidelines for the Calculation of a Selection Index for All Schools and Colleges Except Engineering," in *Gratz and Hamacher v. Bollinger and Patterson: Joint Appendix*, 182–196.

12. Stohr, *Black and White Case*, 49–50.

13. The breakdown of the 150-point scale is drawn from Stohr, *Black and White Case*, 49–50, and "The U-M's New Admissions Policy: Race Counts More than SAT, Service, Essay Combined," *Michigan Review* 16, 9 (April 1, 1998): 5. The *Michigan Review* is a conservative student-run publication at the University of Michigan.

14. Jodi S. Cohen, "Denial Shatters Dream: Southgate Woman Key Figure in University Bias Suit," *Detroit News and Free Press*, November 12, 2000, 8A; James Taranto, "The Woman Who Fought Racial Preference," *Wall Street Journal*, June 28, 2013, https://www.waj.com/articles/SB10001424127887323419604578570041957165544.

15. "Jennifer was sure that something had gone horribly wrong. She understood that Michigan used affirmative action in admissions, though she knew nothing of the specifics. Her thoughts flashed to a Hispanic classmate who had been admitted to Michigan with lower grades than hers." It was with this thought in mind that she asked her father if they could sue. Stohr, *Black and White Case*, 2–3.

16. Jennifer Gratz, "Discriminating toward Equality: Affirmative Action and the Diversity Charade," Heritage Foundation: Backgrounder No. 2885, February 27, 2014, 3, http://thf_media.s3.amazonaws.com/2014/pdf/BG2885.pdf.

17. Kenneth J. Cooper, "Deciding Who Gets in and Who Doesn't," *Washington Post*, April 2, 2000, https://www.washingtonpost.com/archive/politics/2000/04/02/deciding-who-gets-in-and-who-doesnt/7379588d-3a39-42a6-9a1d-f12ac0086a7a/.

18. *Gratz et al. v. Bollinger et al.*, 539 U.S. 244 (2003), 272.

19. Ibid., 294–295.

20. This is the original quotation from Stephen L. Carter, "When Victims Happen to Be Black," *Yale Law Journal* 97 (1988): 434.

21. *Gratz v. Bollinger*, 539 U.S. 244 (2003), 303.

22. Consolidated Brief, Lt. Gen. Julius W. Becton Jr., Adm. Dennis Blair, Maj. Gen. Charles Bolden, Hon. James M. Cannon, Lt. Gen. Daniel W. Christman, Gen. Wesley K. Clark, Sen. Max Cleland, Adm. Archie Clemins, Hon. William Cohen, Adm. William J. Crowe, Gen. Ronald R. Fogleman, Lt. Gen. Howard D.

Graves, Gen. Joseph P. Hoar, Sen. Robert J. Kerrey et al., as Amicus Curiae in Support of Respondents Barbara Grutter v. Lee Bollinger, et al.; Jennifer Gratz and Patrick Hamacher v. Lee Bollinger, et al., February 19, 2003, 6–7.

23. The attorney general's recognition in 2021 that the top domestic threat in the United States is posed by "those who advocate for the superiority of the white race" underscores the continuing urgency of—and the continuing resistance to—the concept that racial (and other) diversity is something to be valued. Eileen Sullivan and Katie Benner, "Top Law Enforcement Officials Say the Biggest Domestic Terror Threat Comes from White Supremacists," *New York Times*, June 15, 2021, https://www.nytimes.com/2021/05/12/us/politcs/domestic-terror-white-supremacists.html.

24. The following statement by Thomas could be inserted into one of Bell's parables about the permanence of racism without anyone realizing that it does not express Bell's views: "Man, quotas are for the black middle class. Look at what's happening to the masses. . . . They are just where they were before any of these policies." Nina J. Easton, *Gang of Five: Leaders at the Center of the Conservative Crusade* (New York: Simon & Schuster, 2000), 195. What is interesting about the similarity between Bell's and Thomas's assessment of the Black masses is the fact that Bell is demonized as a racist by the anti–civil rights movement, while Thomas is lionized as a hero.

25. David Brock, *Blinded by the Right: The Conscience of an Ex-Conservative* (New York: Three Rivers Press, 2002), 135–137, 269–270, 313–314, 96.

26. Ibid., 97, 99.

27. Ibid., 97.

28. *Gratz v. Bollinger*, 539 U.S. 306 (2003), 372.

29. Lani Guinier, "Quota of One," *Journal of Blacks in Higher Education* (Autumn 1993): 32.

30. Anthony Carnevale and Jeff Strohl, interview by the author, June 23, 2020; Anthony P. Carnevale, Jeff Strohl, and Martin Van Der Werf, "The Concept of 'Mismatch' at Play in the Supreme Court Fisher Decision Is Empirically Unsound," 2016, https://cew.georgetown.edu/wp-content/uploads/Mismatch-Paper_62016.pdf.

31. Guinier, *Tyranny of the Meritocracy*, 5.

32. "Ward Connerly's Trumpet Blast," *Economist*, March 29, 1997, 34.

33. Taranto, "Woman Who Fought Racial Preference."

34. Jennifer Gratz, "The Path to Equal Rights in Michigan," *Academic Questions* 20 (2007): 242–243.

35. Deborah Whyman, "Should We Drop Race, Gender Criteria—Yes or No? Social Experiment with Children's Futures Will Not Be Tolerated," *Lansing State Journal*, June 14, 1998, 13.

36. Dan Shine, "Schulman Grabs Nomination in Contentious House Race," *Detroit Free Press*, August 6, 1998, 3B; Mary Owen, "State Hate-Crime Bill Gaining Urgency," *Detroit Free Press*, October 15, 1998, 2B; Kate McKee, "Gay Rights Group Sues Legislator over Campaign Literature: Triangle Foundation Alleges Libel by Whyman," *Detroit Free Press*, March 1, 1997, 5A.

37. Taranto, "Woman Who Fought Racial Preference."

23. SHANTA DRIVER TAKES ON THE ANTI–CIVIL RIGHTS MOVEMENT

1. Ben Lefebvre, "Wham BAMN," *Detroit Metro Times*, January 11, 2006, https://www.metrotimes.com/news/wham-bamn-2183650.

2. Jacqueline Boyle, "Michigan Pro-Choice Activists in the Spotlight," *Detroit Free Press*, April 25, 1992, 3A.

3. Chastity Pratt, "13 Arrested during Melee at Meeting: School Board Members Denounce Protesters," *Detroit Free Press*, March 29, 2002, 4B.

4. Nikita Stewart and Richard Wilson, "'I Look at Tony as a Martyr': Lexington Stays Calm as Emotions Flow at Funeral," *Louisville Courier-Journal*, November 1, 1994, A14.

5. "Election Guide," *Detroit Free Press*, September 7, 1989, 2A; "Election Results," *Detroit Free Press*, September 11, 1997, 3B; "Who's Running Now," *Detroit Free Press*, June 23, 1993, 8A; Ralph Orr, "Service Employees Chief Re-elected," *Detroit Free Press*, February 25, 1984, A3.

6. Patricia Montemurri, "God, Trotsky Spur Some to Enter the Race: Mayoral Candidates Share Motivation," *Detroit Free Press*, August 18, 1992, 4B.

7. Driver "was the legal architect of a student-intervenor defense in *Grutter v. Bollinger*." "Shanta Driver," Discover the Networks, https://www.discoverthenetworks.org/individuals/shanta-driver/). See also Josie Huang, "Closer to Living MLK's 'Dream,'" *Portland Press Herald*, January 20, 2004, 10A; Theresa Hogue, "Lawyer Calls for New Civil Rights Movement: Education, Affirmative Action Need Youths' Work, Activist Says at OSU," *Corvalis (OR) Gazette-Times*, May 20, 2004, 1.

8. Ellen Barry, "Making a Civil Rights Claim for Affirmative Action: BAMN's Legal Mobilization and the Legacy of Race-Conscious Polices," *DuBois Review* 12, 26 (2015): 377.

9. "Driver, Shanta: Candidate Details," Our Campaigns, https://www.ourcampaigns.com/CandidateDetail.html?CandidateID=207084.

10. *Operation King's Dream, et al. v. Connerly, et al.*, Case No. 06-12773, 1, 2; Suzette Hackney and David Ashenfelter, "Affirmative Action Ban's Hearing Gets under Way," *Detroit Free Press*, August 18, 2006, 3B.

11. Suzette Hackney, "Election 2006: Michigan; Affirmative Action Ban OK'd," *Detroit Free Press*, November 8, 2006, 9A.

12. "BAMN Attorney Shanta Driver Speech before Entering Supreme Court in Schuette v. Coalition (BAMN)," https://www.youtube.com/watch?v=3pafqILA--s; David Jesse, "Activists Defend Affirmative Action outside High Court," *Detroit Free Press*, October 15, 2013, https://www.usatoday.com/story/news/nation/2013/10/15/supreme-court-affirmative-action-michigan/2986401/.

13. *Schuette v. Coalition to Defend Affirmative Action*, Oral Argument, October 15, 2013, https://apps.oyez.org/player/#/roberts6/oral_argument_audio/22178.

14. Like his successors in 2022, Carl Cohen, who paved the way for *Gratz* and *Grutter* when he publicized the university's admissions grid, objected to the identity component in Barack Obama's decision to appoint Sotomayor to the Supreme Court (though of course, he did not object to the identity component

in the appointments of Scalia and O'Connor). "Ethnic balance on the court is a foolish and hurtful idea," he opined. Niraj Warikoo, "Sotomayor's Latina Pride Stirs Debate: Some Find It Inspirational; Others Say It's Not Right for High Court," *Detroit Free Press*, July 12, 2009.

15. *Schuette*, Oral Arguments.

16. *Schuette v. Coalition to Defend Affirmative Action*, 572 U.S. 291 (2014), 307–309.

17. Ibid., 380.

18. Joan Biskupic, *Breaking In: Sonia Sotomayor and the Politics of Justice* (New York: Farrar, Straus & Giroux, 2014), 211.

19. Sonia Sotomayor, *My Beloved World* (New York: Alfred A. Knopf, 2013), 191, 192.

20. *Schuette*, 572 U.S. 291 (2014), 374, 392.

21. *Fox News Sunday with Chris Wallace*, April 27, 2014, https://archive.org/details/FOXNEWSW_20140427_220000_FOX_News_Sunday_With_Chris_Wallace.

22. Margaret Burnham, "The New Great Dissenter: On Affirmative Action, Sotomayor Gets It Right," WBUR, April 25, 2014, https://www.wbur.org/cognoscenti/2014/04/25/michigan-schuette-v-bamn-margaret-burnham.

24. BLUM TAKES OVER

1. Joan Biskupic, "Special Report: Behind U.S. Race Cases, a Little-Known Recruiter," Reuters, December 4, 2012, https://www.reuters.com/article/us-usa-court-casemaker/special-report-behind-u-s-race-cases-a-little-known-recruiter-idUSBRE8B30V220121204.

2. Following the money in and out of DonorsTrust, one discovers a kind of financial ouroboros: The current chair of the Searle Freedom Trust, Kim Dennis, also chairs the board of DonorsTrust, which she cofounded in 1999. James Piereson, vice chair of the board of DonorsTrust, is also president of the William E. Simon Foundation, a senior fellow at the Manhattan Institute, and past executive director of the Olin Foundation (which, as intended by its founder, closed its doors after distributing all its funds). Piereson also serves on the board of the Center for Individual Rights. See DonorsTrust, "Directors and Staff," https://www.donorstrust.org/who-we-are/directors-and-staff. According to *Mother Jones* magazine, as of 2013, DonorsTrust had raised some $500 million and distributed $400 million to a thousand conservative and libertarian groups. See Andy Kroll, "Exposed: The Dark-Money ATM of the Conservative Movement," *Mother Jones*, February 5, 2013, https://www.motherjones.com/politics/2013/02/donors-trust-donor-captal-fund-dark-money-koch-bradley-devos/; Nonprofit Explorer: Project on Fair Representation Inc., https://propublica.org/nonprofits/organizations/472593047; Biskupic, "Special Report: Behind U.S. Race Cases"; Joan Biskupic, "A Litigious Activist's Latest Cause: Ending Affirmative Action at Harvard," Reuters, June 8, 2015, https://www.reuters.com/investigates/special-report/usa-harvard-discrimination/; Camille G. Caldera and Sahar M. Mohammadzadeh, "Public Filings Reveal

SFFA Mostly Funded by Conservative Trusts Searle Freedom Trust and Donors Trust," *Harvard Crimson*, February 7, 2019, https://www.thecrimson.com/article/2019/2/7/sffa-finance/.

3. *Fisher v. University of Texas at Austin*, 579 U.S. 365 (2016).

4. "Project on Fair Representation Announces Lawsuit Challenging Admissions Policies at Harvard Univ. and Univ. of North Carolina–Chapel Hill," SFFA, November 17, 2014, https://studentsforfairadmissions.org/project-on-fair-admissions-announces-lawsuits-challenging-admissions-poicies-at-harvard-univ-and-univ-of-north-carolina-chapel-hill/.

5. Abigail M. Thernstrom, *Whose Votes Count? Affirmative Action and Minority Voting Rights* (Cambridge, MA: Harvard University Press, 1987), 78, 154.

6. Abigail Thernstrom, *Voting Rights—and Wrongs: The Elusive Quest for Racially Fair Elections* (Washington, DC: AEI Press, 2009), 1.

7. For more on Mercer, see Jane Mayer, "The Reclusive Hedge-Fund Tycoon behind the Trump Presidency: How Robert Mercer Exploited America's Populist Insurgency," *New Yorker*, March 17, 2017.

8. Thernstrom, *Voting Rights—and Wrongs*, 11.

9. Ibid., 9, 157.

10. Charles S. Bullock III and Ronald Keith Gaddie, *The Triumph of Voting Rights in the South* (Norman: University of Oklahoma Press, 2009), xiii.

11. Edward Blum and Abigail Thernstrom, "Executive Summary of the Bullock-Gaddie Expert Report on Louisiana," 1. This document is undated but was likely published in 2006 as part of AEI's effort to block reauthorization of the Voting Rights Act. See Rick Hasen, "The Project on Fair Representation: Minority Voting Studies of Jurisdictions Covered by Section Five of the Voting Rights Act," *Election Law* blog, January 19, 2006, https://electionlawblog.org/?p=4527.

12. Lee Cokorinos, *The Assault on Diversity: An Organized Challenge to Racial and Gender Justice* (Lanham, MD: Rowman & Littlefield, 2003), 47.

13. Frank M. Reilly and Marc A. Levin, Potts & Reilly, L.L.P., "*League of Latin American Citizens, et al. v. Perry, Gov. of Texas, et al.*: Motion for Leave to File and Brief for Edward Blum, Visiting Fellow at the American Enterprise Institute, and Roger Clegg, President of the Center for Equal Opportunity as Amici Curiae in Opposition to the Appellants," 1, 2.

14. Edward Blum, *The Unintended Consequences of Section 5 of the Voting Rights Act* (Washington, DC: AEI Press, 2007), 42, 43.

15. *Northwest Austin Municipal Utility District Number One v. Holder*, 557 U.S. 193 (2009), 204.

16. Ross Ramsey, "Its Name Is MUD," *Texas Tribune*, October 8, 2007, https://texasweekly.texastribune.org/texas-weekly/vol-24/no-16/its-name-is-mud/.

17. Biskupic, "Special Report: Behind U.S. Race Cases"; Morgan Smith, "One Man Standing against Race-Based Laws," *New York Times*, February 23, 2012, https://wwww.nytimes.com/2012/02/24/us/edward-blum-and-the-project-on-fair-representation-head-to-the-supreme-court-to-fight-race-based-laws.html.

18. Andrew Gumbel, "Man behind Gutting of Voting Rights Act: 'I Agonize' over Decision's Impact," *Guardian*, January 5, 2016, https://www.theguardian.com/us-news/2016/jan/05/edward-blum-voting-rights-act-civil-rights-affirmative-action.

19. Seth Stern, "A Senior Rookie," *Harvard Law Today*, May 10, 2016, https://today.law.harvard.edu/a-senior-rookie/; Marisa M. Kashino, "Meet the Lawyer Involved in Both of This Week's Big Race-Based Supreme Court Cases," *Washingtonian*, June 25, 2013, https://www.washingtonian.com/2013/06/25/meet-the-lawyer-involved-in-both-of-this-weeks-big-race-based-supreme-court-cases/; Biskupic, "Special Report: Behind U.S. Race Cases."

20. Anemona Hartocollis, "He Took on the Voting Rights Act and Won: Now He's Taking on Harvard," *New York Times*, November 19, 2017, https://www.nytimes.com/2017/11/19/us/affirmative-action-lawsuit.html.

21. George Talbot, "Meet the Conservative Power Broker behind Shelby County's Landmark Voting Rights Act Case," June 2013, http://www/al.com/wire/2013/06/meeet_the_washington_power_brok.html.

22. *Shelby County v. Holder*, Oral Argument transcript, February 27, 2013, 4, https://www.supremecourt.gov/oral_argument_transcripts/2012/12-96_7648.pdf.

23. Ibid., 5.

24. Ibid.

25. Ibid., 9.

26. Ibid., 10.

27. Ibid., 11–12.

28. Ibid., 14.

29. Ibid., 21.

30. Ibid., 30.

31. Ibid., 31.

32. Justice Ginsburg, with whom Justice Breyer, Justice Sotomayor, and Justice Kagan join, dissenting, *Shelby County v. Holder*, 570 U.S. 529 (2013), 568.

33. Rick Hansen, "The Ed Blum Law Firm," *Election Law* blog, October 7, 2014, https://electionlawblog.org/?p=66467; Sergio Munoz, "The White Nationalist Ties to the Next Big Civil Rights Case," Media Matters for America, December 21, 2020, http://www.mediamatters.org/justice-civil-liberties/white-nationalist-ties-next-big-civil-rights-case. Munoz argues that Blum's organizations—Project on Fair Representation (PFR) and Students for Fair Admissions (SFFA)—are essentially in-house subsidiaries of DonorsTrust. Although SFFA listed PFR as the source of its funds, SFFA's "original bylaws gave its address as 109 Henry Street in Alexander, Virginia, which was not only PFR's old address, but also the longtime early home of DonorsTrust."

34. David A. Graham, "North Carolina's Deliberate Disenfranchisement of Black Voters: A Federal Appeals Court Finds the Impact of the State's Voting Law Can Only Be Explained by 'Discriminatory Intent,'" *Atlantic*, July 29, 2016, https://www.theatlantic.com/politics/archive/2016/07/north-carolina-voting-rights-law/493649/.

35. Courtesy of Assistant Attorney General Kristen Clarke, "Reflecting

on the 10th Anniversary of Shelby County v. Holder," Office of Public Affairs, US Department of Justice, June 23, 2023, https://www.justice.gov/opa/blog/reflecting-10th-anniversary-shelby-county-v-holder#:~text=This%20anniversary%20provides%20an%20important.before%20it%could%20be%20implemented.

36. Gumbel, "Man behind Gutting of Voting Rights Act."

37. Exhibit A: Deposition of Edward Blum, Dkt. 113-1, pp. 1–6, 10–11, *Students for Fair Admissions, Inc., Petitioner v. University of North Carolina, et al., Respondents*, Joint Appendix, vol. 3 of 4 (JA1043-JA1697), JA1050.

38. Students for Fair Admissions v. University of Texas at Austin: Complaint, Case 1:20-cv-00763-RP, July 20, 2020; Defendants' Original Answer, Plea to the Jurisdiction, and Plea of Res Judicata and Collateral Estoppel, Students for Fair Admissions Inc. v. University of Texas at Austin, July 1, 2019, Case No. D-1-GN-19-002739.

39. Raga Jusin, "UT–Austin Faces Third Lawsuit Claiming White Students Were Unfairly Denied Admission under Affirmative Action," *Texas Tribune*, July 22, 2020, https://www.texastribune.org/2020/07/22/ut-austin-affirmative-action-lawsuit-white/#:~:text=The%20lawsuit%2C%20which%20was%20first,denied%20based%20on%20their%20race.

40. Michael S. Collins, "A Matter of Degrees: America's Long Struggle with Affirmative Action," *Harper's Magazine* (September 2017), 70, 74.

41. Circuit Judge Stuart Kyle Duncan, opinion in *Students for Fair Admissions, Inc. v. University of Texas at Austin*, 37 F.4th 1078 (5th. Cir., 2022).

42. Dana Y. Takagi, *The Retreat from Race: Asian American Admissions and Racial Politics* (New Brunswick, NJ: Rutgers University Press, 1998), 148.

43. Ibid., 25–27.

44. Ibid., 33–34.

45. Ibid., 35–37.

46. Ibid., 37–38.

47. Robert Lindsey, "Colleges Accused of Bias to Stem Asian Gains," *New York Times*, January 19, 1987, A10.

48. William Kami, "Some Asians Gain in Admissions to Berkeley," *New York Times*, February 14, 1987, 26.

49. Takagi, *Retreat from Race*, 96.

50. Jeff Weir, "Asian-Americans Upset with Rohrabacher, Admissions Bill," *Orange County Register*, November 20, 1989, B3.

51. Takagi, *Retreat from Race*, 98–99.

52. See Anatol Rapoport, *Certainties and Doubts* (Montreal: Black Rose Books, 2000), 150–152.

53. See Daniel M. Hausman, "Taking the Prisoner's Dilemma Seriously: What Can We Learn from a Trivial Game," in *The Prisoner's Dilemma*, ed. Martin Peterson (Cambridge: Cambridge University Press, 2015), 56.

54. Hugh Davis Graham, *Collision Course: The Strange Convergence of Affirmative Action and Immigration Policy in America* (New York: Oxford University Press, 2002), 136–137, 132.

55. Amanda Ripley's "conflict entrepreneurs" create hermeneutic traps,

including what she calls "conflict traps" that pull people in "despite their own best interests." Amanda Ripley, *High Conflict: Why We Get Trapped and How We Get Out* (New York: Simon & Schuster, 2021), 281, Kindle. My concept of the "hermeneutic trap" grows out of Anatol Rapoport's notion of the "social trap" and out of the fact that, even without a conflict entrepreneur around, certain situations can lead people into prisoner's dilemma–like traps or into modes of interpretation, such as originalism, that some view as hopelessly flawed.

56. Graham, *Collision Course*, 134.

57. Natasha Warikoo, *Is Affirmative Action Fair?* (Cambridge: Polity Press, 2023), 65–66. See also Liliana Garces and Daniel Woofter, Brief of 1,241 Social Scientists and Scholars on College Access, Asian American Studies, and Race as Amici Curiae in Support of Respondent, *Students for Fair Admissions v. Harvard College*, July 29, 2022, 5–9.

58. Warikoo, *Is Affirmative Action Fair?*; Garces and Woofter, Brief of 1,241 Social Scientists.

59. It is important to remember here that "Asian" is a US racial category, not an Indian, Chinese, Japanese, or Korean one.

60. The concept of "general intelligence," which Herrnstein and Murray rely on in *The Bell Curve*, "pretends to be a biological quality that is measurable and heritable, while it is actually strongly determined by cultural priorities." Siddhartha Mukhrjee, *The Gene: An Intimate History* (New York: Scribner, 2017), 349.

61. The fact that race is a mythology—an "imaginary garden with real toads in it," in Marianne Moore's words—does not make its effects any less real, as racial genocide testifies. Marianne Moore, "Poetry," https://poets.org/poem/poetry.

62. Hugh Davis Graham explains that the development of affirmative action "privileged the rights and claims of African Americans. . . . Politically, black claims came first; all other minority groups played a distant tag-along. . . . Politically, [the African American claim] provided the moral power behind the breakthrough legislation of 1964–65. Subsequently, it also provided the rationale for adopting race-conscious remedies under affirmative action." Graham, *Collision Course*, 141–142.

63. Ibid., 141.

64. Ibid., 13.

65. Ibid., 164.

66. Nick Williams, "Lenders Have Increased Proportion of SBA Loans to Minority Small Business Owners," *Star Tribune*, December 28, 2022, https://www.startribune.com/lenders-have-increased-proportion-of-loans-to-minority-small-business-owners/600239078/.

67. "Middle class blacks—they can get a better deal elsewhere in terms of housing," Der said. "Black families have moved to Vallejo (Solano County) and the Central Valley. Black families have left Oakland. Today Blacks constitute a quarter of Oakland's population, in contrast to Blacks comprising nearly one-half of Oakland's population in 1980." Henry Der, telephone interview with

the author, June 15, 2021. Unless otherwise noted, all quotations from Der are from this interview.

68. Henry Der, "Resegregation and Achievement Gap: Challenges to San Francisco School Desegregation," *Berkeley Journal of Gender, Law & Justice* 19, 2 (2004): 429.

69. Henry Der, "The Asian American Factor: Victim or Shortsighted Beneficiary of Race-Conscious Remedies?" in *Common Ground: Perspective on Affirmative Action . . . and It's Impact on Asian Pacific Americans*, ed. Gena A. Lew (Los Angeles: Asian Pacific American Public Policy Institute, 1996), 17.

70. Anthony P. Carnevale, Peter Schmidt, and Jeff Strohl provide fresh evidence against the testocracy in their book *The Merit Myth: How Our Colleges Favor the Rich and Divide America* (New York: New Press, 2020). Carnevale shows that the maintenance of artificial testocratic paradises is not limited to San Francisco parents but extends to those in charge of such places. Asked in a June 23, 2020, interview about the University of California's recent decision to suspend the requirement for SAT or ACT scores until a new, more accurate test could be devised, Carnevale said, "To some extent this getting rid of the SAT can just be a feel-good thing. . . . They're still in the prestige game." The research literature shows, Carnevale said, that students with high scores will continue to submit their SAT results and that schools will encourage them to do so. "The average of only the people who had high scores" will land the school a good spot in the *U.S. News & World Report* rankings. Another likely downside, Carnevale notes, is that "when you take away the SAT, you give more and more power to the admissions system to do whatever it wants. And the business model in most of higher education if you boil it all the way down is—as many kids who can pay full price or most of the price, that's the game. . . . Now in the case of California, at least starting out, the way they're talking about it is different. . . . What they're doing is something people have been talking about for a long time, which is what we really ought to be doing is giving kids achievement tests based on what they learn in high school. . . . [Yet] people who've done it, it doesn't seem to make much difference. In most cases what happens is they just let in more rich kids, or legacies, or state legislator's kids." Here, the prisoner's dilemma turns up in the form of the university defecting from or staying in some kind of minimal coalition with disadvantaged students. Some of the evidence for Carnevale's conclusions can be found in Gary Orfield, ed., *Alternative Paths to Diversity: Exploring and Implementing Effective College Admissions Policies* (Princeton, NJ: Educational Testing Service, 2017), 12.

71. Tunku Varadarajan, "The Duo that Defeated the 'Diversity Industry,'" *Wall Street Journal*, November 20, 2020, https://www.wsj.com/articles/the-duo-that-defeated-the-diversity-industry-11605904415.

72. This analysis is in line with the findings of Orfield, *Alternative Paths to Diversity*, 37.

73. *Students for Fair Admissions v. Harvard*, 600 U.S. ___ (2023). All quotes from the Roberts decision are from this source.

74. OiYan Poon, Megan S. Segoshi, Lilianne Tang, Kristen L. Surla, Caressa

Nguyen, and Dian D. Squire, "Asian Americans, Affirmative Action, and the Political Economy of Racism: A Multidimensional Model of Raceclass Frames," *Harvard Educational Review* 28, 2 (Summer 2019): 209.

75. Hua Hsu, "The Rise and Fall of Affirmative Action," *New Yorker*, October 8, 2018, https://newyorker.com/magazine/2018/10/15/the-rise-and-fall-of-affirmative-action.

76. Annie Ma, "How the Asian American Backlash to Affirmative Action Went Viral: WeChat Has Played a Critical Role in Organizing Anti–Affirmative Action Activists," *Mother Jones*, December 7, 2018, https://www.motherjones.com/politics/2018/12/affirmative-action-wechat-asian-american-harvard/.

77. Arvind Sharma, *Reservation and Affirmative Action: Models of Social Integration in India and the United States* (New Delhi: Sage, 2005), 7–19.

78. Michelle Ko, MD, Ph.D., Department of Public Health Sciences, University of California–Davis Medical School, Zoom interview with the author, July 21, 2023.

79. Exhibit A: Deposition of Edward Blum, Joint Appendix, vol. 3, JA1053; excerpt from Deposition of Edward Blum, May 12, 2017, Dkt. 107-2, pp. 6–8, 10–15, Joint Appendix, vol. 1, JA291.

80. Freddie Sayers, "Edward Blum: My Battle against Affirmative Action; the Legal Strategist Is on the Brink of a Supreme Court Victory," UnHeard, May 29, 2023, https://unheard.com/2023/05/edward-blum-my-battle-against-affirmative-action/.

81. In 2021, not content to submit amicus briefs, the Pacific Legal Foundation challenged a race-neutral change in admissions criteria at a top-ranked Virginia high school, alleging (on behalf of a group of parents and alumni) that the revisions had a discriminatory intent against Asians. See Complaint, Coalition for TJ v. Fairfax County School Board, Case 1:21-cv-00296, filed March 10, 2021.

82. The remarks transcribed here are from a video, "Edward Blum: 'I needed Asian plaintiffs,'" posted by OiYan Poo, https://www.youtube.com/watch?v=DiBvo-05JRj.

83. Carnevale and a coauthor found that, by following fundamentalist beliefs like Blum's and replacing Harvard-style "whole person" reviews with admissions processes centered entirely on scores and grades, 21 percent of Asian students currently enrolled at top schools would not have been admitted. Cited in Garces and Woofter, Brief of 1,241 Social Scientists, 19–20.

CONCLUSION: ESCAPING OPPORTUNITY DESERTS

1. Alarcon, Trinity, and two coauthors cite voluminous research showing "that being treated by a racially diverse care team, or by doctors with exposure to diverse professional or educational environments, greatly increases the likelihood of positive medical outcomes, particularly for minority patients. . . . [F]or high-risk Black newborns, having a Black physician is tantamount to a miracle drug: it more than doubles the likelihood that the baby will live. . . . It is, of course, neither proper nor possible for all minority patients to

be treated by minority healthcare professionals. But medical educators have learned—through both scientific research and years of experience—that health disparities can be minimized when professionals have learned and worked next to colleagues of different racial and ethnic backgrounds." Heather J. Alarcon, Frank R. Trinity, Jonathan Franklin, and Peter B. Siegal, Students for Fair Admissions vs. Harvard, Students for Fair Admissions vs. University of North Carolina: Brief of Amici Curiae Association of American Medical Colleges et al., in support of Respondents, 3–5.

2. AAMC, "The SCOTUS Decisions on Race-Conscious Admissions and Implications for Academic Medicine," Vimeo, July 10, 2023, https://vimeo.com/844552571. Heather McGhee decisively refutes the "zero-sum" view of society (including admissions and much else) in her book *The Sum of Us: What Racism Costs Everyone and How We Can Prosper Together* (New York: One World, 2021) and in an appearance on the *Amicus* podcast on July 15, 2023: "Zero-Sum Justice," *Amicus with Dahlia Lithwick: Law, Justice, and the Courts,* https://slate.com/podcasts/amicus/2023/07/justice-clarence-thomas-is-part-of-a-supreme-court-trading-of-the-politics-of-resentment.

3. AAMC, "SCOTUS Decisions on Race-Conscious Admissions."

4. Michelle Ko, interview with the author, July 21, 2023.

5. Usha Lee McFarling, "How One Medical School Became Remarkably Diverse—Without Considering Race in Admissions," STAT, March 7, 2023, https://www.statnews.com/2023/03/07/how-one-medical-school-became-remarkably-diverse-without-considering-race/.

6. Michelle Ko, "Racism in My Medical Education: An Asian American Physician Calls for More Diversity and a Commitment to Health Equity in US Medical Schools," *Health Affairs* 39, 6 (June 2020): 1090; Michelle Ko, Mark C. Henderson, Tonya L. Fancher, Maya R. London, Mark Simon, and Rachel R. Hardeman, "U.S. Medical School Admissions Leaders' Experiences with Barriers to and Advancements in Diversity, Equity, and Inclusion," *JAMA Network Open*, February 24, 2023, https://jamanetwork.com/journal/jamanetworkopen/fullarticle/2801822.

7. Ko, "Racism in My Medical Education," 1089.

8. Ko et al., "U.S. Medical Schools Admissions Leaders' Experiences."

9. Christopher F. Rufo (@realchrisrufo), Twitter, August 2, 2022, https://twitter.com/realchrisrufo/status/1554605480374374402. In a pair of August 2, 2023, tweets, Rufo elaborated on his bottomlessly cynical but effective strategy: "The Left's linguistic defense on CRT was to say 'CRT is only in law schools' and 'that's not explicitly labeled CRT.' 'Radical gender theory' will neutralize both those defenses: we're imposing the label on a set of concepts and ideologies; debating the specifics is a win for us. . . . We can elaborate on Michel Foucault, Gayle Rubin, and Judith Butler for technical and academic audiences. But for communicating with the average mom . . . 'radical gender theory' hits all the right buttons." In due course, Rufo and his fellow travelers merged the cumbersome "radical gender theory" with easier-to-deploy terms such as "woke" and "DEI" (diversity, equity, and inclusion).

10. See Susan Svrluga, "Conservatives Seek Control over Public Universities

with State Bills," *Washington Post,* June 3, 2023, https://www.washingtonpost.com/education/2023/06/03/republicans-college-bills-dei-tenure/.

11. Christopher F. Rufo, Ilya Shapiro, and Matt Beienburg, "Abolish DEI Bureaucracies and Restore Colorblind Equality in Public Universities," Manhattan Institute issue brief, January 2023, 2, 7, https://manhattan.institute/article/abolish-dei-bureaucracies-and-restore-colorblind-equality-in-public-universities.

12. Svrluga, "Conservatives Seek Control."

13. Anthony P. Carnevale, Peter Schmidt, and Jeff Strohl, *Race, Elite College Admissions, and the Courts: The Pursuit of Racial Equality in Education Retreats to K–12 Schools* (Washington, DC: Georgetown University Center on Education and the Workforce, 2023), 76–77, cew.georgetown.edu/after-affirmative-action.

14. Roy H. Hamilton, Suzanne Rose, and Horace M. DeLisser, "Defending Racial and Ethnic Diversity in Undergraduate and Medical School Admission Policies," *JAMA* 329, 2 (January 10, 2023): 119.

15. Sean F. Reardon, Demetra Kalogrides, and Kenneth Shores, "The Geography of Racial/Ethnic Test Score Gaps," *American Journal of Sociology* 124, 4 (January 2019): 1166, 1209, 1210.

16. Alexander Panetta, "U.S. Court Strikes Severe Blow to Affirmative Action: Here's What's Next," CBC, June 29, 2023, https://www.cbc.ca/amp/1.6892475.

17. Canada China Business Council, *China's Economic Impact on Canada: Trade, Investment, and Immigration* (China Institute, University of Alberta, 2021), 45.

18. "Students for Fair Admissions on Supreme Court Affirmative Action Decision," C-SPAN, June 29, 2023, https://c-span.org/video/?529062-1/students-fair-admissions-supreme-court-affirmative-action-decision.

19. Ibid.

20. Using a Black-white comparison, Richard Rothstein definitively vivisects the argument that economic affirmative action is a good substitute for racial affirmative action in his essay "The Problem with Wealth-Based Affirmative Action: It's Not an Adequate Substitute for Race-Based Programs," *Atlantic,* June 1, 2023.

21. Gary Orfield, "Social Science and the Future of Affirmative Action: The Supreme Court's Fisher II Decision and New Research," in *Alternative Paths to Diversity: Exploring and Implementing Effective College Admissions Policies,* ed. Gary Orfield (Princeton, NJ: Educational Testing Service, 2017), 12.

22. Steve Inskeep, "NAACP's Ivory Toldson Discusses the Investigation into Harvard Legacy Admissions," *Morning Edition,* NPR, July 26, 2023, https://www.npr.org/2023/07/26/1190123330/naacps-ivory-toldson-discusses-the-investigation-into-harvard-legacy-admissions.

23. Julia Harte and Nate Raymond, "Harvard Faces Federal Civil Rights Probe over Legacy Admissions," Reuters, July 25, 2023, https://www.reuters.com/world/us/harvard-faces-federal-civil-rights-probe-over-legacy-admis

sions-2023-07-25/#:~:text=July%2025%20(Reuters).%20%2D%20The,a%20letter%20from%20the%20agency.

24. *Chica Project, African Community Economic Development of New England, and Greater Boston Latino Network v. President and Fellows of Harvard College:* Complaint under Title VI of the Civil Rights Act of 1964, July 3, 2023, 2–4.

25. Natasha Warikoo, *Is Affirmative Action Fair? The Myth of Equity in College Admissions* (Cambridge: Polity Press, 2023), 67–69.

26. Michael Waldman explains that today's Supreme Court "supermajority was installed by a fierce and effective political drive waged over decades. Senator Mitch McConnell called it his 'judge project' and bragged that ensuring that President Barack Obama could not fill a Supreme Court seat for a year was one of his 'proudest moments.' The new Court's first big moves on abortion, guns, and the interests of fossil fuels companies precisely mirrored key goals of the Republican coalition." Michael Waldman, *The Supermajority: How the Supreme Court Divided America* (New York: Simon & Schuster, 2023), 3.

27. Richard Johnson and Lisa L. Miller, "The Conservative Policy Bias of US Senate Malapportionment," *PS: Political Science and Politics* 56, 1 (January 2023): 11.

28. Alexandra Marquez, "Poll: Support Increases for Affirmative Action Programs," *Meet the Press* blog, April 27, 2023, https://www.nbcnews.com/meet-the-press/meetthepressblog/poll-support-increases-affirmative-action-programs-rcna81762.

29. Neil G. Ruiz, Ziyao Tian, and Jens Manuel Krogstad, "Asian Americans Hold Mixed Views around Affirmative Action," Pew Research Center, June 8, 2023, https://www.pewresearch.org/race-ethnicity/2023/06/08/asian-americans-hold-mixed-views-around-affirmative-action/.

30. "More Americans Disapprove than Approve of Colleges Considering Race, Ethnicity in Admissions Decisions," Pew Research Center, June 8, 2023, https:/www.pewresearch.org/politics/2023/06/08/more-americans-disapprove-than-approve-of-colleges-considering-race-ethnicity-in-admissions-decisions/.

31. Jennifer Rubin, "The Economy Keeps Defying Media Expectations: It's Part of a Pattern," *Washington Post*, January 29, 2023, https://www.washingtonpost.com/opinons/2023/01/29/economy-defying-media-coverage/.

32. Eugene Robinson, "Ketanji Brown Jackson Asks the Right Question about Affirmative Action," *Washington Post*, October 31, 2022, https://washingtonpost.com/opinions/2022/10/31/ketanji-brown-jackson-legacies-affirmative-action/. See also Ian Millheiser, "America's Anti-Democratic Senate, by the Numbers," Vox, November 6, 2020, https://www.vox.com/2020/11/6/2155079/senate-malapportionment-20=million-democrats-republicans-supreme-court.

33. Alabama, determined to get another bite at the apple, refused to draw the second Black district, and as I write, the case is heading back to the Supreme Court.

34. John Berry et al., Brief of the Project on Fair Representation as Amicus Curiae in Support of Appellants/Petitioners, May 2, 2022, 2.

35. *Allen v. Mulligan*, 599 U.S. ___ (2023), 2, 6, 9, 14, 18, 22–23, 33.

36. Li Zhou, "The Many Ethics Scandals of Clarence and Ginni Thomas, Briefly Explained," Vox, May 5, 2023, https://www.vox.com/politics/2023/5/5/23712870/supreme-court-clarence-thomas-ginni-ethics-harlan-crow-ethics-violations.

37. "Did John Roberts Really Just Save Voting Rights?" *Amicus with Dahlia Lithwick*, June 8, 2023, https://podcasts.apple.com/us/podcast/amicus-with-dahlia-lithwick-law-justice-and-the-courts/id928790786?i=1000616183375. Roberts's reasoning in the SFFA cases looks even more peculiar in light of his recognition of racism in *Allen v. Milligan*, but one must take one's victories where one can get them.

38. "Americans Split on Recent Supreme Court Decisions," Ipsos, July 2, 2023, https://www.ipsos.com/en-us/americans-split-recent-supreme-court-decisions.

39. Justice Jackson, with whom Justice Sotomayor and Justice Kagan join, dissenting, *Students for Fair Admissions v. Harvard*, 600 U.S. ___ (2023), 23. In his concurrence, Justice Thomas works a furrow he first entered during the Reagan administration and declares that Jackson's statistics on racial health and wealth gaps eclipse "individuals as individuals" and are "constitutionally irrelevant" in the face of the mighty color-blind Fourteenth Amendment. Thomas, concurring, ibid., 49–52. Of course, statistics linking lower educational levels with shorter life spans go beyond the individual. But in African American and similar communities, they have life-and-death importance. See George Howard, Mary Cushman, Claudia S. Moy, et al., "Association of Clinical and Social Factors with Excess Hypertension Risk in Black Compared with White US Adults," *JAMA*, October 8, 2018, https://jamanetwork.com/journals/ .

40. "The End of Affirmative Action," *Amicus with Dahlia Lithwick*, July 29, 2023, https://slate.com/podcasts/amicus/2023/06/the-supreme-court-demolishs-affirmative-action-in-college-admissions.

INDEX

Milton Keynes UK
Ingram Content Group UK Ltd.
UKHW041306300924
1921UKWH00013B/25/J